Jew or Juif?

Hattie Kellert, Montreal, as Miss Jewish Times, *Purim, 1898*

Jew or Juif?

Jews, French Canadians, and Anglo-Canadians, 1759-1914
by Michael Brown

The Jewish Publication Society
Philadelphia New York Jerusalem 5747 1987

Copyright © 1986 by The Jewish Publication Society
First edition   All rights reserved
Manufactured in the United States of America
Library of Congress Cataloging in Publication Data
Brown, Michael (Michael G.), 1938–
     Jew or Juif? Jews, French Canadians, and Anglo-Canadians, 1759–1914
     Bibliography: p. 325
     Includes index.
     1. Jews—Canada—History. 2. Canada—Ethnic
relations. 3. Jews—Québec (Province)—History.
4. Québec (Province)—Ethnic relations. I. Title.
F1035.J5B76 1986   305.8'924'0714   86–10564
ISBN 0–8276–0271–5

Designed by Adrianne Onderdonk Dudden

The abbreviation "JPL" that appears in the photo
credits refers to the Jewish Public Library, Montreal.
The notation "Notman" refers to the McCord Museum,
McGill University, Montreal, Notman Collection.
The notation "Torcong" refers to Toronto Jewish
Congress/Canadian Jewish Congress Ontario Region Archives.
The abbreviation "PAC" refers to the Public Archives of Canada.

For Joshua, Matthew, and Abby,
our first Canadians

Acknowledgments

Although only one name appears as responsible for the present work, many people have, in fact, contributed generously to it. My research was facilitated by the ready assistance of the staffs of the York University Library; the University of Toronto Library; the Jewish Room of the New York Public Library; the Toronto Public Libraries; Yad Yitzhak Ben Zvi, Jerusalem; the Toronto Jewish Congress–Canadian Jewish Congress–Ontario Region Archives; the Bibliothèque Centrale de Montréal; the Public Archives of Canada; the Ottawa Jewish Historical Society; the Jewish Historical Society of Western Canada, Winnipeg; the University of Western Ontario Archives, London; the American Jewish Archives, Cincinnati; the City of Toronto Archives; the Jewish Historical Society of British Columbia, Vancouver; Temple Emanu-El, Montreal; Congregation Shearith Israel, Montreal; Congregation Shearith Israel, New York; and Holy Blossom Temple, Toronto. Special mention needs to be made of the assistance of the staff of the McGill University Library, Archives, and McCord Museum, Montreal, of the Jewish Public Library, Montreal, particularly Mr. Ron Finegold and Mrs. Naomi Carusso, of the Canadian Jewish Congress Archives, Montreal, especially Mr. David Rome, who was kind enough to share information with me and whose bibliographical works are indispensable to any historian of Canadian

Jewry, of Mrs. Evelyn Miller, Montreal, Mr. Julius Hayman, Toronto, and Mrs. S. Metenko Levy, Toronto, all of whom helped me to uncover materials I might not otherwise have found. To the Faculty of Arts of my own university, York University, Toronto, I am grateful for a number of grants from the Faculty Research Fund, which enabled me to conduct research outside of Toronto. I am also grateful to the Institute of Contemporary Jewry of the Hebrew University, Jerusalem, for aid rendered in many ways on many occasions.

Considerable friendly advice regarding the manuscript was offered at various stages in the writing by Profs. Milton Plesur and Arthur Bowler of the State University of New York at Buffalo, by Prof. Ramsay Cook of York University, by Prof. Arthur Goren of the Hebrew University, and by my wife, Frankie Brown. Most especially I benefited from the knowledge and guidance of my teacher and mentor, the late Prof. Selig Adler of the State University of New York at Buffalo, without whose prodding this volume would never have been written. To the extent that their counsel was heeded, the book has been greatly improved. Shortcomings and errors are, of course, the responsibility of the author alone. I am also grateful for the assistance of Prof. Robert Smith of Syracuse University, of Ms. Leslie Parr, Prof. Moshe Davis, Ms. Roni Kleinman, Dr. Sheldon Krakofsky, and my sons, Joshua and Matthew Brown. The patience and wise counsel of my editor, Ms. Barbara Spector, has been invaluable. Most of all, I should like to thank my family for their encouragement.

Contents

Illuʃtrationʃ

Jew or Juif?

CHAPTER ONE

Introduction

Jews have lived in the province of Quebec for more than two centuries. Montreal's was the first organized Jewish community in Canada; and from those earliest days it has occupied a position similar to that of New York among American Jewry, London among British Jewry, or Warsaw in pre–World War II Poland. For most of the period between 1759 and 1914 Montreal was Canada's largest city. It was the port of disembarkation for many immigrants, who then settled in the city. Throughout the nineteenth century and most of the twentieth Montreal was the unchallenged commercial and manufacturing center of Canada, a city that offered opportunity to newcomers, especially those, like Jews, who possessed skills needed by its burgeoning businesses and industries.

A significant proportion of Canada's Jews has always lived in Montreal. In 1851, after almost a century of Jewish settlement in Canada, 181 of the country's 354 Jews lived in the metropolis and another 51 in the smaller centers of Quebec and Trois Rivières, altogether about two-thirds of the Jews in British North America. In 1921, the first census year after the close of the period to be reviewed here, 45,014 of Canada's 125,445 Jews were in Montreal, with another 2,444 elsewhere in the province of Quebec.[1] Despite a great increase in the country's Jewish population, Montreal retained its numerical preponderance until very recently, when Toronto overtook the older center.

As the oldest and largest Jewish community in Canada, Montreal was also the wealthiest and, quite naturally, the seat of power. National Jewish institutions maintained their headquarters there; and until recently Montrealers supplied much of the leadership of Canadian Jewry. The city took the lead in religious and communal developments; and Jewish culture and institutions have flourished there to an extraordinary degree. Montreal Jews also led the way in integrating into the general Canadian community. In the mid-nineteenth century Rabbi Abraham De Sola became one of Canada's best known men of letters. In roughly the same period Montrealers Adolphus Mordecai Hart and Gerald Ephraim Hart, descendants of Canada's pioneer Jewish settler, Aaron Hart, achieved eminence as historians, while the Josephs were among the most prominent and successful businessmen of the day. In more recent times the names of poets Leonard Cohen and Irving Layton and novelist Mordecai Richler, all of Montreal, have been among the most widely known on the Canadian literary scene; and the Bronfman family is to be counted among the foremost business leaders of the world. Especially in the years at the turn of the century, the period upon which the present study focuses, when the Canadian-Jewish community began to grow rapidly in numbers and institutions, Montreal Jewry asserted its leadership by example and by involvement.

For more than two centuries, then, Montreal served as the "capital city" of Canadian Jewry. What happened there influenced developments and attitudes in the rest of the country immeasurably. In fact, in many respects and for a very long time, to speak of Canadian Jewry meant, in large part, to speak of Montreal Jewry. Today Canadian Jewry is an exceptionally vibrant, vital part of the Jewish Diaspora. And yet, in recent years the Montreal community has been in disarray, perhaps even in the early stages of dissolution. The extent to which Montreal Jews have been abandoning their city and moving to places outside Quebec, either elsewhere in Canada or in the United States, is considerable. By all accounts younger, better educated, more mobile Jews are either on the move or thinking about it. The obvious question is, "Why?"

At the root of the current ferment, of course, is the growing strength of French-Canadian nationalism. The coming to power in the province in 1976 of the Parti Québécois, a party that has advocated a form of independence for Quebec, brought matters to a head. The responses of Jews to "the surprising victory of the Parti Québécois" and the growing possibility of separation from the rest of Canada have ranged from the eager enthusiasm of a tiny minority to general "uncertainty and even fear" among the majority of Quebec's Jews.[2] Fewer than 20 percent of the Jews polled a few years ago on the issue of French-Canadian nationalism indicated definite willingness to live in an independent Quebec.[3] The depth of the Jewish response to the rise of French-Canadian nationalism would seem to indicate that, despite their long history in the province of Quebec, Jews do not feel altogether rooted there. It seems to give the lie to the self-image held by many Canadian Jews only a few short years ago, that as a group they could serve as a bridge between French and Anglo-Canadians.[4] And it is somewhat surprising, since Jews have traditionally tended to "understand, even sympathize with the aspirations for self-renewal on the part of French Canadians."[5] A 1967 study of a small sample of Montreal Jews showed that 72 percent of them felt that at least some of the grievances of French Canadians were well founded.[6] During most of their history in Canada, Jews have had a better record of bilingualism (that is, speaking French and English) than most other groups.[7] Such Jewish writers as A. M. Klein and Mordecai Richler have written about French Canadians and their culture with considerable sympathy and understanding.[8] In recent years many Jews, like some French Canadians, have sensed a parallel between the Jewish nationalist revival in Israel and French-Canadian nationalism.[9] And since the 1950s as many as 30,000 French-speaking Jews have settled in Canada, at least half of them in Quebec. Yet, most Jews in Quebec, like those elsewhere in Canada, seem to identify almost exclusively with Anglo-Canada, its language and culture.

Certainly, Jews came to Canada expecting to acculturate to a greater or lesser degree; they were not looking to establish an autonomous Jewish cultural life, such as had existed in eastern Europe before World War II. Moreover, a large number of those who immigrated after 1875—and especially after the turn of the century—knew neither French nor English and thus were set apart linguistically and religiously from both of Canada's national groups. On the face of it, then, Jews might have integrated into either French or Anglo-Canada. Since so many Jews lived in close proximity to both cultures in Quebec, and since the overwhelming majority in that part of the country was French, the failure of any significant number of Jews today to feel a part of French Canada appears all the more odd. And although it is true that there have been numerous expressions of antisemitism and anti-Israel sentiment among French-Canadian nationalists in recent years,[10] such pronouncements have not been altogether absent from Anglo-Canada, nor, indeed, from other countries in the West.[11] By themselves they hardly appear to be sufficient explanation for the alienation of Jews from French Canadians and their national aspirations. And yet, other than Montreal, there are few Jewish communities outside the Arab world today where 80 percent of the population has considered emigrating. Despite the reassurances offered by a number of French-Canadian leaders, there persist among Jews fears of fascism, persecution, and second-class status in the Quebec of the future.[12]

It must be concluded, then, that the reactions of Jews to French-Canadian nationalism cannot be understood in terms of contemporary events alone. In fact, what Jews (and, to some extent, other minority groups in Quebec, as well) hear—and fear—today are resonances of the past, of Jewish experiences in other places during periods of intense nationalistic fervor and, even more, of past Jewish experiences in Canada itself.[13] It is in the past that the seeds of present attitudes and behavior were sown. Jews' identification with Anglo-Canada is not a recent phenomenon; neither are their very serious reservations about French Canada; nor, for that matter, is the strong attachment of most of Quebec Jewry to the English language, to Anglo-Canadian culture, and to the Jewish communities of Anglo-Canada, of Great Britain, and of the United States.

During World War I, North American Jewry was cut off from Europe for the first time. At that critical turning point the Jewish communities of Canada and the United States assumed the shape they were to have for some time in the future. In 1914 the Canadian-Jewish community was over a century and a half old, but only about a fifth of its members had lived in the country for more than a decade, and the community was still quite small. (Several cities in the United States and many in Europe had a larger Jewish population than was to be found in all of Canada.) Nonetheless, already by that time Canadian Jewry had charted the course it continues along today in many areas of its life. The relationship of Canada's Jews with both French Canadians and Anglo-Canadians for many years to come had certainly been established. In that past of British roots, of American connections, of alienation from France and the Roman Catholic Church, and of more than two centuries of experiences in Canada lies the key to understanding the apprehensions of today's Jews regarding their future in Quebec.

CHAPTER TWO

Britiſh Rootſ

England in the Minds of Jews

The first Jews to arrive in Canada came in 1760 with the conquering British armies.[1] Under the previous French regime Jews, indeed, all non-Catholics, had been prohibited from settling and even from visiting the colony. Those Jews, then, who were aware of the British conquest of Canada had special reason to be grateful; and it is likely that the government-mandated thanksgiving service held in the synagogue of New York on 23 October 1760 to celebrate the British victory witnessed a genuine outpouring of sentiment.[2] To a considerable degree Jewish views of Canada have been governed ever since by feelings toward her mother country. At the same time the behavior of Anglo-Canadians toward Jews has been determined in large part by the example set in the mother country.

Throughout the period under review England beckoned to Jews from all over Europe. It was there that many refugees from the Inquisition in Spain and Portugal fled, among them the progenitors of Canada's first ordained rabbi, Abraham De Sola. The De Solas, like many other crypto-Jews, made their way out of Spain on a British man-of-war to England, where they resumed the public profession of the religion of their ancestors. By the mid-eighteenth century, however, most Jews in England claimed origins in eastern or central Europe and not in Iberia. These, too, found the atmosphere of toleration in Great Britain to be in marked contrast to the severe disabilities and even violence they had faced in Austria, the German states, or Poland.[3]

Throughout the nineteenth century and into the twentieth, Jews looked to England as a potential destination. The Odessa correspondent of the London *Daily News* reported in 1888 that the "idea of emigration to England . . . [had] seized the imagination of the poorer classes of Jewish artisans" in that city.[4] The Russian Jewish émigré population in London alone rose from 8,063 in 1881 to 50,160 only twenty years later. At the end of the eighteenth century perhaps 20,000 Jews lived in all the English-speaking countries, most of them in the British Isles. By the end of the first decade of the twentieth century, a quarter of world Jewry, about 3,000,000 people, lived in the English-speaking world, most of them in the United States, but some 300,000 in England and 75,000 in Canada. Although no one could foresee the Nazi holocaust that would obliterate eastern European Jewry, observers were correctly predicting by 1900 that within a century half of the world's Jews would be Anglophones.[5]

Jews looked upon England as a place of economic opportunity. The country was well known as a land of free enterprise, the world leader in trade and commerce. Many Russian Jews came with the dream of working their way up through the laboring ranks to become masters and employers. The sometimes depressed situation of England's work-men was never well publicized among Jews, or else such reports were simply disregarded by eastern Europeans, whose economic situation steadily deteriorated in the nineteenth and early twentieth centuries.[6]

It was less the promise of economic opportunities, however, than the political and moral virtues of England and her colonies that most at-tracted Jews. England, as Rabbi Meldola De Sola of Montreal put it, became "a synonym for all that is good and noble."[7] More sober Jews with less intimate knowledge of British blessings expressed themselves similarly. When George V was crowned in 1911, the editorial writer of Warsaw's *Ha-Zefirah* compared England favorably with ancient Israel, extolling her extravagantly in the language of the Jewish tradition:

> Free England and the English individual . . . have taken most of their beliefs and manners from the Hebrew Bible. They crown their king, appointing him custodian of the national faith; they give him the Torah by which he is to live and from which he is not to deviate, the Torah of Constitution.[8]

Abraham De Sola, rabbi of Montreal's Spanish and Portuguese Synagogue, 1847–1882

Meldola De Sola, rabbi of Montreal's Spanish and Portuguese Synagogue, 1882–1918

Barnett A. Elzas, rabbi of Toronto's Holy Blossom Congregation, 1890–1893, brother-in-law of Meldola De Sola

The atmosphere of religious toleration that prevailed in England beginning in the time of the resettlement of Jews under Cromwell was unique. Whatever the law, Jews in modern times have generally been freer to practice their religion in England and her Anglo-Saxon daughter states than anywhere else in the world, except, perhaps, in Israel. The degree of openness to Judaism in England by the second half of the nineteenth century was virtually unprecedented in Jewish history. In 1887 a new election law permitted Jews to cast their vote by verbal declaration in elections held on Sabbaths and holy days, when they were forbidden by Jewish law to write. English schools, including the Royal Military Academy at Sandhurst, administered examinations on alternative days when the regularly scheduled ones came out on the Sabbath or Jewish holy days. The Sunday laws were amended in such a way that Jews who closed their businesses on Saturday would not be penalized by having to remain closed an extra day.[9]

What especially endeared England to continental Jews was the well-known fact that religious toleration had not led English Jews to mass apostasy or even to the sort of diluting of the tradition that preceded the rise of Reform Judaism in other countries. Perhaps alone among the countries of the world in the eighteenth and nineteenth centuries, England was both a model of religious toleraton and a bulwark of Jewish traditionalism. Taking a cue from the Church of England, British Jews developed centralized institutions like the Chief Rabbinate, the United Synagogue, the Board of Deputies of British Jews, and the Jewish Boards of Guardians of the Poor, as well as parochial schools and a respected newspaper. To be sure, some eastern Europeans felt that in comparison with the many-faceted Jewries of the Continent, England's was but "a miserable, petit Judaism."[10] And some English Jews did abandon their faith. Still, most Jews appreciated the fact that, whereas German-speaking Jewries were wracked by the pangs of reform and counter-reform, and eastern communities were rent by the struggles of secularists and pietists, British-Jewish religious institutions gained strength.[11]

Also striking and attractive about England to other, less favored Israelites was the opportunity offered to Jews for free association with gentiles. By 1850 "Anglo-Jewry was . . . a community of strong religious loyalty, but it was . . . [also] one of some considerable degree of social assimilation."[12] Social integration in the highest circles set the pace for the rest of society. Already in the period before the accession of Victoria, the four royal dukes, the brothers of William IV, had intimate Jewish friends and an appreciation of aspects of Jewish culture. The Duke of Sussex, for example, studied Hebrew and possessed a fine Hebrew library. When the Duke of Kent, father of Queen Victoria, was in Canada with the sixtieth Regiment in 1791, he is thought to have visited the home of and been on friendly terms with Aaron Hart, the first Jew to settle in Canada after the British conquest. It was said toward the end of the nineteenth century that the Prince of Wales, known for his somewhat eccentric tastes, "almost preferred Jewish company" to gentile.[13] The social and religious emancipation of Jews preceded political emancipation in Britain by many years, although vestiges of social antisemitism remained in evidence.[14]

But even political success came more easily in England than elsewhere in Europe. The 1740 Naturalization Act for the Colonies was probably the first legislative act in the Christian world to consider Jews as the equals of Christians. Although emancipation bills for the British Isles failed to pass in 1753 and again in 1830, the Jews continued to make gradual progress in that direction. In 1833 they won the right to be admitted to the bar, in 1835 to become sheriffs, in 1845 to become aldermen and lord mayors, and, finally, in 1858, the right to sit in Parliament. These steps toward full political equality represented but the legal embodiment of the clear voice of public opinion. Jews were returned to various offices by the electorate before they won the right to occupy them. Lionel Rothschild, for example, was elected to Parliament repeatedly between 1847 and 1858, although he was only allowed to take his seat in the latter year. So complete was the political acceptance of Jews by the 1870s that they were in several instances elected as churchwardens. Although an office concerned largely with the distribution of parish welfare funds, it was, nonetheless, connected with the Church.[15]

When Sir Moses Montefiore, known for his piety and devotion to the Jewish people, was given the freedom of the City of London (that is, honorary citizenship) in 1864, it seemed to many Jews the world over—and to some gentiles, as well—that the Messianic era had begun. In his sermon preached on Sabbath Noah of that year, Rabbi De Sola of Montreal quoted the Montreal *Herald*'s judgment on the significance of Montefiore's honor:

> We think we are not over-estimating the importance of the event on which we are commenting, if we consider it as an additional assurance . . . that men are daily discovering more and more,—that, though of diverse creeds

Aaron Hart, Canada's "First Jew," from a contemporary miniature

McCord Museum, McGill University, Montreal

Notman

William Sebag-Montefiore, newly arrived in Canada in 1913

Torcong

Solomon Jacobs, rabbi of Holy Blossom Congregation, Toronto, 1901–1920, here shown as a young man in England

Jews in New Hirsch colony, Manitoba, around 1910. The settlement was supported by the Jewish Colonization Association of London.

Inaugural service at the new building of Toronto's Hebrew men of England "Congergation" in 1921. The synagogue was founded in 1909.

and nationalities, they may yet put aside minor differences of opinion and dogma ... and walk hand in hand together, to do the great work, which patriotism and philanthropy point out.[16]

Four years later Benjamin Disraeli, a converted Jew who freely acknowledged his Jewish origins, became prime minister of England. To many Jews this was a sign that the Messiah had actually arrived.

Disraeli not only touted his Jewish ancestry but also wrote proto-Zionist novels and while in office concerned himself with the fate of Jews. Disraeli's political rival, William Ewart Gladstone, is said to have remarked that on the Jewish question Disraeli was "much more than rational, he was fanatical."[17] Such an attitude contrasted radically with that of converted Russian and German Jews, who were often consumed by self-hatred. Although some contemporary English Jews disliked Disraeli's romantic racism and suspected him of harboring conversionist sentiments, most appreciated his Jewish pride and reciprocated his affection despite his apostasy.[18]

As time went on, professing Jews also achieved spectacular success in the British political arena. Sir Marcus Samuel was elected Lord Mayor of London in 1902. By 1904 ten Jews were sitting in Parliament. In 1909 Herbert Samuel (later Viscount Samuel and High Commissioner for Palestine) became the first professing Jew to be appointed to the cabinet. A year later Rufus Isaacs (later Lord Reading) became solicitor general, and then, in 1913 lord chief justice.

Canadian Jews and most others in the world were gratified that "all [or, at least, most] classes of Englishmen ... expressed their support of" Jewish achievements.[19] Their formal acceptance by gentiles made English Jews the models for coreligionists in eastern Europe, in America, in the British colonies, indeed everywhere. Rabbi Bernard M. Kaplan's farewell address to the German and Polish Congregation in Montreal in 1902 is instructive. The rabbi "expressed the hope that Canadian Jews might produce some day such men as Disraeli and Montefiore" and that Jews would achieve in Canada the high station that they enjoyed in the mother country.[20] A later Canadian governor-general, John Buchan, Lord Tweedsmuir, a longtime supporter of Zionism, summed up the British-Jewish connection from a gentile perspective in 1936, soon after his arrival in Canada. He remarked at a Montreal Zionist meeting that in England there had "been no social or political or intellectual barriers put up against" Jews.

They have married our daughters, and we have married their daughters. We have made a Jew our Prime Minister; we have made a Jew Governor-General of India. We have had Jews in the highest places in law and learning.[21]

Tweedsmuir viewed such liberality as the touchstone of England's virtue and the cornerstone of her prosperity. English snobbery and social antisemitism were not well publicized among Jews in Canada or elsewhere, perhaps because of wishful thinking, or perhaps because they seemed benign when compared to the malignant antisemitism of the Continent.

No less important to Jews than the tolerance shown to them and to their religion in Britain was the support that country gave to Jewish interests abroad. Already during the early Victorian era, England emerged as the champion of Jews in international politics. In 1840 Damascus Jews were accused of having murdered a Franciscan monk for ritual purposes. Imprisonments and torture followed, and the threat of a pogrom hung over the Jewish community. Apparently the local French consul had instigated the libel and was then supported by the authorities in Paris. The British, however, moved swiftly to aid the Jews. A protest meeting of Jews and Christians was held at London's Mansion House. Sir Moses Montefiore set out to the East with the good wishes of most Englishmen, including the monarch, to assist his coreligionists. Largely because of British concern, the Jews were saved.[22]

More important for future precedent was British interest in the fate of Jews in eastern Europe. In 1828 the first of many meetings to protest the persecution of Russian Jews was held in London. The *New Monthly Magazine* agreed with the protesters that

persecution for religion is most unworthy and dishonourable....We think ... the right of conscience of the Jew as sacred a thing as that of the professors of our own faith.[23]

In 1843 Czar Nicholas I, on a visit to England, was approached by prominent gentiles on behalf of Russian Jews recently expelled from border areas. A year later the foreign minister, the Earl of Aberdeen, who, as prime minister in 1853 would have charge of piloting the Jewish Disabilities Bill through the House of Lords, used the friendly offices of his government to alleviate the situation of Russian-Jewish expellees. (Aberdeen's grandson, the seventh earl, served as governor-general of

Canada from 1893 to 1898, and during his tenure was known as a friend of Jews. In 1894 he attended Passover services at Montreal's Temple Emanu-El, an unusual demonstration of friendliness.) After 1880 Britain's concern for eastern European Jews came to have special importance. It was from London that the first outcries against the pogroms of 1881 were raised; and it was there that the first money was contributed to assist in resettling the refugees.[24]

The tocsin was sounded at a mass meeting at the London Mansion House on 1 February 1882, chaired by the lord mayor and attended by a cross section of British society. The speakers included England's most prominent figures: the earl of Shaftesbury, the bishop of London speaking for the archbishop of Canterbury, Cardinal Manning of the Roman Catholic Church, Professor James Bryce, later ambassador to Washington, Nathaniel Rothschild, Robert Browning, the poet, the high commissioner of Canada, Sir Alexander Tilloch Galt (through whom negotiations were conducted regarding settling some of the refugees in the Canadian West), and a host of others. At the meeting was formed the interfaith Mansion House Committee, which labored for the next two years collecting money for the refugees and assisting them to resettle in Europe, North America, England, and Palestine. The Committee's efforts on behalf of Jews were noted with the greatest appreciation everywhere in the Jewish world. Especially pleasing was the fact that in England support for beleaguered Jews came not only or even mostly from other Jews, but from the public at large.[25]

In Montreal and elsewhere Jews became accustomed to looking to British Jewry to elicit

> the all potent aid of Her Majesty's Government [in inducing] . . . the Czar . . . to establish an efficacious and permanent vindication of the inalienable rights of his Jewish subjects.[26]

Canadians also began to aid the Russian Jews themselves, consciously following the precedent set in the mother country. In 1881 and 1882 Montreal Anglo-Canadians participated in mass meetings protesting the Russian atrocities. A relief fund was set up for the refugees under the leadership of John Redpath Dougall, the editor of the *Daily Witness*. English-language newspapers in Montreal pleaded the cause of the Jews, as did those in England, urging all citizens to welcome victims of the pogrom to Canada should they come. The course of events following the outrages of 1903 to 1905 was similar. In November 1905, a mass meeting was held in Montreal to protest the wave of Russian depredations and to raise money for the sufferers. Speakers included the principal of McGill University and other Anglo-Canadians. That same month in Toronto a protest meeting attended by the mayor and the premier of Ontario, among others, was held at the McCaul Street Synagogue. That meeting dispatched a petition to the king requesting his aid for the Jews of Russia and urged their admission to Canada. Anglo-Canadians also added their voice to British protests during the blood libel trial of Mendel Beiliss toward the end of the period under review.[27]

Even avowed antisemites became disgusted by the unrestrained activities of the Russian mobs. Goldwin Smith, University of Toronto professor and high priest of Anglo-Canadian culture, brought his antisemitism with him when he immigrated from England. Rarely did he miss an opportunity to snipe at Jews and at Judaism. *The Week,* published by him in Toronto between 1883 and 1896, was one of the forums he regularly used for his fulminations against Jews. In 1890, however, even *The Week,* usually a defender of Russian policies toward Jews, was moved to cry out against the "atrociously cruel treatment to which the Jews are being subjected by the Czar."[28] About a year later the journal opened its columns to one of the Russian-Jewish refugees, who wrote movingly of the tribulations of his coreligionists.[29]

British sympathy for the Jews of Russia proved an impediment to the country's adherence to the Franco-Russian alliance in the years prior to World War I. When England finally became the third party to the Triple Entente, many Englishmen—and not only Jews—expressed their chagrin. Yiddish-speaking Canadians could not comprehend the 1908 visit of their "protector," King Edward VII, to his nephew, "the Russian Crown Criminal."[30] They hoped that he would at least use his good offices on their behalf. Jewry's "great ties of loyalty to Britain" were solid enough to survive the new alliance, although Jews never ceased to expect Britain to influence Russia in ways that were probably impossible.[31]

The persecution of Jews elsewhere in Europe also evoked a response in Britain during the period under review. Serbian and Romanian outrages were protested by the British government and public alike. So, too, was the prosecution of Alfred Dreyfus in France. At the time of the second Dreyfus trial in 1899, some fifteen thousand Londoners demonstrated in Hyde Park. England even worked her tolerant magic on the Roman Catholic Church. Whereas the Church in France, Canada, and even the United States was generally opposed to Dreyfus's cause, the largest Catholic newspaper in England, *The Tablet,* was openly Dreyfusard, frequently condemning French antisemitism.[32]

Perhaps the most consistent British effort on behalf of Jews had to do with the Holy Land, which had been closely linked with England from the onset of the nineteenth century. Through their writings Englishmen began to arouse interest in the connection between contemporary Jews and their ancient land. Such British travelers to the Holy Land as Alexander William Kinglake wrote of the country and of the Jewish connection with it. Kinglake's most popular book, *Eöthen, or, Traces of Travel,* enjoyed several editions including one in 1871 by Adam, Stevenson and Company of Toronto. Disraeli himself made a pilgrimage to the Holy Land in 1830. His letters and subsequent novels—*Contarini Fleming* (1832), *Alroy* (1833), *Tancred* (1847), and *Endymion* (1880)—exuded enthusiasm for Jerusalem and suggested the possibility of a Jewish restoration under British tutelage. In Canada and elsewhere both Christians and Jews came to expect that Disraeli would indeed facilitate that restoration.[33]

The most influential work of English literature to deal with the restoration of the Jews was George Eliot's *Daniel Deronda* (1876). The novel took the reading public by storm, and it was published and reissued all over the English-speaking world. The American-Jewish poetess Emma Lazarus claimed that Eliot's novel did more to further "the spirit of Jewish nationality" than any work previously published.[34] In English-speaking Canada the publication of *Daniel Deronda* was the literary event of the 1870s. The book appeared in separate editions in Toronto and Montreal in 1876; and the *New Dominion Monthly* printed long extracts, calling the book "the great novel of the year."[35] Eliot's work was read and reread in homes all over Canada.

There were other literary reverberations in Canada of the interest of gentile Britishers in a restoration of the Jews to their homeland, especially during the 1870s. Mary Ellen Ross, Montreal's own female novelist, expressed Zionist sentiments in her novels, *The Legend of the Holy Stone* (1878) and *The Wreck of the White Bear, East Indiaman* (1870). The apostate Jew, Charles Freshman, in *The Jews and the Israelites* (1870), declared that he had come to believe in restoration, even before the mass conversion of his former coreligionists. The Manitoba *Free Press* editorialized in 1873 on the possibility of an imminent Jewish restoration to be sponsored by Disraeli. In 1876 the Reverend Dr. J. W. Beaumont, an Anglican priest in the diocese of Huron (now London), published his

Judea for the Jews under a Joint Protectorate of the Great Powers of Europe.
It may be more than coincidence that Beaumont's diocese was headed
at the time by Bishop Isaac Hellmuth, a Polish Jew, who had become
an Anglican during the time he lived in England.[36]

Interest in the Holy Land on the part of Britons was not merely a
literary exercise. It was accompanied by increasing political involvement
during the period under review. More and more Englishmen came to
believe like Governor-General Lord Tweedsmuir that "a Jewish national
home" in Palestine would serve "the interests not only of the Jewish
race, but of civilization" and, not incidentally, of the British Empire.[37]
During the Napoleonic Wars, England fought naval battles off the coast
of the Holy Land and Egypt. Earl Ashley (later, as Lord Shaftesbury,
prominent in relief efforts on behalf of Russian Jews) suggested that
Jews resettle Palestine in an 1840 memorandum to Viscount Palmerston,
the foreign minister. In 1878 Sir Edward Cozalet and Laurence Oliphant
proposed a plan for the mass settlement of Jews in the Holy Land, which
received the approval of the prime minister and the foreign secretary.
Neither plan won an enthusiastic response from the Turks, who ruled
the country. Apparently, however, the latter proposal did influence some
of the victims of the 1881 Russian pogroms, who became the first "Zion-
istic" settlers in the Holy Land and sought to establish a modern Jewish
society there. In 1878, at the time of the Congress of Berlin, an anonymous
German pamphlet, apparently erroneously attributed to Disraeli, *Die
Jüdische Frage in der Orientalischen Frage,* suggested that Great Britain
establish a protectorate over a new Jewish state to be established in the
Holy Land. Although the proposal fell on deaf ears at the time, it would
one day be revived with success in the Balfour Declaration of 1917 and
the subsequent British mandate over Palestine secured under the League
of Nations.[38]

British interest in Jewish restoration was not limited to gentiles. At
a time when well-to-do European and American Jews seemed largely
concerned with assimilating in their own countries, many British Jews,
including some of the well placed, shared the enthusiasm of gentiles over
Palestine. In his extensive travels on behalf of beleaguered brethren, Sir
Moses Montefiore, who was connected to the Rothschilds by marriage,
undertook seven trips to the Holy Land. On these visits he asserted not
only his own concern for the welfare of his coreligionists, but the power
of his government on their behalf. Other Jewish individuals and organizations over the years, in the spirit of *noblesse oblige* acquired from
the British aristocracy, also came to the aid of Jews in the Holy Land.[39]

With the birth of Zionism, interest in Palestine ceased to be a matter of sentiment or of theoretical speculation. Although a number of prominent British Jews dissociated themselves from political Zionism, others expressed support for the new movement, as did many gentiles. Theodor Herzl early recognized the potential importance for his new organization of gentile and Jewish Zionist sentiment in England and first tested his revolutionary idea of a reborn Jewish state in that country. In 1900 on the occasion of the fourth Zionist Congress in London, Herzl and others capitalized on the historic connection of the British people with the Zionist idea.[40]

On Easter Sunday, 1903, the spectacle of the most bloody pogrom to date, in the Russian city of Kishinev, horrified a world not yet accustomed to such barbarism. Later that year the British government seemed to be responding directly to the massacre in offering the sixth Zionist Congress a territory in east Africa to be used as a colony for their long-abused eastern European brethren. There ensued a sharp debate over the proposal between those in the Zionist movement who felt that only Palestine would make an appropriate Jewish homeland and those who favored accepting any offer of territory for Jewish settlement. Canadian Jews, perhaps because of their British loyalties, were more enthusiastic about the proposal than many others. A Montreal meeting urged the Zionists to accept the British offer, but also to remain mindful of the ultimate goal of settlement in Palestine. Eventually the offer was rejected by the Zionists and withdrawn by the British government. Among Jews, however, it served as testimony to British concern. Among non-Jews the offer furthered the anticipation that some day Britain intended to make the Holy Land a colony and to settle it with Jews.[41]

The British enthusiasm for Zionism found more than an echo in British North America. From the establishment of the World Zionist Congress in 1897 Canadian Jews flocked to the movement. Especially notable was the involvement of wealthy Canadian Jews, who took their social and political cues from British Jews of similar station. (Wealthy American Jews of the period tended to remain aloof from Zionism.) The Federation of Zionist Societies of Canada was headed for most of the period under review by the Anglophile Montreal socialite, Clarence I. De Sola; his brother, Rabbi Meldola, was one of its best known spokesmen. In Toronto the English Jew, Alfred D. Benjamin, was a leading Zionist. And there were many others. Among Anglo-Canadian gentiles of the period Zionism received almost universal approbation. At the 1907 convention of the Federation of Zionist Societies held in Ottawa, two government ministers appeared on the program, assuring the delegates "that Zionism had the support of the [Dominion] Government."[42] In a letter of greeting to Federation president De Sola, the king's representative in Ontario, Lieutenant Governor Sir William Mortimer Clark, exhibited unrestrained enthusiasm:

> I trust that nothing will be permitted to divert your people from their efforts at bringing about their repatriation and the preservation of their nationality. All schemes of foreign colonisation only tend to the disintegration of your race. I congratulate you on having associated yourself with the Zionist movement. It is a cause which must prevail, for the gift of Palestine to your nation by the Almighty was absolute, and "He that scattered Israel will gather them" in due time.[43]

In one respect Britain's relationship with Jews deteriorated over the years. The wave of immigration from eastern Europe peaked in 1882 and again in 1886. Parliament went on record in 1881 and again the next year as outraged at the pogroms; and the refugees were welcomed to the country. As immigration continued unabated, however, "anti-alien" resentment began to appear in several quarters, some of them Jewish. Like all new immigrants, Jews lived together in certain areas, most notably the East End of London, where they displaced the native population. To those Englishmen with nativist tendencies, Jews appeared as "an army of locusts eating up the British inhabitants or driving them out."[44]

Partly because of the high unemployment rate (2.1 to 7.5 percent between 1880 and 1910, a time when women had not yet entered the work force *en masse* and families were still supported by one wage earner), the English working classes were growing restive. In 1904 Winston Churchill, preparing to stand for Parliament in a heavily Jewish riding in Manchester, was certain that "English working men are not so selfish as to be unsympathetic towards victims of circumstances or oppression."[45] In fact, however, many were. In 1882, 1894, and 1895 the Trades Union Congress passed resolutions hostile to immigration. In 1903 Welsh miners at Dowlais set upon Jewish mine workers, who prudently decided to emigrate to Canada. In 1911, again in Wales, this time in Tredegar, Jewish mine workers were attacked by their gentile co-workers, "as a direct result of the serious labor upheavals . . . [then shaking] the whole of England."[46]

There were some manifestations in turn-of-the-century England of the kind of Judeophobia that had sparked central and eastern European outrages. The debate over the salubriousness of the Russian-Jewish presence took place largely within the confines of social Darwinism. Opponents of the Jews saw them as an inferior race, whose presence might pollute the "superior" English stock. Even socialists like Sidney Webb warned ominously that while the English birthrate was declining, those of Irish Catholics and of German, Russian, and Polish Jews were rising. (Webb's wife, Beatrice, whose grandmother insisted she was of Jewish birth, also had ambivalent feelings about Jews and was a vehement opponent of Zionism.) In 1901 William Evans Gordon organized the British Brothers' League to fight alien immigration. That same year he and fifty-one other M.P.s founded the Parliamentary Alien Immigration Committee to sponsor restrictive legislation.[47]

Some British Jews began to fear for their own status in the country. Communal leader Lucien Wolf expressed alarm at

> the rush of aliens [who] threaten...to swamp and transform the high English character of the community...and [at] the un-English characteristics of the newcomers...calculated to imperil the happy relations of the English Jews with their Christian fellow-citizens.[48]

Louis Zangwill, the brother of novelist Israel Zangwill, offered a solution to the problem:

> A horde of our fellow-beings...arrive at our shores in...batches only to find themselves between the devil and the deep blue sea.... Now I think the best course of all would be at once to consign them to the deep sea.... I am sure that would be...the most effective way of finally extinguishing this most burning question.[49]

If it was an attempt at humor, it was unlikely to amuse Russian-Jewish victims of pogroms. In Canada and elsewhere Jews became very critical of such "un-British" sentiments.[50]

The rising "anti-alien" feeling led to the passage of the Aliens Act of 1905, which severely restricted immigration into England. Many British Jews were relieved that "the alien no longer seeks these shores."[51] Most, however, felt keenly the open espousal of antisemitism in respectable British circles and feared that relations between British Jews and gentiles would never be quite the same again. The country's image abroad was tarnished, although not sufficiently to stem the tide from eastern

Europe entirely. Many there still believed Jews in England to be "more secure than in any other land," although immigrants were now being diverted from Britain to the colonies, to America, and even back to Europe.[52] Perhaps because of the worsening situation at home, Russian Jews tended to overlook British nativism; and they were altogether unaware that men like Professor Goldwin Smith exported British antisemitism to the colonies. In fact, however, during the latter years of the nineteenth century neutral observers noticed an upsurge of anti-Jewish sentiment in the British Dominions parallel to that at home.[53]

But even antisemitism had a bright side in England. Englishmen at home and in the possessions often felt ashamed of having taken up the anti-alien cause. Arthur Balfour, who had earlier expressed doubts about the desirability of Jewish settlement in England, became instrumental in the issuing of the 1917 declaration bearing his name, which promised Jews a homeland under Britain's aegis. (In his last days Clarence I. De Sola suffered from the delusion that he had played a major role in convincing Balfour of the need for a Jewish home.) Goldwin Smith and other avowed antisemites also supported the Zionist cause. If the British did not want Jews in Britain or in Canada, they felt constrained to find a place for them elsewhere.[54] In addition, it was almost universally agreed that English antisemitism was of the mildest nature in comparison with that of eastern and central Europe. Gladstone declared in 1890 that he had no more fear of an agitation in England against the Jews than he had of one against the law of gravity.[55] A decade later Theodor Herzl proclaimed England "one of the last remaining places on earth where there is freedom from Jewish hatred."[56] Their assessment was optimistic but not altogether unjustified.

Jews in the Minds of Britons

The behavior of Englishmen toward Jews was not fortuitous. Rather, it was based on firmly held beliefs and attitudes. Since these ideas crossed the Atlantic with the emigrants from the British Isles and took root to some extent in British North America, they are of significance here. Four conceptions were particularly important.

Throughout the eighteenth and nineteenth centuries and even later Englishmen looked upon their domain as a haven for the persecuted of other lands. Already in the late seventeenth century England had provided a home to many of the Huguenots driven from France after the revocation of the Edict of Nantes. Other victims of persecution also found refuge in England over the years, including a large number of Belgians during World War I. During the period under review one of the most frequently expressed British and Anglo-Canadian images of Jews was as victims of gentile—and especially Christian—depredation. It was an image that could not but prick the consciences of Englishmen attuned to foreign persecution. In Britain the widespread discussion of the Jewish plight in eastern Europe, in Arab lands, and elsewhere reinforced the image. In Canada, Montreal poet Isidore G. Ascher evoked the sympathies of his readers, writing poignantly of Jewish suffering at Christian hands. Rev. John Douglas Borthwick's anthology of poetry on biblical themes, *The Harp of Canaan,* included a number of poems that highlighted the victimization of Jews. By 1871 it had already enjoyed two Canadian editions. In both *The Wreck of the White Bear, East Indiaman* and *The Legend of the Holy Stone,* Mary Ellen Ross portrayed victimized Jews. Widely read travel books reported the "hardships, privation and trials" of Jews in Jerusalem, Morocco, Gibraltar, and elsewhere.[57] In short, Jewish suffering was presented often and sympathetically during these years. Given their feelings of obligation toward the oppressed both Britishers and English Canadians would naturally respond.[58]

A second and no less important intellectual underpinning of the British attitude toward Jews was English reverence for the rule of law. Although the revolutions that swept across Europe after 1789 promised liberation to Jews and other minorities, they often did away with individual rights and privileges, respect for religion, and other values crucial to a peaceful Jewish existence. Moreover, an inflamed mob, whatever its original purpose, could often turn against Jews. Respect for the law and disdain for mob rule were characteristic of England as of nowhere else. As the famous Jewish traveler of the mid-nineteenth century, I. J. Benjamin, sensed, "the strict enforcement of English law under an English government" was to be one of Canada's greatest attractions to Jews.[59]

Yet another ingredient in Britain's approach to Jews in the nineteenth century was the romantic view of Jews as exotic bearers of past grandeur, still possessing special life-affirming powers, sometimes even as a "superior race." Wordsworth's "A Jewish Family," Sir Walter Scott's *Ivanhoe,* Browning's "Rabbi Ben Ezra," George Meredith's *The Tragic Comedians,* George Eliot's *Daniel Deronda,* and much of Disraeli's writing were popular expressions of this view. To be sure, antisemitism found its advocates among some nineteenth-century men of English letters, such as Coleridge, Byron, and Charles Lamb. Others, like Dickens and

Thackeray, could not transcend traditional stereotypes of Jews. But the image of the Jew as exotic, romantic hero was, on the whole, more appealing in that romantic age.[60]

Anglo-Canadians, of course, read and studied English literature. In their own works they adopted from that literature its image of Jews. Thomas Stirson Jarvis believed Jews to be "the most interesting race on the face of the earth," in whose "virtues and vices, wisdom and folly, customs and prejudices, is seen a height and depth which man cannot fathom."[61] In the nineteenth century it was Mrs. Ross, who gave fullest expression to the Jewish mystery. With obvious reference to the Hebrew Bible, she attributed Jewish power to God's continued blessing:

> The old words which the Prophet was forced to deliver against his will, "Be thou strong, be thou glorious Israel!" are in full force to the present day, the mysterious downtrodden people raise their hand, and the nation or man they would help, rise[s] in power as the great swelling billows of the ocean.[62]

The most peculiar of the ideas underlying British philo-semitism in the Victorian era—at least to later generations—was that of Anglo-Israel. One of the favorite avocations of people since the advent of Christianity has been the search for the "lost ten tribes of Israel," those Israelites carried off by the Assyrians in 722 B.C.E., never again to appear on the stage of history. While it can be safely assumed that the Israelites assimilated into the society of their captors, such an assumption has been a difficult one for fundamentalists to accept, for if "Israel" has indeed disappeared, then the biblical prophecies addressed to her can never be fulfilled. Among many North Americans and Europeans the belief pervaded that the Indians were the lost ten tribes. The proponents of Anglo-Israel theories believed the Anglo-Saxons to be descended from those ancient Israelites.

The first person to proclaim widely the connection between ancient Israel and the Anglo-Saxons was the self-styled "nephew of the Almighty," Richard Brothers. Brothers' strange career led him from Placentia, Newfoundland, where he was born in 1757, to the British navy and eventually to a British jail as a declared lunatic. Lunatic or no, not a few people believed his claim that his "family was separated from the Jews" in 294 C.E., and that other Anglo-Saxons were similarly descended.[63] One of those who took up the cudgels quite forcefully was another Anglo-Saxon born in British North America, Henry Wentworth

Monk, who, although no lunatic, was undoubtedly highly eccentric. Like Brothers, he spent much of his life in England.[64]

Brothers believed that there were two kinds of Hebrews, contemporary Jews, "the visible Hebrews," and the "vastly superior mass of 'Invisible Hebrews' . . . separated from the recognized body of their people long centuries earlier. These were now scattered amongst the nations of Europe, especially in the British Isles."[65] Brothers and Monk assumed that both branches of the Jewish people would soon be gathered together in Palestine in fulfillment of the biblical prophecies. According to Brothers the "Government of the Jewish Nation" would *"under the Lord God* be committed to" him, the "visible Prince and Governor of the Jews."[66]

British Jews at first took Anglo-Israel theories with good humor and little seriousness. The *Jewish Chronicle* of London declared such ideas to be "very funny."[67] Jewish skeptics insisted "that the evidence in favour of the claim . . . [of Anglo-Saxon descent from Jews, be] of a more conclusive character," if they were to believe it.[68] Whether Jews accepted the relationship or not, by the last quarter of the nineteenth century attempts were being "universally made [in England and elsewhere in the English-speaking world] to prove the Anglo-Saxon race to be . . . [Jews'] kith and kin."[69] At the very least these efforts helped to promote a feeling among English gentiles of closeness to Jews and of a common fate with them.

By the 1950s some of the most vicious antisemitism in Canada was originating in Anglo-Israel circles, perhaps because of disappointment over the failure of "the visible Hebrews" to accept Christianity and Christian Anglo-Israel stewardship. Seventy-five years earlier, however, the most outspoken philo-semitism in Canada came, as it did in England and to some extent also in the United States, from believers in Anglo-Israel theories. As a child, Monk, the Moses of the movement, had been sent into "exile" in England for his schooling. He felt the separation from family and friends in Canada keenly, comparing it with the almost two thousand years of the Jews' exile. Monk was restored to his homeland; and he sought such a return for Jews to their homeland.[70]

Over the years Monk preached extensively in his native country as well as in Britain and the United States. At a utopian colony on the shores of Lake Erie, he met Laurence Oliphant, one of the earliest proponents of mass Jewish settlement in Palestine, who was later active in Russian-Jewish relief. He corresponded with American proto-Zionists Mordecai Manuel Noah and Warder Cresson about the fate of the Jews and in 1873 founded the Palestine Restoration Fund to buy up vacant land in the Holy Land for Jews. That project received favorable press notice in Canada; and a number of Canadians contributed subscriptions of fifty pounds to the Fund. As would Theodor Herzl after him, Monk foresaw a Palestine governed and peopled by Jews, which would serve the world as a model state. Having recognized himself as the "third Isaiah" yet in 1855, it is not surprising that Monk devoted considerable energy to the establishment of a world organization of nations to ensure peace on earth. That peace, he felt, could be realized only when justice was done to the Jews.[71]

Between 1880 and 1890 there was a flurry of Anglo-Israel activity directly related to Jews. In the former year Monk and his friend and supporter, the painter William Holman Hunt, launched a British campaign to end war. The starting point of the campaign was to be the elimination of antisemitism. Britain would acquire Palestine for Jews, and a bank of Israel would finance resettlement. The London *Jewish World* as well as *Hamagid* and *Hamelitz* in eastern Europe welcomed the scheme. A year later the Russians unleashed their pogroms. In response, Monk proposed the immediate establishment of a "Jewish National Fund" (later called the "Emigration Fund") to assist in resettlement, chiefly in Palestine. He upheld the Dominion of Canada as a model of biracial harmony for a projected "Dominion of Israel" and returned home in 1884 to publicize his ideas. (Despite its decreasing plausibility in a Canada that sometimes seemed at the point of breaking in two, the notion of the country as a binational model for Jews and Arabs in Palestine had a long life. In 1947 Senator W. A. Roebuck of Toronto was still speaking in such terms.)[72] The pogroms of 1891 inspired Monk to renewed activity. He suggested that Queen Victoria invite all persecuted Jews to settle in England, an idea supported by the Ottawa *Journal* and other English-language Canadian papers. The queen, however, was silent. Five years later in Ottawa, Monk published his last manifesto— "Stand Up, O Jerusalem, that the Land of Israel may soon become like the Garden of Eden, 'The Joy of the Whole Earth,' now that the 'Federation of the World' and 'Parliament of Man' has at last become an Imperative Necessity." In it he pleaded once again for the return of the Jews to Palestine under his own leadership and British tutelage. Like Monk's earlier pleas, this last convinced only those already committed.[73]

Monk's lack of success did not discourage other believers. In 1890 Rev. W. H. Poole published his *Anglo-Israel in Nine Lectures*. The book was a collection of discourses that the popular preacher had delivered across Ontario and Quebec. Poole reminded readers that Jesus had appeared to the Jews alone. The minister believed that the ancient people of God continued to "inspire . . . thoughts and command . . . attention."[74] By the first decade of the twentieth century Anglo-Israel was estimated to have some two million adherents in Great Britain and North America. Poole and his contemporary Anglo-Israelites seemed rather less the lunatic fringe of philo-semitic Protestantism than had their predecessors. Poole's work was commended to Protestants by the Anglican Bishop of Toronto and by ministers in a number of towns in Ontario and Quebec. Newspapers from the Cobourg *Sentinel* to the Montreal *Star* and the widely read *Dominion Illustrated* also endorsed the volume. Goldwin Smith thought Anglo-Israel preposterous. But Canadian Jews welcomed the doctrines and, at least in public, expressed no skepticism.[75]

The Anglo-Israel theories, despite their currency and persistence, remain odd byways of intellectual history. They can be understood, however, as a bizarre extension of the closeness that many Protestants— especially Anglo-Saxons—felt to the Hebrew Bible and its laws and prophecies. The Protestant Reformation had been an attempt to strip away later accretions to the "pure word of God," as it had been revealed in the Bible. Moreover, many Protestants, in particular those belonging to dissenting sects, saw themselves as the embodiment of the old Israel; they were, thus, reenacting historical and religious experiences of the Jewish people. Most did not see the connection the way Brothers and Monk did. But the bond between Jews and Protestants was an acknowledged one in England and her possessions. It was an ingredient of no small importance in the British philo-semitism of the Victorian era.

In both the mother country and Canada, then, in the religious sphere Jews seemed to be (and, in fact, were) very close to the majority faith in the period under review. Even those Protestants who considered Anglo-Israel ideas extreme generally had an interest in the Hebrew language and the Hebrew Bible (or Old Testament, as they called it), which was a natural by-product of the quest to "return to the roots" of Christianity. Protestant ministers preached frequently on themes from the Hebrew Bible and often had more than a passing acquaintance with the language in which it was written. They saw Jews as the embodiment of the Protestant ethic: "temperate, home-loving, intelligent, industrious and ambitious."[76] Sir J. William Dawson, long-time president of McGill University, knew Hebrew and devoted some of his scholarly energies to works on Palestine and the Hebrew Bible. Professor Brodie Brockwell of the same institution encouraged both Christians and Jews to study Jewish culture and the Hebrew language. Canadian school books presented Israelite history as the essence of "religious and moral lessons."[77] Even those who had left the fold of Judaism ranged themselves in the ranks of the admirers of the Hebrew Bible. Along with many gentiles, Isaac Hellmuth and Charles Freshman, both apostate Jews, defended the integrity of the Bible during the debate over the Documentary Hypothesis. Goldwin Smith and his followers claimed that Jews practiced a debased form of religion. George Coulson Workman, a prominent Methodist minister and professor of Old Testament Studies at Victoria College, Toronto (later of Montreal Wesleyan College) rose to the defense:

> No nation other than the Jews entertained such a lofty conception of the Deity as a transcendant moral person; and no religion other than Judaism laid such emphasis on justice between man and man, on mercy to both man and beast, or on meekness and humility before God.[78]

This was an affirmation of Judaism with which many—although certainly not all—of Workman's fellow British and Canadian Protestants agreed. No believing Jew might have claimed more.[79]

Sentiments such as Workman's had very practical implications. For one thing, leading Anglo-Canadians were prompted by their religious convictions to support Zionism as the modern fulfillment of biblical prophecies. Sir William Mortimer Clark's statement to the 1907 convention of the Federation of Zionist Societies of Canada represents the clearest articulation of such thinking. Others found different means of aiding Jews. Dr. Edwin Clay, a very religious philo-semitic Free Baptist, was immigration agent in Halifax in the years before World War I. Clay saw to it that almost no Jews who arrived at that port of entry were refused admission into the country.[80]

In the period before World War I there was, then, a very strong attachment of Jews to England and her possessions and of England to Jews. The Jews' attachment was based on their assessment of England's actions toward her own Jewish community and toward world Jewry and was enhanced by the knowledge that the British Empire was perhaps the most powerful force in the world and by an appreciation of "the high standard of English culture."[81] On the part of Englishmen at home and in the British possessions the attachment stemmed from the Protestant affinity for Jews and their Book and also from their perception of their country as a place of law, order, and justice for all, of religious toleration, and of basic fairness. Whatever discrimination and antisemitism (thinly masked as "anti-alien" sentiment) existed seemed mild and ephemeral in the light of the growing understanding between Jews and Anglo-Saxon Protestants and by comparison with the widening gulf that separated Jews from other European peoples. All of this was well known in Canada, where attitudes and behavior regarding Jews were greatly influenced by trends in the mother country.

British North America: The Unknown Land

If nineteenth-century Jews knew a great deal about England and entertained the warmest sentiments for her, they shared with most other Europeans an "appalling ignorance" regarding England's North American possession, Canada.[82] Jewish books about North America seldom mentioned Canada. The most basic information about Jewish life there was lacking. Even late in the century Canada remained to readers of the Hebrew press *terra incognita,* just "a country in North America."[83] Reports appearing in eastern European Jewish journals were fewer and less complete than those about other lands open to immigration, such as Australia and South Africa, not to mention Great Britain and the United States. Even scholarly accounts of Jewish emigration to North America omitted mention of Canada. British Jews were no better informed about their North American brethren. In 1845 the London *Jewish Chronicle* ran a major article on Jewish emancipation that discussed France, Belgium, and the United States. Canada, a British possession that had granted Jews full political rights thirteen years earlier, was not mentioned. Lucien Wolf's 1886 *Chronicle* essay, "Old Anglo-Jewish Families," talked about both the Meldola and the De Sola families, the ancestors of Rabbi Abraham De Sola. Canada's illustrious rabbi had died only four years earlier, yet Wolf seems barely to have heard of him. He merely stated that "connections of the family are still living in London and in Canada."[84] Aggravating the ignorance regarding Canada and the country's unfavorable image among gentile Englishmen was a feeling in the 1880s that British North America "had ceased to fulfill the natural functions of a colony and would some day go the way of all colonies." (Jews' ignorance of Canada was sometimes reciprocated by Canadians' ignorance of Jews. In 1891, for example, the otherwise authoritative *Lovell's Historic Report of the Montreal Census* reported that the majority of the city's Jews were natives of "Judea"!)[85]

In contrast to their very positive image of the mother country, most of the little that Jewish and gentile Europeans knew of Canada in the nineteenth century was negative. Reports told of the bitter cold of Winnipeg, of the 1886 Passover eve floods in Montreal, which prevented Jews from making their festival preparations, of widespread, virulent antisemitism, especially in Montreal, of all "the hardships and difficulties which immigrants eager to establish themselves in Canada encounter: the difficult climate, the primitive conditions of business and industry."[86] The impact of such disheartening news was heightened by reports of a small and weak Jewish community. Disgruntled newcomers accused Canadian Jews (not always deservedly) of being inhospitable to immigrants and of exploiting them. In 1883 news spread in Europe of a Jewish bordello owner in Winnipeg who enticed Jewish maidens to the wild prairies. As late as 1913 a Montreal Jewish correspondent felt as if Canadian Jews had shipped the *Shechinah,* the divine presence (which according to Jewish tradition accompanies Jews wherever they go in their exile), back to Europe.[87] Toward the end of the eighties Herman Landau, a London Jew of eastern European origin and sometime agent of the Canadian Pacific Railway, dreamed of a major Jewish settlement in British North America. He tried to interest Baron Maurice de Hirsch— the Jewish philanthropist and railroad magnate of German origin, Hungarian fortune, and French residence—in Canada. De Hirsch, eager to aid eastern Jews in resettling, expressed some little interest but preferred Argentina as more promising in the long run. Canada seemed to almost everyone a far-off country, rather like China, with which it was occasionally coupled in news columns. There, human life in general and Jewish life in particular were not deemed likely to flourish.[88]

By the 1880s Canada's image among Europeans had begun to change. Indeed, Canada itself had begun to change during the closing years of the nineteenth century. The country elected a Liberal government in 1896, headed by Wilfrid Laurier. Among other innovations the Liberals introduced a vigorous immigration policy to people the West. It brought large numbers of non-English and non-French settlers to Canada for the first time and coincided with the need for large numbers of Jews to find new homes in the wake of Romanian oppression, Russian pogroms, and widespread, grinding poverty throughout Jewish Europe.

Several factors combined in those years to make immigration to Canada less risky and more attractive. In 1887 the British Colonial Office established an Emigrants' Information Office in London, which attempted to match up prospective emigrants with employment opportunities in the Empire. The notices from this office about Canada and elsewhere reached Jews even in eastern Europe. In 1904 a Jewish Emigrants' Information Society was set up in London, the work of which closely paralleled that of the Colonial Office. One of the first acts of the Jewish Society was to send its secretary on a fact-finding mission to Canada; within a short time Canada became "the field that most attracted" its clients.[89] A second factor facilitating the outflow to Canada of transmigrants (the term used for people who had immigrated to England and then emigrated elsewhere) and native-born Englishmen at the turn of the century was the tariff war that raged among North Atlantic shipping companies between 1902 and 1904. The fare declined from just over six pounds in 1902 to two pounds the following year. The number of Jewish emigrants from England to North America tripled correspondingly from 1903 to 1904.[90]

An additional incentive for emigration was provided by the Canadian government. Between 1905 and 1909 Canada paid steamship agents a bounty of one pound for each immigrant of British or western European stock diverted to Canada. Steamship companies had always promoted their Canadian routes with hard-sell methods, sometimes dishonestly representing the less popular Canadian ports as "American." Undoubtedly the bounty strengthened this inclination. It is probable that Jews were among those induced to emigrate to Canada during this period and that some transmigrant Jews "passed" for native Britishers. This was especially likely if the transmigrants had been resident in England for any length of time.[91]

The Canadian government's extensive immigrant recruiting campaigns do not seem to have reached the Jewish pogrom victims, probably by design. But, in time, as more Jews settled in Canada, they themselves wrote back to Europe about opportunities in the Dominion. Jews published their own propaganda literature telling prospective immigrants about homesteading possibilities and the growing prosperity and importance of Montreal. The opening of new synagogues and the growth and development of the Canadian Zionist movement also received notice.[92]

For Englishmen, a factor that served to brighten Canada's image was the rising tide of imperialist rivalry at the end of the 1890s. Then came the Boer War. These events led to a greatly heightened sense in Britain of the Empire's importance. Editions of the *Jewish Year Book* after 1900

covered Canada thoroughly. The 1902–03 issue included colonials in its
"Who's Who in British Jewry" for the first time. By 1902 the once
apathetic *Jewish Chronicle* was claiming that "the happiest thought of
English Jewry is that it can play a part, however humble, in the evolution
of His Majesty's dominions beyond the sea."[93]

   Although there was some hesitation about sending more immigrants
to Canada than the Dominion could absorb, the passage of the Aliens
Act, the renewed interest in Empire, and the rising tide of emigration
from eastern Europe made it more fashionable to stress Canada's "vast
open spaces" and "enormous economic possibilities." Now there was
thought to be plenty of "room . . . for the Jewish fugitives" in Canada.[94]
The once "harsh and primitive" climate of British North America now
was said to offer the "bracing moral and physical conditions" necessary
for building healthy Jewish minds in healthy Jewish bodies.[95] The economic prosperity of the "Laurier years" helped, of course. On the eve
of the depression of 1907 the *Jewish Year Book* unsuspectingly rhapsodized
about the "phenomenal prosperity" of Canada, predicting that the future
of "its rapidly increasing Jewish population may be looked forward to
with confidence."[96] Canadian nativism went unnoticed or was declared
to be nonexistent "outside a small section of [French-Canadian] fanatics
in the province" of Quebec.[97] In Canada "the toleration of creeds" was
now considered to be "part of the religion of the people."[98] And the
Jewish community there was pictured as growing more independent day
by day.[99]

   For Jews, at least up to World War I, one of Canada's chief attractions
remained the fact that it was a British country. Moreover, often the
British tie was one of the few altogether accurate pieces of information
Europeans had about Canada. Readers of the eastern European Jewish
press were reminded from time to time that "the state of Canada is
governed by Britain"[100] and that all Canadians, "even though many of
them are French, are loyal to the government of England."[101] This was,
of course, an oversimplified view of Canadian affairs, but one that shaped
Jewish perceptions. It was also one Jews were eager to hear, for England
continued to hold the imagination and admiration of Jews the world
over. Some Jews and gentiles were wary of the monarchical connection and preferred the republican United States, where, they felt, "the
wind of freedom" blew "much, much more . . . than in . . . Canada."[102]
Others, however, were drawn to Canada, precisely because of that connection.[103]

Immigration to Canada from the British Isles

It is estimated that between 1759 and 1875 approximately a million and a half people left the British Isles for Canada. Although there is no way of discovering exactly how many of these immigrants were Jews, from what is known of the Jews in Canada during these years, it can be assumed that, as with non-French gentiles, most of them came from or through Great Britain. Of the fifteen Jews to sign the first prothonotary's register of the Spanish and Portuguese Synagogue in Montreal in 1832, eight had been born in Canada and the other seven in England. Later records also indicate British origins for many Canadian Jews. From the mid-nineteenth century, agencies and organizations in England and in Canada kept a count of emigrants, but their figures are at best reliable only for those people with whom they were directly concerned. It is certain, however, that as time went on the number of Jewish emigrants from Britain to Canada grew.[104]

After 1880 the face of Jewish Canada changed radically. In 1881 there were but 2,443 Jews in all of Canada; by 1911 there were 75,681. In 1881 there were but five Jewish congregations in Canada and an additional four *minyanim* (small prayer groups). Thirty years later there were scores of congregations, large and small. (The general population of Canada also expanded rapidly in these years. But in the first two decades of the twentieth century, when most of the Jewish growth of the period occurred, the Jewish population grew eleven times faster than the general.) The demographic makeup of Jewish Canada also altered. In the earlier period almost all of Canada's Jews were English-speaking and had British or American backgrounds. After 1881 the Anglicized Jews were joined by Yiddish-speaking Jews from eastern Europe, many of whom had not been acculturated in an English-speaking country.[105]

In determining the "Britishness" of Canadian Jewry census figures are of very limited usefulness, because they do not deal with the transmigrant phenomenon. These people, however, and their children actually contributed significantly to the Anglicization of Canadian Jewry. The transmigrants were, of course, not British; and some of them had remained in England for too short a time to absorb much of English culture. This was increasingly the case after 1881. Others, however, had settled down, perhaps married an English spouse, and assimilated to a considerable degree. Usually, the transmigrants left family and friends behind when they emigrated, creating a lasting personal bond with the mother country. Moreover, most transmigrants had negative feelings about their countries of origin in eastern and central Europe. Those who left after 1881 remembered Russian and Romanian depredations. Even if incompletely Anglicized, they were generally very eager to think of themselves as British and not as natives of the eastern Europe they had fled.[106]

In general, the appeal of settlement in the colonies grew in the British public mind in step with the increasing number of welfare recipients, especially in times of economic stress. From the late eighteenth century onward Britishers considered both their own colonies and the United States to be safety valves, protecting them from poverty, overpopulation, and underemployment. By 1870 some one million people in England were being supported by the poor rates. As immigration from central and eastern Europe swelled the Jewish population, the infant mortality rate in the London ghetto rose alarmingly. In 1858 there were approximately one thousand regular attendants at the Jewish soup kitchens in London, representing some five to six thousand Jews, over 10 percent of the Jewish population. Twenty-five years later almost one-quarter of London's Jews were on relief, mostly supplied by Jewish community institutions. Among these were the first thousand Russian-Jewish refugees to enter the country. In 1875 Rev. Aaron Levy Green, a well known London rabbi, addressing a group of Jewish workingmen and their families, insisted that the only way to relieve overcrowding in Britain was though emigration. The rabbi quoted Lord Dufferin on the prospects of Canada in order to encourage his listeners to consider settlement in that little known place.[107] His speech was echoed throughout the Victorian era by clergymen, humanitarians, and politicians of all stripes and creeds.

As noted previously, a variety of factors drew Jews to England during the period under review. Some of them, however, had come simply because they could not afford the fare all the way to America or because their route to America involved a stopover in England. Pogrom victims in particular had to leave unexpectedly and in haste, often with only enough money to get as far as England. Sometimes emigrants planned to stop just long enough to earn the rest of the passage to North America. England was relatively close, and it was a free country. Moreover, England was the only country in Europe where, by the mid-nineteenth century, there existed an extensive network of Jewish welfare services. Consequently husbands might go on to North America after depositing their families in England, where they could live on charity dispensed by Jewish institutions. Most men sent for their families after they had established themselves. Sometimes, however, husbands abandoned their families altogether or waited for British institutions, eager to be rid of their charges, to provide the fare to North America.[109]

Some Jews, of course, had intended to stay in England and only after their arrival there became interested in moving on to North America, particularly to Canada, of which they had previously known little or nothing. If other family members had gone, they encouraged later emigrants to follow, sometimes paying their way. Others found it more difficult to make a living in England than they had anticipated. Especially during hard times such people tended to leave, expecting to "find regular employment and better wages in Montreal" or elsewhere in the colonies or America.[110] Often, too, emigrant aid societies encouraged poor immigrants to decide to leave by offering them passage out of England or even directly from their country of origin to America. In so doing these agencies were, in part, responding to public pressure, especially after the turn of the century. In 1902, for example, the London *Standard* was urging that Romanian Jews "be systematically directed to Canada." The *St. James Gazette* suggested both Canada and South Africa as appropriate destinations, but not Whitechapel (the Jewish district of London), "where we have more than enough."[111]

In order to assist the poor in their departure and to help them get a start in the New World, various religious and humanitarian societies were founded over the years. Some of these groups aimed to establish group settlements. Others provided inducements to individual emigration. Unmarried women, children, and criminals were especially popular objects of concern among non-Jews, immigrants among Jews. By 1850 there was a host of general and special interest emigration societies concentrated in London and in Scotland, where poverty was worst. These societies, both Jewish and gentile, continued to send paupers to the colonies even after World War I. Between 1882 and 1930 the British Dominions Emigration Society aided some thirty-five thousand emigrants. During the same period the United British Women's Emigration Society, with forty-six branches throughout the United Kingdom, trained women as domestics before assisting them to leave the British Isles.[112]

Jews founded a number of emigration societies both to alleviate the suffering of the poor and to lessen the burden upon the English Jews who supported them. As already noted, some of the settled Jews were themselves quite concerned that the British-Jewish community not be swamped by eastern European immigrants. In fact, Jews were among the first Britishers to consider assisting paupers to emigrate. As early as

1752 one London congregation sought to charter several ships to send one hundred poor families to North America. Just a century later the Jews' Emigration Society was founded in London. Well into the twentieth century that society was aiding native English Jews and immigrants who had been in the country at least ten years to leave. In 1903, a typical year, it assisted 181 Jews to emigrate, 23 of them to Canada. In 1853 the Jewish Ladies' Benevolent Loan and Visiting Society of London, in imitation of the Ragged School scheme, sought without success to send out poor, young Jewish women to the colonies. The Jewish Association for the Protection of Girls and Women in London was more successful, sending as many as several hundred girls a year abroad, some of them to Canada. The London Board of Guardians of the Jewish Poor was formed in 1859, and Boards of Guardians were also established in other major British-Jewish centers. Along with their relief and welfare activities, they engaged in emigration work. The Liverpool Board, in its first annual report in 1877, boasted of having aided 164 applicants, among whom were "recipients merely passing through Liverpool on their way to . . . America"; it was doing "all in its power to prevent newcomers from settling in the town," thereby safeguarding Jewish Liverpudlians from the ignominy of being associated in the popular mind with poor, uneducated immigrants.[113] It may be assumed that furthering emigration continued to be one of the main activities of the Liverpool Board.[114]

By 1879 the London Board of Guardians of the Jewish Poor had established a special Emigration Committee to deal with what was becoming an increasingly important part of its work. Between 1880 and 1907 the Board assisted as many as 1,700 Jews a year to leave the country. After 1907 the Aliens Act was in force, and the number dropped steadily to a low of 162 in 1914. Canada was never the main destination of those assisted. In fact, the first year in its history that the London Board sent more emigrants to the colonies and the United States rather than back to eastern Europe was 1906. Even in subsequent years large numbers were returned to Russia. But especially after 1900, a fair proportion of Board-assisted emigrants headed for British North America. Since agencies in other countries were seldom seriously concerned about London's congestion (the ostensible reason for the emigration activities of the Board of Guardians) emigrants were sent wherever possible. Native English Jews and those who had lived in England for long periods of time could not be sent to Russia. After the Aliens Act went into force these constituted a much larger part of the Board's case load, and consequently the destination of emigrants changed. Also, the passage of that act heralded the beginning of the closing of the gates of the West. The Board may well have begun to hesitate to return Jews to their Russian prison once escape became unlikely.[115]

In Canada the Boards of Guardians sometimes worked with the Baron de Hirsch Institute of Montreal and other groups. In 1884 the London Board sent Benjamin Cohen to Canada and the United States to investigate immigration possibilities. In 1909 that Board together with the Jewish Colonization Association sent out Osmond d'Avigdor Goldsmid to discuss coordinating efforts with the Montreal society. Most of the time, however, the Board simply assisted emigrants without planning for resettlement. People were forwarded to Canada in midwinter, when there was no work for them, and sent to maritime ports, where there was no Jewish agency to assist them. The London Board prided itself on never sending out medically unfit emigrants. Yet, on occasion, its charges arrived in Canada suffering from trachoma or some other disease and thus were unable to enter the United States or even Canada, which had less stringent regulations. In such cases, Canadian Jews generally had to pay for the treatment of their coreligionists or for their deportation. Occasionally the Londoners made promises to prospective emigrants as inducements to leave England, trusting that local worthies in Canada would make good on the pledge. Because of the small size of the Canadian-Jewish community and its meager, if growing, resources, it was not easy to redeem such commitments. But the Board in London saw its main job to be the furthering of emigration and not assisting in resettlement. In all fairness, it must be said that the Board's resources were overtaxed and that British Jews were, on the whole, most generous. A few Canadian Jews had great fortunes and could have helped. They were less than openhanded.[116]

After 1881 the task of assisting genuine refugees in England—those who had fled eastern Europe because of an immediate threat to their safety—fell to the Mansion House Committee and to its successor, the Russo-Jewish Committee. Through such projects as the acquisition of agricultural lands in the Canadian prairies, the committees attempted to assist refugees not only to emigrate, but also to resettle in new homes. The two groups granted funds to the Baron de Hirsch Institute to be distributed to newcomers to Montreal for their immediate needs and to help them to find permanent homes. On the whole, these committees acted more responsibly than the Boards of Guardians, perhaps because their sole task was aiding refugees, and they did not have to concern themselves with the needs of the existing English-Jewish community.[117]

The best funded of all the Jewish emigration societies in London was the Jewish Colonization Association (hereafter referred to as JCA), established in 1890 by Baron Maurice de Hirsch with an endowment of two million pounds. Six years later at de Hirsch's death, it received a further six million pounds. These funds, fabulous for the day, were used to resettle tens of thousands of Jews from eastern Europe, mostly in the New World. Although the chief areas of interest of the JCA were Argentina and the United States, Canada, too, received some attention.[118]

In 1890 the Young Men's Hebrew Benevolent Society of Montreal received a grant of twenty thousand dollars from the Baron, which it used to erect its first building, Montreal's first Jewish settlement house and school. Subsequent grants were forthcoming for the work of the Society, which changed its name in gratitude and expectation to the Baron de Hirsch Institute. The JCA worked with the de Hirsch Institute in forwarding individual emigrants to Canada and in looking after Jewish agricultural settlements in the West. For some years it acted independently in Canada and through its affiliate in New York. Although, for a time they were considered to be potentially most promising, the agricultural settlement activities of the JCA reached a few thousand Jews in Canada at most. The absorptive capacity of modern agriculture turned out to be more limited than expected, while that of industrial cities was proving limitless.[119]

Besides these major agencies, others also endeavored to channel transmigrants and native English Jews toward Canada. Nathaniel, the first Lord Rothschild, sponsored the emigration of two hundred Jewish families to British North America, while his wife, Emma, paid for transporting the pet lamb of one of the Jewish children. Israel Zangwill's Jewish Territorial Organization sought to establish an autonomous Jewish province somewhere in the world other than Palestine. Negotiations were undertaken with Canada after the turn of the century. They proved abortive, as did those with other countries.[120]

From early on there was criticism of the emigration schemes in England, because they were suspected by many of being an attempt to avoid an unpleasant problem by foisting it upon the colonies. In the colonies resentment also grew. Established settlers did not care to have their countries become dumping grounds for the human refuse of the mother country. Canada, as the Canadian *Jewish Times* noted in 1908, was "by no means inclined to shoulder the social burden of Europe!" Already in the 1830s there had been considerable protest in Canada. One French Canadian objected in 1831 to "the injustice of sending us excess population, poor and without resources, which humanity then demands we assist at our own expense."[121]

Some suspected that French-Canadian objections to immigration were politically and racially motivated, masking a desire to prevent any augmentation of the English population. But Anglo-Canadians, and among them Jews, also complained. The presence of some six thousand Irish orphans in Montreal in the late 1840s frightened everyone, especially since they had an unusually high mortality rate. The sudden influx of destitute Jews in the same years necessitated the creation of Montreal's first Jewish welfare organization, the Hebrew Philanthropic Society. At its first annual meeting (which was apparently also its last) the complaint was heard that there was "pour[ing] into Canada an unprecedented amount of [Jewish] immigration . . . of the worst possible description."[122]

To be sure, not all Canadians resented the new immigrants. Many Anglo-Canadians eager to build up their control of the country and others who believed that the country could only prosper if it were settled welcomed the newcomers, even the paupers. Rabbi Abraham De Sola arrived in Montreal in the Irish famine year of 1847. At the time he was the only Sephardic (of Spanish extraction) Jew in Montreal. In 1859 he urged the London Sephardim to forward to Canada destitute brethren in order to build up a community.[123] There was, however, sufficient opposition to immigration to influence the new Dominion government to issue an order-in-council in 1868 forbidding the landing of immigrants unable to care for themselves. This stemmed the tide of paupers, Jewish and gentile, for a time.[124]

In 1908 Bruce Walter, the Canadian Commissioner of Emigration in London, still found that "the work of English charitable and religious societies was giving him much anxiety."[125] Again Canada tried to limit pauper immigration with an order-in-council forbidding further assisted immigration. It followed by some years a similar ruling in the United States. From then on immigrants to Canada, even from the British Isles, were supposed to pass a medical and character examination, to have a job waiting for them in Canada, and to possess fifty dollars with which to begin their new lives (at times reduced to twenty-five dollars). Despite the orders-in-council, assisted immigration of Jews and others continued. Over the years the work of the English-Jewish societies succeeded in effecting a considerable enlargement of the Canadian-Jewish population. It also created bonds between Jews in Canada and the mother country. Jews who had never set foot on English soil were aided by the societies; and they, too, often came to regard England as their adopted mother country, out of gratitude to the Russo-Jewish Committee or the JCA.[126]

It was not only the poor and the unemployed who came to Canada. Both Jews and gentiles who came from England represented all walks of life. Most of those aided by either the Jewish or the government information bureau later in the nineteenth century were artisans or unskilled workers. Cigarmakers, tailors, cabinetmakers, and other skilled workers composed a fair number of the working-class Jews who left for Canada in the three decades prior to 1914. Others came as servant girls, nursemaids, and cooks.[127] A few working-class Jews in England were attracted to Canada because of the opportunity offered for settlement on the land. Already in 1893, well before the election of Laurier and the vigorous immigration policy of Clifford Sifton, the *Jewish Chronicle* was encouraging its readers to think of settling "in the backwoods of Canada."[128] Of those who answered the call, many were imbued with a desire to redress the imbalance of the Jewish economy, in which businessmen were perceived to be over-represented and agriculturists under-represented. They wanted to prove to antisemites and to themselves that Jews could be productive. Others simply wished to farm. In 1906 a group of Jews from England, South Africa, and eastern Europe established a Jewish agricultural settlement at Melfort, Saskatchewan, which they called Edenbridge. (This was the Anglicized version of the Yiddish, *Yidden-bridge,* or "Jewish bridge.") Four years later they were joined by additional Jews from England, who had first tried to set up a cooperative farm near London. A few others came over the years, but of those Jews intending to settle on the land, only a few actually did so. Of those, most failed as farmers. They were insufficiently prepared for Canadian conditions, and they usually had too little capital. Jews, however, were not unlike other immigrants from the British Isles. Of the Irish only 1.9 percent settled on the land during the period under review; of the Scotsmen, only 5.2 percent did so.[129]

As a rule, "the higher in the British social scale a man stood, the less likely" he was to emigrate to North America.[130] But some well-placed Jews and gentiles did emigrate from England to Canada during the period, sometimes seeking to enhance or restore their fortunes. The examples of Joseph Samuel Leo and William Sebag-Montefiore are instructive. Leo was born in London in 1859. He came from a wealthy and distinguished family that moved in English scholarly circles. He was himself educated at University College, London. Leo emigrated to Canada in 1883, where he founded the first optical company in the country, an enormously successful enterprise. William Sebag-Montefiore, a relation of Sir Moses Montefiore, belonged to the decaying gentry. In 1912 he resigned his army commission and emigrated to Canada. During World War I, Sebag-Montefiore rejoined his regiment, serving in Palestine as well as in Europe. Later he returned to Canada, where he married into the wealthy, pioneer Joseph family. The first and the second wives of Sebag-Montefiore were daughters of Horace Joseph.[131]

Some Englishmen were motivated to emigrate to Canada by a sense of adventure. As an outpost of the Empire, Canada was far off and still largely unsettled. The very qualities that made the country unattractive to many were those that attracted others in a period of general restlessness. Marcus Hyman was the son of a London rabbi of eastern European origin. Before emigrating to Winnipeg in 1913, Hyman had served as tutor to the son of the Gaekwar of Baroda in India. He moved from one end of the Empire to the other, like not a few restless Englishmen of the day. Samuel Kronick was a delegate from Kovno, Lithuania, to the fourth Zionist Congress in London in 1900. He liked London better than Kovno, remained there for nine months, and then moved on to Canada, abandoning his Palestinian ideal. One eastern European Jew who had emigrated to London in the early 1890s was overwhelmed by the splendor of the parading Royal Canadian Northwest Mounted Police during the pageants of the Queen's Diamond Jubilee of 1897. He determined to make the country of the RCMP his own and left England for Canada. People already uprooted from their homes and accustomed to wandering found it relatively easy to move on.[132]

Another group of Englishmen who emigrated to Canada during this period were those who married Canadians. Especially before the turn of the twentieth century, when the Canadian Jewish community was still very small, it was often difficult to find a suitable mate. There was a very high rate of intermarriage in these years, and a high rate of bachelorhood and especially spinsterhood as well. (Jewish women have apparently always been more reluctant to intermarry than men.) Those who sought a Jewish mate often had to search outside the tiny Canadian community, either in the United States or in Europe. Aaron Hart established the pattern, when he returned to England to marry his cousin, Dorothea Judah of Portsmouth. Even after it had become easier to find a Jewish mate in Canada prominent Canadian families continued to value an English marriage for snobbish reasons. Montefiore Joseph, the son of Quebec businessman and banker Abraham Joseph, found a wife in England in 1882. Five years later his cousin, Rabbi Meldola De Sola, married Katie Samuel, daughter of the minister of London's Bayswater Synagogue. Many other Canadians followed suit.[133]

Perhaps the most influential group of British-Jewish emigrants to Canada was the clergy. Many British clergymen—although generally not the Anglicans—were eager to emigrate in the nineteenth century. Clerical incomes were low and social status generally commensurate. The situation of rabbis reflected that of clergymen in general. There was during the period a determined effort on the part of some communal leaders to upgrade the status of the rabbinate. As the *Jewish Chronicle* ruefully noted, however, it was the Jews of "America and the colonies" who seemed "alive to the importance of" such a change and not British Jews.[134] Although the Chief Rabbinate gained in stature throughout the century, the synagogue rabbinate in general languished. Often as a result, better educated and more ambitious clergymen, such as Morris J. Raphall and Abraham De Sola, looked to North America, Raphall to New York and De Sola to Montreal. Actually De Sola's departure was hastened by his losing the election for the post of *hazzan* (cantor, and in the case of Sephardim, rabbi as well) at the venerable Bevis Marks Synagogue in London. He was defeated by David Piza, the lackluster *hazzan* of Montreal.[135]

All of the earliest officiants in Canada's first congregation, the Spanish and Portuguese Synagogue of Montreal, came from England. The first regular minister of the congregation was Jacob Raphael Cohen, who arrived in Montreal in 1778. After a stormy career there (his tenure ended in a lawsuit over salary) Cohen moved on to Philadelphia and New York, following what would become a well-trodden path for clergy: England to Canada to the United States. Following Cohen came two men whose exact terms of office are uncertain: Raphael de Lara and Isaac Valentine. (Valentine probably had no formal training for the ministry and perhaps only volunteered his services to the congregation. In the census of 1842 he listed his occupation as "clerk.") Apparently both returned to England. In 1838 after a steady decline of lay interest in the congregation, some of the more traditional members insisted that a search be undertaken for a more suitable minister. Despite the low annual salary of five hundred dollars that was offered, Rev. David Piza agreed to come from London to serve as preacher, *hazzan,* teacher, and *mohel* (ritual circumciser). He remained until 1845 when he returned triumphantly to England as the newly elected *hazzan* at Bevis Marks.[136]

Abraham De Sola, Piza's successor, had the class and culture often

Marcus Berner, rabbi of Hirsch, Saskatchewan and part-time farmer, around the turn of the century

JPL

Isaac Hellmuth, Polish Jew who converted to the Anglican Church in England, as Bishop of Huron (London), Ontario

University of Western Ontario, London, Archives

Gatehouse of "Glenedyth," the ancestral "demesne" of Samuel Nordheimer, as it appeared in the 1890s

Jewish lads—The Queen Esther Cadets in 1914

associated in the New World with Englishmen. He also had the breeding. On both sides he was descended from learned and respected families. The De Solas had lived in England for about a century. His father, David Aaron, was senior minister at Bevis Marks, an enlightened man, a cultured and very traditional Jew. His mother was the daughter of Dr. Raphael Meldola, the *Haham* (Chief Rabbi) of the London Sephardim. His father provided the young Abraham with "a careful education," which, coupled with proverbial "diligence and perseverance," combined to make a man who became the epitome of culture and intellect in the Montreal of his day.[137] De Sola arrived in Montreal in 1847 and served as rabbi of the Spanish and Portuguese Synagogue until his death thirty-five years later. He represented a living link with the mother country for Montreal Jews. He traveled there; he cooperated with British-Jewish charitable endeavors and particularly with Sir Moses Montefiore. He looked to English rabbis for approval and to England for a wife for the son who would succeed him as rabbi.[138]

Other Jewish clergymen who came to Canada from England during the period under review were less distinguished than De Sola. To his own congregation in 1862 came a ritual animal slaughterer from Brighton, whose reputation had not preceded him across the Atlantic. After a few months the man had to be fired, when he was found drunk on the Sabbath. The first minister of Montreal's second synagogue, the German and Polish (later, the English, German and Polish, and now, Shaar Hashomayim), was the Reverend Samuel Hoffnung, formerly of Cheltenham, England. Three of the four rabbis to serve Toronto's Holy Blossom Congregation between 1890 and 1920 came from England. Other British and transmigrant rabbis served in Winnipeg, Victoria, and the Hirsch agricultural colony in Saskatchewan between 1880 and 1914. Converted Jews also came to Canada from Britain. One apostate transmigrant was the Anglican bishop of Huron, Ontario, Isaac Hellmuth. Born a Polish Jew, Hellmuth was instrumental in founding Huron College in London in 1861, now the University of Western Ontario. He served as bishop for eleven years before returning to England to live out his years. Another apostate, Sabeti B. Rohold of Glasgow, was superintendent of the Presbyterian Jewish Mission in Toronto from 1908 to 1923.[139]

Immigrants provided one kind of link with the mother country for Canadians; tourists provided another. As travel became cheaper and faster in the latter years of this period, Englishmen began to visit Canada for short periods. Some came to visit relatives, some on business, and others just to tour the American frontier of the Empire. Of the Jews who came, some left their imprint on the Canadian-Jewish community, although most served to renew the British bond through their presence alone. In 1892 L. S. Davis and Lewis Levy spent considerable time in Montreal. While there they participated in the work of the Young Men's Hebrew Benevolent Society–Baron de Hirsch Institute. Five years later Mr. D. Barish of Liverpool also attended meetings of the Institute during a visit to Montreal. *Noblesse oblige* was not left at home when English Jews traveled.[140]

The most noteworthy Jewish visitor from England during the period was the Right Honorable Herbert Samuel, postmaster general, who paid an official visit to Canada in 1913. Most of the activities on his tour were not, of course, related to Jews, although Samuel, a committed Jew and an avowed Zionist, did not neglect his coreligionists. In Montreal he visited the Baron de Hirsch Institute and other Jewish institutions. One of his best publicized appearances was at the Montefiore Club, where he addressed a distinguished audience of civic leaders and the Jewish membership. Samuel was not the most important member of the cabinet; and his mission to Canada was probably not politically noteworthy. To Canadians of all stripes, however, his Jewishness was symbolically important. Both Jews and gentiles in Canada were for the first time confronted on home territory with a British Jew who had risen to high political office. He was, moreover, posted to Canada by the British government. Such achievement was at the time still unthinkable for a Jew in Canada. No Jew had even sat in the Dominion Parliament since the first Jewish M.P., British-born Henry Nathan (Conservative member for Victoria), had retired in 1874. In 1887 Arthur Wellington Hart had actually written to Prime Minister Sir John A. Macdonald and to Governor General Lord Lansdowne protesting Jews' exclusion from the political life of Canada. (As late as 1931 the percentage of Jews in public service was less than one-fifth that of Anglo-Canadian gentiles.) During Samuel's visit both Jews and gentiles were moved to comment on British tolerance. Prominent Canadian Jews surely found their affection for the mother country reaffirmed and, at the same time, their feelings toward Canada called into question.[141]

The traffic across the Atlantic between England and Canada was not all one-way during these years. Although life in Canada had become steadily more civilized in the nineteenth century, London and even provincial British cities still offered more cultural amenities as well as better developed Jewish communities than any place in Canada. Moreover, despite the Canadian inheritance of a measure of British tolerance, fair play, and sympathy for Jews, prejudice remained in greater evidence than in England, as the career of Herbert Samuel demonstrated. As a result, not a few well-placed Canadian Jews removed to England. Among those who emigrated were members of Canada's oldest Jewish families, including granddaughters of pioneer Henry Joseph of Berthier, themselves third-generation Canadians. The most numerous returnees were well-to-do businessmen. Some had been leaders of the Canadian-Jewish community and one, a successful politician. From Toronto the Lumleys and the Brahmses, who had come to Canada in the 1840s, returned to London in the 1860s; in 1908 Frank D. Benjamin, businessman and longtime president of Holy Blossom Temple, returned. From Montreal the Mosses, Levys, and Benjamins all returned to England in the early years of the period under review. In later years the exodus increased. From Victoria, Henry Nathan, former member of the Dominion Parliament, left for England in 1880. (In 1954 Abraham A. Heaps, longtime member of Parliament from Winnipeg, who had emigrated to Canada from his native Leeds at the turn of the century, followed in Nathan's footsteps by returning to the land of his birth.)[142]

Luckless Canadian Jews also returned to England, especially after 1880. In 1908 the *Jewish Chronicle* remarked that for the first time in memory more people—Jews and gentiles—had left Canada for England during the preceding depression year than had set out in the opposite direction. The Baron de Hirsch Institute paid for the return to England of a number of unsuccessful immigrants over the years. On several occasions undesirables were deported at the expense of the Canadian government.[143]

Most Anglo-Canadians did not, of course, leave permanently for England, although significant numbers sought ways to spend at least some time there. By the close of the nineteenth century Canadians who could afford it were traveling often to England on holiday or for social occasions. They tended to do so rather more often even than the increasingly peripatetic Americans. In June 1895, for example, Rabbi and Mrs. De Sola made the crossing to attend the wedding of the daughter of Hermann Adler, the Chief Rabbi of the British Empire. The ceremony was held in the synagogue presided over by Mrs. De Sola's father. Well-to-do Canadian Jews began to summer in England. Toronto's Canadian-born Sigmund Samuel, whose father was an immigrant from England, maintained two homes, one in Canada and one in England. Samuel, a most enthusiastic Anglophile, tried twice in the period just beyond that

בְּרוּךְ הַבָּא

THE RT. HON. HERBERT L. SAMUEL.

BANQUET FOR MR. HERBERT SAMUEL.

To be Given by Montefiore Club—Reception by Community at the Baron de Hirsch Institute.

The distinguished Jewish visitor to our shores, the Right Honorable Herbert Samuel, M.P., Post-Master General of Great Britain, is due to arrive in Montreal on Wednesday, October 8th. He will spend about a week in Montreal and will take the opportunity of visiting various Jewish institutions in our city.

An invitation has been extended to him by the Montefiore Club, and he has consented to be their guest at a banquet to be held on Thursday, October 9th. On this same evening he will visit the Baron de Hirsch Institute where he will be welcomed to Montreal on behalf of the Jewish community. The gathering, to which thousands of invitations are being sent out, will be an auspicious one. A splendid welcome will be accorded by the Montreal Jewish community to its distinguished visitor. The event will be unique in Canadian-Jewish history, for this is the first occasion upon which Canadian-Jews have extended honor to a co-religionist who occupies a British Cabinet position.

The *Jewish Times* welcomes Postmaster General Herbert Samuel to Montreal in 1913 under review to enter "the finest club in the world," the British Parliament. He ran unsuccessfully both times.[144]

Especially after the turn of the century students from Canada were drawn to England's superior universities, where graduate studies were far more advanced than in Canada. Israel Isidore Rubinowitz, upon completion of his B.A. at McGill in 1904, was named Rhodes Scholar for British Columbia. While at Oxford, Rubinowitz occasionally assisted Herman Landau in propagandizing for Canada among British Jews. A second Jewish Rhodes Scholar of the period was Simon Abrahamson of Manitoba. Among other Canadian-Jewish students in England was Abraham Charles (Bram) De Sola, son of Rabbi Meldola, who earned a B.A. at McGill in 1910 and then another at Oxford two years later. He returned to Montreal and then went back to Oxford to receive a Master of Arts degree in 1921.[145]

Throughout this period England represented to many Canadians the global cultural and intellectual center, a place where recognition counted for much more than in Canada. (Such an attitude persists today. Witness the recent long sojourn of Canada's most successful contemporary Jewish novelist, Mordecai Richler, in London.) Isidore Ascher, one of the earliest Jewish law graduates of McGill, had been brought to Canada as a boy by his businessman father. Better known as a poet and literary figure than as a lawyer, he published poems in various North American journals and, in 1863, a well-received volume of poetry, *Voices from the Hearth*. Like so many other Canadians of the day, Ascher looked upon acclaim in Canada as less significant than acclaim in the mother country. In 1864 he returned to England, where he lived until his nineties as a minor but not unsuccessful litterateur. The Montreal Jewish opera singer, Pauline (Lightstone) Donalda, was another Canadian who sought fame in England. The high point of her career was a command performance at Covent Garden in 1905. And Rabbi Meldola De Sola returned to England as often as he could to occupy the pulpit to which his father had not been elected. He was extremely proud in 1895, albeit on a summer Sabbath with few congregants in attendance, to be the "first preacher not connected with the [Bevis Marks] congregation . . . to preach . . . [there] within 10 years."[146]

For other Canadians the tie with England was more prosaic, involving business connections. The import-export trade was a favored occupation among Jews, partly because they had family and friends in other countries with whom they could trade. Often the products and the foreign trading partners of Canadian Jews were British. Some successful Canadian Jews established British branches of their companies. Others served as the Canadian branch managers of British firms. In this respect, Canadian Jews were, of course, no different from other Anglo-Canadian businessmen.[147]

For most Canadian and British Jews, the immigrant and the itinerant traffic as well as the international business connections fostered familial and friendship networks that were kept up and renewed over the years. Consequently, despite the distance that separated them, people celebrated and mourned together. When John Moss died twelve years after his return to England from Canada, the Canadian *Jewish Times* had not forgotten him. On the occasion of the death of former Montreal city councillor, Samuel Benjamin, in London in 1893, decades after he had left Montreal, the flag of the Montreal city hall was lowered to half staff in his memory. Some Jews moved permanently from England to Canada or from Canada to England. Others traveled for their education, for adventure, to augment their reputations, to imbibe culture, on business, or for pleasure. Increasingly the England–Canada route was a two-way street.[148]

Communal Bonds

In addition to the personal ties of sentiment, origin, and experience binding Canadian Jews to England in their first century and a half in the New World, there developed a communal bond no less important. Canadians sought religious guidance from those British leaders and institutions they had known before emigrating; British congregations provided material and spiritual assistance to fledgling Canadian synagogues. Canadian Jews also affiliated with secular British-Jewish fraternal and communal organizations. Other Canadians of British origin were behaving in a similar fashion.

To some observers Canadian congregations before World War I seemed to be "only very slightly in touch with . . . England."[149] This was to some extent the case. As noted already a number of Canadian rabbis had close ties with the mother country, and yet neither the Sephardic *Haham* nor the Ashkenazic (i.e., referring to Jews originating in eastern and central Europe) Chief Rabbi ever held the same power over Canadian congregations that he held over other colonial Jewries or, for that matter, over certain American congregations in the eighteenth century and the first decades of the nineteenth. There were close ties and sometimes strong sentiments, but Canadian Jews evidenced the religious independence that would generally characterize American Jews later on. Montreal's Spanish and Portuguese Synagogue illustrates the nature of Britain's tenuous hold. Whereas the Spanish and Portuguese Synagogue in New York was one American congregation that leaned heavily upon London for religious guidance and leadership, the Spanish and Portuguese Synagogue of Montreal tended to look more to New York. As England did in so many areas of Canadian life, she seemed content to plant the seeds and allow them to grow to maturity by themselves.[150]

Still, as many nineteenth-century observers also perceived, the general Canadian "religious environment . . . [was] British" during the period.[151] English conservatism rather than American radicalism characterized religion in Canada during these years; and Canadian Jews continued to be inspired by the vitality of British-Jewish religious and cultural life. The rabbis who came from England were "immensely proud of . . . [their] British birth."[152] Together with the Anglophile Meldola De Sola, they helped to maintain the English hue of Canadian Judaism and, no doubt, were in part sought out for that reason. Although "in many ritual matters, such as the introduction of the organ and having a female choir," various Canadian congregations made their own decisions, they still felt themselves to be "nominally under the jurisdiction of the Chief Rabbi of England,"[153] who remained their spiritual mentor even though he exercised no real authority.

In the earliest years Montreal and Toronto Jews turned to England for religious rulings, which no one in Canada had the knowledge or the authority to issue. In 1844 Rev. Piza asked *Haham* Meldola of London what to do when he was unable to gather a *minyan* (the quorum necessary for public prayer). Meldola refused to sanction public prayer without a *minyan* and recommended that Piza work harder to encourage his congregants to attend services. Perhaps because the learned London rabbis seemed out of touch with harsh colonial realities, not many such questions have been recorded. But Abraham De Sola, the successor of Piza and grandson of Meldola, desired and obtained the imprimatur of the then Sephardic *Haham,* Dr. Benjamin Artom, for his new prayer book in 1878, which he dedicated to Sir Moses and the late Lady Judith Montefiore. Montreal synagogues borrowed from England the form of prayers, the custom of holding special services when members of the royal family were buried or crowned, and even synagogue names. "Shaar Hashomayim" was the Hebrew name of Bevis Marks. "German and

Polish" was the English name of the Ashkenazic community in London.[154]

The two old Montreal congregations retained a certain British orientation throughout this period. In 1886 the bylaws of the German and Polish Congregation still specified that

> the prayers shall be read in the Hebrew language and according to the custom of the English, German and Polish Jews, as now exemplified in the great synagogue, (Duke's Place) London, England.[155]

Similarly the minute books of the Spanish and Portuguese Congregation stipulated in 1892 that

> services would continue to be held according to Spanish and Portuguese Orthodox rituals and customs ... as ... practised ... by the Bevis Marks Synagogue, London.[156]

The English rabbis at Toronto's oldest congregation, Holy Blossom, preserved a conservative British atmosphere. In like fashion the Baron de Hirsch School in Montreal looked to England for religious models at the turn of the century. The course in "religious knowledge" taught there was "the same as that used in all the Jewish schools in England."[157]

In the early years England was one of the likely sources for the liturgical appurtenances needed for Jewish worship. (The other was the United States, relations with which will be discussed below.) When it was first established, the Montreal Spanish and Portuguese Congregation turned to the "Portuguese Congregation" of London for Torah scrolls, which that congregation "thought proper to send ... as a present."[158] As late as 1873, Rabbi De Sola requested that one of his congregants visiting in London send to Montreal prayer shawls, which were in short supply.[159]

Throughout much of the nineteenth century it was common for established synagogues to assist new congregations; they in turn aided others. Appeals to England for funds were made by Montreal Jews whenever they contemplated a major project. Rev. Isaac Valentine turned to the Chief Rabbi in 1832, informing him that Canadian Jews had recently received full political equality with Christians and could now sit in the legislature.

> It now only remains for us to erect a Temple for ... worship. ... Being few in number and many of those few, having large families we find it impossible

to purchase a Lot of Ground and build a Synagogue and House for the Reader and Sexton without asking for assistance.[160]

That appeal went unanswered, but later requests met with more generosity.[161]

Eventually, Canadians began to send funds to England. Like other immigrants from Britain, Jews remitted money to their families left behind. Canadians also began to make charitable contributions in England. In 1854 Rabbi De Sola received a plea from the Chief Rabbi, Dr. Nathan Marcus Adler, to aid "Jews in the East." On that occasion and on others De Sola collected small sums in Montreal, which he forwarded to England. Sir Moses Montefiore usually acted as bursar. By the 1890s various English-Jewish philanthropic organizations were soliciting contributions in Canada, and they received a limited response. Canadians continued, for the most part, to be on the receiving end during the period. Most Montreal Jewish institutions requested aid at one time or another from the more charitable and better established British Jews. So, too, did Jews in other Canadian cities. In time, however, British Jews grew less willing to proffer aid, since they were aware that Canadians could now rely on their own resources.[162]

Yet another Canadian Jewish tie to the religious world of England was unique and concerned Meldola De Sola, a born meddler. He was possessed by a dybbuk that urged him on to endless and often tasteless opposition to the Reform Movement everywhere. The rabbi kept a scrapbook filled with his own letters, mostly pseudonymous, to newspapers in Canada, the United States, and especially England. In 1895 as "Querist" De Sola chided the British Chief Rabbi for being soft on Reform. Masquerading as "An American Jew," he complained that London's Jews' College produced only Reformist rabbis, like his own brother-in-law and former Canadian colleague, Barnett A. Elzas, who served for a time in Toronto. (De Sola went so far as to name Elzas in his letter, and perhaps one reason for the pseudonym on this occasion was the family connection. Still, De Sola's style was well known. Many of the *Jewish Chronicle*'s readers undoubtedly guessed the "American Jew's" identity and thought him quite tactless.) De Sola pursued his quarry with houndlike determination. When the English-born, liberal New York rabbi, Maurice Harris, was invited to preach in a London synagogue, Rabbi De Sola stirred up an enormous brouhaha. Ultimately the Chief Rabbi felt compelled to forbid the appearance. Whereas the

Chief Rabbi held only limited sway in Canada, De Sola could exert considerable influence in the mother country.[163]

In addition to the religious connection with England, Canadian Jews maintained a wide variety of organizational ties, especially after 1875. Canadian-Jewish Freemasons were members of the London Lodge of Joppa in the 1870s. In the initial years of the Zionist movement, Canadian Jews affirmed their affiliation with the new movement through the offices of like-minded Britishers. Canadians did not at first bother to travel to Zionist congresses, preferring to delegate Britishers, such as Jacob de Haas (who later emigrated to the United States), as their proxy. It was only at the fourth Zionist Congress that Canadian Jews were in attendance, perhaps because it was held in London, the capital of the Empire. There, Clarence I. De Sola, the Canadian delegate, was regarded as a rather strange curiosity by Zionist leaders accustomed to thinking of Canada as very remote. At a reception that both attended, Theodor Herzl found De Sola "the most interesting thing" in London.[164] Canadian contacts with British Zionism continued along the same lines in the last years of the period under review.[165]

Other British groups, such as the Grand Order of Israel [Sick] Benefit Society and the Union for the Protection of Jewish Girls, also established branches in Canada. Of wider significance was the Anglo-Jewish Association (hereafter referred to as AJA), the self-defense organization of British Jews. The Montreal branch of the AJA dates to the end of the 1870s. A Toronto chapter was organized in 1880. Although in the early 1880s the Torontonians engaged in immigrant aid work, the activities of the Canadian chapters were largely limited to fund raising. The AJA preferred to concentrate its substantive efforts "on the other side of the Atlantic."[166] As was recognized even at the time, however, the AJA in Canada performed an important function quite accidental to its stated purposes. The group served to "unite . . . the Jews of the British Empire" and to Anglify them.[167] It was characteristic of the assimilatory power of the AJA that for many years the president of its Toronto chapter was the Alsatian Jew Edmund Scheuer; in Montreal another French Jew, Moise Schwob, served for some time as vice-president. Both chapters had a fair number of eastern European members as well.[168]

Yet another British-Jewish organization that successfully spread to Canada during the period was the Jewish Lads' Brigade. Modeled on the Church Lads' Brigade, the Jewish Lads was largely a product of the jingo atmosphere that pervaded England and her colonies during the

Boer War period. By the time of the death of its founder, Colonel Albert E. W. Goldsmid, in 1904 the Brigade had enlisted some four thousand members, most of whom were in the British Empire, although there was also a chapter in New York City. Colonel Goldsmid had been instrumental in Montreal's forming "one of the first [companies] in the Colonies of the Empire."[169]

Drilling and military exercises at the Baron de Hirsch School in Montreal were begun as early as 1895, although the first official company of the Brigade, the Hirsch Cadets, was organized only in 1897. By 1903 there were three additional companies in Montreal. A year later a group was formed in Kingston, Ontario, and in 1905 one was set up in Toronto. Along with units of the Church Lads' Brigade the Toronto company was inspected in 1906 by the visiting Prince Arthur of Connaught. After that time interest in the group languished, as the jingo fever abated somewhat.[170]

Of British-Jewish organizations only the AJA and the Jewish Lads' Brigade made any real impact in Canada, although neither of them attracted large numbers to its fold. (Even in England membership in these two organizations was limited.) Altogether, however, the various formal communal and organizational ties bound a significant number of Canadian Jews to the mother country in the period before World War I, including many for whom such a connection was somewhat artificial. The Baron de Hirsch School of Montreal was established by settled Jews in order to Anglify eastern European immigrant children and to prepare them for entry into the city's Protestant schools. "In consequence of the recommendation of the Rt. Hon. Lord Strathcona," (then Canadian high commissoner in Great Britain), W. H. Baker, principal of the school in 1904, "caused a selection of the pupils . . . to open a correspondence with children in" various Jewish schools in London.[171] To cement ties of Canadian youngsters with England the London Jewish Board of Guardians regularly presented medals to the pupils of the Montreal school. In such fashion even Canadian Jews of Eastern origin came to identify with England and to look upon her as their adopted mother country.[172]

Canadian Jews and British Affairs

Canadian Jews, like other Anglo-Canadians, often found themselves involved in the life and affairs of England almost as much as if they lived there. During the nineteenth century and afterward they kept up with the affairs of British Jews and took part in them. Abraham Joseph of Quebec recorded with pleasure in his diary in 1837 the elevation of "one of our creed . . . to the high office of Sheriff of London." When the wife of Sir Moses Montefiore died, he received condolences from Montreal Jews. Canadian Jews joined with the rest of their brethren all over the world to mark the hundredth birthday of Sir Moses in 1884. In Montreal the Montefiore Social and Dramatic Club gave a grand ball. The two oldest congregations attempted unsuccessfully to bury their rivalry and cooperate in celebrating. In the end, however, the German and Polish Congregation held a mass meeting to honor the centenarian and sent him a memorial. The Spanish and Portuguese Congregation held its own standing-room-only thanksgiving service at which one of the hymns sung was a Hebrew rendition of "God Save the Queen." In Winnipeg that same year the two pioneer congregations also held special commemorative services. Toronto's Holy Blossom Temple marked the occasion, as well. Years earlier the Jewish women of Toronto had honored Sir Moses by changing the name of the Toronto Hebrew Ladies' Sick and Benevolent Society (*Chebra Gemilas Chesed,* organized in 1868) to the Ladies' Montefiore Hebrew Benevolent Society.[173]

The political achievements of British Jews were considered by Canadians to be in some sense a mark of their own progress. Outsiders as they generally were in the Canadian political arena during most of the nineteenth century, it is not surprising that Canadian Jews derived vicarious glory from the accomplishments of their coreligionists in the mother country. When David Solomons (later Sir David) was elected mayor of the City of London in 1855, and when Baron Lionel Rothschild was finally seated in the British Parliament three years later, congratulatory letters were sent from the Spanish and Portuguese Congregation in Montreal. When Sir Samuel Montagu was elevated to the peerage in 1907, the Baron de Hirsch Institute sent its felicitations. Other British Jews over the years were similarly saluted. In turn, the few political successes of Canadian Jews sometimes elicited a response from the mother country. When, for example, in 1866 Lumley Franklin became mayor of Victoria, Chief Rabbi Nathan Marcus Adler wrote him a letter of congratulations in Hebrew.[174]

After 1890 Jews like other Anglo-Canadians involved themselves in general British affairs, particularly those of the royal family. In 1892 both the Reform Temple Emanu-El and the Spanish and Portuguese Congregation in Montreal held special services for the recently deceased

Duke of Clarence and the Catholic Cardinal Manning, who had spoken out on behalf of the oppressed Jews of Russia. When Victoria died in 1901 and at the death of Edward VII nine years later, special services were held in many synagogues across the country. Happy occasions also involved Canadian Jews in British events.[175]

Between 1880 and 1914 the British connection of Canadian Jews took on an added dimension. By the late nineteenth century the imperial tie in Canada had developed into "a strong emotional attachment, glowing with new pride and fresh hopes and aims, vitalized by important national interests and . . . ambitions."[176] Many Canadians were conscious of living in an out-of-the-way place on the fringes of civilization. To compensate, "their proudest claim [became] that they belonged to this magnificent and powerful [British] state and that in time they would share in its worldwide work."[177] The British connection became all the more important as the power and glory of Canada's southern neighbor grew. Canadian advocates of the imperial connection believed that Canadians were or should be "British in their historical associations, political ideals, their preference for law and order, and their capacity for self-government."[178] Anglo-Canadian school children were now taught that only "the conquest of Canada by the British" had saved the country from "ignorance and repression."[179] To Anglo-Canadians Canada was a "British country," and that was the best thing about it.

A number of political events toward the end of the period under review contributed to the rise of imperialist sentiment in both England and Canada. The 1887 and 1897 jubilees for Victoria evoked an emotional outpouring of self-praise and self-congratulation among all the Queen's subjects. Enthusiasm for British institutions and freedom was especially marked during these confident years; and it seemed to many as though they were present "at the birth of a new order."[180] The Diamond Jubilee in 1897 infected even many French Canadians "with the pride of belonging to so great a nation,"[181] for they too recognized that their own liberty was considerable under British rule. A typical example was Sir Adolphe Chapleau, the lieutenant governor of Quebec. Speaking to the 1897 convention of the Central Conference of American [Reform] Rabbis meeting in Montreal, Chapleau, in the characteristically unrestrained language of the day, praised the "great British constitution under which we live, with its Magna Carta of civil, political and religious liberty."[182] In the flush of this enthusiasm Prime Minster Wilfrid Laurier, rather against his own previous inclination, accepted a knighthood.[183]

Jews, of course, had their own unique ties with England, ties that made it easy for them to join the imperialist bandwagon with great fervor. From the pulpit of the Spanish and Portuguese Synagogue in Montreal, Victoria was proclaimed "the personification of all that is good and great in woman."[184] Rabbi Meldola De Sola turned Jewish holidays into British celebrations. In his 1901 sermon for Hanukkah, the traditional festival of Jewish religious freedom, he preached on the theme, "British Freedom Is Appreciated." A New York Yiddish-speaking Jewish revivalist who went to Montreal in 1898 to preach found even the Jews of eastern European origin there to be "one hundred per cent British patriots."[185]

There was a certain negative aspect to the upsurge of imperial sentiment in Canada at the turn of the century. It was to some degree associated with anti-Americanism. Canadians had been shocked by the statements of President Grover Cleveland and Secretary of State Richard Olney during the Venezuela Boundary Dispute of 1895, as the administration seemed to be implying that no country in the Americas—including Canada—had a right to maintain permanent ties with a European power. The Anglo-American Alaska Boundary Dispute, which directly involved Canadians, added fuel to the fire just a few years later. But it was the 1897 Dingley Tariff that most excited resentment north of the border, since it hit Canadians in their pocketbooks. The imperial connection offered an alternative to the American connection; and tariff preference within the Empire seemed to be the answer.[186]

By far the most important of this string of events was the Boer War. Paradoxically, the war made Anglo-Canadians more British for its duration while simultaneously arousing their own sense of national self. Among French Canadians, most of whom opposed the war, much of the good will created by the Victoria jubilees was dissipated. They tended to identify with the Boers, another small, non-British people with a particular way of life who were being overrun by the British juggernaut. At the core of imperial sentiment was a feeling of Anglo-Saxon racial superiority, which became blatant during the war fever. The abuse heaped upon the Québécois for their lukewarm support of the British war effort further heightened the tension. The English-language yellow press, most notably the Montreal *Star,* was the chief culprit. The war proved to be one of the milestones on the path of rising intercommunal tension in Canada.[187]

Jewish reaction to the war was at first mixed. Eastern European Jews, having themselves been trodden down by an oppressive empire, tended to sympathize with liberation movements and the struggles of minorities.

On the other hand, most Jews felt affection for England. In South Africa itself, Jews were faring rather better under the British than under the Boers. Many, like Rabbi Joseph Hertz, later Chief Rabbi of the British Empire but then a rabbi in Boer Johannesburg and an advocate of religious liberty for Jews and Catholics, favored the British cause.[188]

In Canada as the war continued, there came to be but one possible side for Jews, that of England. Opponents of the war began to scapegoat Jews. It was claimed by many, among them Professor Goldwin Smith, that the war was "the dirty and bloody work of . . . greedy Jew financiers." Since some of those who sought to exploit the mineral resources of South Africa were of Jewish origin, it was alleged that the British were fighting for Jewish interests. French-Canadian papers covering such events as military parades wrote at greatest length about French Canadians, but they also wrote respectfully about Anglo-Canadian soldiers. Jews, however, received no mention. Their martial talents were of no interest to French Canadians, then growing increasingly antisemitic. The Canadian *Jewish Times* remarked in 1900, that "all anti-Semites are pro-Boers."[189] The paper was referring mainly to French Canadians. Pro-war Anglo-Canadians, on the other hand, welcomed Jews to their ranks. All the Montreal English papers enthusiastically reported Jewish war sermons and the activities of the Jewish Lads' Brigade. In 1901 the *Herald* called the Lads "among the smartest of Montreal's junior soldiers."[190]

Out of genuine feeling for Britain and, no doubt, also because they were accepted as partners in the imperialist camp, Jews responded. Perfervid pulpit oratory became the order of the day. As might be expected, Rabbi Meldola De Sola led the way, telling his congregation in 1901 that the Boers were indiscriminate murderers, "guerillas [who slaughtered] . . . men who care for their wives and families." Kruger was "an infamous despot." The rabbi knew of

> some people who profess to admire the Boers. We know how to characterize such admiration when we reflect that among their other iniquities, the Boers have treated the natives with unspeakable cruelty; . . . abused the flag of truce, . . . killed the wounded, and mutilated the dead.[191]

De Sola's was not a lone voice, although his was less controlled than others. Rabbi Aaron Mordecai Ashinsky of Montreal, of eastern European origin, exulted in a Winnipeg speech in 1900 that with the victory in South Africa, the Anglo-Saxon "race would finally govern the whole world."[192] Jews all over the Dominion gave money to the Canadian

Patriotic Fund. In response to the general eagerness for military drilling and for teenage cadet training the Jewish Lads' Brigade expanded. A few Canadian Jews found their way into the ranks of the soldiers on active duty; two of them, Drs. Lightstone and Harris, were later decorated in Montreal by the Duke of York. Another died of the fever at Blömfontein. For Jews, as for Anglo-Canadians in general, it was "a pleasant, little fight," although more drawn out than originally anticipated.[193]

One of the major vehicles for imperialist sentiment in the late Victorian era was the imperial federation movement, which proposed free trade among the various polities of the British Empire, an Imperial Parliament with full colonial participation, and unified imperial defense, especially in naval matters. The Imperial Federation League was founded in 1884, and the first chapter in Canada was established in Montreal in 1885. From there it spread to Ontario and the Maritimes; although the movement never completely captured Anglo-Canadian support, its popularity was considerable. The League disintegrated by 1894; but by then the idea of federation had gathered so much strength that advocates were able to carry on propaganda work without the oranizational structure. The passage of the Naval Aid Bill by the House of Commons in 1912–13 showed how strong imperial sentiment remained in Canada on the eve of World War I.[194]

Among Canadian Jews—most particularly in Montreal—there was corresponding interest in imperial federation. David A. Ansell, one of the most prominent leaders of the Montreal Jewish community and himself an immigrant from England, was a spokesman for the movement. He peppered the newspapers with letters on the subject and in November 1886 read a paper, "Welding the Links of Union," before the Montreal branch of the Federation League. The speech, later published as a propaganda pamphlet, pleaded for a "closer degree of union between the various colonies and dependencies [sic], and their mother country, Great Britain."[195]

Other Jews were less outspoken but, on the whole, sympathetic. During its early years Montreal's Montefiore Social and Dramatic Club discussed imperial federation on several occasions. In 1909 the city's Yiddish-language daily, the *Keneder odler,* expressed pleasure that the Imperial Defense Conference then being held in London was working to "unite . . . the English colonies with their motherland." The paper evinced pride in Britain's being "now the greatest military power in the world"; and it was fully confident that in time of trouble, Australia and

Canada, "her two children, would leap to her aid."[196] Although leftists undoubtedly opposed aspects of imperialism as they did in England, the United States, and elsewhere, most Canadian Jews harbored strong imperial sentiments that were connected with their love for Britain and—whatever their native land—with their sense of themselves as real or potential Anglo-Canadians.[197] Also, the sense of mission with which imperialism was infused appealed to a number of Jews and Chrstians who saw it as akin to that of ancient Israel. In the formulation of one of the intellectual leaders of Anglo-Canada, George M. Grant, what the Bible had originally enjoined upon ancient Israel, the British Empire would now fulfill: to make "the world the home of freedom, of justice, and of peace."[198]

The imperialistic sense of mission with its assumption of Anglo-Saxon superiority presupposed that the British race could conquer any people, assimilate them, and improve them. The nationalist and imperialist spokesman of Anglo-Canada, D'Alton McCarthy, proclaimed in 1890:

> This is a British country, and the sooner we take up our French Canadians and make them British, the less trouble will we leave for posterity.[199]

British magic could also be worked upon the Jews. William Lyon Mackenzie King noted in 1897 that Toronto's two to three hundred British Jews were "the most intelligent and prosperous of their race."[200] According to all but the most extreme nativists, the British could "improve" all "inferiors," at least in the intellectual sphere, and assimilate them.

Precisely because the British sense of superiority encompassed a notion of "making British" all who lived under the British flag, there was a place in the Anglo-Saxon constellation for Jews and others. Although they were not always incorporated into the British camp wholeheartedly, as noted earlier, outsiders could acquire at least conditional membership, if they imbibed enough of the spirit and learned to play the game. This was a qualified racism, at least in theory. It provided a link between Jews and others that could be useful and therefore not uncongenial to British and Anglo-Canadians. It was welcomed by most Jews, even if full acceptance was a possibility only for the very rich. Perhaps naïvely, Jews assumed that universal acceptance was a matter of time and would come with acculturation. In the imperialist atmosphere at the turn of the century Canadian Jews, including those with no obvious British connection, worked hard to become Anglified; some even fabricated for themselves the kinds of ties to England they perceived to be prerequisites for acceptance. Those who had a legitimate connection made the most of it, and most Canadian Jews were prepared to forgo some measure of their Jewish identity in return for admission into WASP Anglo-Canadian circles.

It seemed natural at the time for immigrant Canadian Jews from eastern Europe such as Louis Aronson, who had come to Montreal from Russian Poland by way of New York in 1872, to profess themselves "profoundly attached to British institutions."[201] Like Harris Vineberg, those who had acclimated already to Canada were eager to assist later immigrants "to enjoy the privileges of British freedom, British institutions."[202] Those who could joined associations of Englishmen resident in Canada: the Sons of England and the more prestigious Society of St. George. Lewis Samuel of Toronto belonged to both. Among those marching in his mile-and-a-half long funeral cortege in 1887 were many fellow members of the two societies. Other Jews, like Michael Hirsch, born in Montreal in 1864 of British parents, or Samuel's son, Sigmund, of Toronto, were most proud of their "birthright as a Canadian and as a British subject."[203] Rabbi Meldola De Sola, whose father and wife were British-born, was usually very orthodox in religious matters. Yet he, too, was willing to put Britishness before Judaism. The rabbi went so far as to declare that not God's law, but the "authority of . . . our Sovereign Lady the Queen" was supreme in matters of marriage. "As a British citizen," he averred, "I have yet to learn that there is any authority that stands above the crown."[204] On the occasion of the 1901 visit to Canada of the duke and duchess of Cornwall and York (the future George V) the Canadian *Jewish Times* was "mindful of the deep significance of the royal tour." Assuming that Anglo-Israel theories had achieved universal acceptance in Britain, the *Times* declared that the British were

> a race which pays to the Church of Israel the flattering compliment of claiming relationship. . . . [Consequently] our loyalty is . . . British not Jewish, for we merge our race in the empire to which we belong.[205]

In their institutional lives as well as in their personal lives, Canadian Jews cultivated the British image. In 1903 the "Corporation of German and Polish Jews of Montreal" officially changed its name to the "Corporation of English, German and Polish Jews, Shaar Hashomayim." The change was more a reflection of heightened sentiment than of the national origin of the members. In Quebec in 1896 the synagogue was no more than "a dingy room in the third floor of a sailors' boarding-house, far down in the shipping district . . . conducted by Russian Jews." But even those immigrants were "touched with the air of London from the stove-pipe headgear of the men down to the 'fried-egg' of the little chaps."[206] In 1903 transmigrants formed the King Edward Sick Benefit Association in Montreal. Eight years later other Jews of Russian origin in Montreal founded the King George Sick Benefit Society. Although these men had not tarried long in England, they nonetheless felt different from others of eastern European origin. Even with their broken English, they were "people inbued [sic] with British traditions and way of life"; and they segregated themselves from Jews who had not had an English experience.[207] Some of the efforts to appear English were ludicrous. In Toronto "a group of Jewish young men who had either been born or had lived for some time in England, and who were desirous of worshiping in the manner prevailing in England," organized the Hebrew Men of England Congregation in 1909.[208] The name itself sounded odd, and if the manner of worship was "English," it was the style of the immigrant congregations of Whitechapel, not the "high English" congregations of the United Synagogue.

Jews tried to be British even "in their historical associations." Some went so far as to deny their Jewish connection altogether in order to win acceptance by Anglo-Canadian gentiles. Abraham and Samuel Nordheimer were pioneer Toronto Jews. Abraham died on a trip to Germany, but Samuel remained in Toronto and married a non-Jew. The descendants of both brothers belonged to the WASP establishment of Toronto; but apparently the family remained uneasy about its Jewish past and its tenuous British connection. A publicity booklet put out by the family piano firm in 1903 tried to remedy the defective past. Abraham, with his telltale Jewish name, was referred to in the booklet only as "Mr. A., sr." (Mr. A., Jr., was Albert!) "Glenedyth," the home of Samuel Nordheimer, was said to "remind the visitor of the finest of English demesnes and ancestral halls." It bore no conscious traces of the German-Jewish ancestry of its occupants.[209]

The cover-up attempt of Clarence I. De Sola was less self-abnegating but more sweeping. De Sola manufactured a grand English past for almost all of Canada's pioneer Jews. He conferred an English-Sephardic lineage on Canada's first Jewish families, cleansing them of any connection with eastern Europe. To Alexander Harkavy, the noted Yiddish lexicographer, then a Hebrew school teacher in Montreal, De Sola confided that early Canadian Jews had almost all been "men of Poland"

and not of England. Yet, despite objections from some Montrealers, De Sola insisted in his public pronouncements and in print that early Canadian Jews had been descended from Spanish grandees long resident in England, like his own ancestors. Reflective as it was of Jews' consciousness of their incomplete Britishness and nervousness about their acceptability, De Sola's version of history held sway for many years.[210]

Canadian Jews were not alone in creating for themselves an exalted British past during this heyday of imperial sentiment. In general, there was a new emphasis in Canada upon "historical antecedents." A "growing consciousness of history and the past was marked in nearly every department of Canadian culture."[211] French Canadians had a sense of their own past. They found the frantic search for British antecedents among Anglo-Canadians and especially among Jews to be funny, contemptible, and even "treacherous."[212] But by the late nineteenth century the British connection had become an important status symbol in Anglo-Canada. Not unnaturally Jews, increasingly eager to be full partners in Anglo-Canada, sought such a past.

The Knot Tied

Jews everywhere, then, in the eighteenth and nineteenth centuries felt admiration for England. Not a few migrated to Britain or to her colonies. England's relative openness and toleration as well as her championship of Jews in the international arena made it almost inevitable that Jews who had resided there or in one of the colonies would come to look upon themselves as British. Considering British tradition and practice it is also not surprising that Jews were accepted in Britain and in Canada— although not by all—as Britishers. In an early Anglo-Canadian tract Jews were already subsumed under the rubric "British and other Protestant inhabitants."[213] When Aaron Hart died in 1801, *The European Magazine and London Review* remarked simply that he

> was the first British merchant who settled at Three Rivers after that place was taken by his friend General Haldimand in the year 1760.[214]

Such an identification was particularly easy when the number of Jews in Canada was small and many of them had, in fact, come from Britain. Even after large numbers of Jews, mostly from eastern Europe, began to come to Canada, however, the ties of Canadian Jews with England were maintained. The multitude of personal and communal connections of Canadian Jews with the mother country was actually enlarged by the newcomers, who also admired England and who sought to become acculturated. Joining a British-Jewish organization might be a first step in the process. Some were prepared to go much further.

Between 1880 and 1914 the ties of Canadian Jews to England acquired new and greater significance. The Empire itself and, even more, the idea of empire acquired new importance in both Canada and Britain. The ties that Jews had to the mother country facilitated their acceptance into the Anglo-Canadian fold. The nature of the imperialist movement with its exuberant—if at times less than convincing—confidence and sense of racial superiority made it possible for Jews to be considered at least imperfectly British, even if they were not so in any way. Moreover, even though the original Canadian-Jewish community was overwhelmed by eastern European Jews during these years, the Anglicizing process worked to preserve much of the "Englishness" of Canadian Jews. Less now because of origin, but no less because of sentiment, Jews continued to look upon themselves as English Canadians.

CHAPTER THREE

The American Connection

The United States and the Jews

Its European antecedents notwithstanding, Canada is a North American country. From 1759 to 1776, it was the fourteenth American colony of Great Britain. Had the fortunes of war been different, Canada might well have become part of the United States, or part or all of the United States might have remained British, joined with the northernmost colony. Although in 1783 the Treaty of Paris formalized the division between Canada and the thirteen former colonies, people on both sides of the border continued to hope for many years that the countries would be reunited. Moreover, the treaty did not put an end to the intimate cultural, economic, and personal relationships that had already developed among all North Americans of British origin. In fact, as time went on, those ties became closer, despite the border and despite the sometimes divergent political interests of the two countries. For Jews, that Canada was an American country was of considerable significance. By European standards England was remarkably tolerant and open. With its vast economic potential, empty spaces, and social fluidity, however, America represented the real land of opportunity for all eighteenth- and nineteenth-century Europeans and especially for Jews.

Jews everywhere thought of America in these terms. Particularly in eastern and central Europe, Jews beginning to despair of the liberalization of the societies in which they lived, turned to America. There they hoped that the lack of a tradition of antisemitism and the absence of a "Jewish question," together with all the other favorable conditions, might offer them opportunity for a decent existence on an equal footing with Christians. Charles Freshman, the future Quebec rabbi and Ontario Lutheran minister, was typical. While still in Europe and still a Jew, he "had heard wonderful stories of the civil and religious liberty" of America and thereupon "resolved to make that . . . [his] future residence."[1]

Coming *en masse,* Jews put America to the test and were well received. In the freewheeling atmosphere of the American colonies, and then in the young United States, Jews were quick to achieve a degree of public acceptance then unknown anywhere in Europe, even in England. From 1657 on, Jews in New York (then, New Amsterdam) enjoyed most of the privileges and duties of citizenship. By 1850 American Jews were being elected to public office, appointed to positions in the foreign service, and even promoted to important posts in the armed services. By the end of the nineteenth century they had achieved a degree of integration unparalleled in Jewish experience.

The integration of Jews into America was reflected not only in the personal achievements of individuals but also in the institutional and cultural advancement of the community. Early American Jews were not known in Europe for their piety or their intellectual accomplishments. To many America was the *treyfe medine,* the land where freedom often meant the license not to practice Judaism at all.[2] Eventually, however, the United States outdistanced many older European centers culturally and even religiously. World War I catapulted the American-Jewish community to a position of paramount power, leadership, and responsibility among world Jewry. By then the community was prepared to assume that role.

The confluence of Jewish and American interests in the international arena was one of the factors that facilitated the maturation of American Jewry and its willingness to lead. Americans saw themselves as the standard-bearers of democracy and freedom, the champions of the underdog. As such, the government sought on a number of occasions to defend Jews. And the American-Jewish community learned early to flex its muscles. Mordecai Manuel Noah's plan to settle European Jews on Grand Island in the Niagara River between Buffalo and Toronto in the 1820s was a precursor of things to come. During the Damascus blood libel of 1840 and the Mortara kidnapping case in Italy in 1858 Americans voiced their concern at home and abroad over the persecution of Jews. Canadian Jews in 1858, as on other occasions later, joined their protests to those of their American coreligionists.[3] This was the first example of American leadership in such an enterprise, but it was not to be the last. Later during the Dreyfus Affair in France and the persecutions of Jews in Romania and Russia, the American public and often the American government spoke out for Jews and at times extended concrete aid to them. One of the most dramatic events was the renunciation by the United States of the Russian-American trade treaty in 1911 because of Russian refusal to ameliorate the conditions of Jews living within their empire.[4]

As was the case in England, American behavior toward Jews was the manifestation of certain widely held beliefs and assumptions. Americans perceived their country to be the bastion of freedom and democracy. They also shared England's Protestant heritage of affinity with the Hebrew Bible and its language. Some groups, like the early Puritans, saw themselves reenacting the Exodus, coming to the New World to found a new and better Jerusalem.[5] Anglo-Israel theories found ready acceptance in the United States as they did in England and Canada. Henry Wentworth Monk, who preached extensively in the United States, and others considered Americans to be one of the divisions of the "lost ten tribes," along with the British. An extension of such concerns was interest in the Holy Land.[6] Like the British, Americans made pilgrimages and became interested in a restoration of the Jews to their ancient homeland. In 1848 the American consul in Jerusalem, Warder Cresson, became so excited about Palestine and its people that he converted to Judaism. In well-publicized legal proceedings he was at first declared insane. But America was too tolerant to allow such a judgment—that conversion to Judaism was evidence of mental aberration—to be sustained for long. As Michael Boaz Israel, Cresson returned to Palestine, where he lived out his years working for renewed Jewish settlement.[7]

Another of the English ideas about Jews that found currency in the United States was the romantic vision of the Jew as a mysterious bearer of past grandeur and the fount of present vitality. The writer Washington Irving became fascinated with Rebecca Gratz, the Philadelphia Jewish socialite, communal worker, and Sunday school superintendent. His description of the charming, exotic Jewess is said to have inspired Sir Walter Scott's heroine, Rebecca, in the novel *Ivanhoe*. In addition, the image of the Jew as innocent victim of Christianity's depredations was heard as frequently in America as it was in England. Finally, most Americans in the nineteenth century believed their country to be a land of opportunity and equality for all—except people of color. And until the latter years of the century, they felt that there was room for all who chose to acquire a lot in the "city on the hill." Jews were as welcome as anyone else and, in some respects, more welcome than many. The Puritan heritage with its emphasis on Hebrew roots helped. So, too, did the eagerness of Jews to become Americans.[8]

To be sure, antisemitism was not unknown in America during these years. Already during the Civil War considerable anti-Jewish animus had been in evidence. In the latter years of the nineteenth century certain WASP groups, which had held the reins of power in the past, realized they were being elbowed aside by the vigorous newcomers. This decaying gentility often exhibited a most unpleasant antisemitism. Henry Adams, the writer, was their foremost spokesman. With the arrival of large numbers of Russian Jews, underlying tensions between Jews and Christians surfaced. Prejudice against the newcomers was fed by the cult of Anglo-Saxon superiority. As the years went by, it became increasingly clear to Americans and to neutral observers that American xenophobia extended to Jews as well as to blacks, Orientals, Slavs, and others.[9]

But America's dedication to freedom and equality was more in evidence during these years than nativism. Certainly Jews who bore the wounds of Russian and Romanian barbarity could appreciate America's broad tolerance despite its admitted shortcomings. For them the United States was "naturally . . . the ultimate hope."[10] As the American Jewish community gained strength and as more and more Americans came to accept Judaism as one of the major faiths of the country, America appeared to be the new "promised land." In 1888 Alexander Harkavy wrote from Montreal that the United States was God's answer to European persecution, "a new land, which, like a merciful mother, spread her wings over all who sought refuge under them."[11]

Their own good fortune notwithstanding, British Jews, no less than those of the Continent, were most enthusiastic about America. The ambitious saw in the United States a land of economic opportunity even more promising than England or her colonies. Lewis Samuel of London, who eventually settled in Toronto, was drawn first to New York in 1844, where he hoped to find "the streets . . . paved with gold."[12] The well-to-do were attracted to the United States by the promise of social integration more easily achieved than in England's stratified society. In England toleration often meant a willingness on the part of Christians to accept Jews into the fold of Christianity. In America it was not unthinkable for Christians to become Jews. In 1846 the London *Jewish Chronicle* reported with astonishment that

> at New York it frequently happens that gentlemen desirous of entering into the holy state of matrimony fall in love with ladies of the Jewish faith, from whom, however, they receive no encouragement, except on condition of becoming circumcised and embracing the law of Moses. More than twelve individuals, inspired by the one lovely reward held out to them, have lately submitted to those rigorous conditions. The rite is performed by a Portuguese, a most skillful operator.[13]

Although England grew ever more open and tolerant as the century progressed, interest in America did not wane. Even Jews of high standing in British society such as Sir Moses Montefiore appreciated "the broad toleration in religious matters which exists in the United States of America."[14]

The actions of the American government, the sentiments of the American public, and the development of the American-Jewish community in the nineteenth century, then, continued to attract Jews, who came to feel very much at home in their new country. As the American capitalist Erastus Wiman, himself an immigrant from Canada, noted in 1891, "of all the foreign elements" in the United States, Jews invariably became "the most truly American."[15] Many Christian Europeans, although by no means all, shared the Jewish enthusiasm for America.

The United States in the Minds of Canadians

Canadians lived close to the United States. To this day, the large majority lives within 100 miles of the American border. Especially before Confederation in 1867, but afterward as well, they lacked unity and a clear sense of national identity. Sometimes, out of their own insecurity, they tended to be rather more ambivalent about the exuberant United States than were Europeans. They also had reason to fear that "manifest destiny" might turn northward; and they grew increasingly protective of their autonomy. Like other Canadians, the Quebec Jew Abraham Joseph feared an American attack in 1837, timed to take advantage of Canada's weakness stemming from the rebellions of that year. Joseph recorded in his diary rather truculently, "We are ready for them!"[16]

Canadians were heirs to a more conservative, nonrevolutionary tradition. Many Anglo-Canadians viewed American liberty as licentious-
ness, seeing in events such as the Civil War signs that the great experiment
in democracy could never succeed. French Canadians, increasingly eager
to guard their traditional way of life, were coming to perceive Americans
as the *"sansculottes* of the New World," not unlike the citizens of their
bête noire, revolutionary France. Later in the nineteenth century both
French and Anglo-Canadians grew resentful of the creeping Americanization of their country. More than ever they felt the need to assert their
own historical and political uniqueness, despite the similarities between
American and Canadian economics, social structure, and cultural ambience. Where uniqueness was not readily apparent, some Canadians
searched it out and even invented it. Like other Canadians, Jews resented
Americans, "who know little about this Dominion, yet imagine they
know it all."[17] Even the New York–oriented Yiddish-language newspaper, the *Keneder odler* of Montreal, expressed annoyance on occasion
that the United States got "all the advantages" in trade with Canada.[18]

In such an atmosphere Canadian Jews at times became wary even
of their American-Jewish brethren. Certainly they feared American-
Jewish radicalism and tended to blame the presence in Canada of socialism
and other forms of radicalism on "professional agitators from the United
States."[19] Harris Vineberg, one of the leaders of the Montreal Jewish
community and himself of Russian origin, felt that it was the eastern
European immigrants from

New York . . . who bring to Montreal the characteristics which are so objectionable in the greater city. . . . The Jewish workingmen of Canada . . . [are] respectable, reliable people. It should be our great object to see
that they retain that character and frown down every attempt to introduce
New York Ghetto peculiarities into Montreal.[20]

The views of Vineberg and other "respectable" Canadian Jews reflected
Anglo-Canadian suspicion of the United States as well as a tendency in
Canada at the turn of the century and afterward to associate radicalism
with eastern Europeans and to decry it as "foreign."[21]

Ultimately, however, such feelings, while ever present during the
period under review, were obscured by the undeniable reality of an
increasing integration of North American society and certainly of North
American-Jewish society. Even Canadians apprehensive of the United
States looked to that country as a model of dynamism, particularly before

JPL.

The "national pastime" in Montreal—immigrant Jewish boys' baseball team at Fletcher's Field around 1905

Mrs. S. Metenko Levy, Toronto

Supporters of Toronto's National Radical School in 1914. The school became affiliated with the New York Arbeiter Ring.

the Canadian economic and political resurgence that began in 1896. Canadian free-trade sentiment often masked a desire for a union of the two countries. It was felt by many, although seldom openly stated, that the "unrestricted reciprocity" advocated by the Liberal Party prior to 1896 would lead to annexation. Not a few Canadians thought republican government more liberal and freer than their own system and that in becoming "assimilated to the United States, Canada was fulfilling itself as a liberal and progressive society."[22]

In any case most Canadian Jews, like most Jews elsewhere and along with many gentile Canadians, agreed with "the sympathetic European view that the United States, this great experiment in popular republican government, was destined to be the education of the world."[23] In the 1830s and 1840s they shared the annexationist sentiments of most Montreal merchants, who saw in union with the United States greater economic opportunity and a counterweight to the growing reactionary sentiment of French Canadians. At most times they saw in America, as Rabbi Abraham De Sola of Montreal put it, "a land . . . greatly favored, . . . of wisdom, justice, and liberty."[24] Jews, after all, had suffered under the tyranny of kings everywhere, including medieval England. Most of them felt, therefore, that there was little to fear from republicanism. Adolphus Mordecai Hart, the historian grandson of Aaron Hart, was typical in excusing the United States her well-advertised excesses. Hart did not deny that the United States had been "baptized in blood." Nonetheless he saw that country as representing to all mankind "the triumph of human right."[25]

Gentile Anglo-Canadians readily appreciated that for Jews and other oppressed minorities no country, including England and Canada, held as much promise as the United States. The Jewish Baron Ephraim in Mary Ellen Ross's novel, *The Legend of the Holy Stone,* remarked that

> a man of talent has twice the opportunity of distinguishing himself [in the United States] . . . that he has . . . [in Europe], surrounded as he is by people who are envious of his popularity, and ready to detract from his merit in every available way.[26]

To be seen in contrast to European antisemitism, according to the Montreal *Star* a decade later, were

> the rapid strides the Hebrews are making [in the United States] and the influence they possess in whatever city they make their home.[27]

Canada—The Blurred Image

The overwhelming power of the attraction that the United States held out for most nineteenth-century Europeans helped to blur their vision of Canada, a vision that was none too clear in any case. Even after World War I emigrants still "often failed to differentiate between the United States and Canada," assuming that Canada was part of the United States.[28] Frequently chance alone brought immigrants to Canada. Canada's indistinct image in the mind of European Jews was reflected in their terminology. "America" was used in the nineteenth century to designate the United States, North America, and even South America. Newspaper accounts from Canada were frequently datelined "Montreal, North America," or "Toronto, America." Since it was also common to write "Boston, North America," and "Pittsburgh, America," confusion was inevitable. Another linguistic complication was the Hebrew-Yiddish word, *medinah.* That word was (and still is) used to translate the English "country" (*medinat Canada* or *medinot ha-brit* for the United States), and also to designate the English "state" or "province" (*medinat New York, medinat Quebec*). The same word was also used at times for "hemisphere" (*medinat America),* and even, in its older, medieval usage, for "city" (*medinat Vineland).* Jews in eastern Europe, like other foreigners, might well have found North American political divisions bewildering in any case. The task of sorting them out became almost impossible, however, when they were translated unclearly.[29] Even when Canada was mentioned specifically in the European press, accounts were often misleading, reflecting prevailing ignorance. If Jewish newspapers reported Canadian events at all, it was generally in the column reserved for "American" news. As late as 1906 even the London *Jewish Chronicle* could report the election of Louis Rubin as president of the town council of Ashley, North Dakota, under the dateline "Canada."[30]

Actually most nineteenth-century Anglo-Canadians were quite willing to foster the notion that Canada was part of "America." Canadians wishing to populate their country well knew that Europeans favored the United States. Before 1860, 72 percent of all *British* emigrants went directly to the United States, and still others went southward after only a brief stay in Canada. Emigrants from other European countries showed an even greater preference for the United States. In 1890, in answer to pleas from prominent American Jews, Alliance Israélite Universelle leaders in France suggested to their counterparts in eastern Europe that emigrants be directed away from New York and toward Canada and

South America. They were told in reply that "Moses and Samuel . . . rise[n] from their graves" together would not succeed in redirecting emigration.[31] America's virtues were too well known, as, apparently, were the drawbacks of Canada.[32]

Canadian and foreign shipping agents and transportation companies were not unaware of the eagerness of emigrants to reach the United States. Good business dictated that people not be reminded that the relatively unknown Canadian ports were not in the United States. Advertisers in late-nineteenth-century Jewish journals and guidebooks to North America listed Quebec and Montreal as but two of the many "American" ports to which passage might be booked. In London, Herman Landau, urging Montreal upon prospective emigrants, claimed that Canada's largest city was a mere two hundred miles from New York City. (The distance, as Landau undoubtedly knew, was more than twice that!) In its early years the Grand Trunk Railway in its European advertising presented itself simply as a desirable route to the American interior, never mentioning Canada. Although the Canadian line had been designed to tap the trade of the American West, it might have been expected that the Canadian cities through which it passed would be mentioned in its publicity. Thus, untutored immigrants often landed in Montreal and other Canadian ports assuming that they were in the United States.[33]

After the turn of the century the Dominion became better and more favorably known among Jews and other Europeans. Newspaper reports began to differentiate clearly between Canada and the United States. A few books that spoke of both countries with some knowledge were published. One of the most notable, Max Raisin's *Toledot ha-Yehudim be-America* (1902) written in Hebrew, included a brief but accurate section on Canada, which introduced the country to many prospective immigrants.[34]

Partly out of necessity, too, Jews began to investigate Canada seriously. As the movement to restrict immigration into the United States and England gained force around the turn of the century, *Ha-Zefirah* noted that more and more eastern Europeans were becoming "interested in Canada as a land for Jewish immigration." Like reporters in England, that paper's writers now perceived Canada to be "an unsettled country, with plenty of room for immigrants."[35] The growing anti-immigration sentiment aroused the concern of Baron de Hirsch, who had funded much Jewish resettlement. He feared the possibility of fomenting antisemitism in the United States by overpopulating it with Jews and took a second look at Canada. "After careful examination, [he] ... became convinced that the Argentine Republic, Canada and Australia above all" other places offered the "surest guarantee" for a secure Jewish future.[36] Some European Jews, then, headed knowingly for Canada; others, however, came thinking it was part of the United States. Still others chose Canada because it was enough like the United States to be the next best place to go.

The Movement from Canada to the United States

To a great extent, of course, Canada seemed an integral part of America. Canada had a three-thousand-mile-long border with the United States and was relatively unpopulated. People moved back and forth between the countries with ease, maintaining close business and family relations on both sides of the border. Except for the French Canadians, the people of the two countries spoke the same language. In the case of Jews and of many gentiles, Canadians and Americans participated in the same cultural, religious, and fraternal organizations, which were generally based in the United States. Because the distance was so much less and the ease of communication that much greater, these relationships tended to be at least as strong as those of Canadians with Great Britain. Often they were stronger, despite the fact that the United States and Canada were two distinct countries. These ties, as well as those of sentiment towards the new "promised land," bound Canadian Jews to the United States.

Proximity, the open border, and many shared aspects of their social, political, and economic systems made possible a large-scale "population exchange" between Canada and the United States. In the early years Canada witnessed a "strong and persistent ... drift of population ... to the United States."[37] Lord Durham's 1839 report on the state of Canada estimated that 60 percent of the immigrants to Canada during the decade from 1829 to 1839 had gone on to the United States. The rate remained very high until about 1900. It is estimated that between 1851 and 1901 only one of every three settlers remained in Canada, with the rest pushing on to the United States.[38]

The traffic of Jewish and gentile Europeans en route to the United States via Canada was so heavy toward the end of the nineteenth century that Canadians complained of "maintaining an immigration corps to bring peoples to Canada as a way-house to the United States."[39] When the Baron de Hirsch Institute in Montreal sought a new immigration officer in 1903, one of the most important qualifications was that he be able to deal with American immigration authorities.[40] It was reported in 1902 that in the previous two decades over three thousand immigrant Jewish families had gone to Winnipeg to settle there. "Owing, however, to inducements held out to them by their friends in the States, many of these visitors [sic] . . . joined their brethren across the border line."[41] There were but two hundred Jewish families left in the town in 1901, although their number was soon to be considerably augmented. The outward bound included native-born Canadians of French, British, and Jewish background. The dimensions of the Canadian movement toward the United States were startling. The number of Canadian-born living in the United States rose from 717,157 in 1881 to 1,204,637 in 1911. Yet even these figures do not tell the whole story, since many, perhaps most, of those who moved across the border were transmigrants born in Europe, who were often not considered or recorded as "Canadians." In addition there was a considerable movement of the children of Americans born in Canada back to the United States. By 1910 Massachusetts contained more people of Canadian stock than any province except Quebec and Ontario. In that year the eight largest "Canadian" cities were, in order of size: Montreal, Toronto, Boston, Quebec, Chicago, Ottawa, Detroit, and New York. Although the percentage dropped substantially in subsequent years as the population of Canada grew, over 20 percent of all Canadian-born people in the world in 1901 were living in the United States. This diaspora helped to cement a strong bond between the two countries.[42]

Jews and other Canadians who moved southward included the prosperous and the destitute, the well educated and the unskilled. No Jews achieved the stature of the most famous gentile Canadian emigrants, such as business leader Erastus Wiman, railroad magnate James J. Hill, and the famous educator Andrew Dixon White, president of Cornell University. Included, however, were the scions of Canada's "first" Jewish families, who, too, were gripped by the wanderlust of the Great Folk Migration. Gershom Joseph, son of the wealthy pioneer trader, Henry Joseph, and brother-in-law of Rabbi Abraham De Sola, was born in Berthier, Lower Canada. In 1849 he "followed the yellow-brick road" to California, where he made and lost two fortunes. During his fourteen years in the American West, Joseph was associated in business with a French-Canadian emigrant, a cousin of Narcisse F. Belleau (later Sir Narcisse), lieutenant governor of Quebec, and he also doubled as a special correspondent of the Montreal *Herald.* In San Francisco Joseph married an American wife of French origin, Céline Lyons, with whom he returned to Montreal in 1863. There he became a respected lawyer, later serving as president of the Spanish and Portuguese Synagogue when his nephew, Meldola De Sola, was rabbi.[43]

Most who crossed the border did not return. Frank N. Hart, a member of Canada's oldest Jewish family, was the first Jew to complete his medical studies in Canada. A member of the initial graduating class in medicine at McGill University in 1835, he left Montreal almost immediately for St. Louis, Missouri, where he practiced medicine for the rest of his life. Another member of the Hart family, Esdaile Cohen David, the youngest son of Dr. Aaron Hart David, had emigrated to Long Island some years before his death in 1890. Abraham Pinto Joseph, the oldest son of Montefiore Joseph of Quebec and great-grandson of Henry Joseph, emigrated to Pittsburgh after receiving a degree in electrical engineering from McGill. One turn-of-the-century writer claimed that within five years of the founding of Hamilton's Anshe Sholom congregation in 1882, all of the founding families had left Canada for Buffalo, Chicago, Milwaukee, and Appleton, Wisconsin.[44]

Jews, like other Canadians, often moved south in search of a better livelihood. In the booming United States, Canadians hoped to find the economic security that had often eluded them in Canada, even during the prosperous "Laurier years" at the turn of the century. The destitute were often assisted in this endeavor by Canadian-Jewish agencies, which, along with their coreligionists in England, looked upon emigration as the ideal solution to poverty. At the least it removed the problem from sight, and at best it enabled the poor to find jobs elsewhere. Synagogues in Montreal, Hamilton, and Toronto provided indigent members with the means to purchase a one-way ticket south. In 1883, at the outset of the influx of eastern European Jews to Montreal, the local Jewish community panicked, and immigrants were sent as far afield as possible. Some reached North Dakota, where they almost starved to death. By 1886 the number being sent out of Montreal was so great that the Young Men's Hebrew Benevolent Society succeeded in getting wholesale rates for its clients on the Delaware and Hudson Railroad, the main route from Montreal to New York City.

Until 1906, when the American government cracked down on the practice, the Baron de Hirsch Institute devoted much energy to the export of poor Jews to the United States. As one of its reports frankly stated, "in all cases where" pauper Jews "had relations, friends or acquaintances

Rabbis Isaac Landman and Nathan Gordon of Montreal's Temple Emanu-El, among a group of American Reform rabbis in 1906

American transmigrant Rabbi Israel Kahanovitch (center) and Winnipeg kashruth officials, 1907

Rev. Henry Singer ("Singer, the meshummad," or apostate), a transmigrant, in debate with Toronto Jews, 1912

City of Toronto Archives (James Collection 2348)

Mrs. Clarence De Sola, the former Belle Maud Goldsmith of Cleveland, Ohio, in 1902

Notman

in ... the United States," they were promptly dispatched to them.[45] In some years as many as a fourth of all Jewish arrivals to Canada were helped by the Baron de Hirsch Institute to emigrate to the United States.[46] Apparently some officials of the Hirsch Institute, in their zeal to be rid of immigrants, smuggled out those unable to meet American immigration requirements. A minor scandal erupted in 1905 when the sensationalist Montreal *Star* focused public attention on the immigrant-running activities of Institute officials. Two years later the Institute had to dismiss an employee, who was proved by an irate American commissioner of immigration in Montreal to have been engaged in immigrant smuggling.[47]

Not all these emigrants went to the United States in search of a better livelihood. Some made the move to join relatives or to marry. Canadians, in general, tended to intermarry with Americans far more readily during these years than with Canadians of other provinces. Canadian Jews often sought a mate in the United States, because their own small community provided only a limited choice of partners. And it was easier and less costly to pursue a courtship in the United States than in England or Europe.[48]

Canadians were also attracted by the larger and better developed cities of the United States, where intellectual and cultural opportunities abounded as they did not in the northern backwaters. By 1902 New York had become the largest Jewish city in the world and was particularly appealing, even for other American Jews. Reuben Brainin, editor of the *Keneder odler* just before World War I and a major contributor to the development of the Jewish community of Montreal, departed for New York after a relatively short stay in Canada, despite ambivalence about Jewish life in the larger city. New York alone in North America offered the particular kind of Hebrew cultural circle he sought.[49]

In addition, throughout the period Jews interested in a good Jewish education found it necessary to leave Canada. (Even today there is no institution of higher Jewish learning in Canada.) In the eighteenth century Aaron Hart sent his four sons to Philadelphia and New York to live with Jewish friends and to receive a Jewish and a general education. In 1873 Lewis Samuel of Toronto packed his older son, Samuel Samuel, off to a New York boarding school where he might "receive a good Jewish education, better than Toronto's first transient Hebrew teachers could provide."[50] Unfortunately the boy died of diphtheria after only a few months in New York. At the turn of the twentieth century Leon

Judah Solway of Toronto had to be sent to New York when he expressed an interest in rabbinical training.[51]

Secular education and professional training also attracted Canadians to the United States just as others were drawn to England. In the late nineteenth century even staunch nationalists such as Stephen Leacock went to the United States for doctoral studies, since Canadian graduate schools were still in their infancy. Among the Jews who studied there in the early years of the twentieth century were Montrealers Solomon Vineberg and Nathaniel Fineberg.[52] Jews had a unique motive for doing graduate and professional work outside of Canada. At the turn of the century most schools in North America restricted the number of Jewish students. Since there were very few universities in Canada altogether, it was often necessary for ambitious Jewish students to look elsewhere, especially with regard to professional schools. The most numerous group of Jewish émigré students consisted of those in the medical professions— medicine, nursing, and dentistry. Physicians often left for postgraduate study in the United States (and continued to do so until well beyond the period under review); many of those eventually returned to Canada to practice.[53]

Although educational and cultural facilities were improving in Canada as the nineteenth century drew to a close, committed Jews still often found the Jewish community too confining or too uncultivated. Rather than recruit newcomers or strengthen existing institutions, they left for the United States. The assimilated were similarly drawn southward to the more developed centers.

The Movement from the United States to Canada

Simultaneously with the movement of large numbers of Canadians to the United States during this period there occurred a smaller but still significant countermovement of Americans to Canada. Some of the same forces that propelled Canadians southward motivated Americans to move northward. The movement was inaugurated with the northward push of the British armies from New York in 1759. Its dimensions grew over time. Between 1881 and 1911 the American-born population of Canada rose from 77,753 to 303,680, while that of Quebec and Ontario, where most Jews lived, rose from 64,859 to 85,519. In addition a large number of partially Americanized transmigrants moved to Canada, as did a significant number of the children born to Canadians living in the United States. Contemporaries estimated that by 1898 half the Jews in Canada had come from or through the United States. Between 1900 and 1920 perhaps 65,000 more Jews immigrated to Canada from there.[54]

The movement northward began slowly. At the beginning of the period Americans, like Europeans, were ignorant of Canada. Jews were no exception. On a trip to the United States in 1844 Quebecker Abraham Joseph noted that "Americans entertain a horrible opinion of Canada. It is generally considered" in the United States, Joseph went on to say, that every Canadian is "locked up in flannel and buffalo skins for 8 mos. without even putting a nose outside a door." Almost half a century later, in 1889, at a lecture at the YMHA in New York City, Ferdinand Shack decried the "ignorance about Canada which prevails in the United States." Shack knew of a "college professor living in New York going to Montreal in summer to cool off."[55] In 1892 the New York *Jewish Messenger* chided its readers for their apathy regarding Canada.[56] An article on "The Jews of Canada" in the 1893 *American Jews' Annual* discussed only the period before 1853.[57] In 1898 the Canadian *Jewish Times* still found its American colleagues printing "frequent gross, inexcusable misrepresentations of persons and things Canadian."[58]

After the turn of the century things improved somewhat. In 1900 and 1901 Carroll Ryan, the gentile editor of the Canadian *Jewish Times,* published a series of articles on Canada in Baltimore's *Jewish Comment.*[59] Other periodicals also began to cover the country more carefully. Perhaps because he knew Canada at first hand, Alexander Harkavy included a well-written section on British North America in his Yiddish-language *Compendium of Mathematical, Physical, and Political Geography* (1911). Abe Cahan, the editor of New York's largest Yiddish-language daily, the *Forverts,* in his Yiddish-language *History of the United States* (1912), discussed Canada's French era in full. These two works helped American Jews who read Yiddish to acquire at least a superficial acquaintance with Canada. Still, that knowledge was limited, even in the first decades of the twentieth century, and a good deal of what was known was uncomplimentary. Although Carroll Ryan asserted that "Israel [was] happily at home in Canada," he could not gainsay the existence in 1901 of virulent French-Canadian antisemitism.[60] New York's Yiddish papers were as sensitive to antisemitism in Canada as they were to its manifestations everywhere else.[61]

American Jews were also aware of the relative weakness of the Canadian-Jewish community in comparison with their own. The partisan antics of Rabbi Meldola De Sola gave Montreal the image of a bastion of the most "ignorant and fanatic orthodoxy."[62] To most American Jews dedicated to separation of church and state, religious involvement in public education in Canada appeared dangerous. Many felt that Quebec's system worked to the particular disadvantage of Jews.[63] When Americans did decide to come to Canada, they felt they were taking a risk. Herman Abramowitz, longtime rabbi of Montreal's Shaar Hashomayim Synagogue, arrived at his post in 1902 from New York. He later recalled that coming to Canada "was like pioneering on distant foreign fields."[64]

Not a few Americans who emigrated to Canada during the pre-1914 period went because they viewed Canada as an extension of the United States. American periodicals often treated Canada as another part of the United States. Canadian items were "domestic news" and not "foreign news" in the *American Israelite* and the *American Hebrew*. The annexationist movement retained considerable strength into the early twentieth century on the American side of the border, and few felt that the United States would have difficulty in digesting her northern neighbor.[65]

Canadians, hungry for Anglo-Saxon immigrants, were even more eager to present their country as congenial to Americans than they were to convince Europeans of their American credentials. Official recruiting literature pictured Canada as a country that shared American democracy—"government of the people, for the people and by the people."[66] The country's newly found prosperity was said to resemble that of the United States. So too did the boosterism of her natives. Carroll Ryan claimed that

> Jewish immigrants [to Canada and others] have found . . . a veritable land of promise, where they have experienced but little difficulty in . . . laying the foundations of future fortunes.[67]

A significant factor impelling Americans to move at the end of the nineteenth century was the disappearance of the American frontier. To the land-hungry, Canada represented the "last, best West." A vigorous Canadian government recruiting policy, sparked by a desire to settle the country rapidly, dovetailed with mistaken American fears that their own lands were all occupied. From the 1890s on, the Canadian government offered direct subsidies to American newspapers agreeing to publish favorable articles about life in Canada. Under the direction of Minister of Agriculture Clifford Sifton, paid agents fanned out over the United States to canvass potential immigrants to Canada. Singled out for special attention were ethnic and religious groups that were thought to be more likely to "hold . . . landless offspring on farms."[68] Although the Jews were not a preferred group, they too were influenced by the campaign.[69]

Very few Jews emigrated from the United States at any time. Unlike others who came to America to earn enough money to live comfortably in Europe, Jews came to stay. Remembering the pogroms, they felt little nostalgia for Russia or Romania, and they were acutely aware that whatever the drawbacks of America, no place was better. From 1908 to 1924 Jews had the lowest rate of emigration from the United States (5.2 percent) of any immigrant group. (Romanians with 65.9 percent had the highest rate, but even the Irish, the group closest to the Jews, left with much greater frequency, 10.1 percent.) The Jews stayed no matter how difficult conditions became.[70]

That some Jews did leave the United States for Canada is probably testimony to their assumption that that country was very much like the United States if not actually a part of it. In fact, American Jews in Canada tended to retain their loyalty to the United States. In 1931 Jews in Canada had the third highest rate of naturalization of all immigrant groups. American-born Jews, however, ranked fourteenth. Like the Canadians who moved south the Jews who came to Canada from the United States during the period under review were both natives and immigrants, well-to-do and poor, educated and unskilled. Most came from the New York City metropolitan area, where about half the Jews in the United States lived from around 1850 on. Others, however, came from all over the United States.[71]

The economic motivation for moving to Canada was one of the strongest. There is evidence of poor Jews, immigrants and natives alike, drifting into Canada from the United States in 1847, in 1863, in 1878, and at other times. Later during the prosperous "Laurier years," Canada attracted Jewish and gentile Americans just as it did Europeans. Contemporaries boasted that "many ghettoites from New York . . . discovered that industrial and social conditions in Canada . . . [were] better than in that congested region."[72] The extent and severity of poverty in Canada and its attendant ills were sometimes underestimated.[73]

Some who came to Canada from the United States during these years to seek their fortune had been dispatched by American societies for aiding the indigent and the immigrants. Americans sought to export poverty, as did their Canadian and British counterparts. The Hebrew Emigrant Aid Society, hastily set up to deal with the emergency created by the unprecedented immigration of 1881/82, worked during its brief lifetime to disperse immigrants from New York City. In May 1882, a typical month, it shipped more than fifty newcomers to various destinations in North America, including seven to Montreal.[74] In 1901 the Baron de Hirsch Fund in New York established the Industrial Removal Office to help reduce the growing "congestion of the immigrant population in ... the East Side" of the city.[75] Fear of antisemitism as well as genuine concern for immigrants living in noisome slums motivated the organization; in its twenty-one years, it assisted almost eighty thousand Jews to resettle in other cities all over the continent. Yet another agency that encouraged Jews to leave New York was the Hebrew Immigrant Aid Society (HIAS), a later incarnation of the 1881 Emigrant Aid Society. In 1912, a typical year for HIAS, the Society assisted 844 clients to depart New York for other American cities as well as for Cuba, Panama, and Canada.[76]

For some of the immigrants Canada proved to be the land of opportunity. Although no American Jews were as spectacularly successful in their new Canadian home as the gentile American immigrant William C. Van Horne, one of the builders of the Canadian Pacific Railway, some did very well. Mark Workman, who emigrated to Montreal from his native Buffalo in the 1870s, became a director of the Dominion Steel Company and chairman of the board of the Eastern Trust Company in Montreal. Abraham Blumenthal, who came from New York City, became a prosperous Montreal businessman and served on the Montreal city council from 1912 to 1918. David Dunkelman, an immigrant from Poland who became the owner of Canada's largest clothing chain in the 1920s, started out in North America as a bankrupt Brooklyn retailer.[77]

Matrimony brought American Jews—particularly women—to Canada just as it took Canadians to the United States. Women generally followed their husbands, and contemporary mores dictated that women could not seek out their mates. Typically Canadian men sought brides in the more populous United States and then brought them back to Canada. American-Jewish men, who lived in larger communities, were less likely to seek partners in Canada.[78] These international marriages frequently involved the more prominent families. The wealthy were more mobile; community leaders were more concerned about the religiosity of their children. In 1816 Elkalah Seixas, daughter of the minister of the Spanish and Portuguese Congregation of New York, Gershom Mendes Seixas, was married to Benjamin Solomons of Montreal. Some years later Sara Gratz Moses, a niece of Rebecca Gratz, was married to Jacob Henry Joseph of Montreal, another of the sons of Henry Joseph.

Later in the century Abram Moses Vineberg, Clarence I. De Sola, and others married American Jewesses. Sometimes American emigrants returned to the United States to marry. Rabbi Herman Abramowitz, for example, then eleven years in Montreal, returned in 1913 to marry Theresa Bockar of Staten Island, New York. The less illustrious followed suit when they could.[79]

Sometimes Americans came to Canada to lose a spouse. In 1884 Rabbi Meldola De Sola performed a marriage ceremony for Jacob Gluffen, a recent immigrant, and Dora Greenut of Montreal. It was discovered soon after that Gluffen already had a wife in the United States, and he was subsequently arrested for bigamy. A similar case involved a Philadelphia milliner who fled to Montreal in 1908 with his paramour. The Baron de Hirsch Institute assisted in tracking down the adulterous hatter, who was later brought to trial. Not all searches for deserting husbands were successful. The Baron de Hirsch Institute noted in 1906 that societies in the United States and Europe had helped "many . . . deserted wives" to travel to Montreal on a fruitless search for their missing mates.[80] Most arrived penniless and became charges of the Institute. In 1913, according to the National Desertion Bureau in New York, an extraordinary number of wife deserters was still disappearing annually across the northern frontier of the United States.[81]

Besides bigamists and adulterers, other types of criminals fled from the United States in search of anonymity in Canada during these years. *Hamelitz* noted in 1884 that the number of Jewish thieves in Canada "was not small" and that most of them had come to Canada from the United States. Among them was Mother Mandelbaum, the "Queen of the [New York] fences," who took flight over the forty-ninth parallel in that year.[82] Criminals, of course, often seek to escape justice by skipping over borders, and Canada's image as a primitive and unsettled country undoubtedly encouraged fugitives to think that disappearing in the northern wastes would not be difficult.

Nineteenth-century wanderlust seized Americans as it did others, and some headed north. Joseph Simpson (whose father and mother were from Germany and Nova Scotia, respectively) was born in Charleston, South Carolina in 1825. In 1849, like the Canadian Gershom Joseph and thousands of others bitten by the gold bug, he set out for California. In 1863, the same year that Joseph returned to Montreal, Simpson removed to Toronto. There he became a successful textile merchant, active in the Jewish community and well accepted by upper class gentiles. Myer Runkel, born in Frankfurt, was taken in 1820 as a child to Charleston, South

Carolina, where he undoubtedly knew Simpson. In 1848 Runkel emigrated to Montreal, where he engaged in business for eighteen years. He then returned to the United States, settling first in Cincinnati and later in New York City. There were numerous others who followed such a path.[83]

Wars, too, occasion moves. And, indeed, various wars in North America stimulated traffic both northward to Canada and southward to the United States. Ideology was sometimes a motivating factor. During wartime, some Americans fled to peaceful Canada to avoid becoming involved. Adventuresome Canadians went south to volunteer in American wars, looking for the excitement unavailable at home. (In the years after the period under review Americans eager to participate in the two world wars before their own country had entered the struggles volunteered in the Canadian armed forces, while during the Viet Nam War, Americans fled to Canada to avoid the draft.)

Out of "loyalism or at least homesickness for British institutions," many residents of the thirteen original American colonies moved north during the Revolution or immediately following. From that time "United Empire Loyalists" made up a significant part of the Anglo-Canadian population. Among them were a number of Jews, such as Montreal merchant Levi Michaels and his son, Myer. "Most of the Loyalists had relations and friends still residing in the States, and although they differed with them over the issues of the Revolution, they were interested in one another's personal fortunes and opinions. Letters and occasional visits kept their friendship alive."[84]

If the thirteen original colonies produced their loyalists, Canada had its share of rebel sympathizers. Among these also were Jews. Levi (Levy) Solomons of Montreal was purveyor to American hospitals in Canada during the American invasion. Exiled to the United States for his sympathies, he was eventually allowed to return to Canada. By 1778 Solomons had been sufficiently rehabilitated to be elected an officer of the Spanish and Portuguese Synagogue in Montreal. Two other Canadian Jews who sympathized with the Revolution were the Quebec merchant Eleazar Levy, and Samuel Judah of Three Rivers. Levy, an associate of Aaron Hart, left for New York with the outbreak of war and remained there. Judah claimed to have lent the revolutionaries almost one million dollars, which he was never repaid. The best known of the Canadian-Jewish revolutionaries was David S. Franks. Franks left Montreal for Philadelphia in 1775 to aid the revolutionary cause. He became aide-de-camp to General Benedict Arnold. After being acquitted of complicity in

Arnold's treason, Franks became vice-consul for the United States in Marseilles. Doubtless the French he knew from his Montreal days served him well in France. Thus, although most Canadian Jews supported the loyalist cause during the Revolution (as did their gentile neighbors), and although most American Jews supported the Revolution, some did cross the lines together with the non-Jewish partisans.[85]

The Civil War, although it did not directly involve Canada, also produced a significant movement back and forth across the border. Its bloody horrors sent a wave of draft dodgers, called "skedaddlers," and deserters scurrying over the northern border of the Union. As in more recent times most returned home when they could, although some remained permanently in Canada. The draft law of 1862 produced the first large-scale movement, and "every subsequent order of conscription provoked another wave in the current."[86] At the same time, not a few Canadians headed in the opposite direction to fight "the battle for the glory of the Lord." Both streams contained a representative number of Jews.

During the war Mrs. Samuel Roman's Jewish boarding house on Chenneville Street in Montreal was the "rendezvous for a large number of men from the United States, who found a home under her hospitable roof."[87] In 1861 Joseph Moses, son of Dr. Gratz Moses of St. Louis and nephew of Rebecca Gratz, was packed off to his family in Montreal "to keep him out of the way of mischief."[88] Another prominent Jew, who "sojourned" in Montreal with his wife and mother-in-law during the latter part of the war, was Rev. Gustav Poznanski, late of Charleston, South Carolina. Some Jews emigrated to Canada after having already served in the war, such as Samuel Stern, who arrived in Toronto in 1862. Perhaps they had seen enough bloodshed (Poznanski had lost a son in the Confederate army) or perhaps they wished to avoid further service. It is not unlikely that Gershom Joseph's return to Canada in 1863 and that of other Canadians was hastened by the prospect of military service in the Union army.[89]

As many as fifty thousand Canadians participated actively in the war, most of them on the Northern side. Of these the largest number came from the ranks of Canadians resident in the United States, of whom there were some two hundred fifty thousand in 1860. According to Adolphus Mordecai Hart, four-fifths of the Canadians in the Union forces were French Canadians, who suffered some fifteen thousand dead. Canadian Jews who fought included Hart's first cousin, Arthur Wellington Hart, at one time a newspaper editor in Scranton, Pennsylvania, who rose to the rank of colonel in the Union army. Another was Montrealer Jacob Rubenstein.[90]

Canadian Jews as well as French Canadians generally sympathized with the Union cause in the war. Among Anglo-Canadians there was much more enthusiasm for the Southern cause, just as there was in Britain. French Canadians already had come to view themselves as a subject people, and they might have been expected to align themselves against slavery and perhaps also against a pro-South Britain. Jews retained memories of persecution and found it hard to make peace with the subjugation of others. Although southern Jews and some in the North saw things differently, and although Anglo-Montreal was a "community . . . full of southern sympathizers," Canadian Jews remained stubbornly pro-Union.[91] The Jacob Henry Josephs of Montreal were typical. They held fast to their Northern loyalties even when sympathy for the Southern cause peaked in Canada, as at the time of the Confederate raid on St. Albans, Vermont, organized from Montreal in 1864. They were, no doubt, influenced by their American relatives, who lived in the North.

The Civil War was an American and not a Canadian affair. That it spilled over into Canada clearly demonstrated that, despite the border, North America was in many ways one entity. As was not often the case, Canadians had to choose between English and American sympathies. Jews supported America, partly for historical reasons and, no doubt, partly because their business interests and family connections inclined them to favor a Northern victory. This was one of the few occasions when Jews did not see eye-to-eye with their fellow Anglo-Canadians.

Canadians and Americans, then, moved with ease across the border in the nineteenth and early twentieth centuries, thereby cementing the ties and reinforcing the similarities between the two peoples. Most people made the move in search of a more secure livelihood. Others, however, emigrated to receive an education, to marry, or to find a community that better met their needs. Some Canadians sought a larger and more developed Jewish community, a trend that persisted despite the rapid growth of both Montreal and Toronto by the turn of the century. And, in general, Jews followed the emigration patterns established by other Canadians, Americans, and transmigrants. Most notably, however, Jews gravitated toward the country that, more than any other, seemed to offer a secure and bright future to them as individuals and as Jews—the United States.

Personal and Communal Bonds

As they did in their relationships with coreligionists in England, Canadian Jews established a variety of links with American Jews. These ties—personal, economic, religious, and communal—paralleled the connections of gentile Anglo-Canadians with Americans. Such ties greatly influenced the character of Canadian Jewry.

The border areas of the two countries were at all times very much one economic and social unit. Citizens of both countries crossed the border to shop and to market their goods. Doctors and clergymen ministered to patients and congregants on both sides of the border. Even after the completion of the Canadian transcontinental railroad system, it remained easier and more natural for traffic to flow north to south rather than east to west. All major Canadian centers of population were close to the American border. Both Montreal and Toronto, where most Jews lived, were less than one hundred miles from the United States, and even the Hirsch agricultural colony in Saskatchewan was only fifteen miles from the border. Proximity to the United States facilitated contacts of all sorts in a period of increasingly rapid communications and mobility.[92]

The most immediate bond between American and Canadian Jews was that of family and friends. In addition, sentimental ties remained strong. American Jews who emigrated to Canada during the period reserved "a warm corner in their hearts for the 'Stars and Stripes'," while Canadians in the United States kept up associations with their place of birth.[93] Hiram N. Vineberg, for example, was for a time president of the McGill Graduates' Society in New York; I. G. Ascher, a founder of the Young Men's Hebrew Benevolent Society of Montreal, kept in touch with the affairs of the Society long after he had moved to New York.[94]

With the improvements in communications, especially the railroads, over the course of the nineteenth century tourism and family visits across the border grew more frequent. Prosperous Jews participated in these exchanges alongside other Americans and Canadians able to afford travel. American Jews with Canadian relatives went to Canada to visit. Canadians more frequently went south. They were to be found at popular American watering places even during the turbulent Civil War years. Abraham Joseph toured New York, Philadelphia, Baltimore, Washington, Richmond, Norfolk, Hanover, New Hampshire, and Burlington, Vermont in 1844 and 1845. In Philadelphia he met Rebecca Gratz and

Isaac Leeser, the best-known American-Jewish clergyman of the day, and was unimpressed. Joseph's brother and sister-in-law, the Jacob Henry Josephs, were regular visitors to Cape May, New Jersey, Silver Spring, Maryland, and Saratoga, New York, in the mid-nineteenth century. They also frequently visited their family in Philadelphia. Rabbi Abraham De Sola traveled more than most. His journeys, often undertaken in connection with publishing ventures or to deliver an address, also included considerable social visiting in the United States. In New York City he visited his sister, Jane Belais, and his nephew, Rev. H. Pereira Mendes, who was minister of the Spanish and Portuguese Synagogue after 1877. He was invited to special events in Plattsburg, just across the border from Montreal, and he spent time with the fashionable people of the day, such as Rebecca Gratz in Philadelphia to whom he was distantly related by marriage.[95]

By the end of the nineteenth century travel between the two countries was swift and inexpensive. "The average Canadian . . . [became at least] as familiar with an American as with a Canadian of another province."[96] The social columns of the Canadian *Jewish Times* record frequent visits to New York, Chicago, Detroit, Boston, Philadelphia, and other American centers. Old Orchard, Maine, became a favorite vacation spot of wealthy Montreal Jews. Abraham De Sola and two of his sons, Meldola and Clarence I., would all die while visiting in the United States, Abraham in 1882, Meldola in 1918, and Clarence in 1920.[97]

Americans also traveled a great deal to Canada by the end of the century. The urge to visit a foreign country was great, and transatlantic travel was still slow and costly. Canada provided an inexpensive foreign alternative. Probably the most noteworthy American-Jewish tourist in Canada during the period was Oscar Straus, the first Jew to serve in a cabinet position in the United States. In 1906, as Secretary of Commerce and Labor, he came to Canada partly on government business. While in Montreal he visited the Baron de Hirsch Institute. Like the later visit of Herbert Samuel, the Jewish postmaster general of Great Britain, that of Straus probably served to underscore to Canadian Jews the fact that their brethren in other English-speaking countries were advancing farther and faster in public life than they themselves were. It surely added luster to the image of the United States held by Canadian Jews.[98]

Complementing the ties of sentiment and blood in cementing the Canadian-American connection were business relationships. During the latter part of the nineteenth century, trade between the United States and Canada grew manyfold in contrast to earlier years when Canadian trade with Great Britain generally outstripped that with the United States. By 1876 Canadian imports from the United States exceeded those from Britain, and by 1905 they reached an annual value two and a half times that of goods imported from Britain. After 1875 the annual value of Canadian exports to the United States approached and sometimes exceeded the value of exports to Britain. This growth took place in the face of increasingly high American tariffs and lower British tariffs.[99]

Canada's "national policy" encouraged the establishment of branch plants. The movement of capital, machines, and know-how was accompanied by the movement of people. American speculators and entrepreneurs were to be found everywhere in Canada in the nineteenth century. American stocks were traded on Canadian exchanges, and New York quotations were telegraphed to Canada. Even the Roman Catholic Church in Quebec participated with American firms in development schemes.[100]

Many Canadian Jews were petty traders, secondhand dealers, and retail merchants. As such they had few American business ties. Others, however, participated in the continentalization of Canadian business. American-Jewish firms established Canadian branches. Canadian-Jewish firms sold American-made products or otherwise traded across the border. Canadian Jews traveled to the United States to sell their wares, and Americans came north to do the same. The correspondence of Aaron and Ezekiel Hart records such transactions already in the eighteenth century. In the journal he kept from 1800 to 1806 Montrealer Samuel David recorded the frequent business trips to New York of Myer Michaels. These were not unique ventures even in those earliest years. At all times a great many Canadians went south to shop, where goods were cheaper and of greater variety than at home. Occasionally even disreputable business was conducted across the border. In 1856 Montreal's Spanish and Portuguese Synagogue "rebuked" its own sexton "for smuggling articles from the U.S." into Canada. Half a century later a New York Jew was jailed in Kingston, Ontario, for smuggling furs into Canada. There were others, of course, over the years.[101]

A few Canadian Jews were involved in the increasing penetration of Canada by American big business after the turn of the century. Lester Rice, a native of Russia, who worked for the Metropolitan Life Insurance Company, was transferred from New York to Montreal in 1904. Archibald Coplan, another Russian-born Jew, had worked for an American company while still in Vilna. He was transferred first to Germany, then to the United States, and finally to Ottawa in 1905. Early in the century, Mortimer Davis of Montreal sold his giant Canadian tobacco firm to the

American Tobacco Company, an international monopoly. Davis then served as president of the firm's Canadian operations. He was also a director of the United States Rubber Company.[102]

Like businessmen, Canadian laborers had growing contacts with their American counterparts, who influenced much of the early unionization in Canada. Americans sent union organizers north to support Canadian laborers in their strikes and also exported some of their own labor problems. In 1912 a Montreal tailors' strike was largely a spillover from the major strikes that had occurred earlier that year in New York and other large American cities. Already by 1909 Canadian-American labor ties were sufficiently close for the American Federation of Labor, headed by the English-born Jew, Samuel Gompers, to hold its annual convention in Toronto.[103]

Jewish labor unions in Canada were generally the offspring of American parent unions. In 1890 the first congress of Jewish labor organizations in North America, held in New York City, decided to found a central union, the Hebrew Labor Federation of the United States and Canada. Among the few delegates from places other than New York were Montrealers. The Jewish or largely Jewish unions with the closest American connections were those in the needle trades. In Montreal and Toronto, as in large American cities and especially New York, eastern European Jewish immigrants flocked to the burgeoning textile and clothing industries. In Canada, as in the United States, they were quick to organize. Jewish tailors in Montreal established the first Canadian branch of the United Garment Workers of America in the early 1890s. The Cloakmakers' Union, the Amalgamated Clothing Workers, the Capmakers' and Pantsmakers' Unions, and the International Ladies' Garment Workers' Union also established branches on both sides of the border during the period.[104]

Business was not the only aspect of North American life that was becoming continentalized during these years. So, too, were cultural and intellectual affairs. Not only for Jews but for all non-French Canadians the hubs of the intellectual universe lay outside Canada. The European centers were far away. It was, however, no more difficult for Montrealers and Torontonians to communicate with New York than it was for them to communicate with each other. Although intellectual and scholarly activity developed in both cities in the nineteenth century, they remained provincial outposts for a long time. When, in 1849, Rabbi Abraham De Sola received the coveted appointment of lecturer in Oriental languages at McGill University, the "university" had only a handful of students, a muddy, broken-down campus, and an unpaid faculty including the principal.[105] In contrast the United States had larger cities, older institutions (Harvard had been founded in 1636), and, by the mid-nineteenth century, an established intellectual tradition. If the United States had rough cultural edges by European standards, it was classical Athens by comparison with Anglo-Canada. Understandably, then, Canadians with intellectual aspirations, and the Jews among them, wanted to be part of the American scene. Just as frequently they invited American intellectuals to come north to enlighten them.

Adolphus Mordecai Hart, one of the early intellectuals of Canadian Jewry, wrote on American themes and published in the United States. He lived for seven years in New York, where he was active in Democratic Party pamphleteering and other activities. It is an indication of the extent to which Canadians were at home in American intellectual and political circles that Hart could cross the border, write effective tracts on behalf of New York governor and Democratic presidential candidate Horatio Seymour, and then return home to Montreal to practice law and write political tracts dealing with Canadian issues. Hart's son, Gerald Ephraim, continued the paternal tradition, living in Jacksonville, Florida, for a decade beginning in 1913, where he published and edited the biweekly *Southern Sun*.[106]

Abraham De Sola published and lectured extensively in the United States. He wrote for the *Occident and American Jewish Advocate* in Philadelphia, the *Jewish Messenger,* the *Asmonean,* and the *American Hebrew* in New York, and the Cincinnati *Hebrew Review*. The prayer book he edited was published in Philadelphia. His writing and public appearances in the United States were of sufficient number to invite offers from American lyceum agents wanting to represent him and to make him a welcome guest in American publishing houses.[107] From the significance the rabbi placed on his American connections and his desire to be accepted by the more sophisticated American public, it is possible to infer a great deal about Canadian attitudes toward the United States. In 1872 the rabbi delivered the invocation before the United States House of Representatives. He was not the first Jew to do so, but he was the first foreigner; and although the event merited some note, only a provincial on the make could possibly have made the fuss over the appearance that De Sola did. He and his friends regarded it as the capstone of his long career. At home and in letters to England the appearance was touted— no one of De Sola's acquaintance remained ignorant of the great event. The dubious claim was put forth that the invocation had been commanded by President Ulysses S. Grant. The rabbi's attitude bore all the marks of a sense of inferiority regarding the United States, one not unique to De Sola among Canadians of the Victorian period.[108]

By the turn of the century Canadians who could were shuttling back and forth between the two countries, speaking and publishing on both sides of the border. On one occasion the prime minister, Sir Wilfrid Laurier, addressed a banquet in New York, and the Montreal Jewess Edith Ballon, a music student, also appeared on the program. Goldwin Smith was a frequent visitor to the United States as were other Canadian scholars; and American guests were a must at Canadian cultural events of all sorts.[109]

Canadians belonged to American scholarly and intellectual associations. Max Steinkopf of Winnipeg, for example, a cousin by marriage of Oscar Straus, was treasurer of the Archaeological Institute of America for a number of years during the period. Other Jews participated in American-Jewish cultural organizations. Clarence I. De Sola was a member of the American Jewish Historical Society and an active participant in its proceedings.[110] Canadians grew accustomed to reading American journals and books, perhaps because up to 1906 Canadian postal rates for American periodicals were significantly lower than those for British and other "foreign" publications. But even thereafter reading habits did not change a great deal.[111]

Minority groups in Canada, with their small and recently arrived populations, tended to rely more heavily than other Canadians on the United States for their cultural fare. Only in 1910, for example, did Canadian Slovaks first try to publish their own journal, and even then it had to be edited and produced in Chicago. Although Italians in Canada after 1895 had their own paper, *Corriere del Canada,* they tended nonetheless to read Italian-American publications.[112] Canadian Jews had no periodical of their own until 1897. They read the *American Israelite,* the *American Hebrew,* the *Jewish Messenger,* and the *Hebrew Standard.* The amount of Canadian news in those journals, in comparison with what English journals printed, indicates that most Canadian Jews preferred the American publications. Some Canadians, most notably the Rabbis De Sola, wrote for the American-Jewish press; and after 1897 Canadians freely reprinted articles from it. On occasion Canadian Jews wrote for the general American press.[113]

When Montrealers established a Yiddish-language paper in 1907, they still found themselves dependent on the United States. Technicians came from New York to set up the *Keneder odler,* which throughout its history has provided full coverage of the New York–Jewish scene. (So, too, did other Montreal papers. The *Star,* for example, had a regular column, "New York Gossip," at the turn of the century.) Harry Winberg, one of the founders of Toronto's Yiddish daily, *The Hebrew Journal,* had spent years in the United States.[114]

Yet another Canadian-Jewish cultural institution that drew heavily upon the United States for models and manpower was the Yiddish theater. A Russian-Jewish immigrant from New York first brought Yiddish theater to Montreal. Two years later, in 1898, a whole troupe of American players from Boston immigrated there. The French-Canadian Monument National was transformed into a Jewish playhouse by "Yiddish theatrical companies from New York" early in the present century. In Toronto and in Winnipeg, as well, the New York Yiddish theater was much in evidence.[115]

In the religious sphere, as well, there were extensive exchanges between Canadians and Americans during these years. Contemporary lists of ministers show that Canadian Christians depended heavily on the United States at least in the early nineteenth century, in part because Canadians had not yet begun to train clergy on a large scale. Along with England the United States was Canada's chief source of Jewish ministers and of lesser synagogue officiants as well. The United States was the main destination of departing Canadian clergy throughout the period. In later years pulpits were exchanged frequently.[116]

Generally the Jewish clergy who came to Canada before the last years of the nineteenth century were immigrants from Europe and not native Americans. Often they were not first-raters. In the latter years of the period under review the Canadian pulpit became largely Americanized; and the caliber of men attracted to Canada improved. Toronto, Hamilton, Ottawa, Winnipeg, Regina, and other cities were served during the turn-of-the-century years by clergy who came from the United States. In Montreal all during the period the American presence was especially marked.[117]

During the tenure of Rev. David Piza at the Spanish and Portuguese Congregation in Montreal between 1838 and 1845 Myer Levy of New York came to fill in for Piza from time to time. In 1846 when the newly hired Abraham De Sola could not arrive in Montreal before the High Holy Days, the congregation turned again to Levy. One of the earliest sextons of the synagogue, a Mr. Mendells, came from the United States. He never performed his duties satisfactorily, yet constantly demanded higher wages. Letters were written to New York and Philadelphia in

*Yiddish author Sholem Asch in Montreal on his "American" tour in 1910.
Note Asch's fellow tourists in the background.*

an attempt to find a replacement. At last Mendells was sent packing to an unsuspecting congregation in the western United States. The assistant minister of the Spanish and Portuguese congregation from 1882 to 1902 also came from the United States. Abraham Kirschberg had spent a number of years in New York before coming to Montreal, and he had close family connections there. Other lesser officiants over the years also came from or through the United States.[118]

In 1881 the Anglophile German and Polish Synagogue of Montreal took on its first American rabbi, Rev. Samuel Marks of Chicago. Since 1898 that pulpit has been occupied exclusively by rabbis who were Americans or who had graduated from American seminaries. In that year Bernard Michael Kaplan, a recent graduate of the Jewish Theological Seminary in New York, was summoned to the congregation. Kaplan remained in Montreal for four years, after which he left for Sacramento, California, where he assumed the leadership of a Reform pulpit. Kaplan's successor in Montreal was Herman Abramowitz. Like Kaplan, Abramowitz was Russian and a graduate of the Jewish Theological Seminary in New York. He proved enormously popular in Montreal, serving in the congregation until his death in 1947.[119]

Some of the synagogues of the eastern European immigrants, who came to North America after 1875, were also headed by clergymen who had been at least partially Americanized. Israel Kahanovitch, longtime chief rabbi of Winnipeg, had spent a year in Scranton, Pennsylvania, before moving north. Solomon Beir Sprince, rabbi of Montreal's Beth Midrash Hagodal Chevra Shaas Synagogue after 1902, had previously served in Paterson, New Jersey, and Portland, Oregon. Sprince's predecessor in Montreal was Aaron M. Ashinsky. Rabbi Ashinsky, who had a major impact on the Montreal Jewish community during his five years' residence in the city, had spent a decade in the United States before coming to Canada and returned there after his stay in Montreal. Ashinsky knew English well and before coming to Canada had become acquainted with American communal innovations, such as the afternoon Hebrew school, which he introduced to Montreal. In Toronto the Goel Tzedec Synagogue, the membership of which consisted of up-and-coming eastern European immigrants and their children, brought Rabbi Julius Price, a native of Worcester, Massachusetts, and a graduate of the Jewish Theological Seminary, to its pulpit in 1913. Price attempted to introduce some "American" innovations during his three-year tenure at Goel Tzedec, which were ill received by a number of the congregation's members.[120]

The most American of all Canadian-Jewish pulpits were those of the few Reform congregations. Hamilton's Reform synagogue, Anshe Sholom, engaged as its first rabbi, Wolf Landau, late of Zanesville, Ohio, and Honesdale, Pennsylvania. Most of Landau's successors came from the United States as well. Winnipeg's Reform Holy Blossom Congregation had a short life; its only rabbi was D. A. Bonnheim, who had come from Las Vegas in 1904. In less than a year the rabbi had left Canada for the United States, and the congregation had changed its name and become more traditional. When the Toronto Hebrew Congregation engaged its first clergyman, they hired Rev. Hyman Goldberg of New York, a combination rabbi, cantor, and ritual animal slaughterer. Following Goldberg's departure the congregation was served by a succession of lesser officiants who came from the United States as well as, briefly, an American rabbi, David H. Wittenberg, who came from nearby Buffalo. A more important Americanizing influence at Toronto's Holy Blossom than that exerted by the synagogue's clergy was the push in the direction of Reform, which came from synagogue members who had lived in the United States.[121]

In Montreal's Temple Emanu-El the American influence was most pronounced. Among the laymen who founded the congregation in 1882 were several who had become acquainted with Reform Judaism while living in the United States. Since 1901 every rabbi of Emanu-El has been a graduate of the Hebrew Union College in Cincinnati, the Reform seminary, or of its New York branch. The most distinguished American rabbi to serve the congregation during the period under review was Nathan Gordon, who was born in Russia and reared in New Orleans. In 1908 Gordon succeeded to Abraham De Sola's old post at McGill as lecturer in Oriental languages. In 1916 Gordon became a lawyer and subsequently acted for many years as president of the temple of which he had once been rabbi.[122]

Since there were always many fewer Canadian than American congregations, Canadian clergymen seeking a new pulpit naturally looked to the south. Those who had originally come from the United States were generally drawn back. For others, eager to become part of the freewheeling Judaism of the United States, more conservative Canada served as a halfway house on the journey from Europe. Barnett Elzas and Abraham Lazarus, for example, both of whom had come to Toronto's Holy Blossom Congregation from England, went on to more successful careers in less traditional American congregations. Isidore Meyers, who came to Shaar Hashomayim in Montreal from Australia

in 1896 and moved on to San Francisco a year later, is another example
of a European who paused in Canada on the way to the United States.[123]

Discontented clergymen, like other Canadians during this period,
were attracted to the United States in hopes of finding greater opportunity
there. When Jacob Raphael Cohen had to sue the Montreal congregation
for his wages in 1782, he moved to New York. Abraham De Sola himself
threatened to leave Montreal for Philadelphia in 1850, when his salary
fell into arrears. Two years later he was elected to the ministry of Micve
Israel Congregation in Savannah, Georgia. He chose not to leave, however, as he did not in 1868, when he was offered the prestigious pulpit
of the recently deceased Isaac Leeser in Philadelphia.[124] Joseph Kornfeld
was a Montreal rabbi who came from the United States and returned
there. Rabbi of Temple Emanu-El from 1904 to 1906 Kornfeld left the
pulpit some time after his return to the States. Later he became minister
to Persia under President Warren G. Harding and, still later, an insurance salesman. Service in Canada and other places had apparently left
the rabbi thoroughly disillusioned with his sacred vocation.[125]

From the earliest years Jewish clergymen crossed the border to assist
congregations that were without a rabbi. During the thirty-odd years
between about 1810 and about 1840, when Montreal Jews had no regular
clergyman of their own, it was not uncommon for a rabbi and especially
a *mohel* (ritual circumciser) to make the arduous trip from New York
to attend to their needs. The *mohel* would ride circuit circumcising all
the male children born since the previous visit. In later years that favor
would be reciprocated, when Montreal *mohalim* visited Plattsburg and
other American border towns to initiate Jewish males into the covenant
of Abraham. In the early years Toronto was similarly served.[126]

Once railroad transportation became fast enough to make it practi-
cable, there was considerable exchange of pulpits between New York
and Montreal. Rabbi Morris J. Raphall of New York came to Montreal
to speak at the cornerstone-laying ceremony of the new German and
Polish Congregation in 1859. A year later at the consecration of the
completed building, another New York minister, Samuel Meyer Isaacs,
was the speaker. Interestingly, both men had emigrated to the United
States from England (although Raphall was Swedish-born and Isaacs,
Dutch-born), and both retained strong ties to the mother country. When
Abraham De Sola died in New York in 1882, his nephew Henry Pereira
Mendes and several lay leaders of New York's Spanish and Portuguese
Synagogue accompanied the corpse back to Montreal. Mendes delivered
the eulogy at the funeral. Americans frequently preached at Toronto

and Montreal synagogues on special occasions in subsequent years.[127]

Although as a group they were less conspicuous in the much larger American-Jewish community, Canadian religious figures made guest appearances in the United States with some frequency especially during the latter years of the period. Rabbi Abraham De Sola preached in New York synagogues and officiated at weddings and other ceremonies in Plattsburg and Ogdensburg, New York, and in other places. Meldola De Sola was a fixture in New York, where he often preached at the Spanish and Portuguese Synagogue and elsewhere. At meetings of the Union of Orthodox Congregations, of which he was one of the founders, De Sola's outspoken presence was always felt.[128]

Even former Jews of the convert subculture moved north and south during these years. In the 1870s the newly converted Charles Freshman and the earlier Canadian apostate, Isaac Hellmuth, exchanged visits with "Mr. Meyer, a converted Jew of New York."[129] The Toronto Jewish Mission was run by Rev. Henry Singer, a converted Polish Jew who came from Boston in 1897 and left for Detroit in 1919. In 1911 a two-and-a-half-hour riot in Toronto followed the proselytizing sermon of a Jewish convert to Christianity from Louisville, Kentucky.[130]

The religious connection between the American- and Canadian-Jewish communities consisted of much more than exchanges of clergymen. During his long tenure in Montreal Abraham De Sola was so well known from his writings in American publications that he received questions about religious practice from American Jews; and gentiles wrote to him about converting to Judaism, healing by electromagnetism, and any number of other questions. In the early years New York was an important source of liturgical supplies for Canadian Jews, and Winnipeg's first congregation turned to Chicago for a Torah scroll. Later, American prayer books came to be used in many Canadian synagogues. The unleavened bread eaten on Passover was imported by many who "preferred New York biscuits" to those baked in Montreal or Toronto.[131] In New York's Spanish and Portuguese Synagogue a perpetual memorial prayer was recited on certain holy days for Rabbi Abraham De Sola after his death. From time to time Americans from Boston to Austin, Texas, gave religious artifacts to the Spanish and Portuguese Congregation in Montreal. In 1918 after the death of Rabbi Meldola De Sola his widow reciprocated by presenting a Torah pointer in his memory to the Spanish and Portuguese Synagogue in New York.[132]

Requests for charitable contributions crossed the border in both directions, although, because of their small number, Canadians tended more often to be the recipients. At times, however, especially in the later years, they sent funds to needy American Jews. Although giving charity is considered a religious obligation by Jews, the contributions were often given for "secular" purposes. In 1853, for example, Montreal's Spanish and Portuguese Synagogue came to the aid of yellow fever victims of New Orleans's Shangarai Chassed Congregation. In the early twentieth century Toronto's Pride of Israel [Sick] Benefit Society sent needed funds to striking Jewish workers in Rochester, Chicago, and New York.[133] These were not isolated instances. In later years Americans, like their British counterparts, grew reluctant to aid the increasingly prosperous Canadians especially as American needs for charity multiplied with the large influx of Russian-Jewish refugees.[134]

Probably the most far-reaching American-Jewish religious influence on Canadian Jews was ideological. The religious movements into which American Jewry came to be organized spilled over into Canada, where all three branches found their adherents; and by the early twentieth century Canadian Judaism, too, began to be organized along tripartite American lines. The most American of the movements was Conservatism, the center of which was the Jewish Theological Seminary of New York. The Seminary, which served Americanizing elements of the eastern European immigration, established a Montreal branch, largely for fund raising, in 1904. The sponsors were Hiram Levy, Lazarus Cohen, and Rabbi Herman Abramowitz of Shaar Hashomayim Synagogue. Over the years that synagogue became one of the leading institutions of the Conservative movement. Rabbi Abramowitz felt that Conservative Judaism had arrived in Montreal

> just at the right time. Radical religious tendencies had begun to manifest themselves and were making headway. But these were checked . . . by the successful harmonization of Jewish tradition with modernity [that characterized American Conservatism].[135]

Many members of Toronto's Goel Tzedec Synagogue were also moving toward the Conservative movement by the end of the period under review.[136]

In fact, Canadian Jews, with their British connections, were never religiously innovative. From the beginning those who were affiliated with Conservatism found themselves on the ideological right of the movement. Montreal's Shaar Hashomayim Synagogue remains today one of the most traditional Conservative congregations. The radical tendencies of American Reform made many Canadian rabbis and congregations wary about even slight deviations from Orthodoxy. Meldola De Sola, when invited to become a member of the new Jewish Theological Seminary, refused, fearing it was not sufficiently traditional for his tastes. Already in 1893 De Sola and his brother, Clarence, were agitating in the United States for the formation of an "Orthodox organization." Five years later the Union of Orthodox Congregations was formed with Rabbi De Sola as its first vice-president. He remained an active member until his death. A number of Canadian congregations affiliated with the new Union during the last two decades under review.[137]

Not surprisingly, the oldest of the American-Jewish denominations made slow headway in Canada. As late as 1953 there were but three Reform congregations in the entire country. Reform rites were adopted in 1882 in both a Hamilton and a Montreal synagogue, although the two congregations and their rabbis were not quick to affiliate formally with the Union of American Hebrew Congregations or the Central Conference of American Rabbis. Only in 1901 did Montreal's Temple Emanu-El join the Union. In 1897, when the Central Conference of American Rabbis held its convention in Montreal, Rabbi Hartog Veld, the host rabbi, was not yet a member. No Toronto synagogue belonged to the Reform Union until after World War I, when Holy Blossom formally affiliated. But, as noted previously, that Temple, with American encouragement, had been moving steadily in the direction of Reform for years.[138]

Around the turn of the century American-Jewish life witnessed an increasing variety of communal activities accompanied by the growth and proliferation of quasi-secular institutions. America was becoming a land of organizations and institutions, and American Jews were following the patterns established by their gentile neighbors. The new organizations represented a response both to an increasingly complex society and to the growth of leisure time. As was the case with Jewish cultural and religious affairs, organizational life embraced the whole continent, although to some extent Canadians transformed American models and ideas to meet Canadian conditions.

The Social Gospel movement, with its belief in human improvement through the reform of society, appealed to both Jews and gentiles. Like their American and English cousins, Canadian Jews established Young Men's and Young Women's Hebrew Associations (YM-YWHAs). Modeled along the lines of the YM and YWCAs, they were designed to provide a wholesome setting for uprooted and newly urbanized people to meet together. In Montreal the YMHA was founded in 1908. Four years later it was the second largest in the world, with over twelve hundred members, just behind New York's "Y". By 1913 the movement had spread to Vancouver and Winnipeg, and attempts were being made to found a "Y" in Toronto.[139] Other institutions copied from New York included the Montreal Jewish Library, which had modest beginnings as a reading room in 1903, and the Jewish People's University. The latter was founded by Reuben Brainin in 1914 to provide adult education for the Montreal Jewish masses. Its work was similar to the pioneering program Brainin had seen in the Educational Alliance settlement house on New York's Lower East Side.[140]

Two of Canadian Jewry's major institutions were direct translations of American models, although they evolved out of local needs and acquired their own distinctly Canadian personalities. By 1914 Montreal Jews, like their counterparts in many American communities, had become increasingly concerned about the waste and duplication in Jewish welfare services. Up to that time some thirty American-Jewish communities had already managed to federate their community services. At the behest of the Baron de Hirsch Institute, Montreal's largest and most successful agency, some Montrealers were sent to study the New York Jewish Federation. They recommended that Montreal adopt the New York model "and show the way to the rest of Canada."[141] Federation was eventually achieved in Montreal; and an American was hired to head the new superagency. Other communities followed suit, including Toronto in 1916, just after the period under review.[142]

Perhaps more significant was the movement for a national Canadian-Jewish organization, the Congress movement, that would unite most Jewish organizations in the Dominion under one roof. Its origins lay in the early years of the twentieth century, and it began to gather steam seriously in 1914. It did not achieve even limited success, however, until 1919. Not a little inspiration was gained from the short-lived Kehilla (united community) movement in New York City. And the American Jewish Congress, finally established in 1918—originally intended to be a Zionist, national, popular umbrella organization for American Jews—provided another model. This was also a period when the union movement among Protestant churches in Canada was gaining strength. That, too, may have provided a spur to the Jewish Congress movement.[143]

American Jews provided more than just the models for their Canadian coreligionists. Most American Jewish organizations of the period—charitable, fraternal, and national—actually colonized Canada by establishing Canadian branches or enlisting Canadian members in American chapters. Immigrant aid work, especially, lent itself to internationalization. Hebrew Emigrant Aid Societies existed in Montreal and Toronto in 1881 and 1882 as well as in American cities from New York to St. Louis. In June 1882 the various societies convened a conference in New York "to arrange for the proper reception and distribution of Russian refugees." Among those who attended the conference were Mona Lesser and Ferdinand Boas of Montreal and Mark Samuel of Toronto. Boas became a national director of the Hebrew Emigrant Aid Societies and Lesser was one of the nine members on the rules committee.[144]

This conference marked the beginning of joint American-Canadian efforts on behalf of Russian refugees, although it was not a very promising start. The delegates recommended that immigration cease at once. Sir Alexander T. Galt, Canadian high commissioner in London, telegraphed that Canada could accept no additional refugees. The American delegates, largely of German-Jewish origin, were no more eager to have them in their country. The later Hebrew Immigrant Aid Society was a more successful venture, although Canadian participation was minimal. In 1913 the National Board of Directors of the Immigrant Aid Society had 918 American members, two Canadians, and one Puerto Rican.[145]

There was more Canadian-American cooperation in the North American operations of the Jewish Colonization Association–Baron de Hirsch Fund, with headquarters in New York. When originally asked for help by the Young Men's Hebrew Benevolent Society of Montreal in 1890, the Fund refused. It was felt that its endowment had been given by Baron de Hirsch for use exclusively in the United States. After the turn of the century, however, the Fund undertook to assist Jewish settlers in Canada as well as in the United States. Assistance was given through the daughter agency of the Fund, the Jewish Agricultural and Industrial Aid Society. Loans were made to individual settlers; and the Society sent its personnel to Canada to inspect and advise. Eventually the Baron de Hirsch Institute of Montreal assumed responsibility for all purely Canadian matters.[146]

Successful cooperation also characterized the new Zionist movement, although for the most part Canadian Zionism developed independently of the American organization. In 1892, even before the first Zionist Congress, New York's Shavey Zion Society had set up a branch in Montreal. A year later a joint Canadian-American delegation from the Society traveled to the Holy Land to investigate settlement opportunities, since the group expected that its members would actually settle in ag-

ricultural colonies there. After the delegates returned a fund was established to purchase lands for colonization, although few Canadians or
Americans ever took advantage of it. Toward the end of the period
under review Canadian and American Zionists cooperated in planning
various settlement schemes. Among the most noteworthy was the American Zion Commonwealth, which during the 1920s was the largest pur-
chaser of land for Jewish settlement in Palestine. It was mostly Europeans
rather than North Americans, however, who settled on those lands.[147]

Other American Zionist groups also established early beachheads in
Canada. Perhaps the most firmly entrenched was the labor Zionist organization, Poalei Zion, the forerunner of the present-day Israel Labor
Party. Born in Europe, by the turn of the century it had a widespread
network of chapters including several in the United States. In 1905 the
New York chapter established a branch in Montreal, and a year later
there were groups in Toronto, Winnipeg, and Hamilton. In 1910 the
American Poalei Zion held its annual convention in Montreal, bringing
to the city major Zionist figures and greatly stimulating Canadian interest
in Zionism. During its entire history the Canadian group has remained
within the orbit of the New York headquarters. Other Zionist organizations that spread from the United States to Canada were the left-wing
Farband Labor Zionist Order, the Orthodox Zionist organization, Mizra-
chi, and the Federation of Young Judea.[148]

Not only formal organizational ties linked Canadian and American
Zionists. They cooperated in various other ways as well. The Zionist
Yiddish orator, Zvi Hirsch Masliansky, visited Montreal from time to
time after 1898. Other Zionist personalities from the United States visited
all over Canada between 1897 and 1914. Sometimes Canadian Zionists
addressed their *confrères* in the United States.[149] Zionists, who were mostly
first-generation eastern European Jews, tended to think of themselves
as Jewish nationalists and usually regarded Jews, wherever they lived,
as their *landslayt* (countrymen). In their eyes the Jewish world of North
America formed a cultural continuum, and all gentiles, Canadian, American, or other, were *goyim* (foreigners, outsiders).[150]

Perhaps the most "American" of all Jewish organizations were the
fraternal orders, which originated in the United States. They served as
mutual aid societies and as social clubs providing vital services for their
members in an era when governments offered little in the way of social
welfare benefits. Jews figured prominently in bringing the largest nonsectarian European order, the Freemasons, to America. Aaron Hart was
accepted into New York's Worshipfull Trinity Masonic Lodge No. 4

just three months before his arrival in Canada in 1760. From the first, Canadians affiliated with the American-Jewish orders, such as the B'nai B'rith, the Ancient Jewish Order Kesher Shel Barzel, and the Deborah Ladies' Aid Society. They also joined American lodges of gentile orders, such as the Masons, when Canadian lodges placed impediments in the way of Jewish membership. Toronto Jews established all-Jewish chapters of two gentile American orders, the Oddfellows and the Order of Chosen Friends.[151]

The oldest and most successful of the Jewish orders was the Independent Order of B'nai B'rith (hereafter referred to as IOBB). Most of its early members were German Jews, who were not very numerous in Canada. Perhaps for that reason the Ancient Jewish Order Kesher Shel Barzel was initially more successful in Canada, and the IOBB got off to a slow start. The first Canadian lodge of the B'nai B'rith was established in Toronto in 1875, thirty-two years after the founding of the order. Six years later a lodge was established in Montreal and in 1886, an additional one in Victoria, British Columbia. The Canadian lodges were under the jurisdiction of American "Grand Lodges," the eastern ones under New York and the Victoria lodge under San Francisco. But Americans were more enthusiastic about the IOBB than Canadians. By 1894 the Toronto lodge had surrendered its charter; and in 1903 Montreal gave up as well.[152]

A dramatic upsurge in the Canadian fortunes of the IOBB came about in the second decade of the twentieth century. By that time the order had lost much of its "German" aura and was considered very "American." In the United States eastern European Jews eager to Americanize now flocked to the IOBB. In Canada there was renewed interest. Influenced in part by American immigrants such as Rabbi Nathan Gordon new Canadian IOBB lodges were established in Winnipeg (1909), Vancouver (1910), Edmonton, Regina, Fort William, Ontario, Montreal (1913), and Victoria (1914). As if to emphasize the orientation of the order, the new Regina lodge was named after the prominent American Jew, Louis D. Brandeis, who just three years later would become the first Jew to sit on the United States Supreme Court.[153]

Other orders to come to Canada from the United States were The Sons of Benjamin and The Independent Order B'nai Jacob. Larger and more influential in the community was the left-wing Arbeiter Ring or Workmen's Circle, a combination fraternal order, labor union, and mutual benefit society. Eleven years after its founding in New York in 1895 the Circle reached Montreal. There it enlisted large numbers of members, including some organized in the Karl Marx Branch and others in the Meyer London Branch. The latter was named after the American-Jewish socialist, who was later elected to Congress from the electoral district that included New York's Lower East Side. The Circle reached Toronto two years after it came to Montreal. The Pride of Israel, a smaller, left-wing, American order and sick benefit society, established a Toronto branch early in the twentieth century.[154]

One other American-Jewish organization that attracted significant numbers of Canadian members during the period was the National Council of Jewish Women (hereafter referred to as NCJW), which dated from 1893. Although Rabbi Meldola De Sola eventually became an outspoken critic of the National Women, because of the Reform leanings of several of its organizers, it was his wife who had brought the group to Canada three years after its founding. At Mrs. De Sola's invitation the then president of the NCJW, Miss Sadie American, came to Montreal to proselytize the local ladies. The first Montreal chapter president was Mrs. De Sola herself, who traveled to Toronto in 1896 to spread the gospel. Soon there was a Canadian division with Mrs. De Sola as vice-president. In 1909 the NCJW held its first "international" congress in Toronto; and since then Canadian chapters have existed in major Jewish centers.[155]

Besides all these popular organizations, several American-Jewish organizations appealing to special interest groups also appeared on the Canadian scene during the latter years of the period under review. In the first decade of the twentieth century a Jewish Literary Society was organized in Montreal in close cooperation with parent groups in New York. In 1907, the Jewish Chautauqua Society had chapters in Toronto and Hamilton as well as in sixty-one American cities. It sought to spread Jewish culture, much as the general Chautauqua Society attempted to spread Christian and general culture.[156] In 1913 the Jewish college fraternity, Zeta Beta Tau, formed its first Canadian chapter at McGill. A year later a Canadian, Nathaniel S. Fineberg of McGill, was elected Supreme Sofer at the fraternity's New York convention. Among the sponsors of the fraternity in Montreal was Rabbi Herman Abramowitz, who had belonged to it while a student in New York.[157]

The multiplicity of Jewish organizations in the United States on the eve of World War I seems staggering, but, of course, the same was true of gentile community life. Organizations old and new enjoyed an "astonishing growth" between 1880 and 1914. These organizations, Jewish and gentile, spread into Canada often through the agency of American immigrants. There they "had a marked assimilating effect."[158] Because of these institutional connections French political economist André Siegfried felt that Canada's whole "way of living . . . [was coming] completely under the influence of New York."[159] Despite its strong bonds with England, the Canadian-Jewish community now seemed "nearer the United States than England, not only topographically, but also typographically."[160] In fact, by the close of the period under review "the Jews of Canada . . . [seemed well] ahead of their neighbours in maintaining an *entente cordiale* with the United States."[161]

Ties of sentiment and birth and personal and communal bonds, then, connected Canadian Jews with the United States all during the nineteenth century, no less and sometimes more than they connected them with England. In the first half of the nineteenth century most American Jews were of German origin, whereas many Canadian Jews were of British origin. Later most on both sides of the border were of eastern European stock. But whatever their background, Canadian Jews were quite ready to adopt American habits and sentiments. Given the number of Canadians with American antecedents, the attachment of Jews everywhere in the world to the United States, and the appeal of the vital, large, and variegated American-Jewish community, it is not surprising that Canadian Jews prior to 1914 evinced genuine enthusiasm for "the great American republic."

Perhaps even more than other Anglo-Canadians at the turn of the century, Jews maintained a high level of interest in American affairs. Events in the United States touched them almost as much as they did Americans. In 1901 when President William McKinley was shot, Meldola De Sola, like other Montreal clergymen, offered special prayers and, after the president's death, he spoke warmly of his "noble . . . character."[162] The *Keneder odler* kept its readers informed about all contemporary American issues from trust-busting to the Philadelphia general strike of 1910. It even took sides in American presidential elections.[163]

American national holidays were celebrated in partial manner by Canadian Jews. Lincoln's birthday inspired an enthusiastic annual article in the *Keneder odler,* and it was a matter of course for the paper "to honor the Pilgrim Fathers" on Thanksgiving Day.[164] In 1892 Montreal's Temple Emanu-El held a service in honor of the four hundredth anniversary of the discovery of America. The service concluded with "an invocation for the citizens of the United States . . . who had so nobly treated all the persecuted."[165] Canadian involvement in American-Jewish affairs continued to increase over the years. The two hundred and fiftieth anniversary of the settlement of Jews in the United States was celebrated in 1905 by Canadian Jews as if it were their own anniversary.[166] On the twenty-fifth anniversary of the death of Isaac Leeser, Meldola De Sola mourned the "national loss" from the pulpit of his Montreal synagogue.[167] Canadian Jews followed with interest news about the Jewish agricultural school at Woodbine, New Jersey, the Jewish theater in New York, and the New York Yiddish press—indeed about all topics of Jewish interest.[168]

Although anti-American sentiment was not absent from Canada during the period, as noted earlier, the Canadian-American relationship remained, for the most part, impervious to the vicissitudes of international affairs. There were, of course, the dislocations of the American Revolution and the War of 1812, which affected Jews as they did other North Americans.[169] But except for these two brief periods, the interchanges that generally marked Canadian-American relations continued despite political differences and experienced an upsurge when tensions abated. (Rabbi De Sola's appearance before Congress occurred just after the conclusion of the Anglo-American Treaty of Washington in 1871.)

Even between 1864 and 1871, the low period of Canadian-American relations—marked by the Fenian Raids, by American annexationist pressure, by the possibility of an American-British war over the Alabama Claims and other issues related to the Civil War—Jews, like others, continued to move back and forth across the border freely. American-Jewish journals arrived in Canada; Rabbi De Sola continued his peregrinations; emigration from Canada to the United States continued apace. In later, less tense years the United States consul was a regular guest at Montreal Jewish functions, such as the laying of the cornerstone of the new Baron de Hirsch Institute building in 1901. To a great degree, then, Canadian Jews of the period under review felt that they were "Americans" and acted as if they were.[170]

The North Atlantic Triangle

The admiration felt by Canadian Jews in the Victorian era for American freedom and opportunity, which was manifested in the multiplicity of relationships they built up with the United States, was typical of the general Jewish attitude toward America. They might well, however, have conflicted with the loyalties that all Canadians, especially Anglo-Canadians, were expected to have toward Great Britain. In general, as noted previously, the links of Anglo-Canadians with the mother country remained strong during the period under review; but for the most part, the British and the American affiliations of Canadian Jews did not conflict.

Even after the American Revolution, Britain continued to transmit ideas and culture to the United States and, of course, to Canada as well. She also continued to export goods, capital, and men to a receptive North America and to import a great deal in return. From this traffic arose shared "tastes and . . . social and political principles."[171] Moreover, Englishmen, and certainly English Jews, also greatly admired the freedom and opportunity that seemed synonymous with America. Over the years there was created a "North Atlantic Triangle," an Anglo-Saxon civilization comprising Great Britain and her two North American daughter states, the United States and Canada.

By 1850 there were approximately three thousand English Jews in the United States and a few hundred more in Canada. After the conquest of Canada, one of the main routes from England to Canada was via New York. The first Jews to settle in what would later be Canadian territory were English Jews who arrived in Nova Scotia in the 1750s after stopovers of varying durations in New York and Newport. Aaron Hart had spent some time in New York before settling in Trois Rivières in 1760. After the American Revolution, too, English Jews and eastern and central European Jews who had passed through England on their way to America continued to make their way to Canada via American ports. It was not uncommon for relatives to be scattered among all three countries.[172] Traffic between the United States and England as well as three-way traffic with Canada increased near the end of the period under review, as thousands of Jews annually described the triangle. Between 1904 and 1912 from 3,300 to 14,000 Jews a year emigrated directly from England to the United States, while others emigrated to the United States from England by way of Canada. Still others went from England to Canada by way of American ports cementing bonds among the three countries and their Jewries.[173]

In addition to those who had actually lived in all or two of the three countries, there were others who traveled among them, sojourning for various periods of time. They, too, helped to create the ambience of the English-speaking, North Atlantic world. Canadian doctors in the early days of the country frequently studied in both the United States and England before returning home to practice. Aaron Hart David, distinguished Montreal physician, received his medical degree at Edinburgh in 1835 and studied in the United States as well. Dr. David kept up professional ties in both countries, retaining his personal friendships even while he served as surgeon to the Sixth Fusilliers during the Fenian Raids of 1870.[174]

Other intellectuals moved about in a similar fashion. Sir J. William Dawson, longtime president of McGill and the guiding spirit behind that university's growth from a country school to a major university, spoke and published in England and the United States and was a member of scholarly societies in both countries. In 1875 he delivered the Phi Beta Kappa Oration at the Harvard commencement, and some years later he refused the presidency of a large American university. His Jewish counterpart was his contemporary and McGill colleague, Abraham De Sola. De Sola's life—that he was born in London, lived most of his adult life in Montreal, and died on a visit to New York—is symbolic of the role he played in the "North Atlantic Triangle." Even war proved to be a uniting factor. At least two Canadian Jews felt sufficiently enthusiastic about both the United States and England to go to war for both countries. Joseph Franklin, a Montrealer born in eastern Europe, and Dr. Hyman Lightstone, also of Montreal, fought as volunteers both in the Spanish-American War and the Boer War.[175]

The interconnection of the three countries was perceptible at the communal level as well as at the personal level. Immigrant aid work was frequently coordinated among London, New York, and Montreal. The B'nai B'rith lodges in all three countries looked to Grand Lodge No. 1 in New York as headquarters. Jewish labor unions in England and Canada looked to the more developed American unions for leadership. In some areas both North American countries learned from England. In others England learned from North America. There was give-and-take of all sorts in both directions across the Atlantic.[176]

In the religious sphere as much as in any other Canada combined both English and American elements. Although the Anglicans and Roman Catholics do not fit the pattern for obvious reasons, most Protestant denominations and Judaism in Canada are blends of elements from all three countries. The first two presbyteries to be established on Canadian soil were founded by emigrants from Scotland. By 1833, however, the Niagara Presbytery in Upper Canada was composed entirely of former American ministers. Canadian Baptists have almost always numbered in their ranks emigrants from both New and old England. The Methodists in Upper Canada were for a long time subordinate to the American Methodist Episcopal Church, causing them to be suspected of disloyalty to Britain at times. During the same period the Methodists of Lower Canada were subordinate to the British Wesleyan Church. Finally in 1855 the two groups came together in an independent Canadian church. In later years other Canadian denominations also maintained connections with coreligionists in Britain and the United States.[177]

Canadian Judaism likewise had roots in both England and the United States. For Judaism as for the Protestant denominations, Canada was a way station between the two countries. It was symbolic of the nature of Canadian Judaism that the bylaws of the Spanish and Portuguese Synagogue in Montreal in 1857 specified that the "fixed prayers shall forever be read in the Hebrew according to the customs of the Great Portuguese Synagogue in London" and that the "hours for commencing the morning service . . . be the same as in the Portuguese Synagogue in New York."[178]

A cursory glance at lists of prominent Jews gives some indication of the importance in the Canadian Jewish community of the triangular relationship. In S. J. Birnbaum's 1912–13 series of articles in the Canadian *Jewish Times* on "The History of the Jews in Toronto," every Jew mentioned had either a British or an American connection or both.[179] Of the eighteen identifiable Jews mentioned in Ross Hamilton's *Prominent Men of Canada* (1932), nine came from either the United States or Britain. A more representative sampling is offered by Arthur Daniel Hart in *The Jew in Canada* (1926). Hart compiled profiles of 302 Jews prominent in Canada in 1926 or earlier. Of these, 148 had lived either in Britain or the United States. Still more had close relatives—children or siblings—living in one of the two countries. The breakdown by groups offers an even more telling picture. Of the clergy, 15 of 21 had American or British experience; of the journalists, 1 of 3; of the doctors, 15 of 29; of the businessmen, 75 of 133; of the women, 11 of 19. Clearly, then, English or American experience was an advantage in rising to a position of influence in the Canadian-Jewish community. It was also likely to strengthen the American and British ties of that community, since these leaders set the pace for others.

The degree to which English and American Jews rose to the top of Canadian-Jewish society paralleled the success of gentiles in the general society. British companies tended to bring over British personnel for top positions and American companies, Americans. In 1931 the number of American-born in responsible positions in Canada was 43 percent higher than the percentage of American-born in the general population.[180] Similarly, the North Atlantic relationship helped Canadian emigrants and Britishers in the United States. Although no systematic studies exist, indications are that Canadians in the United States over the years achieved a high degree of success. So, too, did British immigrants to whom the United States seemed less a "foreign" country than "this 'Greater Britain' in which we have made our home."[181] These immigrants, of course, did not have to overcome the language handicap that confronted others.

Reinforcing the transatlantic movement of people, ideas, and institutions was the political rapprochement between England and the United States at the turn of the century. After the mid-1890s, when Britain awoke to the German peril, she became increasingly eager to better her relations with the United States. Outstanding issues were resolved, sometimes at Canada's expense or so, at least, many Canadians felt. Americans at the time were also eager to better relations with Britain. The WASPs then in the driver's seat in the United States sensed that they were losing power to the newcomers and began to play up Anglo-Saxon unity. Their racism derived partly from Darwin and De Gobineau and partly from fears that the new, post-1880 immigrants from southern and eastern Europe, including Jews, would be hard to assimilate and would threaten Anglo-Saxon hegemony. In Canada the growing friction between French and Anglo-Canada stood in the way of the development of a strong all-Canadian nationalism. Instead, both groups went in search of roots and connections with which to buttress their positions. The alternative to Americanization for Anglo-Canadians was pro-British imperialist sentiment. But that was a problematic alternative, for there were simply too many shared interests and values between the United States and England for imperial sentiment to cancel out North American sentiment. In the end both were strengthened.

The North Atlantic Triangle, then, thrived during the period under review, combining American and British elements and some Canadian. It was a relationship that allowed Anglo-Canadians to live with the growing Americanization of their country while retaining and even fortifying their British connections. The rising tide of Anglo-Saxon racial spirit in Canada helped to create a spirit of unity with all English-speaking peoples. Anglo-Canadians, after an initial spurt of sympathy for Spain in the Spanish-American War, came around to almost unanimous support for the cause of the United States. Canadian churches retained their ties to fellow communicants in both the United States and Britain. Canadian universities manifested the "Anglo-Saxon influence ... in two forms—English and American."[182] And Canadian Jewry was, simultaneously, both very British and very American. By the turn of the century there was a growing feeling in Canada and in the United

States and Great Britain, that the citizens of all three countries were "Anglo-Saxons, All."[183]

The North Atlantic relationship was far more important in Anglo-Canada, with its yet weak sense of nationhood, than it was in either Great Britain or the United States. Over the years there developed a rationalization of that relationship in Canada, which included a new sense of Canada's importance, of unique mission. As intellectual leader, George M. Grant, and others saw it, Canada's "divine mission" was now to be the creation of a British North America, which would become a "living link" between England and the United States. Canada would heal the breach of 1776, mediating between the two great Anglo-Saxon peoples.[184]

Canadian Jews in the Victorian era, then, shared with gentile Anglo-Canadians an American connection and a British connection, which made them part of an increasingly integrated North Atlantic world. Their bonds with England and America were, in part, unique. The admiration and affection they felt for both countries stemmed in large measure from the exceptionally tolerant manner in which both treated Jews. Those feelings were reinforced by the willingness of both countries to defend Jews in the international arena. Jewish affection was reciprocated by many Americans and Englishmen, who felt an affinity for Jews and for their heritage. To Canadian Jews the concept of a North Atlantic, Anglo-Saxon relationship was particularly congenial, since it allowed them to reconcile two ideals: England and America. Canadian Jews boasted of their dual loyalty, their admiration for the "Stars and Stripes" and their "wholehearted . . . British citizenship."[185] It made sense in the Canadian context for Meldola De Sola to sign letters to newspapers at times, "An American Jew," at other times, "Briton," and on still other occasions, "Canadian."[186] Dependent upon and intimately connected with both England and the United States, Canadian Jews found the North Atlantic relationship to be a means to their own Canadianization or, more correctly, their Anglo-Canadianization.

CHAPTER FOUR

The French and Roman Catholic Relationship

France, the Church, and the Jews

If nineteenth-century Jews in general grew attached to England and the United States, their feelings about France were ambivalent at best. The French Revolution promised freedom, equality, and brotherhood to all, including those previously denied such rights; and in 1791 France became the first European country to grant Jews political emancipation. From that time on French Jewry became increasingly integrated into the life of the country. Already early in the nineteenth century a few Jews began to play a major role in the industrial and commercial development of France. Others entered politics and even the military. During what has been termed the "golden age" of French Jewry, the years between 1906 and 1918, from three to six Jews were serving at any given time in the Chamber of Deputies, while others advanced in different spheres. On occasion, too, as in Britain and the United States, France supported Jewish causes abroad. For these reasons France merited Jewish approbation.[1]

For the most part, however, Jews were not enthusiastic about France. To begin with, under the *ancien régime,* France had been a most unpleasant place for Jews. They enjoyed few rights and little sympathy. In

contrast to Britain, France did not allow Jews—or other non-Catholics—
into her foreign possessions, including New France (that is, Canada).
Even members of the Jewish Gradis family of Bordeaux, whose trade
with New France was vital for the life of the colony in its last fifteen
years, were barred from entering it. And after the Revolution the free-
doms granted to Jews showed signs of being transitory. For a time after
1791 France and those territories it conquered enjoyed a good measure
of liberty. Most Jews expected that full equality in all areas of life would
soon be realized. Under Napoleon, however, the Revolution began to
regress toward tyranny. In 1808 an Imperial Decree effectively suspended
Jewish emancipation in France for a decade. In the conquered areas,
such as the Duchy of Warsaw, a major center of eastern European Jewry,
Jews were to receive no civic rights whatsoever for ten years. Napoleon's
rule did not last ten years. Nonetheless some unpleasant memories of
the French lingered among Jews and others as well.[2]

Within France itself some of the most basic of human rights were
denied to Jews in the early nineteenth century. There were various towns
in Alsace, where most French Jews lived, that tried to bar Jewish settlement even after emancipation. The 1808 decree, among its other restrictions, forbade foreign Jews to immigrate into France and forbade
even French Jews to move into Alsace, deeming that the area had reached
the saturation point of Jewish settlement. Despite emancipation, most
French Jews remained poor in the first half of the nineteenth century.
They had little in common with the Rothschilds, the Pereires, the Foulds,
and the Reinachs, except for their ancestral religion and their newly
gained fatherland. Yet, the collectivity of French Jewry was held responsible for the alleged sins of the wealthy by a large number of
Frenchmen, who thought of all Jews as capitalist exploiters. As a result
even wealthy financiers sometimes felt insecure in France. Under the
First Empire, Jews purchased little real estate even when they were
allowed to do so; Parisian Jews were reported on several occasions to be
eager to dispose of their worldly goods, so that they might be prepared
for flight out of France. This unease was not altogether dispelled under
later, post-Revolutionary regimes. Such treatment was a far cry from
the vaunted ideals of the Revolution and stood in sharp contrast to
developments in Great Britain and the United States.[3]

The inability of the French to decide whether to grant Jews civic
equality or to deny it to them resulted in part from the very nature of
revolutionary doctrine. While the Enlightenment tradition preached
equality and freedom, it also stressed rationalism and hence, irreligion.

Edmund Scheuer, "grand old man" of Toronto Jewry, in the early years of the twentieth century

Torcong

Notman

Moise Schwob, Montreal jeweler and communal leader, 1885

JPL

Adolphe Coblentz, pioneer settler of Winnipeg

Enlightenment figures such as Voltaire harbored a strong dislike for Christianity and had even less use for Judaism, which they believed to be a more primitive religion. Moreover, some of the fathers of the Enlightenment had had unfortunate dealings with individual Jews they encountered and, in any case, did not conceive of France in pluralistic terms, as so many Americans and Englishmen thought of their countries.[4]

Another reason for the seesaw career of French Jews was the lingering strength of the forces of reaction. If French revolutionary tradition was ambivalent in its thinking about Jews, the conservative, monarchical, clerical, counterrevolutionary tradition, which remained quite strong throughout the nineteenth century, was unequivocal. Jews were anathema. Their freedom and whatever influence they had—usually blown out of all proportion—were associated with the fall of the *ancien régime*. Those who yearned for a restoration of the old order sought to restore Jews to their former place outside the French body politic. Opponents of "the revolution utilized antisemitic propaganda . . . to discredit . . . revolutionary acts."[5] It was widely believed in rightist circles, even in the twentieth century, that "democracy, the rights of man, [and] anticlericalism" were "Jewish values," which served to "corrode . . . French traditions and strengths."[6]

Fundamental to Jews' problems in monolithically Catholic France was their position in the eyes of the Church. In fact, of course, no Christian denomination has been free of antisemitism or, at the least, of anti-Judaism; and no country has been free of discrimination against Jews. The Crusades, the Inquisition, the expulsions from Catholic England in 1290, from Catholic France in 1394, and from Catholic Spain in 1492 remained etched in the memories of nineteenth-century Jews. So, too, did the outspoken antisemitism of Martin Luther and many of his followers. Charles Freshman, who saw the matter from both a Jewish and a Christian perspective, felt that one of the main "stumbling blocks" to the conversion of the Jews to Christianity was their "oppression and persecution . . . by professing Christian countries," Catholic and Protestant alike.[7]

As time went on, however, it began to seem possible for Jews to differentiate between Catholics and Protestants. To nineteenth-century Jews, influenced by emancipation and Enlightenment, the Roman Catholic Church seemed to rely heavily on superstition, approaching idolatry in its veneration of saints. Almost all Jews felt that the gap between Judaism and Catholicism was much larger than that between Judaism and Protestantism. Indeed, that had also been the claim of the Protestant

Reformation. Many Protestants felt an affinity with the older Hebrew Bible and sought justification through its revelations rather than through those of the New Testament. Moreover, on the whole (although certainly with exceptions), Protestants in the eighteenth and nineteenth centuries were emerging as friends of the Jews. The Roman Catholic Church often appeared as their enemy, a perception that found an echo in the thoughts of many Protestant Americans, Canadians, and Englishmen.[8]

To no small degree Jews had an easier time with Protestants than with Catholics because of the different conceptions the two Christian faiths held of the proper relationship between religion and society. Protestantism looked upon religion as one aspect of life. However important religion might be to them, Protestants recognized broad areas of life outside its purview. In those secular realms they could easily find common ground with non-Protestants. Catholicism, on the other hand, viewed no area of life as inherently secular. Religion was meant to be all-encompassing, sanctifying every area of human behavior, infusing every human act with Christian content—leaving, strictly speaking, no room for cooperation with non-Catholics. In countries where they were not in the majority, such as England and the United States, Catholics made their peace with the "Protestantization" of life and found common interests with people of other faiths. In places such as Italy, Ireland, France, and Quebec, however, where they were the overwhelming majority, Catholics felt obliged to endeavor to preserve the Catholic character of society. In Canada the goal was clearly understood in the nineteenth century by Catholics and non-Catholics alike to be *"the establishment of a people profoundly Catholic in this land, which was given to them as an inheritance."*[9]

The presence of Jews and the toleration of Judaism presented a threat to Catholic hegemony. As the traditional Antichrist of Christian theology as well as symbol of the modern, secular world, Jews became the focus of Catholic animosity in the nineteenth century, along with other groups whose rise represented the triumph of the secular: Freemasons and socialists. Such hostility was manifested less in some places, such as Italy, more in others, such as France and Quebec. Often, as in Quebec, it was out of all proportion to the numbers or real influence of Jews.[10]

The conflict between Jews and Roman Catholics was not limited to the theoretical realm in the nineteenth century. Theory became incarnate in historical events. One of the most important was the Mortara Affair, which erupted in 1858, when Edgar Mortara, a Jewish child of Bologna, was taken forcibly from his parents by the papal police. Sometime earlier the child, when ill, had been surreptitiously baptized by his Catholic nanny. When Church authorities heard about the baptism, they kidnapped the child, secreting him in a monastery. His parents never recovered him, and he became a monk.

As might be expected Jews the world over were up in arms, supported by many Protestants although very few Catholics. In their agitation against the papal authorities, however, they were generally cautious. The *New York Times* remarked that Jews there

> were especially . . . [careful] to express . . . towards their Roman Catholic fellow citizens respect for the sincerity of their religious belief, and a desire to avoid wounding their feelings or their prejudices.[11]

In places with a Catholic majority, such as France and Quebec, Jews were still more circumspect. Alexander Levy (Levey), president of the Spanish and Portuguese Congregation of Montreal, admitted before a mass meeting in New York that Montreal's Jews feared speaking out about Mortara in Canada, where "those with whom we are in daily intercourse are . . . subject to the Church of Rome."[12] Catholics, equally aroused over what they felt to be their right to claim a baptized soul, exhibited less restraint regarding their Jewish fellow citizens. In the mid-nineteenth century American Catholics often spoke of Jews as "Christ-killers" and "perverted Israelites." (They tended to be somewhat more delicate in referring to Protestants, who were mere "heretics, rebels and enemies of the one, true Church.") In less pluralistic societies the rhetoric was often sharper.[13]

The Mortara Affair left a bitter aftertaste. In Montreal and elsewhere Jews did not quickly forget the treatment of Mortara in Italy, where the majority of the inhabitants were professing Catholics. As late as 1876 the London *Jewish Chronicle* reminded its readers that the current pope was the pope of the Mortara case, and that the "papal system" had inflicted "tortures . . . on . . . innocent Jews with fiend-like fury."[14] He was also the pope who had authorized expulsions of Jews from certain areas in the Papal States in 1862, recalling unpleasant memories of the expulsions that had characterized medieval Catholic Europe.[15]

European Catholic anti-Judaism surfaced in a number of sensational events in the waning years of the nineteenth century and the early years of the twentieth. A well-publicized blood libel occurred between 1882 and 1884 at Tisza-Eszlar, Hungary. (Quebec's *La Vérité* was one North American organ that assumed the accusation to be warranted.) In 1892 a similar if less spectacular episode occurred at Ingrandes, France. That same year an outbreak of virulent antisemitism and ritual murder accusations occurred in several locations in Europe, and the "ultra-montane organs in France, Germany and Italy . . . [proved to be] among the most fanatical Jew-baiters."[16] Three years later Pope Leo XIII conferred his blessing on an antisemitic conference meeting in Linz, Austria, and somewhat later he publicly identified "the four enemies of the human race" as socialism, Freemasonry, anarchism and Judaism.[17]

In Russia the Roman Catholics proved that they were the equals of the state church in Jew-baiting. In 1906 a pogrom devastated the Jewish quarter of Bialystok in Roman Catholic Lithuania. Catholics inside Russia and out, even in Britain, insisted that the Bialystok Jews had been responsible for their own destruction. In 1913 there occurred one of the ugliest spectacles of the new century. In Kiev, the Russians brought to trial Mendel Beiliss, an unwitting Jew, on charges of ritual murder. Although it was easily proved that Beiliss had not been anywhere near the scene of the murder when it occurred, the trial continued, the "evidence" consisting of testimony about the alleged Jewish practice of sacrificing Christian children. The only "theologian" to testify against Beiliss and to verify the ritual murder charge was a Roman Catholic priest.[18]

The arm of the Church seemed to reach out everywhere to attack Jews, even to British territory. In 1893 the small Jewish community in Ireland began to fear for its safety. They were thankful for British rule, which seemed to be at times the only thing standing between them and a pogrom. A decade later, in 1904, trouble did break out when, at the instigation of a Catholic priest in Limerick, the thirty-five Jews in that town were subjected first to an economic boycott and then to a hostile riot. That Jews under British sovereignty could also feel the full force of Catholic antisemitism was not encouraging to Canadian Jews, especially those of overwhelmingly Catholic Quebec.[19]

Particularly disturbing to Jews as well as to Protestants in the nineteenth century was Catholic ultramontanism, the doctrine that the Vatican had the right to interfere on behalf of Catholics in the affairs of any state. Since the forces of political reaction in France, Quebec, and elsewhere often spoke in the name of the Church and sought to restore it to the position it had held before the 1789 Revolution, the threat of interference seemed concrete and real. The *Jewish Chronicle* spoke for world Jewry and for many Protestants as well, when it expressed concern over the Roman Church's "tremendous efforts . . . to re-conquer the terrain which it [had] lost during the Reformation in England."[20]

In France traditional Church teachings in combination with more modern notions about the undesirability of Jews fostered exceptional hostility between the two religious groups. The Catholic Church was disestablished by the Revolution and ravaged by its excesses. Jewish influence, one of the traditional demons of the Church, hitherto almost unknown in France and now quite perceptible in some quarters, served as a simple explanation of a bewildering historical process. Revolutionary folklore included the widely held belief that Jews had been foremost in acquiring nationalized Church property. Hysterical rumors that Polish Jews were invading France to buy up the churches and substitute the Old Testament for the New swept the country after 1789. Almost a century later in 1876 a "general assembly of the Catholic Committee of France under the honorary presidency of Cardinal Guibert, Archbishop of Paris, . . . deliberated on the means to be adopted in order to counteract Jewish influence in the civilized world."[21]

Anti-Jewish prejudice was also a prominent feature of nineteenth-century secular French intellectual life, especially in literary circles and among social "scientists." The founder of modern racial antisemitism was not a German, but the French aristocrat le Comte Joseph Arthur de Gobineau. His *Essay on the Inequality of the Human Races* (1854) was a pathbreaking work, which offered a rationale for the ostracism of Jews from society and ultimately, under the Nazis, for their murder. Whereas Christian antisemitism might demand that Jews be relegated to an inferior status, racial antisemitism could and did, after 1933, lead to a demand for their total elimination. Maurice Barrès, one of the founders of modern Fascism, translated Gobineau's "scientific" work into political language. He spoke with candor on Jews and Protestants, whom he did not like much better:

> Our difference in blood strengthens my repugnance towards Protestantism (secular education different from mine) and towards Judaism (race opposed to mine).[22]

Literary antisemitism was not unique to France in the nineteenth century, but it flourished there with extraordinary vigor. There were exceptions, such as Emile Zola and Alexandre Dumas, the younger, who portrayed some Jews sympathetically. More common, however, was a literary stereotype of the debased Jew. Jews were frequently depicted as "grotesque and obnoxious" upstarts with "all the vices that can possibly be associated with parvenus" and the like.[23] Even worse, they were presented as foreigners, outsiders. Jewish characters in nineteenth-century French literature often bore German names, a device not without justification, since, in fact, most French Jews originated in German-speaking Alsace. Still, at a time when Frenchmen were coming more and more to view Germany as their greatest enemy,[24] it could only reinforce existing negative images.

Adolphe d'Ennery, a minor French playwright, explained in the 1880s why he never included Jewish characters in his plays:

> The reason is very simple. I believe that in the theater one should not fly in the face of public sentiment. The first duty of an author is to please his audiences; that is, to respect their tastes and habits. Were I to present a Jew, then, I . . . would have . . . to make him a usurer, a scoundrel, or a traitor. . . . That would have been unpleasant, for I myself am of Jewish origin.[25]

Gentile French authors, and even some other Jews, had no such scruples. Major literary figures, such as Gyp, Alphonse Daudet, and the Brothers Goncourt, were vicious antisemites, who gave free rein to their feelings in their works. Anarchist journals and even more "respectable" writing often referred to Jews as *"youtre"* and *"youpin,"* French equivalents of "kike." There was a kinship between French and English literary representations of Jews; both saw them as exotic and mysterious. The English, for the most part, highlighted the exciting and adventurous aspects of the mystery. The French chose to accentuate the dark and nefarious.[26]

In addition to harboring and fostering well-publicized theoretical objections to Jews, nineteenth-century France was a laboratory of applied antisemitism. In her diplomacy, France generally placed herself on the side of the persecutors of Jews. In the Damascus blood libel affair of 1840, as noted earlier, Britain and the United States denounced the fabricated and dangerous charge of ritual murder. France supported it. In fact, the French consul in Damascus had been the one to accuse the local Jews of the anonymous murder of a Capuchin monk. Foreign Minister Louis Adolphe Thiers backed him up. It was all apparently a ploy to curry favor with the Church, which France sought to use as an instrument for aggrandizing her power in the Middle East. Britain, of course, played the same game in backing Jewish and Protestant interests in that area. But Jews could hardly be faulted for seeing a moral difference in the attitudes of the two countries, and not just a formal one. Britain, to achieve her aims, defended the defenseless, whereas France, to obtain hers, persecuted them.[27]

Later in the century, in the age of French imperialism, antisemitism followed the flag. Although the Jewish position in North Africa had been perilous throughout the nineteenth century, it actually worsened after the arrival of the French. A wave of pogroms swept Algeria in 1898–99. Not only Jews, but also Canadian and American observers, felt that the French government had approved of the attacks, perhaps because they diverted attention from the resentment of the local population toward their French rulers. Although for the most part North African Jews had welcomed the French presence, they soon learned that the "French government had not brought them equality or protection."[28]

The French alliance with Russia provided further convincing evidence to Jews that France was not their friend. Zadoc Kahn, the Chief Rabbi of France, wrote in a pastoral letter of 1891 in praise of the recently concluded Franco-Russian entente, which had "so brilliantly raised the prestige of our country."[29] But outside France everyone, antisemite and Jew alike, recognized the real import of the alliance for Jews. British nativist Arnold White remarked "the partnership in antisemitism involved by the Franco-Russian alliance."[30] Benjamin Sulte, French-Canadian historian, felt that the Russian ukases represented the embodiment of French antisemitic theories, as did the Canadian *Jewish Times*.[31]

As France and Russia moved closer together, it became ever more difficult in France to express sympathy for the suffering Jews of Russia, so widely supported in Britain, the United States, Anglo-Canada, and elsewhere. In 1881–82 the French responded to the Russian pogroms with the formation of a gentile Comité de Secours pour les Israélites de Russie under the chairmanship of Victor Hugo. Among its supporters were the Cardinal Archbishop of Paris and both leftist and monarchist newspapers. Jews, too, spoke out in defense of their Russian brethren. In 1891 Alphonse de Rothschild refused to help float a major loan to Russia because of the recent wave of pogroms. Since France had become Russia's chief banker, the Rothschild bank's refusal was a gesture of more than symbolic importance. But all in all the response of Paris to Russian depredations was muted compared with that of either London or New York. In 1909 French Jews, beginning to feel somewhat more self-confident, attempted to persuade their government to protest Russian discrimination against French Jews traveling in Russia, but without success. As attacks on "international Jewry," which allegedly worked against the Franco-Russian alliance, were stepped up, Frenchmen critical of Russia's treatment of Jews grew to "fear . . . to express their opinions openly" on the issue.[32]

In any case there had always been definite limits to the sympathy of Frenchmen, both Jewish and gentile, for Russian Jews. Intellectuals were especially insensitive to the Jewish plight. The Jewish critic, Bernard Lazare, who would later emerge as one of the main supporters of Alfred Dreyfus, was typical. He asserted in 1890 that Eastern Jews were "contemptible people . . . [having] no ties with any nation, no affection for any nation." He advised that French Jews "kick out these lepers who corrupt them, . . . vomit up the rottenness that wants to creep in."[33] Unlike England, where such sentiments were considered uncouth and usually unspeakable, in France they were *de rigueur*.

Most Frenchmen wanted none of the refugees in their own midst. Immigrants arriving in France were often left helpless and without work. Many provincial Jewish communities refused to accept a single refugee. Those Jews who tried to hire eastern Europeans in their factories found that the antisemitic prejudices of French workers inhibited them. Even after 1905, when anti-Jewish sentiment in France abated, Jewish immigrants were unwelcome. They "were singled out [by Jews and non-Jews alike] as importers of inferior moral standards and squalid living conditions."[34] Most French Jews were unwilling even to help the immigrants move on. Unlike their American and British coreligionists they sought mainly to wipe their hands of the problem.[35]

The outstanding manifestations of *fin-de-siècle* French antisemitism came not in response to foreign stimuli but as a function of domestic politics. After 1870 French reactionary politicians staged a strong comeback. The Third Republic was nearly toppled on more than one occasion by a combination of clerical, monarchical, and military interests seeking to restore the old order. Jews, as symbols of the new order, or causes of its advent if the propagandists were to be believed, became prime targets. After France's defeat by Germany in 1870 French antisemitism became increasingly open and vocal. By the end of the nineteenth century it "was as it once had been—overt, strident, and brutal."[36] Even the citizenship of French Jews was called into question by some.[37]

Some of the key events in the rising tide of French political antisemitism were: the collapse of the Catholic Union Générale bank in 1882, popularly attributed to Jewish machinations; the publication in 1886 of Edouard Drumont's *La France Juive: Essai d'histoire contemporaine;* the founding in 1889 of the Ligue Nationale Anti-sémitique; the 1891 proposal of thirty-two deputies in the Chamber of Deputies to expel the Jews anew from France; the Panama Scandals of 1892 in which several Jews were implicated; the founding the same year of Drumont's newspaper, *La Libre Parole;* and, from 1894 to 1906, the Dreyfus Affair, which rocked the nation.

The Dreyfus Affair, or simply, *"l'Affaire,"* as it came to be known, marked the climax of pre-World War I antisemitism. It began in 1894. Captain Alfred Dreyfus, a Jew on the French general staff, was convicted of selling military secrets to Germany. The case made relatively little stir at the time; and most people assumed Dreyfus to be guilty. Dreyfus, however, maintained his innocence. His family supported him, and gradually a movement for a new trial gathered force. By 1897 the captain had become a *cause célèbre* and not only in France. Especially in the English-speaking world the assumption grew that Dreyfus had been convicted falsely. Inside France, however, there was deep division that split the country into two camps; the captain's Jewish origins were at the center of the controversy. Support for Dreyfus was equated with support for the revolutionary tradition and for Republican France. Belief in Dreyfus's guilt was dogma for those who sought the downfall of the Republic. Not until 1906 did the Affair come to a complete close with Dreyfus's vindication. It left a shattered France, which felt the effects of the schism for years afterward.

Most Western Jews, especially those in France, had not at first leaped to Dreyfus's defense. In eastern Europe, however, where ethnic solidarity was stronger and the scapegoating of Jews more common, doubts about the captain's guilt had been expressed early. From the start both *Hamelitz* and *Ha-Zefirah* gave the case broad coverage. By 1898 most Jews outside of France, like most gentiles, had climbed on the pro-Dreyfus bandwagon. After the Affair, Jews everywhere, except possibly in France itself, came to question the promise of liberal Western civilization.[38]

All of the outstanding episodes of French antisemitism were followed carefully the world over. No one who read the daily press could remain ignorant of them, and many were alarmed by what they learned. The Dreyfus Affair, in particular, brought deep-seated animosities to the surface and made France a synonym for antisemitism to Jews. In 1890 the *American Hebrew* expressed its concern about events in France. Baltimore's *Jewish Comment* warned in 1901 that the growth of antisemitic feeling in France, especially among legislators, was becoming dangerous. The London *Jewish Chronicle* remarked in 1904 that every French election—local or national, whatever the real issues—ultimately hinged on the candidates' position toward Jews. In Montreal the Protestant *Daily Witness* feared a massacre of French Jews in 1898, while later the *Keneder odler* kept its readers well informed about all manifestations of anti-semitism in France.[39]

Yet another reason for Jewish suspicion of France was the notorious assimilationism of the French-Jewish community. In contrast to British Jews, French Jews were known for their weak Jewish connections, moribund Judaism, and ineffectual, assimilationist institutions. The "hatred borne the Jews by French society in general" resulted in widespread self-hatred and even antisemitism among French Jews.[40] Ahad Ha-Am, the popular Russian-Jewish essayist and influential Zionist theorist, thought turn-of-the-century French Jews with their "extreme zealot patriotism" to be moral and intellectual "slaves."[41] Their lack of attachment to the ancestral faith, in contrast to the traditionalism of British Jews, was well publicized. *Hamelitz* noted with sarcasm in 1903, that although "there might possibly be a few Jews left in France," there was "no French Judaism [left] at all."[42] Even the Reform *American Israelite* remarked that "French civilization does not seem to have had . . . a very good influence on the religious life of the Jew."[43] Chief Rabbi Zadoc Kahn, himself an ardent French patriot, sadly remarked the decline of French Judaism in his 1899 Yom Kippur sermon. The rabbi was particularly grieved to note that the attrition in belief was far worse in France than in the United States or England.[44]

French Jews failed altogether to provide adequately for Jewish education or religious life in the nineteenth century. The organized Jewish communities, the *consistoires,* and the defense organization, the Alliance Israélite Universelle, might have become the instruments of a viable Jewish life, but they did not. It is characteristic of French Jews that— although they were shaken by the stance of their government during the 1840 Damascus Affair and recognized the need for an organization to lobby for Jewish interests at home and abroad—it took them twenty years to found the Alliance. Only with the added shock of the Mortara Affair in 1858 were they galvanized into action. And even thereafter, the Alliance "devoted itself to the dissemination of the French ideal of Jewish emancipation and assimilation."[45] Assimilation, needless to say, was not a consciously desired goal of the mass of European Jews; emancipation, which insisted upon assimilation as a precondition, was at best a mixed blessing.

If nineteenth-century Jews had special reasons, then, to feel estranged from France, it is also the case that dispassionate non-Frenchmen in that period might have had their own reasons to respect Britain more. The

British Empire was at the pinnacle of its power. France, already after the defeat of Napoleon I, was on the decline. Her political affairs were chronically unsettled and marred by frequent revolutions. Following her defeat by Prussia in the war of 1870, France's image suffered further damage. In a century of Western growth, France's population and economy remained static. The "corruption of French public life" at the turn of the century was infamous.[46] Gerald E. Hart, Canadian-Jewish insurance salesman, numismatist, and historian, expressed a widely held opinion in 1888 in claiming that corruption had long been the French way of life.[47] Many foreigners including Arnold White felt that French antipathy toward Jews illustrated the decadence of the country.[48] When the Duke of Orleans made "common cause with the Jew-baiters of Paris," the Canadian *Jewish Times* accorded him the title "Ex-Royal Degenerate."[49] Certainly the French attitude toward Jews stood in marked contrast to the more civilized position taken by most residents of the English-speaking world.

For Jews the decline of France signaled not only moral bankruptcy at home but the political impotence of French Jews on the international scene. After 1870 the Alliance Israélite Universelle was reduced for a time to a state of helplessness. French Jews, unlike their British coreligionists, were in no position to help fellow Jews in distress in faraway lands, even had they so desired. During the Congress of Berlin in 1878 the Alliance Israélite Universelle turned to Britain's Disraeli to guarantee Jewish rights rather than to their own government.[50]

In European-Jewish circles at the end of the nineteenth century there still remained sympathy for France, the country that had initiated Jewish emancipation in Europe. Moreover, French Jews themselves were staunch patriots. Between 1871 and 1910 the Jewish population of Alsace-Lorraine, ceded to Germany after the Franco-Prussian War, dropped by over 25 percent through the emigration to France and to America of Jews who would not live under the rule of the enemy of France. The family of Captain Alfred Dreyfus were among the patriotic émigrés. So, too, was Jules Hirtz, who left for Montreal.[51]

On the whole, however, France was known as a place that was not particularly hospitable to Jews. Few tried to go there from elsewhere, even when they were permitted to do so. This included eastern Europeans, who were desperately searching for new homes. Even as thousands were pouring into Canada, tens of thousands into England, and hundreds of thousands into the United States, a mere eight thousand eastern European Jews went to Paris between 1876 and 1901, and a very few more to the provincial cities, although France was closer to Russia than any English-speaking country. France was a country of Jewish emigration in the nineteenth century, the only country in western Europe that actually lost Jewish population. Significantly, French gentiles rarely left the country.[52]

Judaism and Jews in the Minds of French Canadians

Their own experiences coupled with preconceptions about France and Roman Catholicism, then, prepared nineteenth-century Jews settling in French Canada for conflict. The concepts and attitudes to which French Canadians were heirs similarly prepared them for the inevitable clash. In some ways the ground was even shakier for Jews in French Canada than in France itself. As their foremost nineteenth-century historian, François-Xavier Garneau, put it, French Canadians hearkened back to the France of the *ancien régime,* to that genuine "soul of France [which] ceases not to spread its warmth and vitality over the people of its race and tongue" everywhere in the world.[53] The Revolution had destroyed the France of which French Canadians had once been a part. As a result, Enlightenment, revolutionary ideology, the only one which held out any promise for Jews in France, often met with an inhospitable welcome in Canada. And, indeed, in French Canada antisemitism and Catholic anti-Judaism proved a volatile combination during the period under review. As noted above, prejudice against Jews had been no stranger to France's North American colony. Under the British, especially in the latter half of the nineteenth century, the even more carefully distilled antisemitism of Catholic Europe and especially France made its way across the ocean to Quebec where it blended well with the local variety.

The language and themes of French antisemitism successfully took root in Quebec during the nineteenth and early twentieth centuries. From French journals and street slang French-Canadian antisemites adopted the terms *"youpin"* and *"youtre."*[54] The image of the "obscure menace" of Jewish power found its way into French-Canadian literature already in the early nineteenth century. Writers frequently represented the English as a "frank, open threat" to French Canadians; but the Jews were "a hidden, subtle, cunning threat" to the Church and the French-Canadian way of life.[55] The arguments used by *Le Canadien* and by Pierre Bédard, the French-Canadian parliamentary leader, during the 1807–09 debate over whether to seat the Jew Ezekiel Hart in the Lower

Canada Legislature pointed the way.[56] Another milestone was the novel of Pierre Joseph Olivier Chauveau, *Charles Guérin* (1846–1854). Chauveau, who served as premier of Quebec from 1867 to 1873, presented a stereotypical Jewish moneylender, Shouffe, "the oldest and richest Jew in the country." Chauveau's Shouffe had one purpose in life: "to persecute, to condemn, to seize and to sell."[57] The novel was sufficiently popular to be reprinted in 1900; and it paved the way for later imitators. In French-Canadian literature of the period, as in most French literature, there was a place for Jews and other "strangers" only as caricatures. The literary stereotypes also attached to live culture in Quebec. In 1905 Sarah Bernhardt, the most renowned actress of her day, a Frenchwoman and a Jewess, played Quebec. There she was greeted with cries of "Down with the Jewess!" She fled the town fearing for her safety.[58]

The French fears of "Jewish finance" and of control of the press by Jews and their alleged allies, the Freemasons, became fairly widespread in French Canada at the turn of the century. Montreal's *La Croix* called for the suppression of the "big, Freemason papers" in 1905, taking pains to quote "the [French] Jew [Adolphe] Crémieux" on the importance of the media, thereby associating Jews with Freemasons in the minds of its readers.[59] Attacks on the financial power of Jews had a mechanical, automatic quality about them. French Canadians were frequently threatened with French and German-Jewish financiers: the Rothschilds, the Ephrussis, the Oulds (sic), the Bleichröders. No one bothered to mention the few Montreal Jewish millionaires, since not reality, but a stereotypical scapegoat, was what mattered. The Rothschilds were more famous than the Josephs and for that the more useful in reinforcing myth. The European names also served to connect the campaign against Jews in French Canada with that in Europe.[60]

In spreading the antisemitic gospel in Quebec, Canadians availed themselves of the aid of Europe's most successful antisemitic polemicist. The writings of Edouard Drumont became almost as popular in Quebec in the last decade of the nineteenth century and the beginning of the twentieth as they were in France. In 1893 there appeared a short-lived *La Libre Parole* in Montreal. Three years later W. A. Grenier tried again with *La Libre Parole Illustrée,* a more lively tabloid. The second Canadian incarnation of Drumont's journal received favorable notices in other French-Canadian papers. The publication was welcomed as a "new brother" and "a most independent liberal."[61] One of the most prominent features of the first issue of *La Libre Parole Illustrée* was "a satire against the Jews, after the fashion of the celebrated journal of Drumont."[62] After a few months Grenier's journal, like the earlier Canadian *La Libre Parole,* folded, but not because of its unpopularity or its antisemitism. The editor had attacked the Laurier government in an impolitic and indiscreet manner, especially the minister of public works, J. Israel Tarte. Grenier was jailed for libel; and without him the paper expired.[63]

Others in Quebec were more successful than Grenier at propagating Drumont's creed. *La Croix,* a "Catholic and Independent Review" published in Montreal from 1903 to 1930, included frequent contributions from the master. *Le Nationaliste* and *L'Action Sociale* also reprinted him frequently, as did *L'Etudiant,* the student newspaper of Laval University. The latter journal was silenced as a result of the protests of Jews and others to the university authorities. In 1910, however, the leader of French-Canadian nationalism, Henri Bourassa, founded *Le Devoir.* Almost overnight that paper became the spokesman for French-Canadian nationalism and the respected paper of the Quebec intelligentsia. Writing for it were the leaders of the nationalist movement in the province. From the start *Le Devoir* featured Drumont's writings, lending them respectability in Quebec.[64] *Le Devoir* also wrote in praise of French fascist Maurice Barrès and the antisemitic mayor of Vienna, Karl Lueger, whom the paper's correspondent, Omer Héroux, called, "the most magnificent example of moral courage."[65]

The most scurrilous journal of all was *Le Pionnier,* published by L. G. Robillard at the turn of the century. Robillard faithfully reprinted articles by Drumont and added some of his own in the same vein, such as his 1902 series, "Jewry the Enemy." Robillard and his journal distressed Quebec Jewry considerably. He was finally charged with libel by the editor of Montreal's mass circulation daily, *La Presse,* Jules Heilbronner, who was himself of Jewish origin. Subsequently it was revealed that Robillard was a swindler as well as an antisemite, having embezzled the funds of the Union Franco-Canadienne insurance scheme of which he was the treasurer. Flight from Canada ended Robillard's publishing and insurance ventures much to the relief of Montreal Jews.[66]

Drumont's influence in French Canada extended not only to the press but to the military, the Church, and other quarters. In 1904 one of the French-Canadian officers at the Royal Military College in Kingston revealed himself as a disciple; Catholic priests became Drumont's acolytes, speaking and writing openly of their sympathies. In the wake of the Dreyfus Affair and its accompanying agitation certain religious orders were suppressed in France, and many priests "had to leave . . . their native land for that country's good."[67] In Canada these émigré priests "did their little best to play the role of [anti-Jewish] agitators."[68] In 1908 at the annual convention of the Association Catholique de la Jeunesse Cana-dienne (hereafter referred to as ACJC), French Canada's most prestigious and largest youth organization, it was suggested that a French-Canadian Ligue Antisémitique be established along the lines of the French league inspired by Drumont. The Canadian league was not organized, but the Ligue des Droits du Français, founded in Quebec in 1913, served much the same purpose. It, too, was a copy of a French original, the organization of the same name founded by Maurice Barrès.[69]

When one considers Drumont's popularity in French Canada and his preoccupation with the Dreyfus Affair, it is not surprising that *l'Af-faire* became an issue of great importance for French Canadians. So long estranged from France because of its revolutionary, democratic, secular ideology, they found in *l'Affaire* a cause in the motherland to which they could relate with enthusiasm. Anti-Dreyfusard sentiment may have been more widespread in French Canada than in France itself. The "little journals," the "independents," which tended to antisemitism in any case, were the most outspoken. These included *La Libre Parole, La Croix, Le Pionnier, La Feuille d'Erable,* and *La Semaine religieuse de Québec. La Vérité* outdid them all in writing freely of the "Christ-killer race" of Dreyfus and recommending that the Jews return to the ghetto. When Emile Zola came to Dreyfus's defense, *La Vérité* attacked him as a pornographer.[70]

Contrary to later popular belief, the "respectable" French-language newspapers in Canada did not give Dreyfus much better treatment than the fringe press. Montreal's large daily, *La Patrie,* is a case in point. In November and early December 1897, as the movement for a retrial got under way, the paper printed a number of articles neutral in tone, even friendly to Dreyfus's cause.[71] Then occurred an abrupt about-face. On 3 December 1897 an article and an editorial appeared, both of them anti-Dreyfusard and antisemitic. The paper declared that Dreyfus was guilty and that the "Jewish syndicate," which sought to destroy France and to assume power there itself, stood behind him.[72] Later that month came a vitriolic attack on Zola by the French antisemite, Henri Rochefort, and an interview with Alphonse Daudet. Daudet hinted darkly that Jews had tried to bribe him into taking Dreyfus's part. *La Patrie* reasserted on Christmas Eve that "the guilt of the traitor [Dreyfus] was well-established."[73] After the second trial in 1899, when the captain was again convicted, *La Patrie* confidently expected that the Affair would end. The paper upheld the honesty of the judges and the validity of the secret trial.[74] Most people the world over, and almost everyone in English-speaking countries, considered the proceedings to have been a travesty of justice, as indeed they turned out to have been.

The attitude of *La Presse* was more ambivalent than that of *La Patrie,* perhaps because of the Jewish origins of its editor. The coverage given by *La Presse* to all the Dreyfus proceedings was rather scanty and sporadic, almost as if the paper were attempting to avoid the issue. (In like manner, in 1913 when Mendel Beiliss was finally acquitted of ritual murder in Russia, *La Presse* took no notice of the event.) Since *La Presse* was a mass circulation paper, however, and its readers were interested in the outcome of the trials, it could not refrain altogether from giving voice to popular opinion. In January 1898, for example, the paper assured its readers that "real" public opinion was convinced that Dreyfus's first trial had been just and honest and that spokesmen in his behalf sought only to attack the army and the Church.[75]

Both *La Patrie* and *La Presse* usually treated Jewish matters fairly. That they were biased on the Dreyfus issue and at such variance with the opinion of most Anglo-Canadians is illustrative of how the case, like other aspects of French and Catholic antisemitism, became domesticated in Canada. In France the Affair became the focal point of the battle between the forces of republicanism and those of reacton. In Canada it became a divisive issue in the growing antagonism between French and Anglo-Canadians. The two groups were at loggerheads on the issues of imperialism (the imperial connection, the Boer War, and Canadian naval aid to the imperial forces), religion (the Jesuits' Estates Act, the Catholic schools in Manitoba), and language (the French-language question in Ontario and the West). Each side sought to buttress its position in Canada through Old World connections. Foreign affairs took on great symbolic significance for Canadians; local issues were lent added legitimacy when they were associated with the great international questions of the day. The English-language press in Montreal, like that of much of the English-speaking world, was unanimously Dreyfusard; the *Daily Witness,* the *Gazette,* the *Star,* and the *Daily Herald* all supported the Jewish captain. French Canadians, on the other hand, almost all desired his conviction; in fact, Dreyfus's guilt became a nationalist article of faith. Such a belief accorded well with the long-standing antisemitism of many nationalists, especially because it was also held by the Catholic-monarchist-reactionary forces in France—those very Frenchmen who were seeking to restore to France the old order, about which many French Canadians waxed nostalgic.

As might be expected in traditionalist French Canada, Roman Catholic anti-Judaism was even more easily transplanted from Europe than "scientific" or secular antisemitism. Although in no way a new phenomenon in Canada, Catholic anti-Judaism gathered strength toward the end of the period under review as the industrialization and secularization of Quebec society got up steam. It blended well with the ideas and concepts of modern racism, as it did in France and elsewhere. Pilgrim literature, much of it written by priests, was one of the main vehicles for introducing contemporary currents in European thought to Canadian anti-Judaism. The pilgrims visited the Vatican and European shrines and religious leaders on their travels, as well as the Holy Land, and they often returned to French Canada newly recharged with the traditional anti-Judaism of their Church and informed about new notions as well. Their works were very popular in an age when entertainment was rather limited and piety admired.

One of the priests to make the journey from Quebec to Jerusalem toward the end of the nineteenth century was l'Abbé Léon Provancher, whose book of travels appeared in 1884. (Four years later Provancher founded the widely read and openly antisemitic Church journal, *La Semaine religieuse de Québec*.) Provancher included in his work a recapitulation of the crucifixion not remarkable for its historical accuracy and sufficiently lurid to appeal to the basest instincts of his readers. Provancher told of "the soldiers of the high priests [who, in point of fact, as Provancher probably knew, had no soldiers at their command], their hands dripping with blood like the hands of criminals," leading away the innocent Jesus. The priest assured his audience that the "lying Jews" of Jesus' day lived on in the modern world. They were to be found in the guise of "free thinkers, atheists, the impious," and, of course, the Jews.[76] L'Abbé J. F. C. Delaplanche made the pilgrimage to the Holy Land a few years after Provancher. This ecclesiastic found it hard to comprehend the "blindness" of the Jews whom he met in the Holy Land, who stubbornly refused to accept the messiahship of Jesus. Delaplanche recommended nonetheless that Christians regard contemporary Jews with "compassion." They were, after all, but the "Jewish debris" of the ages.[77] The *abbé's* book appeared in 1887 under the imprimatur of Cardinal Taschereau of Quebec.

In 1894 yet another *abbé*, Jean François Dupuis, traveled to Rome and Jerusalem from Quebec. In Jerusalem he visited the Wailing Wall. Dupuis was moved to "pity the unhappy people" he observed there. They were, he said, "a people without a homeland, without a religion [sic!], rejected by God and man." But pity was not to be overdone. Christian doctrine, the priest reminded his readers, taught that the sufferings of Jews were well deserved and "incurable, the result of many sins."[78]

One of the more entertaining pilgrim books was Abbé Henri Cimon's *Aux Vieux Pays*. Cimon had a better than average observer's eye and some literary talent as well. His book, first published in 1895, was by 1917 in its third edition and had sold more than eleven thousand copies, almost all of them in French Canada. Cimon was a professor at the Séminaire de Chicoutimi; and the 1917 edition of his book bore the imprimatur of the bishop of Chicoutimi. Cimon admired the "incredible endurance" of the Jews. But he found it less remarkable than "the hardness of their guilty hearts." The Jews were "blind," the *abbé* claimed, "scourged by God."[79] Those he met in Jerusalem had a "greedy countenance." And all of them belonged to "a deicide race."[80]

Twentieth-century pilgrims were no kinder to Jews and Judaism. The Reverend Father Frédéric de Ghyvelde, a French Canadian of Dutch origin, was renowned in Canada for his charity and mild manners. Ghyvelde was also a literary collaborator of Abbé Provancher. He chose to relate in his *Album de Terre Sainte* only one legend dealing with Jews. It was the Barabbas tale.[81] The most vicious of all the pilgrim books from the Jewish point of view to appear during the period was that of Joseph A. l'Archevêque, *Vers la Terre Sainte* (1911). L'Archevêque was a Recollet friar of Acadian origin from a New Brunswick monastery. His description of the Jews of Jerusalem reads like a quotation from later German propaganda:

> We see the crooked noses, the stooped backs, the ghastly faces. These are people of appalling debilitation . . . [who exibit] the degeneracy peculiar to their race.[82]

It was not only the Jews of Jerusalem who disgusted the friar. He found contemporary Jews everywhere menacing:

> What is on the mind of contemporary Jews? One meets now Pharisees weighed down under the law, Pharisees interested in money. There are also those pretentious Jews, the devotees of cunning, the cowards; but be what they may, their . . . mentality is all the same: faithfulness to the outmoded rituals of the Talmud, war on Christianity and continual efforts to monopolize power. To dominate, that is the life and the happiness of any true Jew.[83]

The friar was sufficiently important to merit a private audience with the pope on his return from Jerusalem.[84]

Pilgrim literature was not the only forum used by the French-Canadian clergy to propagate anti-Judaism. The press was another, *La Semaine religieuse de Québec* being the outstanding example. This was also an age when people were moved to action by sermons. In 1908 the Reverend Curé Belanger of St. Louis Parish in Montreal urged his flock in a regular Sunday sermon to refrain from selling real estate to "strangers." No one doubted who those strangers were. The Canadian *Jewish Times* expressed the hope that Belanger had not voiced "the real sentiments of our fellow Canadians of French origin . . . [or] the mature thought of the Vatican."[85] But the paper feared that French-Catholic antisemitism in all of its fury was becoming acclimated in Canada. And the Belanger case was not an isolated incident. In 1910 as a result of a priest's relentless attacks on local Jews, the Quebec city council determined to impose a special tax on "Jew peddlers," hoping thereby to limit the number of Jewish settlers in the town.[86]

The greatest antisemitic spectacle of French Canada in these years was also a reverberation of events in Europe; and it emerged from what seemed like a remote, trivial occurrence. Ernesto Nathan, a British-born Italian Jew who was also a socialist and a Freemason, had been elected mayor of Rome. Some Roman Catholics felt that the election of a Jew to the mayoralty of the Eternal City was a direct insult and considered Nathan part of the Jewish-socialist-Freemason conspiracy to destroy "the one true Church."[87] Catholics outside Italy, on the whole, took the matter more seriously than the Italians, who had, after all, elected the man. When in 1910 Nathan mildly rebuked the pope for past interference in Italian political affairs, some Catholics became enraged. French-Canadian ultramontanists were particularly aggrieved and sought a way to express their feelings.

The first move was to bring pressure upon the Montreal city council to protest Nathan's speech. In a hastily conducted meeting on 10 October 1910, the council, under the leadership of Mayor Guerin, an Irish Catholic, voted to censure the mayor of Rome officially. It was an extraordinary act from the legal point of view. The vote, however, was unanimous, largely because it was taken at the beginning of a meeting when the five Protestant members of the council were not yet present. They had been expected to oppose the motion, although they may have deliberately absented themselves hoping to buy peace on an issue not yet perceived to be of real significance.[88] The pope was grateful for the support of the

Montrealers. Through Cardinal Merry Del Val, who had once served as papal legate in Canada, he conveyed his thanks to the "illustrious" city council of Montreal for protecting his honor.[89] Mayor Nathan himself took the censure with good humor. He found the Montreal council ignorant of international law and generally "grotesque." His letter of reply to the council was never officially read before that body.[90]

The matter was not allowed to die. The *Daily Witness* and other English-language papers found the council's action an unpardonable confusion of politics and religion and a typical example of ultramontane interference. The Protestant Ministerial Association protested the action, and almost "the entire Hebrew population of Montreal" was aroused.[91] Jews failed to understand how Catholics managed to tolerate frequent criticism and even anti-Catholic polemics from Protestants but would not suffer the slightest criticism from a Jew. Many felt that they should work to unseat Mayor Guerin, "now revealed in his true light," as mayor of only Christian Montrealers.[92] As the antisemitic pressure mounted, Rabbi Herman Abramowitz wondered aloud why all Jews were being condemned for the words of one. A few fearful Jews "deplored" the sentiments of Nathan, who, they claimed, was only "nominally a Jew" in any case.[93] Most, however, were discovering that the Church was involved in politics, even in Montreal, much as Nathan had charged.[94]

Partly to head off the considerable sentiment for revoking the censure motion, partly to curry favor with ultramontanists, and partly to display the strength of French-Canadian Catholicism, Archbishop Bruchési of Montreal and others determined to hold a mass meeting to demonstrate support for the city council and to condemn Ernesto Nathan. The meeting was set for 16 October in the Monument National, the French-Canadian theater, located in the Jewish ghetto of Montreal, which was often used as a playhouse by Yiddish troupes.

For several days preceding the rally *La Presse* and other newspapers carried bold advertisements urging a large turnout. That paper helped to inflame Catholic opinion by featuring such articles as "L'Anti-pape du Rome."[95] Omer Héroux, the nationalist leader, wrote in *Le Devoir,* that Ernesto Nathan was "hereditary hatred of the Church incarnate."[96] Montreal Jews were startled and alarmed at the ferocity of such sentiments, and they protested the meeting planned by "the anti-Semitic archbishop."[97] The English-language press supported them. The *Daily Witness* found it incredible that Catholics could be so exercised, since they themselves often used strong invective against Quebec Protestants.[98]

Narcisse, Manitoba, farming colony named for French-Jewish leader Narcisse Leven, in recognition of the aid of the Jewish Colonization Association of Paris and the Alliance Israélite Universelle to Jewish farmers in Canada

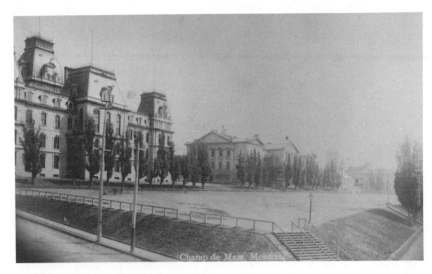

PAC (C-42675)

Champ de Mars, Montreal, scene of 1910 demonstration against Mayor Ernesto Nathan of Rome and local Jews, as it appeared at the time

PAC (C-49508). Photo by Quéry Frères, Montreal

Jean Bruchési, the archbishop of "Catholic Montreal," a leader of the demonstration

And the *Star* published an article on Nathan, whom it called "one of the ablest mayors Rome had ever had."[99]

The meeting itself was a smashing success. The crowd, numbering approximately twenty-five thousand according to press reports, quickly overflowed the Monument National. It was then marched in procession to the Champ de Mars. Students of Laval University and members of the ACJC were out in force, no doubt encouraged by their teachers and priests. At the Champ de Mars the crowd was addressed by Archbishop Bruchési, Henri Bourassa, provincial secretary Jérémie Décarie, and Mayor Guerin. Letters were read from prominent Quebec ecclesiastics. Slogans shouted in the background echoed those of Europe: "Down with the Jews!" "Down with Nathan!" "Down with Freemasonry!" "Down with the Emancipation!" Bruchési presented Mayor Guerin to the crowd as "the mayor of Catholic Montreal," while calling Mayor Nathan "an insulter, a blasphemer, and a liar." Henri Bourassa told the audience that Nathan's attack on the pope was just a variation of the two-thousand-year-long battle of the enemies of the Christian religion. The reference was obvious to all. It was a performance, the likes of which had not previously been seen in North America.[100]

When the meeting ended, the battle was still raging. Catholics in Quebec were not to be outdone by their Montreal coreligionists. A week later they staged what seemed to the correspondent of the *Keneder odler* a "much worse and blacker demonstration." In the province's capital city with its tiny Jewish community, a

> few hundred students . . . marched holding a big picture of Ernesto Nathan. . . . The procession stopped near the Champlain Monument opposite the bishop's palace. Some students made fiery speeches against the Jews using barbarous expressions of the most extreme antisemitism, expressions heard only from hooligans in dark and troubled lands [such as France and Russia]. The local Jews are very frightened and have remained in their homes, fearing to go out lest they be attacked. After the Catholic hooligans made their speeches they sang "O Canada!" with their dark hearts and burned the picture of Mayor Nathan.[101]

In Montreal there was a counter-rally on 24 October. Jews and Protestants charged that the affair had "done a good job of destroying any friendship there was among religious groups in Montreal." According to the *Keneder odler* some seven thousand people attended. No French-language paper and, strangely, no English-language paper took note of the counter-rally.[102]

Catholics calmed down after the demonstrations. *La Vérité* was pleased that "the insulter of the Pope has been spat upon."[103] It was hoped by many that the demonstration had at least taught local Jews where real power in the province lay. Among Protestants there was considerable lasting resentment. The *Daily Witness* pointed out that in denouncing Freemasonry, the Catholics were denouncing the king. (As had been his predecessor, George V was an active Mason.) Moreover, some of the Catholics had gone so far as to claim that the pope was their rightful king. Such an extreme ultramontane claim bordered on sedition.[104] For Jews, however, the implications of the affair were potentially the most serious; and they recognized that fact. Soon after, the *Keneder odler* received an anonymous letter threatening open war on Quebec Jews if they got out of line again. The letter affirmed that "one word from a Catholic priest is enough for us to attack the Jews."[105] The warning was not taken lightly. The paper refused to let its readers forget the rally and continued to write about it for months after the English and French press had already dropped it. With their fresh memories of Russian atrocities, Jews could not gloss over the incident.

Allied with the priests as propounders of traditional Catholic anti-Judaism and as purveyors of other varieties of French antisemitism were Catholic laymen of all stripes. One of the most influential organizations where laymen and clerics joined forces in combatting Jewish influence was the ACJC. The annual convention of this youth organization, which always attracted prominent French-Canadian Catholics, was invariably marked by strong and openly expressed anti-Jewish sentiments. Day-to-day work of the ACJC involved lobbying against Jewish interests, most notably open immigration. Earlier on, French Canadians and even many Anglophone Catholics had exhibited the same coolness to Jewish refugees shown by Frenchmen in France. Almost no French Canadians attended the mass meetings to protest the Russian atrocities or contributed to relief funds. In 1905 Montreal's Archbishop Bruchési was invited to the meeting called to protest the Kishinev pogrom, attended by so many of Montreal's Anglo-Canadian civic leaders. The archbishop declined, stating that, although he disapproved of Russian brutality, his attendance at the public meeting would be "inopportune."[106] Some of the French Canadian papers over the years justified Russian barbarity directed at Jews. Although it moderated its stand after 1893, up to that time *The True Witness,* the mouthpiece of English-speaking Canadian Catholics, also opposed allowing Jewish refugees into Canada.[107]

The ACJC was concerned with theoretical issues as well as practical ones. L.-C. Farly addressed its 1908 convention, held at Laval University, with a "learned" and vitriolic speech on the subject of "La Question Juive." Farly pointed out to his youthful listeners that Jews were considered anathema in France, Germany, and Russia. Drawing upon the works of Drumont and the notorious German antisemite, Adolf Stöcker, the contents of the diatribe were familiar to those who knew European antisemitic works. The Jews were "a deicide race"; they bore "the mark of Cain [and] the mark of Judas."[108] With unwitting ignorance and irony Farly accused Jews of rejecting the Bible for the Talmud, "which apologizes for all crimes [by] offering dispensation." The God of the Talmud was "a liar and a perjurer."[109] According to Farly Jews believed that women were "vile beasts, whom a man might use as he pleased."[110]

Farly's speech went beyond most pre-1914 European racism, even adumbrating Nazi theories. He advocated the "isolation of the Jew."[111] Converting them was of no use, for although "the body be baptized, the soul would remain forever faithful to Israel."[112] Intermarriage between Jews and Christians was to be avoided, and Catholics should not even work for Jews.[113] Farly warned his listeners about their own safety. Just as Jews had conquered France, they were now about to overrun Montreal.[114] Farly supported the idea of a French-type antisemitic league in Canada, and he hoped his listeners would form the vanguard of such an organization. For Jews it was disquieting to say the least, for the foremost Catholic youth organization in the country, the molder of young minds, to entertain such views.

The next year the ACJC convention "implored its central committee to undertake every means practical to interrupt the immigration of Jews to Canada."[115] In 1913 the bishop of Cloutier told the youngsters that Jews were a menace to religion and morality. That same year, the year of the Beiliss trial in Russia, the Montreal ACJC chapter sponsored a public lecture by Abbé Antonio Huot. Huot devoted most of his lecture to attempting to substantiate the allegation that Jews practiced ritual murder, quoting liberally from the German antisemite, August Rohling, whose work, *Der Talmud Jude,* had recently been published in France in translation. Outside of the ACJC such charges were also heard. Already in 1884 Abbé Provancher had said that Jews practiced ritual murder, although he conceded that only dissident Jewish sects did so. His journal, *La Semaine religieuse de Québec,* repeated the accusation regularly over the years. Nationalist leader Armand Lavergne, a close associate of Henri Bourassa and at one time of Wilfrid Laurier, later upheld the charge as well. *L'Action Sociale* and even the mass circulation *La Patrie* lent support to the notion of Beiliss's guilt.[116]

When one considers the tone and substance of the polemic against Jews as well as the "respectability" of their opponents, it is surprising that European-style anti-Jewish riots did not occur. Still, there was some violence. In May 1910 J. Edouard Plamondon, a Quebec journalist, delivered a ringing anti-Jewish lecture to the ACJC chapter in his home town. The overheated audience left the hall and went on a rampage of window breaking and other violence in the Jewish quarter of the city. Two of the Jews whose property was damaged subsequently sued Plamondon for inciting to riot and group libel. Plamondon brought priests to testify to the correctness of his allegations; the Jews brought Rabbi Herman Abramowitz from Montreal to refute them. In a complicated decision following drawn-out proceedings the Jews won their case. But the Montreal *Gazette* doubted that a court decision would lay French-Canadian antisemitism to rest any more than Mendel Beiliss's acquittal was likely to put an end to Russian antisemitism. There were other instances of violence during those years as well. Most, however, were spontaneous acts of hooliganism. British law stood between Jews and French Canadians or so, at least, most Jews felt.[117]

Although the violence was contained, the atmosphere was nonetheless often highly charged; "relationships between Jews and Catholics in Quebec remained . . . most cool."[118] Jews perceived the constant barrage of antisemitic oratory, especially from the pulpit, to be a real threat. Since many of them had but recently experienced Russian savagery, they were all the more sensitive to antisemitism and all the less inclined to discount bombastic rhetoric. But the power of the Church in French Canada seemed unrestrained to non-Jews as well. French political economist André Siegfried asserted in the early years of the twentieth century that it would have been difficult to exaggerate the part played by religion in French Canada at that time.[119] Siegfried found "all the old beliefs . . . preserved" and the body "of the faithful . . . submissive in their attitudes." The 1910 Eucharistic Congress in Montreal and the demonstrations against Mayor Nathan later that same year were signs of the power of Catholicism in French Canada; and the Canadian Church, according to many contemporaries, was "in a condition of deep submission to the Holy See."[120]

The Church in Canada had never accepted the idea of complete separation of church and state, and, to a great degree, the British had acquiesced in such a view already in the years immediately following the conquest. The ultramontane "Programme Catholique," drawn up in 1871, suggested how politics and religion in Canada were to be intertwined. The Church was to reserve the right even to determine who were acceptable candidates in elections. Although only a minority of churchmen approved of the program, and ultramontanism steadily declined in the last quarter of the nineteenth century, it represented a line of thinking that was congenial to many. It was not congenial, of course, to Quebec Jews, who sought to become part of the body politic on an equal basis with other citizens. And it was very different from prevailing British and American views of the role of religion in the state.[121]

When it came to a choice (as it did only infrequently) between obedience to Rome or to French-Canadian nationalism, French Canadians, it should be noted, usually chose nationalism. But from the first in Canada, and certainly from the time of the British conquest, the Church was "the most powerful factor in the preservation of the French Canadian races." French Canadians and others believed that the Church alone maintained the survival of the French people and tongue in North America, a judgment that was not mistaken. From the mid-nineteenth century the Catholic clergy in Quebec actively promoted the French-Catholic homogeneity of the province. They sought to colonize unsettled lands with French Canadians and to attract back to the province those who had emigrated to the United States. They also tried to encourage French Canadians to buy out the properties of Anglo-Canadian settlers in the rural areas of Quebec.[122]

As noted already, French-Canadian antisemitism fitted into wider French and Catholic frameworks. But it was also part of the racial and religious xenophobia directed at everyone in Quebec who was not French and Catholic. Jews, other immigrant groups, and, as well, Anglo-Canadians, especially in the rural Eastern Townships, had good reason to complain of French-Canadian antagonism. All of them were treated like "strangers." As Louis Hémon remarked in his classic novel of French-Canadian life, *Maria Chapdelaine:*

> when the French Canadian speaks of himself it is invariably and simply as a "Canadian;" whereas for all the other races that followed in his footsteps, and peopled the country across to the Pacific, he keeps the name of origin: English, Irish, Polish, Russian; never admitting for a moment that the children of these, albeit born in the country, have an equal title to be called "Canadians."[123]

During the period under review the Church was under attack in many places in the world. France was one such place, as *La Semaine religieuse de Québec* refused to let its readers forget. Because "French-Canadian life was [so] closely bound to clerical life," any attack on either the French Canadians or their Church seemed to be an attack on both.[124] Thus the struggles in Canada over French language rights, over Louis Riel, the rebel leader executed in 1885, and over a host of other issues dividing French and Anglo-Canadians seemed to be attacks on the Church and not simply national disagreements. At the same time attacks on the Church in France and elsewhere appeared to French Canadians as attacks directed at them. Moreover, during the nineteenth century Catholics and French Canadians were subjected to considerable prejudice in Canada and in the United States. To some degree their lack of hospitality towards others was reinforced by the animosity they experienced in North America. And the persistent threats to their cultural individuality from Anglophone North America had the inevitable effect of making them more hostile toward outsiders than they might otherwise have been.[125]

The nationalist response to such attacks was to look toward strengthening everything French and Catholic in Canada. It was natural to look to France and the Vatican, the "mother countries," for inspiration and guidance. By the latter years of the nineteenth century, moreover, there were powerful forces in France that seemed to stand for values and beliefs that were "authentically" French, values divorced from and even opposed to the revolutionary tradition. In this other, reactionary France, French Canadians might legitimately seek their roots. And of this France, which looked to the past with nostalgia, antisemitism was an integral part. Jews, who owed their freedom in Canada as in France to the destruction of the *ancien régime,* were ready symbols of the new order. In French Canada, where their number grew steadily in the nineteenth century, they served increasingly as a symbol of the threat to French Catholic homogeneity. For the fanatics, for the paranoids, for anyone seeking a scapegoat for the ills of urbanization, industrialization, and other trials of the twentieth century, Jews provided a convenient candidate. Their symbolic value was enhanced by their identification as the traditional Antichrist allegedly responsible for many of the Church's setbacks.

Jews, then, occupied a special place in French-Canadian demonology, symbolizing much that French Canada traditionally opposed. United in the campaign to keep Montreal free of the "Jewish peril" were traditional Catholic anti-Judaism with its European roots and long-standing French-

Canadian efforts to preserve the racial and religious homogeneity of Quebec. Added to both was a measure of the newer, nineteenth-century varieties of antisemitism, imported from Europe. The campaign against the Jews also represented a deflection of French Canadian resentment of Anglo-Canadians. The latter were in control of Quebec; and it might have been imprudent to criticize them. Curé Belanger claimed that more than the Anglo-Canadians, the "Jews are our greatest enemy. It is incumbent upon us," the priest added, "to make it harder for them to come here."[126] His statement was less than accurate.

Jews could hardly have been expected to accept with equanimity their symbolic ascription or the attempts to exclude them from the body politic. They reacted strongly in Canada, as they did elsewhere in the Western world when they felt threatened. In an early nineteenth-century pamphlet Moses Hart, a son of Aaron, accused the Church of almost every possible sin.[127] Charles Freshman was more temperate in expression but probably not in sentiment. Hovering on the threshold of conversion, he thought only of Protestantism. He had, he said, "never had much opinion of Roman Catholicism."[128] In Montreal over the years "Catholic" became a dirty word to Jews. Abraham A. Roback, writing in the *Keneder odler* in 1909, considered it a "silent victory for the Jewish people" that the power of the Church was on the wane in Spain and Portugal.[129] The most devastating attack that could be levied against Rabbi Meldola De Sola, according to his Reform critics, was to compare him to a Catholic priest.[130] For Rabbi Aaron Mordecai Ashinsky, the only act more unthinkable than stepping into a Catholic church was crossing the doorstep of a Reform temple.[131] Jews came to admire the Indians, who preferred "a little whiskey" to the ministrations of the Catholic missionaries.[132] And on the holiday of Purim in 1895 the Jews of Montreal's Spanish and Portuguese Synagogue chose an unwitting French-Canadian Roman Catholic to act the part of Haman in a play.[133]

The Jewish relationship with France and the Roman Catholic Church, then, worked to impede Jewish integration into French Canada. The antisemitism of French Canadians, much of it inherited from Europe, as well as the low social status of French Canadians in Canada were calculated to reinforce the negative attitudes of Jews toward everything French and Catholic. In turn, their religion made Jews especially objectionable outsiders to French Canadians. If the British and American connection attracted Jews to Anglo-Canada, their contacts with France and the Catholic Church repelled them in the same direction. There was, moreover, a relationship in Canada between antisemitism and both

Joseph Olivier Joseph, descendant of a pioneer Jewish family, a founder of the St. Jean Baptiste Society, in 1892

Notman

Louis Marchand, son of Louis Marchand, the former Levi Koopman of Amsterdam, of St. Mathias, and Montreal, in 1892

Notman

anti-American and anti-British feelings. The commercial and industrial United States, with its dedication to progress and growth, represented to traditionalist Frenchmen and French Canadians the antithesis of their ideal of rootedness in the land and the ancient Church, "of ordered life and contented immobility."[134] Great Britain, "the nation of shopkeepers" and industrial giant, was disliked for some of the same reasons. But in Canada she was also the conqueror, the destroyer of French-Canadian Catholic hegemony. In French Canada nationalists harbored strong antisemitic feelings, admired Russia, the persecutor of the Jews, and her ally, France; they were lukewarm at best in their feelings for England, the protector of Jews, and the United States, the country in which Jews had achieved the highest degree of freedom and integration. "Antisemitism and Anglophobia are diseases identical in their origin," asserted the Canadian *Jewish Times* in 1902. In Europe

> anti-Semites and other reactionaries, ... whether in France, Germany or Austria, are devoted advocates of Russia and equally determined enemies of England and the United States.[135]

The readers of the *Jewish Times* needed no statement about their own country.

The connection between antisemitism and anti-British sentiment was clearly perceived by many non-Jewish Anglo-Canadians, whose position in Canada was threatened by French-Canadian resentment against them. Anglo-Canadians generally supported Jews in their various struggles with Russia, in France, and with French Canadians. There was certainly an affinity between Judaism and Protestantism and perhaps between Jews and English-speaking peoples. But it is not unlikely that a good measure of the support Jews received among Anglo-Canadians was a reflection of self-interest stemming from anti-French sentiment.

Canadian Jews and Their Tenuous Connections to the Francophone World

The group that might possibly have reduced the distance between Jews and French Canadians were those Francophone Jews who immigrated to Canada during the period under review. Had their old world habits and connections functioned as did those of Jews who came from Britain and the United States, they would have paved the way for integration into French Canada, at least for themselves. In the event, however, their having come from France was no great asset in French Canada. Their number was very small, and their Jewishness was such a liability in both France and French Canada, that they could form no bridge at all. Altogether the immigrant traffic from France to Canada after 1759 is instructive. For about a century it was negligible. In 1871 among the 1,089,040 Francophones enumerated in the decennial Canadian census, there were but 2,908 French-born. Of these not a few were Protestants and Jews. Interestingly many of the French immigrants to Canada resided outside of Quebec and were rapidly becoming assimilated into Anglo-Canada.[136] Of those who went to Quebec most were traders and professionals, who had a difficult time integrating into the society of French Canada with its pastoral ethos.[137]

By the 1870s Quebec was eager to counteract the steady stream of immigrants to Canada from Great Britain and the United States. Advertisements were widely circulated in France and in Francophone Belgium and Switzerland for immigrants. Few responded at first. Around the turn of the century, however, immigration picked up. According to one source, some eighteen thousand Frenchmen and Francophone Belgians came to Canada between 1897 and 1908, although others estimate a substantially lower figure. (During the same period over one hundred thousand Francophone Europeans immigrated to the United States.) Their number, too, included Protestants and Jews.[138]

Of the founders of the Young Men's Hebrew Benevolent Society in Montreal in 1863 one was identifiably French, Jacques Bloch. By 1871 there were at least eight other French Jews in Montreal, among them the jeweler brothers, Maurice and Alfred Schwob, Céline Joseph, and Pauline Auerbach, the wife of Zacharia Auerbach, a Polish transmigrant, who came to Canada by way of France and the United States. In subsequent years others arrived. It was estimated in 1911 that of Montreal's forty thousand Jews some one hundred had been born in France and another fifty in Belgium. Jews from France also went to other parts of Canada. In 1871 Edmund Scheuer, an Alsatian Jewish jeweler, who had been living in Paris, immigrated to Hamilton. In 1877 among the pioneer settlers of Winnipeg were the Alsatian-Jewish Coblentz brothers, Edmond, Anchel, and Adolphe. The 1931 census showed 103 Jews born in France in all of Canada, most of them residing in Quebec.[139]

A small number of eastern European-Jewish transmigrants made their way to Canada through France. Among the earliest were the Leon family, of Polish origin, who were living in Montreal in 1861, where they had arrived after sojourns in both France and the United States. Zacharia Auerbach has already been mentioned. Moscow-born Leon Goldman lived in Paris for three years and then for a time in the United States before coming to Montreal in 1892. Yehuda Kaufman (Even Shmuel), a writer for the *Keneder odler* and later a figure of some note in Israeli intellectual circles, was an eastern European, who came to Montreal after receiving an education in France. Two of the transmigrants were clergymen. In 1894 Cantor S. Solomon went to Toronto's Holy Blossom Synagogue from the Rue Notre Dame de Nazareth Synagogue in Paris. He remained in Canada for seven years before leaving for a Reform congregation in San Francisco. Solomon Beir Sprince, a native of Russia, had served a congregation in Montmartre as well as two in the United States before arriving in Montreal in 1902.[140]

Some French Jews came to Canada because they thought of it as a French-speaking country, although most emigrant French Jews in the nineteenth century, including the many Alsatians who fled their homes after 1870 rather than live under German domination, went not to Canada but to the United States. Among French-Jewish communal leaders there had been some feeling in the early twentieth century that Canada might be a suitable place for agricultural settlement. Ironically, however, there were real concerns in France about the weakness of the Canadian-Jewish community and the possible resulting dangers for Jewish immigrants. In general, Canada and Canadian enterprise, and especially French-Canadian enterprise, had a bad name in France. Most Frenchmen had no more inclination to invest in Canada than to emigrate there. As well, nineteenth-century French Jews were, on the whole, less well informed about Canada than were Jews elsewhere in Europe. Before 1875 only a few articles about Canada had appeared in the *Archives Israélites* and *L'Univers Israélite,* and those were not very informative. Later, too, information was scanty and often discouraging. As France sought to redress her declining fortunes and glory toward the end of the century, some Frenchmen showed renewed interest in their former colony in North America. That interest, however, developed only slowly. Thus it is not unikely that of those few French Jews who came to Canada, some had originally set out for "America" and ended up in Canada more by accident than by design as had so many Europeans from other countries.[141]

(It must be noted that some 40 percent of Canada's Jews chose to live in French Canada during the period under review, most of them new immigrants, who had to make a conscious choice about where to live. It is doubtful, however, that very many, even of those who came knowingly to Canada, consciously chose *French* Canada. For one thing, as noted already, France and French Jewry and the Roman Catholic Church had received ample bad publicity in the eastern European Jewish heartland. French Canada itself was comparatively unknown, although articles that appeared from time to time after 1884 in *Hamelitz, Ha-Zefirah,* and *Hasman* in eastern Europe and in the *Jewish Chronicle* and the *Jewish Year Book* in England told of anti-Jewish feeling in Montreal, the Nathan affair, hooligan attacks on Jews in Quebec, the Plamondon blood libel, and other events.[142] One must assume, therefore, that Jews were simply choosing to ignore the "French fact" in Quebec. And, in fact, Jews lived almost exclusively in Montreal, where there was already a large English-speaking minority. Jews chose Montreal because there were job opportunities, because it was their port of disembarkation, because there was an established Jewish community, because the British—or Anglo-Canadians—were in control, on the whole, despite the presence after 1851 of a French Canadian majority.)

As did their coreligionists from England, Jews from France in Canada maintained ties with their old homeland. Unlike the bonds of émigré British Jews, however, these ties tended to be weak. For one thing, as noted earlier, the French-Jewish community itself was not cohesive. Moreover, in Canada being French meant being identified not with the ruling class, but with the conquered people, whom a later French-Canadian writer would call, "the white niggers" of North America. Unlike Jews of British origin, those from France could not point to their homeland as a model of toleration toward Jews nor as a model Jewish community. They also could not make the argument to French Canadians, as could British Jews to Anglo-Canadians, that Judaism was an integral part of the heritage and culture of the mother country. Still, certain personal and communal ties developed.

Nineteenth-century France was perhaps the most important cultural and artistic center of Europe, and a number of Canadian Jews traveled there to study during these years. Pauline (Lightstone) Donalda studied opera in the French capital. Austrian-born Louis Fitch (Fieczwicz) earned a degree from the University of Paris after he had received his B.C.L. from McGill in 1911. A few Canadian Jews went to live in France during the period, perhaps lured by its more developed cultural ambience. Henri Dreyfus returned to his homeland after many years in Montreal. Gerald E. Hart, a great-grandson of Aaron Hart, was born in Montreal in 1849. He lived for some time in New York, Fort Worth, Texas, and Jacksonville, Florida, as well as in Montreal and Trois Rivières. In the 1920s he retired to France, despite the reservations about the country that he had earlier expressed in print. Later he returned to Montreal. There were probably a few other Canadian Jews who traversed a similar route.[143]

There was some limited trade between Francophone Europe and Canada during these years. A few Jews were involved, including the Schwob family, jewelers who had some important business connections with Switzerland, and Clarence I. De Sola and Jesse and Abraham Joseph, who had ties to large Belgian companies. In 1910 André Weill of the Paris branch of the Rothschilds arrived in Montreal to discuss the establishment of steel mills in Canada. It seems, however, that he had no contact with the Jewish community on that occasion. The closest ties with France were those of Moise Schwob, a founder and then president for four years of the Chambre de Commerce Fançaise in Montreal, a small group of businessmen of French origin, many of them Jews or Protestants. A later president was newspaperman Jules Heilbronner.[144]

There were Canadian Jews appointed as consuls of Francophone countries, probably because of their business connections. Although unimportant, these posts did provide some links with Francophone Europe for Canadian Jews. Schwob served as vice-consul of France in Montreal for a number of years. Jesse Joseph was Belgian consul there for some time, and after his death in 1904 he was succeeded by his nephew, Clarence I. De Sola. Abraham Joseph served for thirty years as vice-consul for Belgium in Quebec. After his death in 1886 his son, Andrew C. Joseph, succeeded to that post. In Vancouver, Samuel Gintzburger, a native of Neuchatel in French Switzerland, served as consul of that country for many years. For the increasingly antisemitic French Canadians, these appointments were probably unpleasant reminders that in Europe Jews could rise to positions of authority, while the fact that Jews were the agents of foreign governments probably tended to perpetuate their image as foreigners.[145]

Canadian Jews also established some tenuous communal bonds with France. A few Montreal Jews belonged to French organizations, such as the Alliance Française. A few had ties with French-Jewish organizations. In the earlier days of the Zionist movement in Montreal, for example, there were contacts with like-minded people in Paris.[146] The experience in North America of the major French-Jewish organization, the Alliance Israélite Universelle (hereafter referred to as AIU), however, illustrates the weakness of Canadian-Jewish ties with France. Within a few years of its founding the AIU had established a number of chapters outside France. Several of them were in the United States, even in such out-of-the-way places as Galveston, Texas, and Keokuk, Iowa. Among its members were some of the most prominent Jews in America. Adolphus S. Solomons, Washington politician, bookseller, and Jewish lobbyist, was a member of the Central Committee of the Alliance and its treasurer for the United States. Solomons had close ties with Rabbi Abraham De Sola of Montreal, his daughter having married the rabbi's favorite nephew, Rabbi H. Pereira Mendes. And yet Solomons never recruited De Sola for the AIU.[147] Edmund Scheuer organized a short-lived branch of the Alliance in Hamilton, the only one in Canada.[148] Efforts to start a chapter in French Canada proved abortive. From 1900 Nissim Behar was the AIU organizer in North America. It is not unlikely that his opposition to Zionism and his militant Americanism ("In America, Boston is our Zion and New York our Jerusalem," the Jerusalem native asserted in 1904) alienated potential Canadian members already wary of any French connection.[149] A century after its founding the AIU was active in the United States, as well as in Mexico and eleven Latin American countries, but still not in Canada.[150] In the early 1890s the AIU developed one significant connection with Canada, the contribution of funds to immigrant aid work. The Baron de Hirsch School and Institute of Montreal received donations between 1891 and 1894 "without which they would have been unable to have kept the school open."[151] The AIU also provided funds to prospective agricultural colonists in Canada's West. This tie, however, was of short duration.[152]

The major Canadian-Jewish communal connection with France was that of the Jewish Colonization Association (JCA), which was headquartered in both London and Paris. French JCA involvement in Canada began with Baron de Hirsch's original gift to the Young Men's Hebrew Benevolent Society of Montreal in 1890, which enabled that group to erect its own building and to pursue immigrant-aid work on a large scale. According to some sources Moise Schwob was instrumental in securing that first infusion of French funds into Canada.[153] After the initial gift the JCA in Paris continued to contribute toward the work of the Benevolent Society, now renamed the Baron de Hirsch Institute and, as well, toward the cost of settling eastern European Jews in agricultural colonies in western Canada. On occasion the JCA joined with the AIU and British organizations in support of existing colonies in the prairie provinces.[154]

Although relations between Montreal and Paris were usually correct, the two JCA groups seem not to have had much confidence in each other. The Canadians were wary of Paris, preferring to deal with English board members rather than directly with the French head office. They expected the Londoners to be "more conversant" with their needs than the Parisians.[155] Paris, on the other hand, was never sure what type of aid "was appropriate" to Canada and kept its involvement in the country "relatively restrained."[156] For a time the French kept their own immigration officer in Montreal, perhaps because they did not entirely trust the local Jews. Between 1900 and 1906 all connections between Montreal and the western colonies were severed by the Paris center. The task of overseeing this aid was given over to the Jewish Agricultural and Industrial Aid Society of the New York Baron de Hirsch Fund. Even after 1906, when the supervision of the colonies was once again entrusted to Canadians, Paris retained the right to nominate three of the six directors of the Canadian JCA branch and regularly sent its own inspectors to Canada to check up on local activities. On occasion Canadians traveled to Paris to attempt to improve relations with the parent group, but tensions did not abate.[157]

There was never any sense on the part of the French JCA that Jews in Canada and France had any genuine affinity. Correspondence from Montreal to Paris was always in English. JCA-sponsored schools in Canada were conducted in English and not in French. At the turn of the century, French Jews were interested in disseminating French culture among "backward" and malleable coreligionists in the Levant and North Africa. They viewed Canada, however, as a British country and were content to let their London coreligionists assume responsibility for aid there. For the most part the autocratic Jewish leaders and bureaucrats in Paris placed more confidence in the Argentinian enterprises of the JCA than in the Canadian. It was easier to maintain control there; the British directors had less of a clear interest in Argentina; and local Jews were not yet sufficiently established during the period under review to insist on a major say in the determination of policy.[158]

There existed, then, during these years traffic between France and Canada and some communal and personal ties between the two countries. But the traffic both ways was light, and the bonds were tenuous at best. Most Canadian Jews showed little warmth for France during the period, except for a few isolated individuals such as Moise Schwob. Canadian Jews shared the feelings of most of the rest of world Jewry that France was no friend of Jews. And they could hardly share the enthusiasm of French-Canadian nationalists for the reactionary forces of France, which, as the Dreyfus Affair had made abundantly clear, remained strong even under the Third Republic.

Not surprisingly, their common origin did not lead to a feeling of solidarity among French Jews in Canada as it did among Jews from Britain. Not in Montreal, where they were concentrated, nor elsewhere in Canada was any attempt made by French Jewish immigrants to organize themselves. This was partly a function of numbers, but undoubtedly it was also a sign of how little they cared to emphasize their French origins in Jewish circles in Montreal or their Jewishness in French-Canadian circles. The behavior of French Jews in Canada stands in marked contrast to that of French-Jewish émigrés in the United States, where it seemed possible to retain both the Jewish and the French attachments. In New York around 1900 there were both a French-Jewish synagogue and a mutual aid society. French Jews and others who had not originated in France, as well, maintained a lively interest in French affairs, despite general Jewish ambivalence regarding France. They affiliated with French cultural organizations even when they had no personal ties to France, and they remitted considerable sums to Jewish philanthropies in France.[159] In the United States a French connection conferred status on anyone who could claim it; in Canada, for the most part, it did not. Although in British Columbia Jews might participate in both French and Jewish organizations in the mid-nineteenth century, Jews of French origin in Quebec generally did not, then or later. They behaved like Protestants of French extraction and, for that matter, like Catholic Francophone immigrants there. "Absorption of [any] immigrants into French-Canadian culture has never been easy, partly because of the conservative parish community, and partly because the nationalists preferred the *status quo*," and partly for all the other reasons already discussed.[160] And Jews were not just "immigrants"! To French Canadians and to most Frenchmen, as Jews they were outsiders, aliens, symbols of the new, the materialistic, and the anti-Christian.

Many of the immigrants probably preferred to affiliate with the Anglophone ruling class; and the Jewish community was a subgroup of the Anglo-Canadian community. Some Jewish immigrants maintained an attachment to France and its culture, usually at the cost of giving up their religion. Even then, however, they frequently remained part of the "French colony" and did not integrate into the French-Canadian community. But the norm was assimilation into English-speaking Canada. Of those who maintained their French identity, many saw their children discard it either through emigration to the United States or through absorption into Anglo-Canada. Some examples are instructive.

Jules Heilbronner has already been mentioned a number of times, and his career in Canada illustrates the choice faced by French Jews. Born in Alsace in 1852, he emigrated to Canada at the age of twenty-two. He became prominent in the French-language press of Montreal, editing *La Presse* for many years. He was also associated for a time with *Le Soir* and *Le Prix Courant*. Because of the role he played in public affairs in Montreal as editor of the largest French-language daily, he received various honors, including appointment to the 1886 Royal Commission, which studied labor conditions in Canada. Everyone knew that Heilbronner was a Jew. Antisemites attacked him as one; Jews included him among their number; his friends included other Francophone Jews. And yet Heilbronner never affiliated with the organized Jewish community. He lived the life of a virtual Marrano.[161]

Jules Hirtz (Hertz), "one of the best-known men in the French colony of Montreal," also lived outside the Jewish community. Hirtz was a well-known druggist. Born in Alsace in 1847, he emigrated to Montreal in 1872, two years before Heilbronner. Having fought for France in the Franco-Prussian War, he opted for Canada as his new home "in order to remain French." In Montreal, Hirtz belonged to the usual French societies. At his funeral in 1910 the consul-general of France was in attendance as well as the presidents of the Union Nationale Française and the Chambre de Commerce Française and several former members of the Foreign Legion. Hirtz apparently knew Hebrew from his early childhood; he advertised his drugstore in the *Keneder odler* as well as in the English and French press. But during his lifetime he remained aloof from Judaism and Jewish organizations in Montreal, such that his funeral was not conducted by a rabbi but by his two sons. (Hirtz's daughter opted out of the French-Jewish identity conflict in another way, by leaving Montreal for the United States.)[162] Doubtless, Hirtz and Heilbronner were not unique in Montreal. Several typical French-Jewish names appear in business directories of the period. It is unknown, however, whether such men as police sergeant Henry Dreifuss, who was treasurer of the Swiss Society in 1880, were of Jewish origin.[163]

The dominant pattern, then, was that of French Jews in Canada acculturating to the English-speaking Jewish community rather than preserving their French identity. Many chose to live in English-speaking Canada, and those in Montreal often affiliated with Anglophone institutions. Jules Rueff was a French Jew who emigrated to Victoria, British

Columbia, in 1860, where he became a prosperous merchant and a prominent supporter of both local Jewish institutions and immigrant French organizations. Rueff returned to France in 1873 because of illness and died there the next year. Samuel Gintzburger emigrated to Vancouver in 1887. John Creed, a native of Belfort, France, emigrated to Toronto in 1912. The Coblentz brothers were probably already Americanized before moving to Winnipeg, since they had lived for a time in Philadelphia and Bethlehem, Pennsylvania. So, too, was Rabbi Sprince, who also paused in the United States between his soujourns in France and Canada. Transmigrants such as Cantor Solomon and the artist Simon Soboloff chose Toronto despite, or perhaps because of, their prior stay in Paris. Edmund Scheuer and his sister, Camilla Levy, lived in Hamilton (Scheuer later moved to Toronto) and naturally became part of its English-speaking culture.[164]

Immigrant Frenchmen—Jews and gentiles—left Canada in the nineteenth and twentieth centuries no less readily than people of other origins. The French connection was too weak to bind them to Francophone Canada. They went to the United States and to South America and other non-French-speaking areas as well. When they left French Canada, moreover, French Jews generally left behind all traces of French culture, easily forgetting whatever motivation they had once had for living in a French-speaking environment.[165]

In 1910 the Chambre de Commerce Française in Montreal inaugurated a "free course of English [sic] for the benefit of our compatriots."[166] Even those with strong attachments to the mother country could sense which way the wind was blowing for them in Quebec. In 1931 the Belgians living in Canada were mostly of Flemish origin. French-speaking Belgians stayed at home. And most Belgians of both nationalities, who were almost all Catholics, became English speakers in Canada. As late as the 1960s Francophone Jews immigrating to Quebec were assimilating to the English language and Anglo-Canadian culture.[167] For Jews, coming from France and speaking French proved to be of no help in acclimating to French Canada during the period under review, leaving affiliation with Anglo-Canada as the only route open to them. For Jews a genuine choice did not exist.

CHAPTER FIVE

Aɟ Part of Anglo-Canada

There were additional factors that were no less important than the international relations of Canada's Jews and gentiles in determining the patterns of Jewish integration into the country. These included internal Canadian developments, language, demography, occupational distribution, social habits, and even religious behavior. Analysis of these factors does not lead to any easy identification of cause and effect. It does, however, complete the picture of influences acting on Jews, Anglo-Canadians, and French Canadians in the period under review, all of which together served to bring Jews into the Anglo-Canadian community exclusively. As is not necessarily the case with the developments discussed until now, the measuring stick for what follows is Montreal, the only place in the country where there were substantial numbers of Anglo-Canadians, French Canadians, and Jews during the period under review. Only in Montreal (and the very few smaller centers of Jewish settlement in Quebec), therefore, was there the potential for Jews to affiliate either with the French or with Anglo-Canadians.

A Common Language

Over the years language proved to be one of the decisive influences on Jewish settlement patterns in Canada. Of no little importance in determining language assimilation was the fact that English was the language of those who ruled and controlled Canada, including Quebec. Even in Montreal, the largest city in French Canada for most of the period, government and business were conducted in English. French Canadians who expected to get ahead in these fields had to know English. Jews and other immigrants who did not know English already learned it for the same reasons—to participate in the economic and official life of the country and also because it was the language of the ruling classes. Whatever other drawbacks there were to French, it was the language (and culture) of the subservient class.[1] In any case, the first Jews in Canada had come either from England or from the British colonies. Their language was English; and the institutions they established in their new country operated in that language.

Most Jews who came to Canada in the period of mass Jewish immigration after 1890 came without much knowledge of either of the country's two official languages. This was true no matter whence they had come. As late as 1931, 94.3 percent of all British-born Canadian Jews claimed Yiddish as their mother tongue; and 91.6 percent of all American-born Canadian Jews did so.[2] Wherever in Canada they settled, however, most immigrants, including Jews, learned English and not French. In 1931 there were 1,301,622 Canadians whose mother tongue was neither English nor French. Of these 1,078,284 had learned English but not French. A mere 6,039 had learned French but not English. A further 69,147 had learned both languages.[3] Even in Quebec immigrants were learning English. Although only 2.4 percent of all Canadian Jews reported their mother tongue to be English in 1931, 94.6 percent of them spoke that language. Only Anglo-Celts, Scandinavians, and Germans reported a higher percentage of English speakers. And of those groups many more claimed English as a mother tongue than did Jews.[4]

In later years when ethnic identity and pride became respectable in North America, Canadian Jews liked to stress the degree to which they, as opposed to their American cousins, had remained faithful to the Yiddish culture and language of Europe.[5] Nineteenth-century observers, however, perceived no such proclivity. Rather they sensed the unseemly haste with which Canadian Jews were discarding the Yiddish language in favor of English. Alexander Harkavy reported from Montreal in 1888

PAC (C-65394)

The "muddy, broken down campus" as it appeared when Abraham De Sola taught there

that Jews there refused to speak Yiddish no matter how broken their English was. "They were ashamed, lest they be recognized as Jews."[6] In fact, in all English-speaking countries during these years, Yiddish was disdained by the children of immigrants and by the immigrants themselves. Moreover, they tended to transfer "this contempt for the language . . . to those who use[d] it . . . [and] to everything . . . conveyed by means of it."[7] In Montreal as elsewhere in North America Jews were trying as hard as they could, not only to speak English, but to assimilate to North American culture and mores. Sometimes Montreal Jews seemed unaware that any language other then English was spoken in the city. Joseph Elijah Bernstein, a Hebrew- and Yiddish-speaking immigrant to Montreal, asserted in 1884 in the Hebrew-language *Hamelitz,* that in Canada, English was "the language of the country."[8] In 1887 when the cornerstone was laid for the new building of the Spanish and Portuguese Synagogue, only English-language newspapers were placed inside. Eastern European Jews came to consider it an insult to be addressed in any language other than English.[9]

In the early years almost all Jewish institutions in Canada functioned in English; and Jews who did not speak that language had to learn it in order to participate in Jewish communal life. This was true no less of French speakers than of Yiddish speakers. The earliest minutes of the Spanish and Portuguese congregation in Montreal were kept in a very good, legible English. In 1875 the bylaws of the De Sola Lodge No. 89 of the Ancient Jewish Order Kesher Shel Barzel, Canada's largest Jewish fraternal order, insisted that "all debates and proceedings . . . shall be transacted in the English language." The Lodge conceded to the chair the right to grant "to any brother" permission "to use any other language."[10] It was probably not French speakers whom the brothers thought to accommodate, however, but German, which was the language of the Grand Lodge of the order in New York and of many other lodges as well. In the latter years of this period the language spoken at large, public Zionist meetings in Canada was usually "the language of the country."[11] When a library was opened in Montreal for immigrant Jews in 1910, it was stocked almost exclusively with English books, in the hope that it would serve as a means "of teaching English to foreigners."[12] As late as 1939 that library, funded by the Jewish community, had a collection of 13,000 volumes of which fewer than 650 were in languages other than English, Yiddish, and Hebrew. Jewish linguistic assimilation in Montreal during the latter years of the period under review even included the Anglicization of Yiddish. The *Keneder odler* frequently used

English words when Yiddish alternatives existed. It never used French words. In fact, the paper Anglicized French terms for its readers.[13]

Some Jews in Canada did know French, of course. The record of Jews has been better in this regard than that of other groups, as noted at the outset. Jewish shopkeepers and perhaps some of the better-educated Jews in Quebec learned some French. Those who had received a good secular education in Europe had often studied French there. Not a few Romanian Jews, who came to Montreal in large numbers after the turn of the century, had learned some French in their native land. A few Canadian Jews with international business connections learned to "speak French like Parisians," although probably not like French Canadians.[14] In 1931, 14.1 percent of all Canadian Jews could speak French, the second highest percentage of any non-French group in the country. But even that small number gives an exaggerated picture of the use of French by Jews. Immigrant Jews were poor. They lived in working-class neighborhoods, often in close proximity to French Canadians. Since many were engaged in retail and secondhand trade, they had to learn enough French to deal with their customers, but they did not speak it among themselves. By 1905 the Baron de Hirsch School in Montreal, run by the Jewish community for immigrant children, was teaching French, although only in the highest classes. Five years later its night division for adults also added French. For most Jews, however, even if they had acquired a knowledge of French, it remained an alien tongue. French was "the guardian of the [Catholic] faith,"[15] the "outworks protecting Catholicism in Canada."[16] As such it was not likely to prove attractive to Jews as a means of communication.[17]

Toward the end of the period, the issue of language became highly politicized in Canada. In Ontario there arose strong opposition to the use of French in public schools. One of the chief opponents of French was the Irish Catholic bishop of London, Ontario, Michael Francis Fallon, who felt that bilingual schools were wasteful and even harmful. In 1912 the Ontario Department of Education formulated Regulation 17, which, in effect, prohibited Franco-Ontarians from receiving their schooling in French. The regulation contributed a great deal to the heightening of tension between French and Anglo-Canadians everywhere in Canada.[18] The year 1912 also saw a counter-demonstration of impressive dimensions in support of the French language in Canada. In June over one thousand delegates assembled in Quebec for a French-language congress. Among those who gathered to pay tribute to the beauty and the political significance of French were the archbishops of Quebec,

Montreal, St. Boniface, and Kingston. Also present were Sir Lomer Gouin, the premier of Quebec, and Sir Wilfrid Laurier. Regulation 17 and the congress made it quite clear that the language one spoke in Canada had political implications. Jews' identification as English-speakers, then, came to have political as well as social and linguistic significance.[19]

Religious and Ethnic Diversity in Common

Although Anglo-Canadians were linguistically homogeneous, ethnically and religiously they were not. And to a certain extent this ethnic and religious diversity facilitated Jewish integration into the community. French Canadians were a "remarkably homogeneous people." They were almost all French in origin and Catholic in religion. Anglo-Canadians, on the other hand, came from different national backgrounds and could therefore more easily accommodate divergence. The diversity of Anglo-Canada can be overstated. In 1871 less than 8 percent of all Canadians were of non-British, non-French stock. But however similar they might appear to outsiders, Englishmen, Scotsmen, Irishmen, and Welshmen felt very different from one another. From early on there was also considerable religious diversity among Anglo-Canadians. In 1871 eight Protestant denominations each claimed at least 1 percent of the Canadian population as members, although none claimed more than 16 percent, and only two had more than 8 percent. In later years variety increased, especially when immigrants of non-British stock came in great numbers after the turn of the century. Among the homogeneous French, Jews were an anomaly; among the more diverse Anglo-Canadians, they might appear to be just one more of the society's many national and religious groups.[20]

The fact that Jews in Canada were almost all immigrants also bound them to Anglo-Canada and separated them from French Canada. As noted above very few French-speaking immigrants came to Canada after 1759. Throughout the nineteenth century, on the other hand, Anglo-Canada was a nation of immigrants, its history "in large measure the history of immigration," as social scientist William George Smith remarked in 1920. The cities, where most Jews lived, tended to be overwhelmingly populated by immigrants. After the turn of the century immigration accelerated. Although not all Anglo-Canadians favored immigration, it was part of the Anglo-Canadian way of life.[21]

There was a practical need, moreover, for Anglo-Canada to encourage immigration. Immediately following the conquest there were perhaps five hundred British civilians in Canada and sixty thousand French. If Britain were to hold the colony—and after the American Revolution, if Canada were to remain an entity separate from the United States—then it had to be populated, and it had to achieve a certain degree of unity. Lord Durham's report on Canada, written after the Rebellion of 1837 had almost severed the country from the crown, suggested two ways to make Canada British to the core. One was British immigration. Another was the naturalization of everyone possible. Both approaches were employed with varying degrees of energy and success at different times.[22]

It has been claimed with some justice that the ease with which it has been possible almost from the start to become naturalized in Canada reflected the desire of the British to bolster their own ranks. Immigration also served that end. Consequently Anglo-Canadians usually supported it, whereas French Canadians opposed it. Canadian immigration agents scouted England, Ireland, and the Continent for prospects in the late nineteenth century and the early twentieth. French Canadians claimed that they deliberately avoided France and Belgium. Whether it was because they were not recruited or, more likely, because there was neither overpopulation nor pressure of urbanization in France, few Francophones came. Immigration benefited only Anglo-Canadians in the developing struggle for cultural domination.[23]

Jews required continued immigration to build up their own community in Canada to a viable size or just to keep it going at all. And Jews from eastern Europe were desperately seeking new homes after 1881. Thus, immigration was one issue over which Jews and French Canadians clashed head on. Nevertheless, not all Jews at all times favored immigration; nor for that matter, did all Anglo-Canadians. In 1875 the Young Men's Hebrew Benevolent Society of Montreal announced in London and New York "that it is imprudent to send emigrants to Canada."[24] Those were depression times in Canada, however, as they were in the United States. No one could assist impoverished newcomers; the community was in no position to assume any added burdens. Even in more prosperous times, there was a strong strain of nativism among Anglo-Canadians directed specifically at Jews and other non-Anglo-

Spode tea service created for Ezekiel and Fanny Hart of Trois Rivières

Horse trough erected in memory of Abraham Joseph (1815–1886) in Quebec

Skating champion Louis Ruben-stein of Montreal in 1893

Mr. Ascher reading to Miss De Sola, Montreal, 1875

Saxon immigrants.[25] Generally, such feelings were submerged, at least during the earlier years of the period under review, by the need for population. The presence of such sentiments, however, helps to explain why Jews felt a strong desire to Anglify themselves.

Migration and Mobility

As the nineteenth century progressed, the Canadian need for additional population for defensive purposes was augmented by a vision of a great country in the making. Westward expansion was a vital component of that vision. Settlement of the West was pioneered by French Canadians, although most French Canadians seeking greater economic opportunity headed for the United States and not western Canada. The large-scale settlement of the Canadian West was undertaken by Anglo-Canadians or Britishers, and, increasingly, during the "Laurier years," by continental European and American immigrants who affiliated with Anglo-Canada. Through the westward movement, ties of family and friendship were created between English Quebeckers and Anglo-Canadians in other parts of the country. These ties also drew Quebeckers into the broader English-speaking world. They served to widen the gap between them and their French-Canadian neighbors. Jews participated in this process.

By the second half of the nineteenth century Jews were beginning to spread out over the expanse of Canada, and their concentration in French Canada began to diminish. Although in the earlier period Quebec contained the majority of Canada's Jews, by 1921 fewer than 40 percent lived there, with almost as many in Ontario and nearly 15 percent in Manitoba. Interprovincial contact should not be overestimated. The Canadian population in general has been much more stable than that of the United States. In 1931 over 90 percent of Canadian-born Jews resided in the province in which they had been born. Nonetheless, there was some contact, creating the beginnings of a national Jewish community in Canada for the first time in the country's history.[26]

Newcomers especially seemed to move from place to place. People left small towns for Montreal and other centers. Polish-born Hiram Levy lived in Waterloo, Quebec, before moving to Montreal in 1884, where he became a successful importer of clothing and trimmings. Ascher Pierce and his family had been pioneer colonists in Oxbow, Saskatchewan, before joining the exodus to Montreal. Other Montreal Jews had lived in rural areas and smaller centers of Ontario, in such places as Lancaster, Lanark, Cornwall, Kingston, and Sudbury.[27]

There was also some reverse movement of people out of metropolitan centers to smaller communities. Most went in search of better economic opportunities. Montrealer Dr. Hiram N. Vineberg, for example, practiced medicine in the early 1880s in Portage-la-Prairie, Manitoba, before leaving Canada for the United States. Immigrants who did not do particularly well in Montreal left for the prairies and for other cities. The Young Men's Hebrew Benevolent Society–Baron de Hirsch Institute sent newcomers to other points in Canada, just as it did to locations in the United States, in an effort to relieve congestion in Montreal and its own financial burdens. In 1908 the Society sent its manager on a tour of forty-five cities and towns in Ontario looking for placement opportunities for immigrants.[28]

In spreading out across Anglo-Canada in the pre–World War I period, Jews were becoming physically removed from French Canadians. This was also true in French Canada itself. In fact, Jews in French Canada had frequently lived at something of a distance from French Canadians. Most of the earliest Jews, who arrived on the heels of the British armies, settled in those towns that had garrisons: Montreal, Berthier, Trois Rivières, and Quebec, where they themselves often joined the militia. They did not, for the most part, settle in rural areas, where most French Canadians lived. (Montreal actually maintained an English-speaking majority throughout most of the first half of the nineteenth century.) With the advance of that century, Canadians moved farther afield in search of economic opportunity, and some Jews did attempt to settle in rural Quebec. Generally they scurried back to Montreal as quickly as possible. Dr. David Alexander Hart, a grandson of Aaron Hart, graduated from McGill in 1874. He practiced medicine for some years after his graduation in the eastern townships of Quebec, an area that had first been settled by the British. By the 1870s, however, it already had a French majority, which was becoming steadily larger. After a few years Dr. Hart followed the English exodus to Montreal.[29]

In general, during the last years of the period under review Jews in the province of Quebec tended to settle only in those areas that had substantial numbers of Anglo-Canadians. In 1891 there were settlements of twenty or more Jews in only three places in Quebec. By contrast, Ontario, with fewer Jews, had nine such communities. By 1921 Quebec had nine Jewish communities of twenty or more people. But Ontario, which still had a smaller Jewish population, had forty-four. When the

Baron de Hirsch Institute assisted immigrants to leave Montreal, it almost never sent them to other towns in Quebec—no matter how desperate it was to rid itself of potential charges. As a result, most of those towns have never had a Jewish resident. This is in marked contrast to small towns in the eastern United States or in Ontario. It is unquestionably a function of the reluctance of Jews to settle among French Canadians and of the latter to receive Jews in their midst.[30]

In Montreal itself there was also a growing separation between the two groups. Jews tended to live closest to French Canadians in their first area of settlement, when they were new immigrants and poor. With each successive move they drew farther away from French Canadians, until by the fourth area of settlement, they were living in exclusively Anglo-Canadian neighborhoods. Jews born in the United States, England, or Canada tended to settle immediately in Anglo-Canadian neighborhoods on moving to Montreal. To Jews, French-Canadian neighborhoods were associated with poverty and the lower-class status of the new immigrant.[31]

It should be remembered that Jews fared only somewhat worse among French Canadians than other immigrants. In 1921 the British immigrant population in Quebec was over 91 percent urban, and most British immigrants were congregated in Montreal. Elsewhere in Canada only 65 percent of British immigrants were living in urban centers in the same year. Slovaks and Italians shared Roman Catholicism with French Canadians, and Italians had a linguistic affinity as well. And yet, as late as 1967, Slovaks were settled in only four locations in Quebec as opposed to twenty-seven in Ontario. In that year over 90 percent of the Italians in Quebec lived in Montreal. It may also be noted that emigrants from Quebec have always included a disproportionate number of English speakers. French-Canadian xenophobia affected all outsiders and not just Jews.[32]

As Jews spread out across Canada, they developed personal and communal bonds with each other, which served to further the growth of a national Jewish community. These ties paralleled those of Canadian Jews with the United States and Great Britain. Relatives and friends were usually left behind when Jews moved to new areas. At the turn of the century the social columns of the Canadian *Jewish Times* show a rising tempo of cross-Canada contact. Although it continued to be more usual for Jews and other Canadians to do business with New York and London, Montreal also became a supply center for the Canadian hinterland. More slowly, Toronto developed along similar lines.[33] Successful companies established branches in Montreal, Toronto, and other large Canadian centers. By 1909, two years after its founding, a considerable amount of the advertising carried by the *Keneder odler* was for Toronto firms; and the paper carried a regular column of Toronto news. Even after the establishment of the *Hebrew Daily Journal* in Toronto in 1912, the *odler* continued to be read there.

Montreal Jews developed ramified religious and communal ties with the rest of Canada. As the nation expanded, religious and fraternal organizations of all denominations within Canada began to look to each other for assistance. Already between 1867 and 1870 "the four largest Churches in Canada became full-fledged national organizations."[34] Jews did not achieve such a high degree of national integration during the period under review, for their numbers did not make it feasible. For the time being London and New York remained necessarily the focuses of Canadian-Jewish life. Still, the Montreal Jewish community was beginning to stake out a claim to national leadership.

In 1856 Toronto Jews organized the first Jewish congregation in that city. The group turned to the Spanish and Portuguese Synagogue in Montreal for a Torah scroll. For a number of years the new Toronto congregation had no rabbi of its own and submitted religious disputes to Rabbi De Sola in Montreal for adjudication. As late as 1871 members of the Toronto synagogue were still seeking guidance from the more experienced Montrealers in running a synagogue. Jews in outlying areas of Ontario and Quebec in the early days of settlement were married and buried in Montreal, since only there were both a rabbi and a Jewish cemetery to be found. Toronto and London, Ontario, members of the Ancient Jewish Order Kesher Shel Barzel looked to Montreal and especially to Rabbi De Sola for leadership. Quebec Jews, like English-speaking gentiles, were constructing yet another complex of relationships that served to draw them away from their Francophone neighbors and into the Anglo-Canadian orbit.[35]

Over the years, as the Jewish population of Anglo-Canada grew, the connections between Montreal Jews and those of the rest of Canada developed further. As had his father earlier Meldola De Sola solemnized marriages for Jews of outlying areas. Although Hamilton Jews usually turned to nearby Buffalo for guidance and inspiration, on occasion in the late Victorian period they looked to Montreal. In 1881 David A. Ansell participated in the examination of Hebrew-school pupils in Hamilton. The following year Rev. Samuel Marks of Montreal's German and Polish Congregation assisted the Hamiltonians in dedicating their new synagogue building. Some years later Marks, then minister of the Reform Temple Emanu-El in Montreal, helped Quebec Jews organize a Sunday school. In 1906 Rabbi Herman Abramowitz presided over the laying of the cornerstone of the new Goel Tzedec Synagogue in Toronto, to which his own synagogue, Shaar Hashomayim of Montreal, had made a substantial financial contribution. While in Toronto on that occasion Abramowitz conferred with Rabbi Solomon Jacobs of Holy Blossom Congregation and Rabbi Weiss of Hamilton on problems of mutual concern.[36]

Montreal communal organizations also had increasing contact with other areas of Canada. In 1893 Ottawa Jews under the influence of the Montrealers organized a Baron de Hirsch Institute of their own. Six years later members of the Relief Committee of Montreal's Institute helped Quebec Jews set up a similar committee there. In 1896, as noted previously, Mrs. Meldola De Sola brought the National Council of Jewish Women to Toronto from Montreal. The Baron de Hirsch Institute maintained its ties with the agricultural colonies of the West. Visitors to the colonies over the years included David A. Ansell, Lazarus Cohen, Rabbis Abramowitz and Ashinsky, and other prominent members of the Young Men's Hebrew Benevolent Society–Baron de Hirsch Institute.[37]

Prior to World War I there was only one Jewish organization in Canada that actually embraced the entire country. Ironically, it was the Federation of Zionist Societies in Canada, dedicated to founding a homeland for Jews in Palestine, that became the first coast-to-coast Jewish organization in the Dominion. In 1899 the Federation came into being with chapters in Montreal, Winnipeg, Toronto, Quebec, and Kingston, numbering altogether some seven hundred members, about half of them in Montreal. A year later membership in Montreal was up 50 percent, and new chapters had been formed in London (Ontario), Hamilton, Ottawa, and St. John, New Brunswick. By the time of the 1907 national convention in Ottawa, there were over forty constituent chapters of the Zionist Federation across Canada.[38]

Zionist leaders, especially those from Montreal, traveled the country proselytizing. Rabbi Ashinsky spoke frequently in Toronto, Quebec, Kingston, and the West. Clarence I. De Sola, president of the Federation of Zionist Societies of Canada from its inception almost to his death in 1920, traveled from Glace Bay, Nova Scotia, to Toronto on behalf of Zionism and to the West as well. So, too, did Rabbi Nathan Gordon.[39]

Unlike other groups that continued to have a strong regional base long after they had supposedly become national, the Zionist Federation included officers from every part of the country from its earliest days. In 1907 its president was De Sola, and there were several other officers from Montreal. But there were also vice-presidents from Ottawa, Kingston, Winnipeg, and Toronto. *Hamelitz* accurately described the unifying effects of the Zionist movement among Canadian Jews:

> Until just a short time ago we knew little about such communities as Halifax and Vancouver. Each one was a law unto itself. Since Zionism arose . . . breathing new life into . . . [all Jews], even such congregations exude a new spirit, the spirit of Judaism. And that spirit has, to a great extent, succeeded in uniting Canadian Jewry.[40]

The cross-Canada ties of Jewish nationalism, too, then, served to bind Montreal Jews to Anglo-Canada and thus to the rest of the English-speaking world.[41]

Economic Ties

In terms of their occupational distribution Canadian Jews had almost always been a part of Anglo-Canada and not of French Canada. The main occupation of urban Anglo-Canadians before 1850 was trading. After that time manufacturing and communications also became important.[42] These, of course, were precisely the occupations in which Jews were experienced. Agriculture, the main occupation of French Canadians throughout most of the nineteenth century, was almost unknown to contemporary Jews. A totally different occupational structure by itself would have created a distance between Jews and French. But some scholars claim that part of the tragedy of the British conquest and the suppression of the Rebellion of 1837 for French Canadians was that their own middle class was eliminated and replaced with an English and Jewish one.[43] If, indeed, this occurred, not only distance but resentment was inevitable.

The first fur traders working out of Montreal after 1763 were Scottish, English, and "some Jews."[44] Aaron Hart and Henry Joseph both founded their fortunes on the fur trade. The import-export trade was a common Jewish enterprise in Montreal and Toronto at a somewhat later period. It was a natural undertaking for Jews, few of whom were more than one or two generations removed from their European roots and who

Notman

Mansion of bachelor Jesse Joseph, pictured here some years after his death

Jesse Joseph (1817–1904)

Notman

Mortimer Davis (1866–1920)

Notman

Home of Mortimer Davis and his family at the turn of the century

Notman

therefore usually had relatives in other countries and often spoke other languages. In Montreal, Alexander Levy was an importer and retailer of cut glass, china, and Sheffield plate in the mid-nineteenth century; the Schwobs were jewelers and diamond merchants with business connections in Europe; John Levey was an importer and processor of tobacco. Among those in the import-export trade in the 1870s was Meldola De Sola, who, before he succeeded to his father's rabbinical post, worked as a broker and commission merchant. In Toronto the hardware firm of Lewis Samuel and his family utilized connections in England from the mid-nineteenth century until after World War I.[45]

Although banking would quickly become an exclusive preserve of gentile Anglo-Canadians, in the early nineteenth century Jews participated as well. Among the forty-three petitioners in 1817 for a charter for the Bank of Montreal, the first in Canada, were a few French Canadians and three Jews, David David, Henry Joseph, and M[oses] J[udah] Hays. Considering the small number of Jews in Montreal at the time, three represented significant involvement. David was a member of the board of directors of the bank for some years. Other Jews who participated in early Canadian banking enterprises were Jacob Henry Joseph and Abraham Joseph, sons of the fur trader of Berthier, Henry Joseph, and Samuel and Abraham Nordheimer of Toronto.[46]

Considerably more significant than their role in banking was the part played by a few Jews in the development of public utilities and communications in nineteenth-century Canada. Jews were instrumental in the establishment of Canadian telegraph and shipping companies, the Montreal street railway, the Montreal Gas Company, and the Quebec Electric Light Company. Except for the Jews, these companies were entirely owned and managed by Anglo-Canadians as were the large business and trade associations. The Montreal Committee of Trade was founded in 1829 with twelve gentile Anglo-Canadian members and one Jewish, but no French Canadians.[47]

By way of contrast, the free professions were occupied during the early years in Quebec largely by French Canadians, whose educational institutions discouraged careers in business or manufacturing but prepared students well for law, medicine, and the priesthood. Jews, on the other hand, usually came to Canada with some business experience. Moreover, most of them were immigrants. The professions, because of the training required, are not generally first generation occupations. There were a few early Jewish lawyers in Montreal, such as Aaron Philip

Hart, Gershom Joseph, and the notary, Lewis Alexander Hart. Dr. Aaron Hart David and his son-in-law, Dr. David Alexander Hart, were two early Montreal physicians. But most Jews in these years refrained from entering the professions, perhaps in part because they were considered to be the preserve of the French in Quebec.[48] In the latter years of the period under review Jews followed Anglo-Canadians somewhat less closely with regard to occupational distribution than they had earlier. When Jews and French Canadians pursued similar occupations, however, tension resulted.

Except for the recession in 1907–08, which Canada suffered along with the United States, the years from 1896 to World War I were, on the whole, boom years. Quebec, however, was less prosperous than Ontario, and, except for Montreal, it industrialized rather slowly. In the second decade of the twentieth century the pace quickened in Quebec, but the province still lagged behind her more prosperous neighbor. The economy of Montreal flourished more than that of the rest of the province of Quebec. The city was the chief export and distribution center of British North America, and its economy was closely tied to that of the country as a whole. Immigrants were attracted by the opportunities that Montreal offered. There was little, however, to attract them to other locations in Quebec, especially for Jews, who would have had to face French Canadian antipathy and might have found shopkeeping uncomfortable. During the "Laurier years" French Canadians themselves were flocking to Montreal, where most became industrial laborers. So, too, did many Anglo-Canadians, particularly those who were new to the country. Increasingly, however, Anglo-Canadians came to occupy the skilled positions and French Canadians, the unskilled; Anglo-Canadians, the managerial and responsible positions, French Canadians, the positions of lower status.[49]

Jews in these years were engaged in both skilled and unskilled labor as well as in trade. As unskilled laborers they worked in the railroad shops, in shipbuilding, and as longshoremen; their fellow workers were often French Canadians. The highest concentration of Jewish artisans was to be found in all branches of the clothing industry and in tobacco processing. In the needle trades many of the other workers were French-Canadians. Because Jews unionized more quickly than did their co-workers, employers frequently played off members of the two groups against each other as a means of keeping labor strife down. Jewish employers in the needle trades as well as gentiles in other industries played this game. French-Canadian employers, on the other hand, generally refused altogether to employ either Jews or Anglo-Canadians in their shops. Those who tried to do so experienced considerable pressure from nationalists.[50]

Large chain and department stores, like heavy industry in Canada, were mostly controlled by Anglo-Canadians, many of them of Scottish origin. On the other hand, petty trade was largely neglected by Anglo-Canadians, at least in Quebec. There, small business was left to French Canadians—who themselves, from Laurier to Bourassa, acknowledged their inferiority in large-scale business and trade. Many professed this weakness to be a virtue that bespoke the French Canadians' lack of interest in progress and material matters. Small enterprises seemed to suit family-oriented French Canadians well.[51]

But small family businesses were precisely those that Jews entered easily and successfully. Little capital was required to get started and not much experience. Moreover, many Jews had conducted such businesses in Europe. Jews, like other eastern and southern Europeans, were accustomed to a low standard of living. They were thus in a position to undersell Canadians used to living better and less skilled in the kind of cutthroat tactics that had been necessary for staying alive in eastern Europe. Around the turn of the century peddling, pawnbroking, and secondhand clothing shops were taken over by Jews in Montreal (and in Toronto), becoming near Jewish monopolies.[52]

Late in the period under review considerable resentment arose among French Canadians. Some became obsessed with the economic successes of Jews, usually exaggerated, allegedly achieved by elbowing aside unaggressive French Canadians. People spoke more often of the power of "Jewish finance,"[53] of the ability of Jews "to realize gain ... from the folly of others."[54] The natural friction created by the proprietor-customer relationship plus that of small business competitors contributed to the mutual dislike of the two groups and to a distorted view of Jewish economic power.[55]

Occasionally such friction caused political reverberations. In an effort to minimize Jewish competition, a special tax was levied on Jewish peddlers in Montreal and Quebec in 1892. A number of Jews found themselves out of work. In 1909 Montreal passed an early closing ordinance, which worked to the special disadvantage of Jews. All shops had to close Sundays. Because of the Sabbath, Jews closed early on Fridays and all day Saturdays. When forced to close early on weekdays, as well, they found it difficult to compete with Christian merchants. Later in the century, after the close of the period under review, this harassment blossomed into a full-fledged attempt to boycott Jewish businesses in Quebec under the slogan "Achat chez nous!"[56]

In the turn-of-the-century years a few Montreal Jews operated large businesses. Jews were still prominent proprietors in the tobacco business and the import-export trade; and they now became proprietors in the garment industry, as well, in Toronto, Montreal, and later in Winnipeg. In the professions there were now engineers, such as Charles Brandeis and Walter Joseph in Montreal. There were a few Jewish lawyers and some Jews in the medical professions, although Quebec did not graduate its first Jewish nurse until the last year of the period under review. A few Jews also participated in "big business," although their number actually declined during the period. After 1890 few, if any, large Canadian corporations ever nominated a Jew to their board of directors. In general, Canadian Jews were under-represented throughout the period, both in the professions and in big business. Those who did succeed in those areas were generally well Anglified. They were, in the parlance of a later day, token Jews.[57]

Some aspects of Jewish economic life, then, were shared with both French and Anglo-Canadians. For the most part, to the extent that their careers paralleled those of French Canadians, friction developed because of the clash of interests. Unquestionably Jews in Canada as elsewhere in the West aspired to the economic position of prosperous Anglo-Canadians. With their middle-class ethos and urban habits few Jews saw themselves as permanent members of the proletariat. Increasingly during this period Jews attempted to enter those areas of the economy dominated by Anglo-Canadians, who, in turn, allowed some Jews to enter "their" fields of endeavor and abandoned other areas to them. But they also set limits to the degree of Jewish penetration they would permit. French Canadians had little control over the economy and saw Jews enter many fields that were once theirs. Often their anger at their subservience was expressed as anti-Jewish resentment. The nationalists were genuinely troubled by Jewish competition. Although Jews suffered less friction with Anglo-Canadians than with French in the economic sphere, this was one area in which they had some difficulty with both groups.

Social Coexistence and Communal Cooperation

Because Jews and Anglo-Canadian gentiles often engaged in similar occupations, lived in proximity to each other, and spoke the same language, there developed between them fairly extensive social relationships. There were other reasons why Jews were acceptable social companions to the English in the early years of the period. For one thing, there were at the time few enough English speakers in Montreal and other towns of Lower Canada; moreover, any frontier society tends not to have firm social boundaries. Thus, people were not likely to snub anyone at all desirable; indeed, Jewish social and political success in the American and Canadian West demonstrates the possibilities for Jews in such an environment. It is no accident that the first Jewish mayor of a large Canadian town was Lumley Franklin of Victoria, elected in 1866, and that the first Jewish member of the Dominion Parliament, Henry Nathan, was also elected from Victoria some five years later. In Toronto and Montreal Jews were most readily accepted by gentiles during the earliest years of British control, before society became stratified. In addition, they rapidly accumulated wealth; and they were generally literate, with at least enough knowledge of Hebrew to read the prayers, among the most cultured people in that rough-and-ready society.

Early Anglo-Montreal exhibited many of the features of a frontier garrison town. Doubtless many of its British residents were of the semi-disreputable sort that one would expect to find in a newly conquered area. If Jews were outcasts because of their religion, others were outcasts for other reasons and not inclined to reject Jews as associates. As the years went by and as the numbers of Anglo-Canadians grew, some of the early intimacy was lost. Nevertheless, a great deal remained.

Jews are said to have participated in many British and Anglo-Canadian social institutions in Canada in the first century of British control. Abraham Joseph of Quebec was a member of the St. George's Society. In Montreal, Jews belonged to the St. Andrew's Society and to the Curling, Beaver, Whist, and Hunt clubs in the first half of the nineteenth century. As was the case elsewhere, Jews in Canada were active in the Masonic movement. One of the first Jews in the country, Chapman Abrahams, who died in 1783, was a Freemason. In 1838 Theodore Hart and Jacob Henry Joseph were inducted into St. Paul's Masonic Lodge just before they left to serve with the militia forces fighting the rebels.[58]

Late in the period under review almost every kind of social and welfare group in Montreal became segregated according to language and religion. Almost no private or communal institutions attempted to include the general population. Hospitals, clubs, fraternal organizations, sports clubs, and educational institutions were maintained either for Catholics or for Protestants, but not for both. A few organizations even distinguished between French and Irish Catholics. Jews developed many of their own institutions in this period, including synagogues, lodges, and unions. There were not yet Jewish schools or a Jewish hospital, however, and some Jews continued to participate in gentile cultural activities. They also continued to join non-Jewish organizations and societies, almost all of them Protestant Anglo-Canadian.

In sports activities in these years Jews joined in with the Anglo-Canadians. One of the most popular recreations of the day was snow-shoeing, and most of the clubs in the province of Quebec were either for English Protestants or French Catholics. Jews who participated in the sport belonged to Anglo-Canadian clubs. The oldest one in Montreal was the Montreal Snowshoe Club, and over the years a number of Jews joined. In Quebec, Jews were members of the Anglo-Canadian Quebec Snowshoe Club. Other sports associations were similarly confessional. The Montreal Amateur Athletic Association was entirely Anglo-Protestant at the turn of the century except for its few Jewish members, such as world skating champion, Louis Rubenstein. Rubenstein also was a member of the Anglo-Canadian Montreal Bicycle Club.[59]

Strict divisions were maintained in charitable and welfare activities in Montreal as well. Protestants were sent to Catholic hospitals only in extreme emergencies. The same was true of Catholics and Protestant hospitals. Since Jews did not open their own hospital in Montreal until 1934, they had to be entrusted either to Protestants or to Catholics for care. Almost always they turned to Protestant hospitals, which took them in. In 1891 a confessional survey of all Montreal institutions was taken. Only the Catholic Hôtel Dieu housed a Jewish patient, a rare occurrence. Jews ordinarily used the Montreal General Hospital, the Royal Victoria Hospital, the Mackay Institute for the Deaf, Dumb, and Blind, the Verdun Asylum for the Insane, and other Protestant healing institutions. They felt particularly attached to the Montreal General Hospital, where a number of Jews served on the Board of Governors over the years and donated large sums of money. Some Jews were also active in support of the Royal Victoria Hospital, the Western Hospital, the Protestant Home for Incurables, and the Verdun Asylum. Only one Catholic hospital, the Notre Dame, seems to have enlisted Jewish support during the period, and Mrs. Meldola De Sola was quite active in volunteer work for that institution.[60]

In children's aid work, orphan care, and juvenile rehabilitation Jews also teamed up with Protestants. The Boys' Farm at Shawbridge was opened in 1910 for Protestant delinquents. By 1914 it housed, in addition to those for whom it had been built, some thirty "Hebrew boys."[61] Lyon Cohen was a trustee of the Farm and secured a subvention for it from Jewish charities. Even animals were helped confessionally during the period in Montreal. The executive committee of the SPCA included many Protestants, Jesse Joseph, and his nephew, Rabbi Meldola De Sola. On occasion Rabbi De Sola wrote one of his anonymous newspaper letters on behalf of the Society's charges. (In Toronto, Rabbi Solomon Jacobs served as governor of the Humane Society in the same period.)[62]

In social and fraternal organizatons there was, of course, the same confessional division found in less intimate circles. Here, too, if Jews gained admittance to any non-Jewish groups, it was to those of Anglo-Canadian Protestants. Fraternal organizations such as the Masons, the Select Knights, the Order of Foresters, the Maccabees, the Knights of Pythias, and the Ancient Order of United Workmen accepted some Jews at the turn of the century. Jewish women joined the National Council of Women and the Imperial Order, Daughters of the Empire. In Quebec an all-Jewish chapter of the Daughters of the Empire was founded in 1914, named after Lord Reading, the Jew who had become lord chief justice of Great Britain.[63]

More exclusive were the social clubs for the wealthy and privileged. In Montreal these clubs included a very few French-Canadian members by the latter years of the period under review. In general, however, they were the preserve of the Anglo-Canadian establishment. Those few Jews who were very wealthy and had achieved the highest status in Montreal's business community were also admitted. Mortimer Davis was a member of the Mount Royal Club, the St. James Club, the Montreal Hunt Club, the Montreal Jockey Club, the Forest and Stream Club, the Royal St. Lawrence Yacht Club, and the Mt. Bruno Country Club. He served as a director of both the Royal Montreal Golf Club and the Montreal Horticultural and Fruit Growers' Association. Gershom De Sola, bachelor brother of Rabbi Meldola, was a member of the Cosmopolitan Club and a director of the St. James Club. Bendix A. Boas belonged to the City Club. There were others as well.[64]

The social integration of Jews and Anglo-Canadians did not all take place within the confines of a club or lodge. In the earliest years of the period most contacts were less formal and some were quite intimate. It has been said that eighteenth-century Montreal Jews, "aside from their distinctive religion, ... associated freely and on equal terms with their English and Protestant fellows."[65] When the widow of Aaron Hart moved to Montreal after his death in 1800, she is reported to have moved in high English mercantile and military circles. Diary excerpts from the Joseph family indicate extensive social intercourse with non-Jews, very few of them French Canadians. Some Jews in the early years integrated into Anglo-Canadian society so thoroughly that they felt little need to associate with fellow Jews. Aaron Hart himself never joined the Montreal congregation, although Trois Rivières was only ninety miles from Montreal, and he was an observant Jew. Later synagogue records indicate that other Jews also neglected to affiliate, although at times they sought the congregation's services. In 1863, when the Young Men's Hebrew Benevolent Society was organized, one of its goals was to help young Jewish men of Montreal get to know each other. Since there were only 403 Jews in the city at the time, it must be assumed that some associated but little with coreligionists. In later years, as the number of Jews increased and social boundaries grew more rigid, socializing between Jews and Protestants. in homes became rather more limited in both Toronto and Montreal. Although such visits did not cease altogether, it was now only the very few "acceptable" Jews who were included. Among the token Jewish guests at a ball given for the visiting Prince of Wales in 1890 was David A. Ansell. (Ironically, the Prince had many Jewish friends in England.) Some years later, when the duke of Cornwall and York (the future George V) and the duchess visited Montreal, Rabbi and Mrs. De Sola were among those presented to him.[66]

In contrast to the closeness that existed between many Jews and some Anglo-Canadians, at least during the early years of the period under review, there was a noticeable lack of social contact between Jews and French Canadians throughout. As noted previously, it was not easy for any "foreigner" to penetrate French-Canadian society. Italians and Poles, although Roman Catholics, more often than not also assimilated into Anglo-Canadian society. Jews were only somewhat more unacceptable than others. Moreover, the gap was not altogether unbridgeable. English and French sources close to the period, as well as the contemporary diaries of Samuel David and Abraham Joseph, noted that in the late eighteenth and early nineteenth centuries Aaron Hart's two sons, Benjamin and Ezekiel, and David and Joseph were all well accepted by both French and English gentiles. Since Jews and French Canadians lived markedly different kinds of lives, however, and often did not understand each other's language, such relationships probably had little chance to develop. The proprietor-customer relationship is not the sort to engender warm personal friendships either. The argument is largely one from silence. Surviving diaries, scrapbooks, and letters from the period offer little evidence that much social intercourse between Jews and French Canadians took place. Rather, most Jews were wary of French Canadians, even in the mid-nineteenth century, long before any large-scale immigration of Jews took place, as the words of Alexander Levy at the time of the Mortara Affair, quoted earlier, plainly show.[67]

Cultural Affiliation

Jews were not much in evidence in the cultural affairs of Anglo-Canada during the first century and a half of Jewish settlement in the country, except in Montreal. There, however, because of the activities of a few individuals, most notably Rabbi Abraham De Sola and the painter, William Raphael, they were rather better woven into the cultural and intellectual fabric, at least in the first three-quarters of the nineteenth century, than into the social. But however little part they played in it, the intellectual and cultural world for almost all Jews was that of Anglo-Canada. Jews did not participate in French cultural and intellectual affairs at all.

Dr. Aaron Hart David was an important figure in the early development of science and medicine in Canada. He served for a time as president of the Montreal Natural History Society and as general secretary of the Canadian Medical Association. He was also a cofounder of the *Canada Medical Journal.* David was longtime dean of the medical faculty at the (Anglican) Bishop's College in Lennoxville, Quebec. At Bishop's one of his colleagues between 1844 and 1854 was the converted Jew, Isaac Hellmuth, professor of Hebrew and rabbinics.[68]

Between his arrival in Canada in 1847 and his death thirty-five years later, Rabbi Abraham De Sola was the intellectual giant of Canadian Jewry and perhaps of all Montreal. The Montreal *Gazette* boasted of De Sola's identification

> with all movements tending to promote the moral and intellectual welfare of our people, [and his] . . . distinguished position in the principal university of the Dominion, [which have] . . . achieved for him . . . a reputation extending over the whole continent, and reaching the scholars of many countries.[69]

There was almost no subject on which De Sola did not publish or lecture. He wrote on the Jews of Poland, France, and Persia, cosmography, the Jewish calendar, and a host of other topics, including Spanish literature. The rabbi appeared at one time or another before almost every cultural and scholarly group in the English-speaking community in Montreal: the Mercantile Library Association, the Mechanics Institute, the Young Men's Christian Association of St. George's Church, the Literary Club, and the Natural History Society, of which he served as president for a time. He was offered a chair in Hebrew at Montreal Presbyterian College but declined; he was appointed professor of Hebrew and Oriental languages at McGill, a post he held for many years, as well as professor of Spanish literature at the same institution. His contacts at McGill included the foremost intellectuals of the period.[70]

Partly because of De Sola, McGill was from its earliest days the favored university of Canadian Jews. Other schools had religious tests— King's College (later the University of Toronto) until 1850, Queen's College in Kingston, until the twentieth century. But at the opening of McGill, Anglican Bishop Jacob Mountain declared that all offices were to be "open either to Protestants or Roman Catholics, and [that] students of all denominations would be permitted to attend."[71] De Sola's appointment to the faculty was evidence that Jews were to be permitted to teach as well.[72]

Besides its nonsectarian credo, the importance given to Hebrew studies at the university and the fact that Hebrew was taught by a rabbi also served to endear McGill to contemporary Jews. Hebraic studies were offered in many North American universities in the nineteenth century, although they were almost always taught by Christians to Christian students. Occasionally, as was the case at Harvard in the eighteenth century or at Bishop's College in Quebec and at King's College in Toronto in De Sola's time, they were taught by converted Jews.[73] Often such studies took on anti-Jewish overtones, with professors preaching the superiority of Christianity over the religion of the Hebrews. At McGill, however, Hebrew was taught by an outspokenly traditional Jew for some thirty years to both Jews and Christians.

In 1858 the university awarded to Rabbi De Sola an honorary LL.D., probably the first such degree given to a professing Jew in the English-speaking world. De Sola explained the honor as a testament to

the spirit of enlightened liberality which has activated the Governors and Faculties of McGill College, . . . evidencing the cheering fact that in Montreal at least there is no bar, unless our own want of self-respect erect it, to prevent the Israelite from reaching the goal which all right thinking men aspire to attain.[74]

Because of Rabbi De Sola, Jews in general, in Montreal and even elsewhere in Canada, acquired an undeserved reputation among Anglo-Canadians similar to that which they enjoyed in England and the United States, as the bearers of high culture. To a certain degree they retained that reputation even after his death. The rabbi had chosen to be "first in a barbarian village rather than second in Rome"; and the "barbarians" were appreciative. De Sola had the bearing of an ancient high priest. His gentile contemporaries saw in him "a gentleman of high intellectual powers." They recognized that "few ... men of Montreal ... centre[d] in themselves more ... sound scholarship."[75] Mary Ellen Ross probably had in mind both De Sola and the Rothschilds ("Baron de Schwartz-kind") when she asserted with admiration and self-deprecation that "the Jews are the only people ... who know anything about the fine arts."[76] With De Sola's "decease the *literati* of Canada felt that they had been bereft of one of their brightest luminaries."[77]

Not quite all the citizens of Montreal were impressed with Rabbi De Sola, however. Nor was it possible for a Jew to succeed in every circle in that bilingual city. To French Canadians the rabbi was a non-entity, for all his achievements; and no glory accrued to his fellow Jews because of his accomplishments. In all his years in Montreal De Sola does not seem to have addressed even one French-Canadian group. Nor did he participate in those few intellectual and cultural ventures that united French and English. For example, the Institut Canadien, founded in 1844, had both French and Anglo-Canadian members and was probably the most exciting intellectual forum in Montreal. De Sola was not among its members. Perhaps he shied away from an institution associated with liberalism and anticlericalism, especially in his first years in Montreal. It is more likely, however, that he was not invited. The French-Canadian press apparently never mentioned De Sola at all, although his fame had spread in the United States and England as well as at home. And he was sufficiently well known in France for the Jewish press of that country to take occasional notice of him. He belonged to the "Jewish North Atlantic Triangle," and he belonged to Anglo-Canada. But he could never cross the barrier into French Canada.[78]

At the turn of the century some increased Jewish participation in Anglo-Canadian intellectual and cultural affairs was evident. As earlier, Montreal remained the center of such activity; there was, however, no one shining star. Rabbi Meldola De Sola did not have his father's stature, although he, too, circulated widely in Montreal, Toronto, and elsewhere. In Montreal he lectured for the Somerville Free Lectures of the Natural History Society, otherwise given only by Protestant Anglo-Canadians. Other Jews active in Anglo-Canadian cultural circles were Feodor Boas and B. Marcuse, who were officers of the Montreal Freethought Club in the 1890s. There were no French Canadians in that group. Gerald Ephraim Hart was prominent in Canadian numismatics and also president of the Society for Historical Studies in Montreal, another Anglo-Canadian group. Joseph S. Leo was the first president of the Canadian Chess Association. Yiddish-speaking immigrants in these years attended the English theater. Elsewhere in Canada Jews were also assimilating to Anglo-Canadian culture. There is no indication that they took even the slightest interest in French cultural affairs.[79]

In Montreal and Quebec during the latter years of the period under review Jews enrolled at McGill in steadily increasing numbers. A few Jews came to occupy senior teaching positions, although none commanded the same attention and respect as Rabbi De Sola in the earlier period, when Jews were more of a rarity. Like Rabbi Nathan Gordon, some Jews were active in the university's learned societies, such as the McGill Oriental Society.[80]

That Jews continued to favor McGill was due not only to its long tradition of tolerance, but also to the absence of attractive alternatives. In 1903, of 559 teachers at Roman Catholic colleges in Quebec, all but 32 were clerics. Education at those institutions was avowedly sectarian. André Siegfried asserted that even at Laval University, the province's largest Catholic institution of higher learning,

> the Church makes a special point of watching over the students entrusted to her care. . . . She is conscious to the full of the strength of the imprint left upon the young men who to-morrow will be the pilots of their race, priests entrusted with the charge of parishes, physicians "co-operating with the priests in works of charity," lawyers, journalists, politicians.[81]

A concomitant of such sectarian education was the strong spirit of antisemitism that seemed to permeate Laval and other Catholic institutions. Such was especially the case in the second decade of the twentieth century.[82]

Despite the antagonistic atmosphere, beginning in 1894 some Jews did enroll at Laval, mostly prospective lawyers, appreciative of the thorough training in law and of the opportunity to gain experience in using French in legal work. Also, since most universities in North America harbored people with antisemitic tendencies during these years, Jews who went to Laval no doubt considered it worse than Anglo-Canadian institutions only in degree. The important thing was to get a university education, which was considered the best way to bring an end to prejudice. In 1913 Mortimer B. Davis endowed a chair at Laval, probably in the hope of neutralizing the anti-Jewish animus of many of the students and faculty.[83]

Religious Affinities

Relations between Jews and Anglo-Canadians in Montreal, at least, were sufficiently close during much of the period under review for Jews to be able to turn to their gentile neighbors even for their religious needs. For more than thirty-five years in the mid-nineteenth century Mr. Fitts, the baker, prepared the Passover matzoth or unleavened bread "for our friends of the Jewish persuasion."[84] Fitts considered it a testimonial to his reliability that he was entrusted with the task, no doubt under close supervision. By 1854, members of the Spanish and Portuguese Synagogue felt so much at home with Protestant Anglo-Canadians that they sought to rest near them for all eternity in the Protestant Mount Royal Cemetery. When advised by Rabbi De Sola that burial in a Christian cemetery was contrary to Jewish law, they agreed to purchase land adjacent to the Protestant cemetery but not in it. Half a century later the Reformers of Temple Emanu-El had fewer inhibitions. After prolonged negotiations, the Temple arranged in 1900 for its members to be interred in Mount Royal.[85]

Intimate social contact could lead, on occasion, to a falling away from the traditional faith. And, indeed, some Jews married gentiles over the years, although more in the early part of the period under review, when there were few Jews in Canada and the choice of Jewish partners was very limited. Not surprisingly most such marriages were contracted with Anglo-Canadian Protestants. The first marriage register in Montreal, that of the Reverend Dr. Delisle, the third Protestant clergyman to officiate in the city, records "very many intermarriages" involving people of all faiths.[86] Among them was that of Myer Solomons to Sarah Combs in 1773. A scandalous affair, at least for that day, involved the intermarriage of Moses Hart, the freethinking black sheep of Aaron Hart's sons. Hart was married in 1799 to his cousin, Sarah Judah. After bearing him three children, Sarah decided she could no longer tolerate her husband's playboy temperament and left him. There was a reconciliation, but in 1814 she left him a second time. Hart then married the widow of Peter Brown, Mary McCarthy Brown. He fathered six additional children, some of whom married French Catholics and others, Anglo-Canadian Protestants.[87]

Apostasy unconnected with intermarriage, despite the closeness of Jewish-Protestant social relationships in the early years, was relatively uncommon. The celebrated case of Charles Freshman stands out because of its rarity. It is significant, however, that Freshman wavered on the brink of conversion for some time, a fact that apparently was widely known among all groups in Quebec. And yet it was only Protestant clergymen who showed an interest in Freshman, visited him, and encouraged him in his new faith. Roman Catholics exhibited no concern for the rabbi's soul.[88]

Conversion and intermarriage were not one-way streets in the early years of the period under review. George Barnard of Montreal applied to Rabbi De Sola in 1850 "to become a member of the only true Religious Faith."[89] Over the years the rabbi received other such requests, although his traditional outlook led him to discourage would-be converts. Apparently, however, there was more openness to the mates of Jewish partners, or, at least, to the children of such unions. Alexander Hart and Mary-Ann Douglas married and had two daughters. Both were considered Jewish and married Jews.[90]

Some Jews did marry French-Canadian Catholics in the early years of the period, and their descendants succeeded in becoming part of the French-Canadian community. The tombstones in the Catholic cemetery of Trois Rivières are testimony to the Harts and Judahs who became French Catholics. Samuel Jacobs, an Alsatian Jew who came to Canada in 1759 as a fur trader, never joined the Montreal Jewish congregation. He married a French Canadian, and his children, including one named Jean-Baptiste Jacobs, were all Catholics. Ezekiel Solomons, on the other hand, married a French Catholic but retained his ties to the Jewish community. Although, as noted, Jewish women have traditionally been more reluctant to intermarry than men, there is at least one recorded case of a Jewish woman who married a French Canadian during the early part of the period under review. The wife of Dr. Seraphim Gauthier, landlord of the young Wilfrid Laurier's family in Montreal, was Phoebe Lyons, the daughter of Lewis Lyons, a wholesale jeweler who had come to Canada from Manchester, England. Against her father's will, Phoebe ran off with Gauthier and upon marriage to him became a Catholic. Her parents finally made peace with their daughter's apostasy, although they themselves remained Jews and eventually returned to England.[91]

Clearly, then, it was possible for Jews to join the French-Canadian community, if they were willing to give up their faith. And yet, the careers of a few Jewish converts to Catholicism cast doubt even on that possibility. Judah Joseph, the brother of Henry Joseph, also emigrated from England to Berthier in the early years of Jewish settlement in Canada. Jewish sources barely mention him, although it is clear that he died young in England, some time after marrying a French Canadian and perhaps apostasizing. His descendants were French Catholics. Among them was Joseph Olivier Joseph, one of the men responsible for the 1870–74 reorganization of the St. Jean Baptiste Society, which subsequently became one of the most important vehicles of French-Canadian nationalism. Joseph Olivier's brother was Emile.[92]

Another Jew who became part of the French-Catholic community was Louis Marchand (né Levi Koopman). Marchand was born in Amsterdam. His father, a diamond merchant, had business interests all over Europe, including France, where he married off a daughter to Achille Fould, a member of one of France's foremost Jewish families and for a time minister of finance. The family also had interests in England, and it was to that country that the young Levi was sent for part of his education. As a youth Koopman also traveled to the United States to visit relatives in Charleston, South Carolina. After returning to Europe, Koopman lost the fortune bequeathed to him by his father. Like others he hoped to restore his fortunes in the New World and emigrated to Boston. From there he made his way to Montreal. After failing to find suitable employment in that city either, Koopman moved on to Saint-Mathias in 1828, where he became a clerk to a local French-Canadian businessman. That year he converted to Catholicism and in the same period changed his name to Marchand. Two years later Marchand married the daughter of a wealthy French Canadian. He returned to Montreal, where he engaged in business and politics, serving on the city council from 1851 to 1860. One of Marchand's grandsons, also named Louis, was married twice. His second wife was Patricia O'Leary, an Irish Catholic, who was the widow of Emile Joseph.[93] The connection may have been coincidence. It is not unlikely, however, that in the closed French-Canadian society, converted Jews acquired a status similar to that of the New Christians of medieval Spain. That is, one did not cease to be a Jew even after conversion.

In the latter years of the period under review there was relatively little intermarriage in the "whole Canadian community."[94] Although there are no entirely reliable statistics for the period before 1926, indications are that intermarriage was lowest in Quebec during these years and that Jews had the lowest rate of intermarriage of any group other than the Japanese. The increasing stratification and rigidity of the entire Canadian society over the years, and especially in Quebec, militated against appreciable intermarriage. And yet, the fears of Rabbi Meldola De Sola, that many Jews would intermarry and some become "genuine converts to Christianity," were not altogether unfounded. By 1931, the first census year for which figures are available, there were 384 Jewish converts to Christianity in Quebec, some of whom had doubtless been converted in Europe. Indeed, De Sola's own son and a niece married Protestants, although after his death and after the close of the period under review. Neither converted.[95]

Of the converts enumerated in 1931, 166 were Protestants and 156 Catholics. This would seem to indicate considerable acceptance of Jews among Catholics in Quebec. It must be remembered, however, that the province was overwhelmingly Catholic. Statistically, the likelihood of a Jew meeting and marrying a Catholic, the usual reason for conversion, was far greater than that of his meeting a Protestant. It is not known, moreover, whether Jewish converts to Catholicism in Quebec belonged to French or Irish congregations. Perhaps a more accurate sense of the willingness of Catholics to accept Judaism can be gained from the rate at which they converted to Judaism. In 1931 there were 263 Christian converts to Judaism in Canada. Of these only four were French Canadians, and of these four none resided in Quebec. As Olivar Asselin candidly asserted in 1911: "The Jew as a rule is further from the French than from the English in religious matters."[96]

The Political Arena

Limited though it was, the experience of Jews as Jews in the Canadian political arena during this period demonstrated their affiliation with Anglo-Canada, as did their involvement in other areas of the country's life. Jews were among the signers of the several petitions sent to King George III asking for the establishment of British law in Quebec (1763 and 1770) and later for an assembly with a guaranteed British majority (1773). Like other Britishers they sought the repeal of the Quebec Act, which had, in effect, granted the status of an established church to the Roman Catholic Church in Quebec. The only French who signed any of the petitions were Protestants. They owed their presence in Quebec to the British no less than did Jews, and they feared the reestablishment of Catholic hegemony with equal apprehension.[97]

A few Jews were elected or appointed to minor political offices in Montreal and elsewhere in Lower Canada during the first century of Jewish settlement, mostly in English constituencies. The one attempt to occupy a major office demonstrated in yet another way how Jews might gain acceptance among Anglo-Canadians but not among the French. Ezekiel Hart was elected to the Legislative Assembly of Lower Canada in 1807. This was the start of what has come to be known as "the Hart Affair."[98]

When Hart took the oath of office on the Hebrew Bible with head covered according to Jewish custom, he was immediately challenged. On 19 February 1808 the House voted not to allow him to take his seat. A month later Jewish residents of Lower Canada petitioned on Hart's behalf, but the House would not even read the petition. In the wake of the refusal to seat Hart, the governor, Sir James Craig, dissolved the House and called for new elections. Once again Hart was elected by the voters of Trois Rivières. When he came to take his seat on 10 April 1809 he had, however, apparently decided that his political career was more important than his religious scruples. This time he is reported to have taken the oath on the New Testament, head uncovered. The House again refused to seat him, now doubting the sincerity of his oath. Again dissolution and new elections followed. By this time both Hart and the voters of Trois Rivières had had enough of principle. Hart withdrew, and the electors chose one of his former opponents.[99]

The "Hart Affair" has been exhaustively discussed in almost every work that even touches on the history of the Jews in Canada.[100] None, however, has ever satisfactorily answered the question of how Hart's Jewishness came to be the focus of a struggle for power between French and Anglo-Canadians. Hart was elected by the voters of both communities, probably carrying a majority of both French and English votes. Hart, himself, claimed that "¾ of [his] . . . voters were Catholic." His main opponents for office, including the one finally seated, were Anglo-Canadians. Throughout the affair, the British government was of the opinion that Jews did not have the right to sit in a British legislature. Sir James Craig at first refused to intercede on Hart's behalf.[101] And yet, the affair was understood at the time and later, as well, as one involving French anti-Jewish sentiment and British acceptance of Jews.

To be sure, Ezekiel Hart was caught in the middle of a dispute not of his own making. It was not really about Jews at all, but rather, about control of the legislature. It was apparently not possible for the French to elect one of their own number to Hart's seat, but it was possible to cause a great deal of unpleasantness over that fact. Supporting Hart rather than a Christian Anglo-Canadian might well have been a way of expressing anti-English sentiment, of casting a protest vote; and then, after the election, Hart's presence in the House as an English-speaking member could easily be used as a stick with which to beat the English. They were, claimed the French-Canadian opposition, "Jew-lovers," protectors of the Antichrist, the traditional enemy of Christians, destroyers of the Christian character of Canada.

The affair brought to the surface dormant attitudes and prejudices. Led on by their chief newspaper, *Le Canadien,* French Canadians both in and out of the legislature verbalized the traditional hatred of Jews associated with medieval Christianity and with the *ancien régime.* Some Anglo-Canadians, most notably Hart's two political opponents, also supported the concept of the sacrosanct Christian character of the Lower Canada legislature.[102] But in the end it was both politically expedient and easier on the Protestant consciences of Anglo-Canadians to support Hart.

The most eminent French-Canadian historian of the mid-nineteenth century, François-Xavier Garneau, tried to turn the guilt for Hart's expulsion around, claiming that the "question of excluding the Jews . . . from the Assembly [arose] in imitation of English custom."[103] But that was surely not the impetus behind the fulminations of *Le Canadien* nor of the parliamentary maneuverings. Hart, himself, remarked that other than the attorney general, his opponents "were all Catholicks," whom he supposed "were led on by . . . their priests. . . ." All the Protestants in the House, on the other hand, "voted for . . . [his] case." Garneau's translator, Andrew Bell, was nearer to the mark than the historian. In a footnote to Garneau's presentation of the affair, Bell added:

Mr. Ezekiel Hart was a merchant in Three Rivers, a highly respectable man, but of English birth and a Jew; and being such, eminently obnoxious [to French Canadians], if only for his double "nationalité."[104]

The "Hart Affair" heightened a growing awareness among Jews that if they belonged at all in Canada, it was to the Anglo-Canadian community.

The affair really came to an end only in 1832, when royal assent was given to "An Act to Declare Persons Professing the Jewish Religion Entitled to All the Rights and Privileges of the Other Subjects of His Majesty in this Province" of Lower Canada (Act I, William IV, chapter 57). Although only a year earlier Samuel B. Hart of Trois Rivières was denied an appointment as magistrate because of his faith, this was a period when most Canadians had little interest in the very few Jews who lived among them. The act received the support of both French and Anglo-Canadians and came more than a quarter century ahead of full Jewish emancipation in the mother country. But the passions stirred up by the affair had not been extinguished, only dampened. They lay smouldering, waiting to be fanned in the future.[105] The "Hart Affair" and its aftermath were the major political events of nineteenth-century Canadian history for the Jewish community. Such momentous events as the Rebellion of 1837 and Confederation thirty years later touched Jews largely as individuals rather than as a group. These events, too, however, (more the first than the second) demonstrated the emerging pattern of Jewish political identification with Anglo-Canada.

The 1837 rebellion was not altogether a French-English conflict. There were people of both communities on both sides. The leader of the revolt in Lower Canada was Louis Joseph Papineau, who had among his followers a number of Anglo-Canadians. The leader of the coordinate rebellion in Upper Canada was an Anglo-Canadian, William Lyon Mackenzie. The Roman Catholic Church, fearing the radical ideas of Papineau and many of his followers and enjoying its privileged status under the Quebec Act, opposed the revolt. But the rebellion was directed at British authority in Canada.

With their British connections and growing fear of French Canadians, it is not surprising that the majority of Jews actively supported the crown. On the eve of the rebellion, when most Anglo-Canadian merchants no longer wished to have any contact with Papineau, he was still welcome at the home of Ezekiel Hart in Trois Rivières. But most Jews, like gentiles of the merchant class, eschewed his company. Abraham Joseph lived in the same rooming house as Papineau in Quebec in June 1837 and found him, "as far as his private conduct" went, to be "a good enough fellow." But he disliked Papineau's "usual abusive style" and confided to his diary that "respectable" people were almost all opposed to the rebel leader. When the rebellion did break out, it found Jews in the militia, a number of them with commissions. After a short time, moreover, it became clear that there was only one possible side for Jews, the side of British authority, (although a few, like Louis Marchand, remained in the rebel camp—in his case, perhaps, to mark his separation from the Jewish community). A group of extremist rebels in Lower Canada declared that "all Jews are to be strangled and their goods confiscated."[106] In Upper Canada, Mackenzie saw the establishment of an explicitly Christian government in Canada as a goal of the revolt; and he allowed himself to become known as an avowed antisemite. As would be the case in later years, as well, opposition to Jews and opposition to Britain went hand in hand. Abraham Joseph was at first reluctant to join the fray, having "no idea of going . . . where I stand a great chance of having my head broken." Soon, however, as the seriousness of the rebellion and its personal implications became clear to Joseph, he took his "first lesson in drilling" and then joined Daly's company of Royal Volunteers. Still, Joseph never enjoyed military life. He recorded in his diary on New Year's Eve 1837, while on guard and unable to join the holidaymaking, that "soldiering is very well, as long as a fellow has the good luck to hold a commission." Benjamin Hart of Trois Rivières was more enthusiastic about defending the crown and later unsuccessfully claimed a knighthood as reward for his services.[107]

After the rebellion most Jews remained identified with the Tory Party, some of them actively, for many years. As such they supported both Confederation and closer ties with Britain. One Jew, Mark Solomon of Toronto, was a delegate to the national convention that preceded Confederation in 1867. The only Jew to serve in the Dominion Parliament before World War I was a Conservative. David A. Ansell of Montreal held no office but was very active in party affairs, exercising all his "great energy in the good cause," as Sir John A. Macdonald, party leader and longtime prime minister, described him.[108] Some Jews knew that Macdonald himself was not altogether untainted by antisemitism. It is unlikely that Arthur Wellington Hart swallowed Macdonald's disingenuous reply to his inquiry regarding the lack of Jewish civil service appointees in Canada. (Macdonald wrote to Hart that he was "unaware of any prejudice" in the government service and assumed that "Jews as a body have taken . . . a wiser course in [voluntarily] avoiding the worries of political life.") In later years Gerald E. Hart angrily claimed that his father, Adolphus Mordecai, had been denied a judgeship in Trois Rivières only because "he was not a Catholic nor a french canadian [sic]." In the end, however, most Jews probably discounted the feelings and actions of Macdonald and others as current intellectual and social fashion. The "father of Confederation" stood for the stronger British connection, and that, after their experiences in Canada and elsewhere, was comfort enough to most Jews.[109]

Like other supporters of the Tories many Jews were disturbed by the "deplorable effrontery" of the Macdonald government during the railroad scandals of the early 1870s (the "Pacific Scandals") and relieved when Alexander Mackenzie's Liberals were swept into office in 1873 saving Canada from one of "the worst swindles."[110] But the scandals were soon forgotten, and Jews like others returned to their traditional loyalties. It was indicative of the Jewish political orientation that in 1877 Rabbi De Sola was invited to join the militant Protestant Defense Alliance, and that the Alliance was prepared to change both its name and its constitution in order to include him. In later years Solomon Vineberg, Joseph H. Jacobs, Mrs. Meldola De Sola, and Mrs. Joseph S. Leo of Montreal were all active in Conservative Party affairs. Jacobs served as honorary secretary of the committee that raised money to erect the Sir John A. Macdonald monument in Montreal, which the governor-general, Lord Aberdeen, unveiled in 1895.[111]

By the turn of the century both Jews and French Canadians in Quebec were moving into the Liberal camp. Bendix A. Boas of Montreal had campaigned hard for Laurier in 1896; Lyon Cohen was very active in the Montreal Reform Club and otherwise in Liberal Party affairs. Within a short time Jews were stampeding into the Liberal ranks except in Ontario, where the Tories continued to reign supreme. There Jews remained loyal to the Conservatives, at least at the provincial level. French Canadians deserted the Tories for a number of reasons, of which the execution of Louis Riel in 1885 was symbolically the most important. Jews transferred their allegiance along with other non-British, non-French immigrant groups, because Liberal economic and immigration policies were more congenial to them and because of a growing conviction that the Conservatives in Quebec and federally were allied with anti-semites. Jews exerted only negligible influence in the Liberal Party, however, even long after the period under review. The first Jewish Liberals to enter the Dominion Parliament were Samuel W. Jacobs, elected from Montreal in 1917, and Samuel Factor, elected from Toronto in 1930. Both men represented gerrymandered ridings with overwhelmingly Jewish populations. It was a given of eastern Canadian politics in the twentieth century that non-Jews would not vote for Jews. In Parliament, Jacobs and Factor occupied a position not dissimilar to that of the court Jews of a bygone age, serving "their fellow believers by procuring from the powers that be a variety of [small] favors intended to be of benefit to most of our important institutions."[112] Neither was able to move the government on the one matter of great importance to Jews in the 1920s and 1930s, open immigration. On one occasion Jacobs threatened to bolt the Liberals and join any party that would come out in favor of immigration. In fact, however, already by the last decades of the period under review neither party was particularly open to Jewish concerns. Again it was Gerald E. Hart who offered the most biting postscript to Jewish political impotence during the period and especially to the lack of political success of his own family:

> Had they been traitors or rebels or even accused of a crime, they would probably have been rewarded with a knighthood, . . . such as [has] . . . been conferred on French Canadians. . . . They were not allowed to be politicians, probably from fear that their transcendent abilities and high education would have displaced several of the eminent semi-educated french canadian [sic] politicians.[113]

Life Styles

A concomitant of the linguistic, economic, demographic, and political affinities of Jews and Anglo-Canadians during the period was increasing similarity of values and style of life. During these years in Canada— and everywhere else that Jewish immigrants settled—their "moral, social and spiritual conceptions" underwent a "vast change."[114] To the extent that Jews correctly perceived Anglo-Canada and were in a position to alter ancient custom, they used Anglo-Canada and not French Canada as a model for change.

In terms of their religious ethos Canadian Jews had much in common with Anglo-Canadians in the early years of their settlement in Canada, a closeness similar to that of Judaism with British and American Protestantism, as noted previously. In general, modern Jews and classical Judaism have been everywhere nearer in orientation to the this-worldly "Protestant ethic" than to Catholic otherworldliness. In 1853 the historian Aldophus Mordecai Hart observed that it had been the spirit of Protestantism and of the Hebrew Bible that had really conquered Canada.[115] Canadian gentiles, for the most part agreed, although the French and the English each placed a different value on the accomplishment. Thoughout the nineteenth century the Hebrew Bible remained dear to the hearts of Anglo-Canadians, not only as a historical record, but as a living document. In mid-century, writers such as Charles Heavysege wrote extensively about biblical themes that were familiar to their readers, who in turn could relate those themes to contemporary experiences. Half a century later many Canadian Protestants were in agreement with the assertion of James S. Woodsworth that "in our own day . . . when ancient prejudices and hereditary hatreds are being overcome . . . when . . . the brotherhood of man is becoming an ideal," the "attitude of the Protestant churches to the Catholic churches and to the Jewish synagogues" should be one of openness and cooperation.[116]

The closeness of Jews to Anglo-Canadian Protestantism was reinforced over the years by the modification of Jewish custom according to the norms of Christianity, a process that occurred in almost all Western countries. Carroll Ryan, the Irish-Catholic editor of the Canadian *Jewish Times,* claimed in 1901 that "the conservative atmosphere of the country" had helped Canadian Jews to maintain their orthodoxy.[117] This was the case to a certain extent, although over the years there was a considerable falling away from traditional Jewish values and practice. The diaries of Samuel David and Abraham Joseph indicate that already in the early decades of the nineteenth century Canadian Jews were broadly latitudinarian in their practices. On 6 April 1803, for example, David wrote in his diary: "A fine clear Cold Morning . . . Began Trimming the Trees in the Orchard. Pesack [Passover]." On Sabbath days Joseph recorded his prayers as one of many activities, including the conduct of business. James S. Woodsworth, the Protestant minister and social and political reformer from Winnipeg, thought young Canadian Jews in the first decade of the twentieth century, most of them eastern European immigrants and their children, to be "cutting loose from the old moorings and venturing forth on unknown seas."[118] Rabbi Meldola De Sola felt that many of his own congregants were "indifferent . . . to the religious education of their children," more interested in "music, painting, drawing, and dancing . . . [than in] Hebrew and religious knowledge."[119] Alexander Harkavy had earlier found Montreal Jews extraordinarily ignorant of Judaism and delinquent in their observances.[120] In 1897 Rabbi Isidore Myers of Shaar Hashomayim Synagogue in Montreal was outraged at being served an unkosher meal at the Montefiore Club. The incident apparently hastened the rabbi's departure from the city. A decade later the Reform Temple Emanu-El served its own members such a meal at an official function.[121]

Not only did personal observance of Judaism weaken, but synogogue ritual altered according to contemporary fashion as well. In Montreal's Temple Emanu-El, where the "more progressive members of the community" worshiped, congregants doffed their hats during prayer, men and women sat together, gentiles sang in the choir, and by 1893 the Temple had introduced a Thanksgiving Day service. By 1911 a presumably Protestant correspondent from the *Daily Witness* observed that services at the "Jewish Reformed Church . . . differed very little from the Methodist service."[122] In the building of Hamilton's Anshe Sholom Synagogue, erected in 1882, there were family pews and an organ. Early rabbis there favored praying in the vernacular with bared heads and even moving the Sabbath service to Sunday. More traditional congregations were also not impervious to change. In 1882 the German and Polish Congregation in Montreal began to recite "a few short prayers in English so that the little ones might understand."[123] By 1913 in Montreal even the orthodox rabbi of the Hevra Kadisha Synagogue was preaching in English ostensibly for the benefit of "ignorant youngsters" in the congregation.[124] The most conservative of Montreal Jews were to some extent "willing to yield . . . to the changed conditions and progressive spirit of modern life in America."[125] In Toronto change came somewhat more gradually and fitfully, partly because the community was of more recent origin and closer to its European roots, less aware of Christian practice and sensibilities. There even so assimilated a Jew as businessman-philanthropist Sigmund Samuel claimed to have observed the Jewish dietary laws all his life. Until 1914 Samuel also closed his place of business on Saturdays. Still, in Toronto as well, Judaism began to assimilate to Anglo-Canada during the period under review.[126]

Changing Jewish values were in evidence in places other than the synagogue and home. European Jews had spent most of their leisure time in synagogue and burial society activities. By contrast, their Canadian-born children, like their Anglo-Canadian neighbors, busied themselves with lodges, beneficial societies, clubs, concerts, plays, and dances. By 1904 the members of Montreal's Temple Emanu-El had become so removed from traditional concerns that no one seemed willing to devote any time to the synagogue at all. Bendix A. Boas, who served as Temple president for seventeen years between 1882 and 1907, found himself acting as "President, Treasurer, Secretary, Collector and Shamos [that is, sexton]." As secretary, Boas was able to record his own reelection by default as Temple president in 1904. Although Jews frequently gathered in organizations with exclusively Jewish membership, their activities were often indistinguishable from those of gentiles. The regular lectures of the Montefiore Social and Dramatic Club are instructive. Prominent Canadians, such as Henri Bourassa and social scientist Herbert Brown Ames, addressed the club members on topics ranging from nationalism to "The Significance of the St. Lawrence Route to Canada." Between 1910 and 1914 the Club heard not a single speaker on a topic of specifically Jewish interest. More recent immigrants and others who had not yet achieved the wealth and position of the members of the Montefiore Club joined together for similar programs in the new YM-YWHA. The Baron de Hirsch School inculcated the same values among immigrant children. Its curriculum de-emphasized Jewish subjects; and, in fact, two-thirds of the teachers as well as the principal were Anglo-Canadian gentiles. There, too, guest lecturers almost never spoke on topics of specifically Jewish interest.[127]

The Canadian Crucible

The tendency of Jews in Canada to affiliate with Anglo-Canada was related to attitudes and sensibilities as well as to the confluence of Jewish and Anglo-Canadian interests and way of life. As already suggested, that French Canadians were a conquered people and Anglo-Canadians the conquerors had a profound effect on relationships between the two nationalities and influenced the ways in which the two groups related to Jews as well. In the earliest years of Jewish settlement, the British victors were a minority in their new country. A kind of cultural imperialism was born out of necessity and out of their confidence that they could assimilate anyone into their "superior" culture. As François-Xavier Garneau put it, England had

> always acted under the belief that, with the help of gold and power, the less numerous races which owed her allegiance would become extinct,— merged and lost in the all-powerful orbit of the nationality of her own people.[128]

There was some talk of pluralism, although that was to be more of a twentieth-century phenomenon. In practice tremendous pressure was put on individuals and groups to acculturate to British culture and mores and to the English language. By the turn of the century, people in all English-speaking countries exuded more self-confidence than ever and felt eminently justified in pressing their demands. England and the United States, prosperous and increasingly powerful, seemed to be "performing the Divine mission of enlightening and civilizing the whole human race."[129] The future seemed to be theirs.

A corollary of British self-confidence and eagerness to assimilate others was a disdain for peoples and cultures not British, and especially for the French. The animosities between France and England were of long standing. And even in the New World "the farther off from England, the nearer was to France." Lord Durham's report saw the French Canadians, with their peasant ideal imported from *ancien régime* France, as the chief impediment to a progressive, enlightened, dynamic Canada. Many Canadians readily agreed that the French "desired no innovations—no improvement of any kind." At best they were harmless and quaint, "fond of pleasure, ... non-reflecting, ... indolent, ... superstitious, [knowing] nothing of that sober, steady love of constitutional liberty that animates every true Briton."[130] At worst they were thought to be intolerant, priest-ridden, backward, and parasitic. In later years as earlier, British immigrants arrived in "Montreal with definite attitudes of superiority towards the French Canadian."[131] Anglo-Canadians, with their "abiding faith in British Imperialism," were quite confident that the "complete assimilation [of all non-British elements] will be quickly realized ... in Canada."[132] In their eyes, French Canadians remained "a conquered race."[133] In contrast to burgeoning Britain and the United States, French Canada seemed increasingly unprogressive and old-fashioned.[134]

As would be expected, Jews shared the British view of the French in Canada. The new Canadian, Sara Gratz Moses Joseph, thought French Canadians in 1848 "particularly amus[ing] ... with their primitive costume," although she noted, too, their "proud defiance of the ... present rulers."[135] Rabbi Abraham De Sola, writing a few years later, was less positive. He was convinced that the "Canadian *habitants*" had become debased by what he believed to be their "unrestrained addiction to blood eating," a practice particularly abhorrent to Jews. The *habitants* were, De Sola conceded, doutbless a worthy, happy, contented [people], ... yet few would charge them with too much intellectuality, enterprise, or with a too free spirit of inquiry either in matters spiritual or secular.[136]

Adolphus Mordecai Hart had a still less benign view of the French Canadians. He feared they would undermine the fabric of Canada altogether:

> While the noble, high-minded English speaking subject of Her Majesty is toiling with his usual perseverance and industry to add to his own means of living, and thereby increase the national capital and wealth of the country, the lazy, indolent, and impassive French Canadian jogs along in his usual way, hoping and trusting that by means of legislation or the patronage of the local Government, he may be enabled to obtain some lucrative office or employment, and thereby obtain a fancied position of superiority over his fellow-colonist of another origin.[137]

Hart railed against clerical interference in the electoral process and against "the peculiar opinions of the clergy and laity of the Romish Church in Canada on matters of nationality, religion, politics, and social economics." In later years as the conflict between Jews and French Canadians became more heated, disdain turned to contempt and amusement, to fear. By the turn of the century, Hart's son, Gerald Ephraim, had become convinced that "the bulk of the habitants ... [were] innately rapacious, [the] ... Papist French-Canadians, fanatical and intolerant of other religions."[138]

It was not only French Canadians whom Anglo-Canadians looked down upon. Like many other Britishers they were convinced that all non-British cultures were inferior. Imperialists and their fellow travelers felt that Canada could become a great nation only if she assumed her share of the civilizing mission of the British Empire and Anglified all non-Anglo-Canadians.[139] For obvious reasons, Jews could not embrace the concept of British superiority in its entirety. Their willingness to integrate into Anglo-Canada by dispensing with some aspects of their own tradition indicates, however, that they did not wholly reject the notion either.

In the mid-nineteenth century Canadians of British stock seemed to be gaining firm numerical ascendancy in the country. Between 1871 and 1938, however, the Anglo-Saxon majority was in steady decline, dropping from over 60 percent of the population to just over 50 percent. Most of the decline was attributable to the large influx of non-British, non-French immigrants after 1896. By this time it had become clear that the French Canadians would not become Anglified. If the immigrants had not been Anglified either, then the Anglo-Canadian character of the country would have been endangered. Cultural balkanization would have become a real possibility and the danger of American annexation, heightened.[140]

Toward the end of the nineteenth century Anglo-Canadians had become less relaxed and less liberal even in their dealings with French Canadians as, increasingly, the theory of minority rights was abandoned for that of majority rule. French-language rights in the Manitoba schools were watered down. The Autonomy Bills of 1905 accomplished the same thing in other western provinces. French-language rights in Ontario schools were ended in 1912, as noted earlier. Such issues as the execution of Louis Riel in 1885 were also resolved to the satisfaction of one group only, the Anglo-Canadians. In Montreal, the largest city of French Canada, there emerged a pervasive "anglicized and anglicizing character."[141] Contemporaries sensed the haughty disdain of Anglo-Canadian Montrealers, who ran the city often without regard for the ever larger French majority.[142] French and other rising young professionals realized "that to advance in their professions they had to adopt much of the culture of the dominant, English-speaking minority."[143]

Immigrant groups felt such pressure even more acutely. Since Anglo-Canadians generally accepted the British model of a homogeneous society rather than a more pluralistic model, the pressures they applied on "inferior" non-British groups were enormous. The public school in Canada was regarded as "a crucible for the creation of a new race, unified in language, customs and thought."[144] If a strong Canada were to be built, and if the non-French majority were to retain cultural and political hegemony, then all the new immigrants had "to be assimilated and developed into British-Canadians."[145] Intellectuals like C. A. Magrath and James R. Conn argued that Anglo-Canadians should take "an active interest in this matter of assimilation."[146] Journalist Howard Angus Kennedy, who favored unrestricted immigration into Canada, declared in 1907 that "even the most backward" of the "Continental races of Europe" might be profitably blended into "the future British race," provided they were initiated through a "rational and patriotic system of education in their new home." Even radicals like James S. Woodsworth looked forward to the homogenization of the non-French population of Canada, and perhaps of all Canadians.[147]

The pressure to Anglify was exerted on Jews in many ways. It came from all quarters, including fellow Jews. At the turn of the century even those Anglo-Canadians most open to the Jewish presence, such as the editors of the Montreal *Daily Witness,* tended to look down on Jewish immigrants as "half-man, half-beast," asserting that

> Jewish children should grow up on the same benches with . . . Christian children, thus imbibing Canadian sentiment and growing into patriotic citizens, and not as strangers and foreigners in this country in which they are born and in which they live.[148]

Well-meaning neighbors might deluge a new Jewish family with English books and papers and make certain that children would attend school. The message was clear and unequivocal.[149] In Montreal, at least, what mitigated such pressures and made them somewhat more friendly than coercive was the fact that all the non-French groups faced a hostile French-Catholic majority—a common danger—by the late nineteenth century. Thus, whatever their true feelings, Jews, Anglo-Protestants, and other non-French groups were rather more inclined to tolerate each other than they might otherwise have been; they understood the necessity for presenting a united English-speaking front.[150]

But it was not only pressure that Jews experienced in these years; many Anglo-Canadians had a positive attitude toward Jews and Judaism. Some of it stemmed from the British inheritance and from their American connections, but much of it was of local genesis. Over the years Anglo-Canadians exhibited increasing curiosity about and awareness of Jews. Carroll Ryan wrote poems about Jewish mysticism as well as about the "happiness of love and joys of the wine cup" at the turn of the century.[151] The English-language press, especially in Montreal, covered Jewish events from gossip to the sermons of Rabbi Meldola De Sola in the same period. When John Douglas Borthwick published his *Montreal History and Gazetteer* in 1892, he invited Clarence I. De Sola to write an extensive section on Jews. At the turn of the century *The Mantle of Elijah,* one of the popular novels of Israel Zangwill, who wrote about Anglo-Jewish life, was published in Toronto. More and more, Jews were incorporated into the Anglo-Canadian landscape.[152]

Anglo-Canadians came to appreciate Jews' tenacity, "continu[ing] . . . to live in hope" despite the ages-long denial of those hopes.[153] Canada, too, was a nation of few people with great hopes for the future. The willingness of Jews to support each other and even to sacrifice personal gain for the good of their people was also greatly admired. Mary Ellen

Ross, as she often did, put such feelings into their sharpest perspective. She found

> every Hebrew, be he great or small, . . . as one man ready to give his all when the time of the promise comes, the time foretold by the prophets.[154]

This was a particularly compelling vision to Anglo-Canadians, who more and more feared the division of their country.

In addition, many Anglo-Canadians seemed eager to assuage the passion of Jewish sufferers, of the pogrom victims, of Dreyfus, and of Mendel Beiliss. A few even sought to atone for the antisemitism of French Canadians. *The Canada Farmers' Sun* offers an illustrative example. The paper was the offficial organ of the Patrons of Industry of Ontario and Quebec, a group that represented a large number of Ontario farmers in the first half of the 1890s. Defense of farmers' interests, the Patrons felt, included opposition to urbanization and to open immigration. And yet *The Canada Farmers' Sun,* which might well have assumed an anti-Jewish posture, welcomed Jewish immigrants to Canada, urging that they be given "just as good a chance to push ahead" as Christians.[155] Rev. J. McPhail Scott, a few years later, reminded Canadians that if the Jew was "unlovely," he had only become what the Christian world "had made him."[156]

Anglo-Canadian support for Jewish sufferers spilled over into sympathy for all Jews. In Toronto gentiles contributed to the immigrant aid activities of the Anglo-Jewish Association in the 1880s and to the construction of the new Holy Blossom Temple in the mid-1890s. (Contributions from non-Jews had been instrumental even in the erection of the earlier Holy Blossom structure built in 1876.) In Montreal similar aid was forthcoming. In 1885, when the German and Polish Congregation was collecting funds for a new synagogue building, dozens of Anglo-Canadians contributed, although only two French Canadians did so.[157] Many Christians donated funds to the Baron de Hirsch Institute and to other Jewish charities over the years, especially businessmen and politicians. Such people, no doubt, sought to retain the goodwill of Jewish customers and voters. At that, however, almost all were Anglo-Canadians, such as former alderman James Robinson, who in 1908 became the first life member of the new YMHA. Without any apparent ulterior motive was Lord Strathcona, who in 1901 made a "handsome donation" to the new library of the de Hirsch Institute.[158]

The contrast with the reception given to Jews by French Canadians is striking. To them Jews were almost "always the object of suspicion."[159] Many French Canadians were aghast at the progress Jews were making in Canada. When Trois Rivières appointed a Jewish harbor commissioner in 1896, *La Libre Parole Illustrée* expressed astonishment at what had come over that "good city, so French!"[160] The integration of Jews into Canadian society and their achieving political influence commensurate with their numbers were seen by many French Canadians as a direct threat.[161] Some French Canadians appreciated Jewish sobriety and industriousness.[162] Others, however, feared that those qualities would enable Jews more readily to overwhelm the "less materialistic, . . . more spiritual" *habitants.*[163] When two Russian-Jewish refugees were burned to death in a Montreal fire in 1901, the Canadian *Jewish Times* reported that one French journal had actually expressed satisfaction.[164] The French-Canadian press took pains to emphasize the religion of any Jew in trouble with the law, although it seldom mentioned that of Protestants or Catholics. (In Toronto, as well, newspapers made a point of identifying the religion of Jewish miscreants. Edmund Scheuer and Rabbi Solomon Jacobs did their best to pressure editors into writing about Jews as they wrote about other Canadians, with some success.)[165] Whatever the French Canadians' perception of Jewish suffering in the period under review, they seem, for the most part, to have considered it well deserved.

Jews hard pressed by the antithetical French were in no position to resist pressure from Anglo-Canadians, even if they had so desired. In any event, however, most Jews who came to North America throughout the period under review desired to change their way of life to some degree and to adapt themselves to Western society. The blandishments held out by Anglo-Canadians made accommodation all the easier. Jews embraced Canadian nationality and patriotism with alacrity during the period under review and Anglo-Canadian culture, as well. In 1931, as noted earlier, just beyond the period, Jews had the third highest rate of naturalization of any immigrant group in Canada. Only Icelanders and non-Chinese, non-Japanese Asians, two very small groups, outranked them. Antisemites condemned Jews' "eagerness to share in the Government of the Country."[166] But most Anglo-Canadians were pleased that Jews were "fully alive to the possibilities the future" held in store for them in Canada and that they hastened "to become British subjects."[167]

CHAPTER SIX

The Third Solitude

Although there were many factors conducive to the absorption of Jews into Anglo-Canada during the period under review, there existed very definite limits to integration, as well. This was particularly the case after 1890, when the growing Jewish population was becoming noticeable in Montreal and, to a lesser degree, in Toronto. To Canadian Jews in these years integration might mean a degree of acculturation at most; for the overwhelming majority of them, however, it could not mean total affiliation. Even Jews whose religious beliefs had become attenuated seldom drifted out of the Jewish community in Canada, as they tended to do elsewhere. Most of them did not anticipate doing so either. Within the Jewish community population growth and the proliferation of institutions contributed to the strengthening of Jewish identification. Of even greater consequence were the strong pressures exerted on Canadian Jews from outside their own community.

Parallel Institutions to Meet New Needs

Almost everywhere Jews have lived they have established institutions to look after their religious and social needs. In addition to their primary

Notman

Montreal's Shaar Ha-Shomayim on McGill College Avenue

Notman

Montreal's Spanish and Portuguese Synagogue on Stanley Street

Toronto's Holy Blossom Congregation on Bond Street

Torcong

purpose, such institutions have served to reinforce Jewish identification, as they did in Canada during the period under review. The first Jewish institution in the country was Shearith Israel, the Spanish and Portuguese Synagogue of Montreal, founded in 1768. The small size of the community, the transiency of many early members, and their religious apathy impeded efforts to provide essential services, such as a rabbi and teacher, a proper building, kosher meat, and a *mohel* (ritual circumciser). Nonetheless, the fledgling congregation acted as a focal point of Jewish religious, social, and charitable activities. For both Christians and Jews in Montreal religion early on acquired an ethnic component; and by 1844 attempts were being made to establish a second synagogue, one using the German and Polish rite. By 1860 the new congregation also occupied its own building. In Toronto and Hamilton, Ontario, the first Jewish institutions established were cemeteries, Toronto's in 1849 and Hamilton's four years later. By 1856 Toronto Jews had succeeded in organizing a functioning congregation, and seven years later there was one in Hamilton and another in Victoria, British Columbia, as well. Other communities followed suit when their numbers permitted.[1]

Nineteenth-century North American governments provided relatively few, if any, social services, leaving such activities to private and church groups. Jewish communities, in any case, had traditionally made provision for their own poor and sick and for the education of the young. In similar fashion, they undertook to do so in the New World. At first the congregations attempted to provide such services for their few members and the small number of other Jews in the community. By 1847 Montreal Jews felt the necessity for a separate Jewish welfare organization—the short-lived Hebrew Philanthropic Society. Its successor, the Young Men's Hebrew Benevolent Society, was founded in 1863 and remains in existence today incorporated into the Allied Jewish Community Services of Montreal. In Toronto it was women who organized the first Jewish charitable endeavors, founding the Toronto Hebrew Ladies' Sick and Benevolent Society in 1868. In the 1870s the American Jewish fraternal orders, the Ancient Jewish Order Kesher Shel Barzel and the Independent Order B'nai B'rith, which were brought to Canada, offered members both mutual aid and a secular framework within which to socialize with other Jews. In 1874 Montreal Jews attempted to found a "Jewish Educational Establishment" to provide for the education of Jewish children in a Jewish school. The proposal foundered, however, on the rocks of rivalry between the two congregations, and because most Jews still felt comfortable in the city's Protestant schools.[2]

Contemporaries and later critics, too, assumed that these early Jewish institutions represented a turning away from the general community;[3] and, of course, in some ways they did. But it was also the case that ethnic organization had been part of the Anglo-Canadian way of life since the early nineteenth century. (With regard to manifestations of ethnicity, Anglo-Canadians, especially in Montreal, were more accepting of pluralism than they were with regard to culture and language.) In 1828 the St. Patrick's Society was founded in Montreal to aid Catholic Irish immigrants. Seven years later the St. Andrew's Society was formed to aid Scottish immigrants. In 1856 a second Irish group was founded, this one for Protestants. There were, as well, a German and a Swiss society in Montreal in those years. In founding their own separate religious and charitable institutions Jews were, in part, then, acculturating to the organizational patterns of Anglo-Canadian society.[4] By 1891, in addition to the ethnic societies established earlier in the century in Montreal, there existed English, Welsh, Italian, and Scandinavian groups as well as those of French Canadians.[5]

As the Canadian-Jewish community grew with the new immigration from eastern Europe that began in the 1880s, the number and variety of Jewish institutions multiplied rapidly. This proliferation was partly a function of numbers, partly a function of more diverse European origins, and partly a continuation of the traditional desire of Jews to provide for their own needs, needs that increased with the growing population. The profusion of new Jewish organizations also represented a typical immigrant response—to seek familiar surroundings within an alien environment.

To a considerable degree the impulse to organize came from outside Canada. Synagogues, of course, were local affairs, as were institutions like the Canadian *Jewish Times* (1897), the Yiddish-language *Keneder odler* (1907), the Toronto Jewish Dispensary (1908), the Montreal Hebrew Orphans' Home (1909), the Montreal Hebrew Free Loan Society (1911), and the Jewish Endeavor Sewing Schools of Montreal (1902) and Toronto (1912). Lodges, cultural organizations, labor unions, benevolent societies, the Jewish Lads' Brigade, synagogue unions, the Anglo-Jewish Association, and Zionist societies, however, tended to be offshoots of American or British organizations, as noted earlier, as were analogous associations of Anglo-Canadian gentiles. Whether local groups or branches of international bodies, these societies all contributed to the development of autonomous Jewish life in Montreal, Toronto, and elsewhere in Canada, providing a setting within which Jews could spend a great deal of their time with coreligionists. Since most Jews in this period lived in Jewish neighborhoods and many worked with or for other Jews, partial segregation became a fact of Canadian-Jewish life.

By the end of the period under review Canadian Jewry—particularly in the two largest cities, but also to a degree in the rest of the country— seemed on the threshold of becoming a third Canadian nationality. The Jewish People's Schools of Montreal, which would make the first major effort to provide all-day Jewish education in Canada, were gestating. The federation and professionalization of Jewish charitable work were well under way in the two larger communities; and the movement toward a national Canadian-Jewish organization, the Canadian Jewish Congress, was also beginning and would achieve fulfillment shortly after.[6] World War I acted as a catalyst in this process. For the first time in their history, North American Jews would be completely cut off from the European Jewry, which had for so long provided much of the leadership for the North American communities. Well before the outbreak of war, however, as noted at the outset, Jews in Canada had begun to prepare themselves for independence.

Perhaps the best yardstick of Canadian-Jewish autonomy was the development of the Jewish national movement, Zionism. Considering that there were but 2,443 Jews in all of Canada in 1881, even the extent of Canadian participation in the precursor movements to Herzlian Zionism is notable. In the 1880s the elitist, cultural Zionist organization founded by Ahad Ha-Am, the B'nai Moshe, had only two members in North America, one of them, Lazarus Cohen of Montreal. In the first years of the Hibbat Zion (Love of Zion) settlement movement Montreal Jews were contributing money to the cause. In 1887 they founded a short-lived Hibbat Zion group under the leadership of Alexander Harkavy. The joint activities of the New York and Montreal chapters of the Hibbat Zion group, Shavey Zion, have already been discussed. That one of the two members of the Shavey Zion commission investigating settlement opportunities in the Holy Land was a Canadian attests to the relative strength of the Montrealers within that organization. A year after the founding of the World Zionist Congress by Theodor Herzl in 1897 the new Montreal Zionist association, Agudath Zion, had become the largest Jewish organization in that city. By 1899 perhaps as many as a quarter of the adult Jewish males in Montreal were dues-paying Zionists; countless others were "parlor pinks." The first Canadian women's Zionist organization, the Daughters of Zion, was founded in Toronto in 1899. As noted earlier, by 1907 the Federation of Zionist Societies in

Canada had chapters in forty-two cities and towns from Nova Scotia to British Columbia.[7]

Not only was Canadian Zionism from the first geographically all-encompassing, it also attracted members from almost all religious elements in the Jewish community. The officers and rabbis of Shaar Hashomayim of Montreal, the one synagogue in the country affiliated with the new Conservative movement during the period, were active Zionists like their American counterparts. Unlike Europe and the United States, Canada saw virtually no Orthodox opposition to Zionism; numbered among prominent Zionists were such Orthodox rabbinical authorities as Aaron M. Ashinsky and Meldola De Sola of Montreal, Israel Kahanovitch of Winnipeg, and Jacob Gordon of Toronto.[8]

Standing in even sharper contrast to Europe and the United States was the position of Canadian Reformers. The members of the Hamilton Reform congregation, Anshe Sholom, were generally friendly to Zionism. Holy Blossom Temple in Toronto permitted Zionist groups to use its premises on a number of occasions. Alfred D. Benjamin, longtime president of the congregation, served on the council of the national Federation of Zionist Societies and as treasurer of the Toronto Zionist Society. Edmund Scheuer, among the most influential members of both Anshe Sholom and Holy Blossom and the chief advocate of Reform, led the Zionist Jewish Free School for girls in Toronto for a time, although he was not an active Zionist. David Wittenberg, rabbi of Holy Blossom in 1899, was one of the organizers of Toronto's first Zionist group. Solomon Jacobs, the congregation's rabbi from 1900 to 1920, also became a Zionist supporter, although he had originally dissociated himself from the movement. (After Jacobs's death Holy Blossom formally joined the Reform movement, and its next two rabbis were American Reformers. Yet, both Balfour Brickner and Ferdinand Isserman were also active Zionists.)[9]

Montreal Reformers tended to behave more like those in the United States than did their coreligionists in Toronto and Hamilton, which was not surprising, since, as noted previously, many of them were of American origin. The members of Temple Emanu-El refused to allow Zionists to gather in their building before World War I and were generally not supportive of the new movement. During the convention of the Central Conference of American Rabbis, which met in Montreal in 1897, the Temple provided a platform for a ringing denunciation of Zionism by the patriarch of American Reform, Isaac Mayer Wise. Nevertheless, even in that congregation where extreme Reform held sway, opposition to Zionism was not unanimous. Nathan Gordon, the congregation's rabbi

Zionist convention in Ottawa, 1912

Prof. Goldwin Smith, critic of Jews and Judaism, in the library of his home, "The Grange," in Toronto in 1909. From a pen and ink drawing by Owen Staples

Fiftieth anniversary dinner for Mr. and Mrs. Jacob Hirsch at Montreal's Montefiore Club, 1913

School committee of Baron de Hirsch Institute, Montreal, 1913

late in the period under review, was an outspoken Zionist who, as noted earlier, appeared frequently on behalf of the movement in Montreal, Toronto, and elsewhere in Canada. (Gordon had been raised in New Orleans, where two of the few staunch Zionists in the American Reform rabbinate, Maximillian and James Heller, served as spiritual leaders.) In later years the Temple's rabbi, Harry Joshua Stern, another immigrant from the United States, would also be active in Zionist ranks.[10]

Early Zionism in Canada encompassed all social strata of the community as well as all religious groups. As noted previously, in Canada, Zionism was endorsed by the "most active and most respected section of Jewry"—the very people who most tended to remain aloof from the movement in the United States and western Europe. At the other end of the social spectrum, in immigrant, working-class circles, there was also only token opposition to Zionism, whereas in Europe and the United States socialists voiced adamant objections to the movement. Some union members were among the most ardent Canadian Zionists in the early twentieth century. Still, now and then complaints were heard about the apathy of Canadian Jewry toward Zionism, voiced by American Zionist orator Zvi Hirsch Masliansky, Rabbi Ashinsky, and others; and during the first decade of the new century some of the wealthier Jews of Montreal and Toronto drew away from the movement. On the whole, however, there was a remarkable degree of faithfulness to Zionism among Canadian Jews in the last years of the period under review.[11]

The growth of Jewish nationalism in Canada is noteworthy not only because of its scope, but also because of the function that the Federation of Zionist Societies performed from the time it was founded through the end of World War I. Zionism appeared in Canada during a period of rapid Jewish population growth. Many of the immigrants inclined to Zionism either out of loyalty to traditional religious ideas or out of commitment to modern Jewish nationalism. They arrived in a community that lacked a well-defined and broadly accepted sense of self-identity. Unlike the United States or western Europe, Canada had not a single Jewish organization with a national network; no group offered an institutional or an ideological framework for Canadian-Jewish life— until Zionism offered both. The Federation of Zionist Societies was the first Jewish group in Canada with cross-country representation, as noted previously, and it remained the only one until the founding of the Canadian Jewish Congress in 1919. Here at last was a Jewish organization that was not an American branch plant and that was capable of uniting Jews all over the Dominion. Beginning in 1900, the annual Zionist conventions were the only nation-wide forums of any sort, and they were invariably used to advance the interests of Canadian Jewry in general. Under the banner of Jewish independence in Palestine, Canadian Jewry, with its growing number and variety of institutions, began to develop into a cohesive, autonomous, national community in Canada itself.[12]

Growing Apart

The widening scope of Jewish life in Canada in the nineteenth century cannot be viewed merely as a function of population growth, particularly in Montreal. There was a special quality to the growing autonomy of Jews. Already in 1839 Newton Bosworth had remarked in his guidebook to that city that "the privileges of *caste* are more jealously maintained, and the lines of demarcation more distinctly drawn in Montreal, than in other cities."[13] This was increasingly the case during the period under review. In class-conscious Montreal there was an almost ineluctable coolness between Anglo-Canadian gentiles and Jews, whom Protestants generally considered to be of lower social status. A factor in the antagonism between Jews and French Canadians was the fact that many Jews considered the French to be their social inferiors. By the end of the period few Jewish businessmen or lawyers in Montreal (or in Toronto, for that matter) had gentile partners. University faculties and hospital positions were being closed to Jews. Almost no jobs were open to Jews in the giant companies owned or managed by Anglo-Canadians or in the few large companies in French Canadian hands. Isolation seemed to be on the rise in every sphere of life, bringing with it friction. In 1884 Joseph Elijah Bernstein wrote from Montreal that he found the city divided into parties: French, English, Scottish, Irish, Protestants, Catholics. According to Bernstein all of them hated one another and could agree on only one thing: a common hatred of Jews.[14] Some years later, the *Keneder odler* made a similar assessment of the situation of Montreal Jews:

> A lot of people think that in Montreal there will be a war between the Protestants and the Catholics. If there is, we Jews will be the first to suffer, from both sides; no less from the Protestants than from the Catholics.[15]

More and more over time, French Canadians seemed to withdraw into their own world, concerned largely with their own narrow interests.

The Catholic Church was far more interested in protecting its faithful from alien influences than in reaching out to others or in working for the good of the general community. French Canadians were developing a survivalist mentality, an outlook to some extent shared by Anglo-Canadians. Many of them were increasingly unreceptive to people of non-British backgrounds, although others, as noted, remained quite open. Anglo-Canadians, and not only the imperialists with their sense of Anglo-Saxon superiority, were also retreating behind fortress walls. Even British immigrants found it hard to acclimate in the years at the turn of the century and formed their own groups within the society. Others had still greater difficulty in gaining the acceptance of Canadian WASPs. In founding their myriads of organizations and institutions during those years, Jews must have been responding at least in part to their lack of complete acceptance by other Canadians. They, too, were erecting walls behind which they would preserve their unique identity.[16]

Instructive in this regard is the behavior of Montreal's Reform Temple Emanu-El, which had been founded in 1882 by people who sought more than anything else to break down the traditional barriers between gentiles and Jews. To accomplish this goal the Temple long refrained from involving itself in the Jewish community. Although Protestant ministers were welcome visitors to the synagogue pulpit early on and the Zion Church was permitted to use the Temple social hall for worship in 1886, relations with other Jewish groups were poor. The Temple refused to allow the Montefiore Social and Dramatic Club, then dedicated to doing good works among Montreal Jews, to rent quarters for meetings in 1882. In 1884 it refused to join with the local B'nai B'rith lodge in a testimonial to Sir Moses Montefiore on his one hundredth birthday. A few years later the Temple board refused to cooperate with other Jewish institutions in trying to sort out the thorny issue of Jews in the Protestant schools. Similarly, in 1892 the board would not participate in a discussion of the plight of the city's Jewish poor. In 1896 the Temple declined to be part of an arbitration board being set up to mediate disputes among Jews, because "such [a] committee . . . would tend to make different . . . the Jews from other citizens."[17] In 1897 the Temple board resigned in a body from the Young Men's Hebrew Benevolent Society, in which its president, Mortimer Davis, had once been active.[18]

Although the Temple succeeded in gaining a measure of gentile acceptance, ultimately such efforts to break down ethnic barriers proved futile. By 1909 the Temple, too, was beginning to retreat behind the rising ethnic walls. In that year Emanu-El appointed two members to the Montreal Jewish Board of Deputies and from that time on began to participate in other Jewish communal activities.[19] In Toronto and elsewhere in Canada by the end of the period under review almost no one entertained the illusion of a Canadian melting pot, which had long tantalized the Americanized members of Temple Emanu-El. All over Canada "the lines of demarcation" were being "distinctly drawn."

Theoretical Underpinnings of Ghettoization

Contemporary Canadian social and political theories, which implicitly or explicitly excluded Jews from the body politic, contributed to the difficulties experienced by Jews in finding a place for themselves in pre-World War I Canada. One of the most serious stumbling blocks was the belief of many Canadians, both French and Anglo, that Canada was a "Christian country." Unlike the United States, Canada had first been settled by people who sought to perpetuate the European religious atmosphere, not to escape it. This was true of the first British to come no less than of the first French. Canada's founding fathers "left their stamp upon the land," and Jews perceived it to be a Christian stamp. Such a heritage was inherently problematic for Jews, many of whom hoped to see Canada become a neutral, secular state.[20]

The general French-Canadian attitude about the relationship of religion and politics during the period under review has been discussed. On the eve of World War I it remained largely unchanged. In 1910 the Montreal city council was reminded by Abbé Garrequet, the Superior General of the Sulpician Order in Rome, that his "predecessors [had] aimed to make Canada ... [both] prosperous and Catholic," in which regard he hoped to follow in their footsteps.[21] Many Anglo-Canadians also insisted on the Christian—albeit Protestant—character of the country. Although, according to early-twentieth-century observer André Siegfried, many Canadian Protestants had ceased to believe in God by the turn of the century, like good Britishers, they thought it bad form to express their unbelief openly. In any case, they mistrusted secularism and did their best to retain in the schools and in the country, in general, a "Christian character—Protestant up to a certain point."[22] As noted previously, the strong Protestant heritage proved to be a powerful force in paving the way for the acceptance of Jews in Canada. But at times it also worked as a counterforce. The negative influence of the Protestant heritage became increasingly evident by the turn of the century, as the growing Jewish population threatened to alter the previously all but universal Christian makeup of the country.

The "constitution" of Canada, the British North America Act of 1867, had implicitly established Catholicism in Quebec and Protestantism in Ontario, at least with regard to schools. In other areas of official life, as well, the Christian character of Canada was palpable. In 1900 a notarial position became vacant in West Montreal. Fellow notaries recommended that Lewis A. Hart be appointed to the post. The appointment was not forthcoming, however, because it was felt the position should be filled by a Protestant, as it had been formerly.[23] In many respects Jews were considered a part of the Anglo-Canadian community, but not when it came to enjoying such emoluments as might be given to Protestants. In unofficial quarters the same attitude often prevailed. The Montreal *Star,* for example, as late as 1897 included only news of Protestants and Catholics in the religious news column, although Jewish news was amply reported elsewhere in the paper.[24] Only the *Daily Witness* of Montreal's English-language newspapers considered Jewish news to be "religious" news.

Outsiders observed the position of Judaism and its followers in Canada with apprehension. Peter Wiernik, a pioneer historian of the American-Jewish community, found turn-of-the-century Montreal Jewry "in many respects like the communities of the United States of similar size." But he feared

> the dissensions between religious denominations [which gave rise to] ... more open partisan hostility to Jews, both on the part of the press and in public life, than in the United States where the government is strictly secular.[25]

The concept of a Christian Canada meant more than the potential or actual exclusion of Jews from certain aspects of public life. In the minds of many, conversion to Protestant Christianity became a necessary concomitant of good citizenship; to that end Jews were subjected to heavy pressures. And whereas missionaries sought, as always, to save the souls of Jews for their own good and for the good of mankind, in Canada they also sought to break "down the racial, national, religious, political and social prejudice that divides our heterogeneous population," in short, to make Protestant Anglo-Canadians out of everyone.[26]

Organized missions to Jews in Canada began in 1892 following earlier, independent efforts. The Church of England Missionary Society established its first Montreal mission in 1901 and some years later set up missions in Ottawa and Toronto. The Presbyterian Church in Canada established its first Jewish mission in 1908 in Toronto, although sporadic efforts had been made ealier. In 1913 the Presbyterians opened a Montreal mission as well.[27] The means used by the missionaries to communicate their message to Jews were many. In 1884 Rev. W. W. Robertson of the Advent Church in Montreal announced his own messiahship and sought to lead Jews back to the Holy Land. Newspapers such as the Montreal *Daily Witness* and *Daily Herald* gave missionary news prime coverage, often presenting conversionist propaganda as fact. In 1898 during Montreal's "Universal Week of Prayer" one day—appropriately enough, a Saturday—was devoted to Jewish conversion. Prayers were offered that "God's ancient people may be brought into the fold of Christianity."[28]

More subtle methods were also employed. In 1898 the famous American evangelist, Dwight L. Moody, suggested during a visit to Montreal that the *Witness* and the Montreal Jewish Mission jointly promote a school for immigrant Jewish children. At the time it was the general wisdom that converts would be more successful than gentile Christians at reaching Jews. Accordingly, in 1901 the Protestant Ministerial Association sponsored the visit to Montreal of three converted Jews, who came to preach to their unregenerate brethren. Several of the resident missionaries were also converted Jews. In Toronto, Rev. Sabeti B. Rohold, whose family came from Jerusalem, and Rev. Henry Singer, a former Polish Jew, held forth for many years at the turn of the century. In Montreal there was the flamboyant Ignatius Timothy Trebitsch Lincoln, who was born in Austria-Hungary and ended his life as a Japanese collaborator in China during World War II. One of the missionaries' favorite methods of attracting young Jewish girls was through sewing classes. These were accompanied by "singing, praying, . . . and lollipop entertainments."[29] Boys were enticed through athletics, and adults, through the offer of medical services. In both Toronto and Montreal even "orthodox-looking men" were in the habit of attending missionary lectures.[30]

Despite all the efforts, Canadian Jews proved "a hard nut to crack," partly because the missionaries met vehement opposition from Jewish community leaders.[31] In Toronto, Rabbi Jacobs wrote and preached passionately against the missions as did other clergymen and laymen. In Montreal, Rabbi De Sola preached fiery sermons and threatened to invoke the law if missionaries forced their way into Jewish homes. In 1902 the Jewish Endeavour Sewing School of Montreal was founded by Rabbi Abramowitz and a number of prominent Jewish women. The school hoped to attract Jewish girls who would otherwise be ready prey for the missionaries' wiles. Ten years later Toronto Jews organized a similar enterprise using the same name. Attempts were redoubled in both cities to insure that Jewish orphans were placed in Jewish foster homes.[32]

The most forceful counterattack against the missionaries was mounted by Lewis A. Hart in his book, *A Jewish Reply to Christian Evangelists* (1906). The work had first appeared in serial form in the Canadian *Jewish Times* and was published as a book by popular demand. In it Hart used his legal and Jewish training to refute Christian claims, pulling no punches. He found the missionaries' efforts dishonest and underhanded:

> There certainly can be no more justification for Christian attempts to pros-elytize the Jews than there would be for a litigant to bribe and suborn the witnesses of the opposite party in a lawsuit; or for the rulers of a country or the generals of an army to buy up the statesmen of another country, or to foster treason and rebellion among the soldiers of another state, with which their own might be at variance.[33]

Hart pointed out "errors" in the New Testament and defended una-bashedly the superiority of the Hebrew Bible. He took great pride in his ancestral faith, which was to him a living religion. He exhorted his readers to stand up to "the endless questions and arguments with which Christian Evangelists are so fond of perpetually afflicting us."[34]

Spurred on by their lay and rabbinic leaders, Anglicized Jews in Canada and the new immigrants alike resisted the ministrations of the missionaries. They steadfastly refused to accept the necessity of becoming Protestants in order to be good Anglo-Canadians. But the pressure was unrelenting. In 1910 the Anglican Lord Bishop of Montreal was still insisting that Christians

> should see to it that the Jew knows the Gospel as we know it. As citizens, at least we should show that we are the friends of the Jews, and that we show our friendship for the race from which our Saviour sprung [sic].[35]

Anglo-Canadians came to desire harmony and homogeneity in their society only somewhat less than French Canadians. In an age that took religion seriously, religious harmony was seen to be an important aspect of social harmony. In French Canada, where Protestants made up an ever-smaller portion of the population, Anglo-Canadians were in need of allies, as already noted. In 1914 Jewish children represented 43.5 percent of the "Protestant" school population of Montreal, and some accommodation with Jews would present obvious advantages to Protestants. Outside Quebec there was no such overwhelming need, and, indeed, Protestants often remained militant throughout the period under review, although, as noted previously, many felt close to the Hebrew Bible, to ancient Judaism at least, and even to Jews. When it was in their interest to do so, they could make room in their society for Jews as Jews. Although they might desire to see Jews "saved," they could also live with them "unredeemed." This did not hold for Catholic French Canadians, who for the most part, were not even interested in attempting to "save" the souls of Jews.[36]

Another conception of Canada discomforting to Jews was that of the country as a bi-national or bi-racial state. In the last fifty years of the period under review the notion of race was a very popular one. As noted earlier, De Gobineau's theories had been accepted by many, especially as reworked by social Darwinists. Although some considered "race" to be open-ended and related more to geography, language, and culture than to biology, others understood it in the biological sense. If, indeed, Canada were a bi-national or bi-racial state in the latter sense, then Jews certainly had no place there. Nor, for that matter, did the "hordes" of gentile non-French, non-British immigrants who flooded the country at the turn of the century. As in Europe, racial theories in Canada often had antisemitic overtones. The bi-national idea (bi-racial ideal) provided a basis for an antisemitic political alliance between Goldwin Smith and Henri Bourassa and their followers.[37]

Whether or not they thought of race as biologically determined, the fathers of Confederation had intended to construct a bi-national state, having had no notion of the country as a melting pot of races. Most French Canadians have generally shared that understanding. Prior to World War I French nationalist leaders, such as Henri Bourassa and Armand Lavergne, firmly upheld the bi-national concept. Anglo-Canadian politicians and intellectual leaders, such as Sir J. William Dawson, George M. Grant, and George Parkin, accepted it as well. Jews were not in a position to challenge this idea, even though it was a concept that took no account of them. They had not been in the country in sufficient numbers early enough to press their interests. Moreover, no alternative conception of Canadian nationality seemed to be available during these years, except Anglo-Canadian homogenization, which was altogether unacceptable to the French.[38] Much later many Canadians would come to understand their society as an "ethnic mosaic." Such a notion would prove very promising to Jews and other minorities seeking to maintain a measure of individuality within the larger nation. French Canadians as well would find the idea of the "ethnic mosaic" advantageous to their survivalist policies. In the period under review, however, Jews and others could justify their presence in a bi-national Canada only by affiliating with one of the two nations, not always an easy task.[39]

One may assume that in no small way, many Jews during the period felt compelled to flaunt their Britishness out of a basic sense of unease as racial outsiders in Canada. The peculiar character of early Canadian Zionism was connected with Jews' difficulty in fitting into the country's bi-national structure. As elsewhere in the West at the time, some Canadians saw Zionism as a charitable movement organized to resettle the less fortunate Jews of Russia and Austria. They did not see Zionism uprooting Canadian or American or British Jews.[40] But Canadian Jews also spoke forthrightly of another kind of Zionism in the early twentieth century. Already in 1883 Joseph Elijah Bernstein had written from Montreal that "only the resettlement of Palestine would extricate the Jews of all countries [including Canada] from the slavery of antisemitism."[41] Some years later Rabbi Meldola De Sola, one of the staunchest British patriots in Canada, expressed the conviction that England, the United States, and possibly "one or two other enlightened countries"—not necessarily Canada—would continue to welcome Jews. Others would not. A Jewish homeland in which even Canadian Jews might some day take refuge, he felt, was an imperative.[42] Still other Canadians spoke of the spiritual poverty of Judaism in the Diaspora. Only a return to Zion, they felt, might effect the regeneration of Judaism.[43] Almost no one in Canada accepted the popular notion of American Reform Jews that Judaism had necessarily to be divorced from a physical land. And, indeed, in the period under review, some Jews from Canada left to settle in the Holy Land, a highly unusual step for North Americans. By 1909 there was a trend among certain groups to enlist in the Canadian army in order to acquire the military skills they felt would one day be necessary in Palestine. In later years Canadian emigrants to the Holy Land would include Jews from assimilated families long settled in Canada.[44]

To a degree, as already noted, Canadian Jews were enthusiastic about Zionism because prominent Anglo-Canadian gentiles gave the movement their stamp of approval. In England and the United States, too, many gentiles, some of them prominent, also favored Jewish restoration. Nonetheless, in those countries many Jews strongly opposed the new movement, whereas in Canada there was almost no Jewish opposition to Zionism before World War I. In fact, in these years Canada, along with two other bi-national states, Belgium and South Africa, had one of the highest per capita Zionist memberships in the world.[45] Canadian Jews correctly perceived that a measure of gentile enthusiasm for Zionism reflected a strong desire to see Jews settled somewhere other than Canada. In 1925, just beyond the period under review, Arthur Meighen, former prime minister and then leader of the opposition Conservative Party, was moved to comment on the meaning of Zionism. "Of all the results of the [first world] war," Meighen said, "none is more important and none is more fertile in human history than the reconquest of Palestine and the re-dedication of that country to the Jewish people." Meighen went on, however:

> I do hope that the Jews in Canada take a proper pride in this great event and that the sons of generations to come may go back to the land of their destiny.[46]

To the Jewish ear, well attuned to slights, the double meaning was unmistakable. To such attitudes a firm Zionist commitment seemed to be an appropriate response, a way of opting out of bi-national Canada, which excluded Jews.

Although most of Canada's Anglo and French leadership understood the country as bi-national, that did not mean that French and Anglo-Canadians lived together in harmony. In fact, the pot of racial antagonism simmered throughout the period under review, especially between 1885 and 1914, as noted previously. Toward the end it occasionally boiled over. Several dramatic events already alluded to served both as milestones and as catalysts of the strife. The first and perhaps the most important was the execution of Louis Riel in 1885. Others were the language question in the West and later in Ontario and the Quebec Jesuits' Estates Act of 1889. The Boer War and then the question of contributions to the British fleet further divided the country. Even a 1908 plebiscite on prohibition proved racially divisive, Anglo-Canadians voting heavily in favor and French Canadians almost unanimously against. The founding of the Association Catholique de la Jeunesse Canadienne provided a forum for strident French-Canadian nationalism. The Eucharistic Congress in Montreal in 1910, the demonstration against Ernesto Nathan in the same year, and the French Language Congress in Quebec two years later were massive, public manifestations of the discontent of French Canada. In Montreal itself economic and industrial growth "reinforced the French character of ... [the city], but ... also fostered the segregation of French and English, the rich and the poor, widening the social gulf between the various ethnic and economic groups within the community."[47]

Increasingly French and Anglo-Canadians came to regard each other as adversaries. There were ever fewer forums in which the two groups came together. They did not even share a common national holiday. There was, in short, an increasingly poisoned atmosphere in the country.[48] Occasionally both French and English might join in venting their spleen on outsiders. Jews—for both groups the traditional symbol of the outsider, the Antichrist in a Christian country, the scapegoat—were in a particularly vulnerable position. It has been claimed by some scholars, as mentioned earlier, that French Canadian antisemitism at the turn of the century had, in large part, displaced anti-British sentiment.[49] The economic "power elite" of Canada by the early twentieth century and even before consisted of a relatively small number of "interlocking directorates," almost all the members of which were WASPs. Their interests in Quebec, at least, were well served by French-Canadian antisemitism, which, although authentic and indigenous in itself, also served to divert attention from the real masters of Quebec and Canada. In Canada as elsewhere antisemitism was "the socialism of fools."

The intercommunal tension in the country was a factor in the steady undertone of racism and especially antisemitism among Canadians after 1875. By 1907 there were anti-Oriental race riots in Vancouver and mounting race hatred in Quebec and Ontario. In 1888 Alexander Harkavy observed that the words "Juif" and "Jew" were equally opprobrious in Canada.[50] Some years later, the well-assimilated Sigmund Samuel portrayed his native Toronto as "one of the most quietly bigoted cities in Europe or America."[51] In 1901 the Winnipeg *Telegram* described prejudice against Jews in Canada as "widespread and deep-rooted." Most Canadian Christians, according to the paper, even in the more free-wheeling West with its ethnic diversity, assumed most Jews to be "low, despicable . . . [people], given to lying, cozening and theft."[52] In the early years of the twentieth century Rev. J. McPhail Scott of Toronto noted an "inborn prejudice" against Jews in Anglo-Canada, which was expressed by "social ostracism."[53] Even the liberal C. A. Magrath was asserting in 1910 that Jews, Slavs and "Iberics" represented "negative immigration."[54]

Some British immigrants to Canada, especially those of the industrial classes, brought antisemitism with them from Britain. Imperialists, with their belief in Anglo-Saxon superiority, easily slipped into racial antisemitism. As Jews climbed the economic ladder, they inevitably elbowed aside some of the older, declining groups, which resulted in resentment in those quarters. In Toronto, Augustus Bridle, among others, complained that Jews were pushing "good Christians" out of their homes and their churches. Bridle preferred Negroes to Jews. Blacks, he felt, knew their place and did not seek to "crowd . . . other populations out."[55]

Although the negative behavior of Anglo-Canadians toward Jews seldom deteriorated to the level of that of French Canadians, there were many manifestations of it during the period under review. Goldwin Smith's journals, *The Bystander* and *The Week,* have already been mentioned. *The Bystander* gave voice to widely held feeling in 1880 in accusing Jews of having "spread themselves abroad to appropriate by usury and other commercial toils the fruits of the toil of others."[56] The journal, which appealed to a cultured and educated readership, asserted that Jews were morally "enfeebled," the practitioners of "a religion of race" who had signally "and steadfastly rejected the Gospel of Humanity."[57] More popular writing also displayed antisemitic convictions. The guidebook of Captain "Mac" (J. McAdam), *Canada: The Country, its People, Religions, Politics, Rulers, and its Apparent Future* (1882), presented Jews as vulgar moneygrubbers, barely able to speak English. Some two decades later John A. Steuart's antisemitic novel, *The Hebrew* (1905), which had previously been published in England, was issued in Canada. The book's main character was a loathsome English-Jewish slum lord and developer of east European origin. In 1911 French-Canadian nationalist Olivar Asselin described for an Anglo-Canadian audience "the invasion" of "exotic babbling" Jews into Montreal, which, he felt, had caused the debasement of Canada's metropolis.[58] Writing in a respected English-language publication, Asselin must have felt confident that his readers would sympathize with the plight of French Canadians. The daily press in Montreal and Toronto, as noted above, seldom hesitated in those years to call attention to the religion of Jewish miscreants. In 1909 the Montreal *Star* was printing advertisements on its front page, promising "no Jewish tricks."[59]

Antisemitism was not only manifested in print. It was difficult for Jewish graduates of Canadian medical schools to find a Canadian hospital to accept them as interns. Many were forced to emigrate to the United States, at least temporarily. Jews found it difficult to acquire fire insurance in these years, since they were alleged to have a predilection for arson. In 1904 the names of some six hundred Jews were stricken from the voting rolls in Montreal. Because their names were "foreign-sounding," it was assumed that they were aliens. By the last years of the period more and more housing was being closed to Jews in Montreal and Toronto. In 1914 *Ha-Zefirah* advised immigrants coming to North America to avoid ships of the Canadian Pacific Line, as sailors and "British soldiers" on board were said to mock Jews and treat them roughly. More serious were two legal trials involving Jews. In 1903 Max Kirt, son of a Montreal Jewish railroad contractor, had to stand trial for murder three times. An antisemitic prosecutor refused to accept the verdicts of acquittal handed down in the first two trials. A decade later in Halifax a ritual animal slaughterer was arrested for cruelty to animals at the instance of the local SPCA. His trial evoked considerable popular antisemitic feeling across Canada and much discomfort among Jews. Apparently the participation of Rabbis De Sola and Jacobs in SPCA activities had done little to endear Jews to Canadian animal lovers. All in all in these years Canadian Jews felt acutely the racial tensions that were part of life in bi-national Canada.[60]

Yet another aspect of Canadian life—the economic—hindered the ready acceptance of Jews. Even during boom years there were real concerns among Canadians about the health of their economy, its ability to withstand the competition of the United States and Europe. Unemployment and underemployment, perceived to be an omnipresent threat, aroused fears that immigrants would take the jobs of Canadians. And Jews were mostly immigrants. Contemporary scientific studies showed unequivocally that immigrants seldom took jobs away from those born in Canada or residing there for some length of time. On the whole, they took jobs that native-born Canadians refused to do.[61] Most people, however, refused to accept the validity of such data, which seemed to fly in the face of common sense and common prejudice. Immigrants appeared to be flooding the labor market at some periods. With their lower economic expectations, they were assumed to be displacing the native population. There was particular concern during the period, even among Jews, about assisted immigration programs, as noted earlier, which, it was claimed, were filling the country with Europe's flotsam. Of course, in periods of economic recession opposition to immigration mounted predictably. Then restrictionist sentiment developed in all circles, and antisemites singled out Jews as its proper targets.[62] Thus, economic objections to immigration often spilled over into xenophobia in general and antisemitism in particular.[63]

Trade unions were among the main opponents of immigration. In 1883–84 they expressed hostility to the addition of thousands of immigrants to the labor pool. In 1888 Montreal "workers and small businessmen" at a public meeting called upon the government to halt immigration, which, they felt, was detrimental to their livelihoods.[64] Again in the 1890s unionists voiced vehement opposition to immigration, especially if it were assisted. By the end of the period under review organized labor was demanding the "total exclusion of Asiatics from Canada" and wide-ranging restriction of others.[65] Union members became especially indignant when employers used immigrants as strike breakers. Such was the case in 1900 when Mark Workman, a respected member of Montreal's Temple Emanu-El, replaced striking union members in one of his textile plants with immigrant Romanian Jews. The Romanians had unknowingly signed on for wages two-thirds lower than those of unionized workers.[66] Similarly, other foreigners were usually unaware, when they were recruited, that they were to be scabs. Once in Canada, however, they were faced with the necessity of earning a living. Even Jewish workers, who tended to support the union principle, found it difficult to extricate themselves from such situations.

A concomitant of economic objections to Jewish immigration was the perception held by most Canadians before World War I that their country was agricultural. As noted already, French Canadians tended to glorify the pastoral; they disdained urbanization and industrialization, seeing in them the seeds of the destruction of their traditional way of life. (In outlying areas where industrialization was undertaken under French-Canadian auspices, often with American backing, there was less antagonism to it.) Objections to industry and commerce were particularly strong in Montreal, where they were almost entirely in Anglo-Saxon, or possibly Jewish, hands.[67] Among Anglo-Canadians a similar, if generally more temperate, ethos existed. Goldwin Smith was not the only one who idolized peasants. Progressives such as James S. Woodsworth were seriously concerned about the evils attendant upon industrialization and urbanization, especially deracination and immorality.[68] One of the main canons of imperialist thought was the "belief that business values were inadequate and insufficient, demoralizing and corrupting," that agricultural values were ennobling.[69] Proponents of immigration during the period under review usually sought agriculturists. C. A. Magrath asserted in 1910 that "the Englishman who fails completely [as a settler in Canada] is almost always a Londoner."[70] Agriculture Minister Clifford Sifton, the champion of immigration under Laurier between 1896 and 1911, spent his efforts in trying to bring farmers rather than industrial laborers to Canada.[71]

Jewish agriculturists were also welcome in these years. In a confidential letter to Harris Vineberg, president of the Baron de Hirsch Institute of Montreal in 1891, Hugh Sutherland, secretary to the Canadian high commissioner in London, Sir Charles Tupper, urged that "Manitoba as a field for Russian Jewish Colonization" be brought to the attention of the Russo-Jewish Committee in London, which was helping to resettle Jewish refugees.[72] A year later the Montreal *Gazette* extended a welcome to would-be Jewish farmers. Throughout 1906 the Ministry of the Interior ran a large advertisement in the Canadian *Jewish Times* advising readers of homesteading opportunities in the northwest. And in 1907 Prime Minister Sir Wilfrid Laurier stated publicly that Canada welcomed Jews, although "we encourage no immigrants except those who are agriculturists, farm labourers, and domestic servants."[73]

But Jews were the most urban of all religious groups; their main occupations were business and industry. As such, many Canadians considered them to be an unsuitable class of immigrants. Alexander T. Galt, then Canadian high commissioner in London, had been very sympathetic to Russian-Jewish refugees in 1882. In later years, however, his enthusiasm for Jewish immigration waned, apparently because of the lack of success Jews experienced on the land in western Canada.[74] Others were much more hostile. In an acrimonious parliamentary debate in 1895 the failure of "Jew pedlars" from the United States to become farmers was aired. In 1907 the Canadian government representative at the Irish International Exhibition in London went so far as to assert that "the Jews in Canada could not be viewed as permanent settlers," the reason being their lack of interest in agriculture.[75]

Jews tried to counteract their urban-business-exploiter image. In 1884–85 a few Montreal Jews founded the Montefiore Agricultural Aid Association to promote Jewish settlement on the land in Canada. The Association was stillborn. After 1890 the Baron de Hirsch Institute in Montreal devoted considerable energy to the nascent Jewish colonies in Alberta and Saskatchewan. On one occasion Rabbi Ashinsky vouched for seventy penniless Romanian Jews who had been refused entry into Canada. Ashinsky personally escorted them out to Manitoba, where they were expected to settle on farms. Rabbi Meldola De Sola and others tried to apprise the Canadian public of the success Jews were having in agricultural pursuits in Palestine and the United States.[76] Generally, however, Canadian Jews remained an urban people. A disgruntled commissioner of immigration in Winnipeg reported in 1906 that "very few of the Hebrew immigrants of the past year had settled on land permanently."[77]

In 1910 after years of effort, there were but 568 Jewish farming families in Canada.[78]

Their detractors saw the failure of large numbers of Jews to settle on the land as evidence of an "invincible desire to peddle rather than to labour."[79] That many non-Jews also failed, perhaps a majority of those who tried, was overlooked, as was the fact that other ethnic groups besides Jews were "underrepresented" in Canadian agriculture. As late as the 1940s the Canadian government was discriminating against Jewish immigrants, ostensibly because they were considered unsuited to agriculture. Canada as an agricultural country, no less than as a Christian country or a bi-national country, was a problematic place for Jews.[80]

Illustrative Events

The various impediments to the thoroughgoing integration of Jews into Anglo-Canada during these years came to focus on one personality and four dramatic issues. Although each of these reinforced the understanding that Jews were a part of Anglo-Canada and not of French Canada, each also established that there were clear limits to Jewish belonging, limits delineated in large part by antisemitism. The most serious of the issues was immigration. Others were the school question in Quebec, Sunday observance, and the Christian character of Queen's University. The personality was Goldwin Smith, who has already been introduced.

Professor Smith represented perhaps the most blatant manifestation of Anglo-Canadian antisemitism during the period under review, certainly within "respectable" circles. Smith was the panjandrum of Anglo-Canadian culture; his base in Canada, the University of Toronto, was one of the intellectual bastions of Anglo-Canada. A British emigrant, who as an Oxford professor was well known for his Liberal affiliations, Smith had taught for some years at Cornell University before coming to Canada. In England, he had also been known for his passionate dislike of Disraeli, a sentiment that was reciprocated. Smith may have transferred his hatred for the Tory Disraeli to the people from whom the prime minister had sprung.[81] Certainly, he gave voice to almost all the nativist and antisemitic ideas to be found in Canada. As an admirer of the peasantry, he sympathized with French Canadians and Russian kulaks, although on occasion he criticized French Canadians for their backwardness. Smith justified Russian pogroms as natural "resistance to Jewish instrusion and oppression," a revolt of "people ... goaded by . . . oppressive usury," (a position he later modified).[82] He believed, or affected to believe, that Jewish finance controlled the world, preying parasitically on non-Jews; he held Jews responsible for *all* wars. They were unpatriotic, fit only to be ostracized and perhaps forcibly segregated in their own country. In Smith's view, any sound, healthy social body would naturally "repel Jewish sentiment" and Jewish settlement.[83] Not surprisingly the professor felt a "sense of estrangement" whenever he had to relate personally to Jews.[84]

Repeatedly he asserted that the problem with Jews was not religious but social and economic. In fact, however, much of his objection was built on religious argumentation. He berated Jews for rejecting the "superior" religion, Christianity, claiming that Judaism was not a religion but a form of tribalism and that its God was but a "tribal God."[85] He castigated Jews for not intermarrying with Christians. Smith went so far as to assert that the Hebrew Bible was a subversive document, the reading of which resulted in "scandals and dangers."[86] He greatly admired modern Christianity's "medieval ancestors [who had] learned the duty of persecution."[87]

Goldwin Smith was a controversialist who enjoyed being at the center of a good fracas. He may possibly have been less averse to Jews than his outspoken views indicated (he attended the opening ceremonies of Toronto's new Holy Blossom Temple building in 1897, for instance), but there is no proof that he did not mean them. Certainly many people took his words at face value, and everyone listened when he spoke. Even those who disavowed him considered the professor to be "the most eminent of Canadians," and that made him all the more dangerous.[88] At the very least Smith offered antisemitism a highly visible and respectable platform, and his words appeared to be buttressed by the "scientific" knowledge of a university professor. Based as he was in Toronto, where Anglo-Canadians were not threatened by a hostile French-Canadian majority, Smith appeared to many Jews to be voicing the real views of Anglo-Canadians. Knowing violent antisemitism firsthand, Jews were alarmed by any manifestation of the disease, however polite, fearing its destructive potential in a country increasingly torn by racial strife. They were concerned, therefore, even though they recognized in Smith a more benign menace than the massive, multifaceted popular resistance of French Canadians to Jews. However widespread his following, Jews also knew that Smith aroused extensive opposition. There were Anglo-Canadians who disclaimed him as "not a product of our society"; and Jews themselves had many supporters.[89]

Of greater consequence than any individual were the several issues that arose around the turn of the century in such a way as to highlight the increasingly ambiguous position of Canadian Jewry. Unquestionably the most momentous of these was immigration. On the one hand, as noted previously, Jews found their way into Anglo-Canada eased by the fact that the society was largely one of immigrants or their children. On the other hand, Jews knew that even those Anglo-Canadians most eager for immigration did not consider them to be the most desirable sort for religious and racial reasons and because they were not farmers. Such feelings were only little in evidence in the first century and a quarter of Jewish life in Canada, because the number of Jews was very small and many of them had already been Anglicized before their arrival in the country. When their numbers became appreciable and their "foreignness" more noticeable, attitudes began to change, especially since the Jewish newcomers at the turn of the century were part of a wave of non-British, non-French immigration for which many Canadians were psychologically unprepared.

Themselves immigrants or the children of immigrants, most Jews were invariably quite sensitive to the debate about immigration restriction that raged in Canada during the last three decades of the period under review. Canadian Jews, like their counterparts in western Europe and America, were acutely aware, as well, of the desperate plight of their impoverished and persecuted brethren in eastern Europe. That was a very personal concern, since most Canadian Jews had close relatives in Europe, who, they knew, might one day want to join them in the New World. It is true that Canadianized Jews, like gentile Canadians, opposed making Canada a "dumping ground for people unable to care for themselves" and agreed that, with its harsh climate, theirs was "the worst country in the world to which the weak and incapable could be sent."[90] Along with their coreligionists in Britain and the United States, however, Canadian Jews, in general, were almost unanimously opposed to immigration restriction.[91]

Some scholars have maintained that prior to 1923 such restrictions in Canada were applied equally to all Europeans, even those of British extraction.[92] Contemporary Jews, however, did not feel that such was the case; and there is considerable evidence to support that contention. It is incontestable, moreover, that government incentives to immigrants were not dispensed equally. Between 1905 and 1909, for example, a bonus of one pound was paid to steamship agents for each immigrant of preferred stock—British, Dutch, French, Belgian, Swedish, Norwegian, Danish, Finnish, and American—diverted to Canada. As a result some 72 percent of all immigrants to Canada between 1901 and 1914 (a period of mass emigration of eastern and southern Europeans to North and South America) came from the United Kingdom and the United States. Although Canada had a much lower rate of immigrant rejection than the United States in these years, the reason may have had as much to do with the way various incentive programs were used to attract "desirable" immigrants as with anything else. In 1900 a large number of Romanian-Jewish immigrants was refused permission to land in Canada following the issuance of an order-in-council prohibiting the disembarkation of "undesirable immigrants." On that occasion the board of the Baron de Hirsch Institute gave a guarantee and "reminded the Government that the Hebrew immigrants to Canada had never . . . been an expense to the Government or a burden upon the country."[93]

In 1906 Henri Bourassa, the acknowledged spokesman of French-Canadian aspirations, turned his attention to immigration, criticizing "a system which peopled the West with a mixture of foreigners, neglecting prospective French and Belgian colonists in favor of Jews from Poland and Russia."[94] Many Anglo-Canadians agreed. In 1908, as noted previously, Canada prohibited assisted immigration altogether, a step that, in particular, disadvantaged the eastern European-Jewish poor and political refugees. In view of the increasing difficulty of getting into Canada, *Hasman* advised its eastern European readers that same year to book passage on British ships, which were more likely to be allowed to land their passengers than American.[95] In 1909, in an article entitled, "Canada Against the Immigrants," the same paper outlined the new impediments facing Jews seeking to immigrate to the Dominion. The article quoted a particularly sharp statement of the commissioner of immigration proclaiming his determination to enforce the immigration regulations according to the letter of the law.[96]

The immigration acts of 1906 and 1910, especially the latter, "vastly expanded the powers of immigration personnel to reject entry into Canada" on the basis of their own judgment[97] Moreover, racial background was now understood to be a valid reason for rejection. Beggars, vagrants, those likely to become a public charge, and assisted immigrants were barred by the 1910 act. All of these were broad categories, which were often applied to Jews with particular severity. A 1910 order-in-council required each adult immigrant to have at least $25.00 and each child between the ages of five and eighteen, $12.50, in addition to a railway ticket to his final destination. The rate of immigant rejection rose dramatically as a result of all these measures, which, as noted by the Jewish Colonization Association annual report of 1911, were being applied to Jews "with the greatest vigilance."[98] In order to assist Jews arriving in Canada in dealing with unsympathetic immigration officials, the Association found it necessary the next year to hire a special agent. Despite his efforts and those of local organizations and individuals, immigration officers in Quebec, "who were to be suspected of antisemitism" in any case, were managing to prevent the landing of qualified immigrants in 1913.[99] In August of that year 125 Russian and Galician Jews were held at Quebec for deportation as likely to become pubic charges.[100]

On the eve of World War I restrictions were tightened still further in ways that affected Jews in particular. An order-in-council that came into effect in January 1914 forbade the immigration into Canada of people who had interrupted their journey to North America with a stopover. Transmigrants, who had always made up a substantial proportion of Jewish immigrants to Canada, were thus barred from entry. In May 1914, another order-in-council excluded from Canada immigrants not having a valid passport or penal certificate from their country of origin. Because many Jews were political refugees from Russia, they could not hope to obtain such documentation. Most other immigrant groups were relatively unaffected by both regulations; and it is understandable why Jews felt that ostensibly impartial rules were, in fact, directed against them.[101] Indeed, Canadian immigration law and practice by World War I not only reflected the uncertain status of Jews in the country but also worked to reinforce that status.

The second major issue highlighting the ambiguity of the Jewish position in Canada was the complicated school question. It arose mainly in Quebec and had a long history. Already by 1841 the dissentient minority in Upper and Lower Canada received the right to establish its own schools. The Education Act of 1861 set up Protestant and Roman Catholic denominational schools in both Montreal and Quebec. In 1869 after Confederation the Province of Quebec made a further refinement. In Montreal the population was divided into four groups for school tax purposes: a Roman Catholic panel, a Protestant panel, a neutral panel into which corporations, non-Protestants, and non–Roman Catholics were to pay their taxes, and a fourth group of tax-exempt owners. Taxes paid into the neutral panel were to be divided between Protestants and Roman Catholics on a per capita basis. In Montreal and Quebec students might choose the school system they wished to attend. No one, however, had the right to choose the system into which he paid taxes. That was determined solely by religion.

These laws were all made without regard to Jews. Willy-nilly the various school acts enshrined a Christian, denominational school system to which Jews did not belong. Generally, during the first century of Jewish life in Canada Jews found their way into the Protestant schools although sometimes they attended Catholic schools or such private schools as there were. By 1870, however, because of their growing numbers in Montreal, it appeared necessary to legislate a place for Jews in the system. The act (34 Victoria, 1870, Chapter 12, section 9, Quebec) gave Montreal and Quebec Jews the right to pay their taxes into either the Protestant or the Roman Catholic panel and to educate their children in either system.

Until 1886 almost all Jewish children went to Protestant schools, and Jewish parents paid taxes to the Protestant panel. In that year, however, a split occurred in the Jewish community. The Protestant School Board of Montreal had been paying for Jewish religious instruction. Earlier still it had given financial support to a school run by the Spanish and Portuguese congregation. Now that congregation insisted that its minister, Meldola De Sola, be engaged by the Protestant board to teach Jewish children. The board refused, and it declared an end to all support for Jewish instruction. The congregation reopened its own school and affiliated with the Roman Catholic board; nonetheless, most Jewish children continued to attend Protestant schools.[102]

Considerable animosity developed between Jews and Protestants and among Jews themselves. Since most of the few wealthy Jewish property owners were members of De Sola's congregation, most Jewish tax money was now being channeled into the Roman Catholic system. Most Jewish children, however, were being educated in the Protestant system, seemingly at the expense of Protestants. (Protestants chose to ignore the fact that landlords obtained the money they paid in taxes from their tenants, and that indirectly, Jews were undoubtedly bearing their share of school expenses.) Agitation increased in 1890, when the Baron de Hirsch School was opened for immigrant Jewish children. That school, which was affiliated with the Protestant board, was supported mostly out of Jewish communal funds to which the wealthy members of the Spanish and Portuguese Synagogue contributed little. Graduates of the de Hirsch school continued their education in the Protestant system like most other Jews, placing an added burden on that system.[103]

After much wrangling and the interference of the provincial government a compromise was effected. The Spanish and Portuguese congregation closed its school, which had been poorly attended in any case. The Protestant board was to receive all Jewish tax money. In return it would subvene the Baron de Hirsch School and hire Rabbi De Sola as a teacher. Still, there remained no little dissatisfaction on all sides. The Jews for their part were accepted into the Protestant schools, but although they paid their taxes and sent their children, they did not have equal rights. They could not be elected to the school board, nor could they even vote in elections. (Only in 1965 did Jews finally gain the right to sit on Montreal Protestant school boards, a right still not uncontested in 1986.) Jewish supervisory personnel were not hired, nor even Jewish teachers. As much as possible, Jews were segregated in all-Jewish classes in mixed schools or removed to schools where the student body was entirely Jewish. In 1902, Jewish children were denied the right to earn scholarships to high school, no matter how good their grades. On the other hand, the Protestant board was discontent with the high cost of educating Jewish children. Irksome, too, was the challenge to the Christian character of the schools, an outgrowth of Jewish pressures for equality with Protestants, which could only have been achieved by secularization. Finally, antisemitism motivated some Protestant figures.[104]

In 1903 Jacob Pinsler sued the Protestant School Board of Montreal for refusing to grant him the high school scholarship to which his grades would have entitled him had he been a Protestant. Pinsler lost. Jews were declared to have no legal rights whatsoever in Quebec schools and to be there only on sufferance. The consequent uproar produced a new school act (Act 3, Edward VII, Chapter 16, Quebec). The new law was a rather inelegant compromise that declared Jews legally to be "Protestants for school purposes." Jewish children were now to attend school by right like Protestant children, although they would not be compelled to participate in Christian religious exercises and would be excused from school on Jewish holy days. Jewish parents were to pay their taxes to the Protestant panel, but they continued to have no say in policy making. They could not vote for school directors nor sit on the school board. No Jewish teachers were appointed in Montreal until 1913 and then only in schools where the pupil population was overwhelmingly Jewish. (In Toronto, Jews had the right to vote and to sit on the school board in the same years, but there, too, no Jewish teachers or supervisory personnel were appointed.)[105]

By 1914, Jewish children, as noted, constituted almost half of the

"Protestant" school population of Montreal; and Jews were growing restive because of their disfranchisement. They were unwelcome in the Catholic system and would not, in any case, have chosen to send their children there. The very nature of education in those schools made them unsuitable for non-Catholics. They were not designed to convey a body of knowledge to prepare students for careers. Rather, their aim was "to build . . . character, will and spirit of sacrifice, so that . . . [Catholics] could perform their duties toward God" in adult life.[106]

Protestant schools were different. Inspired by the "Protestant ethic," they were geared toward preparing their pupils for careers and for the world by imparting a large body of "objective" knowledge. Since their population was drawn from several Protestant denominations, they were necessarily less homogeneous than the Catholic schools and thus more appropriate for Jews. Nevertheless, these schools, too, were "permeated by religion."[107] The unofficial agreement between the Protestant School Board of Montreal and representatives of the Jewish community that had been in effect before the 1903 legislation stipulated that Montreal schools "shall as heretofore be distinctly Protestant, and therefore Christian."[108] At the time most members of the Board were ministers, and their administration reflected an unmistakably "Christian character." Protestant parents expressed considerable discontent about their children having to study with Jews; and in 1910 a number of ministers demanded the expulsion of Jewish children from the Protestant schools. If the Christian character of Protestant education was less oppressive and all-encompassing than that of Catholic education, its constituents took it no less seriously. (In Ontario the situation was better only in the technical sense. Whereas there was no question that Jews had a right to attend the public schools, those institutions were also overtly Protestant in character.) In the period before World War I it was understood by all that Jews had no right to expect neutral, secular education.[109]

In effect, then, Jews had no place in the Quebec schools. They were outsiders in the Protestant schools, admitted on sufferance and lacking rights. Antisemites opposed the presence of Jews even on those terms. In the Catholic schools they were altogether unwelcome. Accordingly, by World War I there was growing sentiment among Jews for establishing their own separate schools, an idea favored most by recently arrived eastern European immigrants. By way of contrast Canadianized Jews who expressed themselves publicly actually favored non-denominational schooling similar to that of the United States, out of a belief that it would educate Jewish and gentile children to be equal citizens.

Ultimately, they felt, only such a system of secular education could clear the way to full Jewish citizenship in Canada. In order to further those ends the board of the Baron de Hirsch Institute voluntarily downgraded its own school to an after-hours religious school.[110] Secularization, however, was generally opposed by both Catholics and Protestants in Quebec and, indeed, elsewhere in Canada. In the early years of the twentieth century, a few gentiles, mostly freethinkers or anticlericals, advocated a unified, secular school system organized along language lines. Majority opinion favored religious education on bi-national lines, the status quo. Sir Wilfrid Laurier and others spoke out publicly and often in favor of retaining the denominational system.[111]

Jews, moreover, were not free to go their own way. Had they wanted to establish their own school panel, they would have encountered opposition from both Catholics and Protestants. Protestants feared the further fragmentation of the nation as well as a diminution of their power in Montreal, were the many Jewish children to be removed from their schools. And many liked the system as it was. Catholics were opposed even though they would have benefited from the establishment of a Jewish panel—a reduction in Protestant power would have augmented their own. But most did not wish to grant legitimacy to Judaism by giving it equal status with Christianity. Some Protestants agreed.[112]

Despite certain shared attitudes, there was still a substantive difference in the practice of Protestants and Catholics that should be noted. True, both were wary of Jews and objected to their presence in Canada; and neither group was willing to accord them equality. But the Protestants, to a large degree out of their own self-interest in Quebec (but without any such interest elsewhere), were prepared to suffer the Jewish presence and to make limited concessions. French Catholics, in general, were not. If neither group liked Jews in their schools, only Protestant Anglo-Canadians offered them the possibility of existence.

The third major problematic area for Jews in Canada was the question of Sunday observance, or "the Lord's Day question," as it was called. Until 1903 Sunday blue laws had been considered a matter for provincial legislation. In that year, however, the Privy Council, on appeal, declared such laws to be beyond provincial competence. Immediately there sprang up a clamor, mostly from Protestants, for a Dominion-wide Lord's Day Act to guarantee the Protestant character of Sunday throughout Canada. Under such legislation Jews, whose Sabbath was Saturday, would be obliged by federal law to refrain from work on Sunday as well. In the case of small shopkeepers an extra day closed might mean the difference between poverty and minimal financial security. A workingman forced to be idle two days a week might not be able to provide for his family, or he might not be able to find work at all.

Feeling among Protestants regarding the proper observance of Sunday had always run high in Canada. In 1887 the Protestant clergy of Montreal "made efforts to suppress all means of amusement and diversion on Sunday." The city council at that time "resisted these attempts to curtail the few privileges the people . . . enjoy [ed]."[113] In 1898 the *Daily Witness,* usually friendly to Jews, informed them unequivocally that they might keep any Sabbath day they wished. They were not, however, to "do anything that would interfere with the public sanctity of the Day, which the great mass of the people observe."[114] By 1901 it was already becoming clear that those who kept the Jewish Sabbath were sorely disadvantaged and heading for difficulties.[115] Even as the campaign for countrywide restrictive legislation mounted, Jews were optimistic, confident that they were standing "on the side of freedom and common sense."[116] British legislation set a comforting example. An act of 1875 permitted British Jews who closed their businesses on Saturday to remain open on Sunday. Sabbath-observing employers in Britain might employ Sabbath-observing workers on Sunday. Canadian Jews sought for themselves no more than the mother country had granted to her Jews.[117]

"Freedom and common sense," however, were not the order of the day. In fact, during the public and parliamentary debates about the proposed legislation, Jews were dealt with rather roughly. Although he would later change his mind, Henri Bourassa attacked Jews in Parliament as "vampires" and urged that they be given no special rights.[118] The Protestant Lord's Day Alliance and its leaders and sympathizers were as severe and unrelenting. The Reverend Dr. J. Edgar Hill, Montrealer and president of the Alliance, asserted that Jews, with their separate ways, were an "anachronism" in modern society, who should be ignored completely in the drafting of Sunday legislation.[119] The 1906 Methodist annual conference also urged a bill without concessions to Jews.[120] Most Protestant members of Parliament expressed a "solid and stolid determination . . . to refuse freedom of conscience to Jews and those Christians [such as Seventh Day Adventists and Baptists] who strive to obey the divine commandment."[121] During the debate many Protestants gave vent to antisemitic feelings usually suppressed. Dr. Hill and not a few others were honest about their aim of securing for Canada "a Christian government in a Christian land."[122]

Jews finally became militant. In 1906 the Baron de Hirsch Institute formed a legislative committee to lobby for Sunday exemptions for Sabbath observers. Help was sought from the Board of Deputies of British Jews, which had succesfully fought a similar battle in Britain. Some support was forthcoming from Canadian gentiles. The Montreal *Star* and the *Gazette* supported the Jewish cause. Less puritanical French Canadians came to realize that Sunday, as they were accustomed to observing it, was threatened, and they, too, now supported the Jewish arguments. Even Goldwin Smith opposed the legislation as it stood. His erstwhile liberalism revived, as he argued against the restraint of personal freedom.[123]

Militancy, however, had come too late. In 1906 a Lord's Day Act that provided no exemptions was passed by the Dominion Parliament. It was subsequently amended to provide for local option enforcement, and this met the objections of French Canadians. In Quebec, at least, it also eased the problems of Jews somewhat, although as late as 1910 the Montreal police were arresting Jewish bakers for delivering bread to their Jewish customers on Sundays. In fact, as recently as 1977 a Montreal synagogue was served a summons for holding a bazaar on Sunday.[124]

Moreover, even the modified Lord's Day Act remained an annoyance to Jews and a reminder that many Anglo-Canadians were unprepared to accord them equal rights. In 1910 an attempt was made to mitigate further the effects of the law. Again, a campaign was mounted to allow those who kept a Saturday Sabbath to work on Sunday. But again, Jews and their supporters were beaten back, as the *Keneder odler* put it, by "the holy English black coats."[125] Again Jews were being told—in this case by Anglo-Canadians—that Canada was not quite theirs, but rather, a Christian country.

The fourth issue to bring home to Jews the ambivalence with which they were regarded in Anglo-Canada was the Queen's University Bill of 1912. To Jews the question was mostly of symbolic importance. From its inception the university in Kingston, Ontario, had been affiliated with the Presbyterian Church. In 1912, however, the university trustees desired to obtain Ontario government subsidies and, more important, to take advantage of the Carnegie Pension Fund for Queen's employees. In order to do so the university had to sever its ties with the Church. The trustees applied to the Dominion Parliament for charter as a "national" university.

Queen's had been accepting Jewish students for some time by 1912. But its most famous principal, the intellectual George Grant, was a Protestant minister known for his coolness toward Jews. Jewish faculty were not appointed. The university charter stipulated that "the profession of Christianity shall be required of the trustees and other officials of the University."[126] Grant and the trustees sought to retain that provision in their new "national" charter.[127] Canadian Jews were irate. If a "national" university could exclude Jews legally and officially, then, indeed, Jews were not a part of the nation. Samuel W. Jacobs later to be a Liberal member of the Dominion Parliament from Montreal, led the campaign for the Jewish community. The battle raged in the press and in Parliament. This time there was considerable parliamentary and public support for the Jewish position.

The charter was finally granted with the Christian provision standing, but the word, "national," stricken out. It was a victory of sorts, for the principle of equal citizenship, but only a partial one, for Parliament was willing to charter a university that maintained a religious test for its faculty and officers. Moreover, the battle had once again aroused animosity toward Jews, this time of such vehemence that many Jews were left frightened and less sure than ever of their position in Canada.[128] It provided further proof, if any were needed, that at the end of the period under review Jews were still outsiders to some extent; the boundaries that separated them from other Canadians were still distinctly drawn.

More at Home; More Insecure

Most Jews came to Canada during the period under review expecting to become part of Western society. They were prepared—eager—to make concessions in exchange for full and equal citizenship in their new homeland, as they were doing in Britain, the United States, and elsewhere. But they were unwilling to give up their religion altogether and sought to retain vestiges of ethnicity: endogamous marriage, a social life largely within the ethnic group, the retention of many Jewish values and customs.

French Canada proved to be out of bounds for Jews, both because they themselves were not eager to join it and because French Canadians were entirely unprepared to have them. To the extent that they could before World War I, Jews affiliated with Anglo-Canada in the various ways that have been described. Because of the uncertain reception they received even among Anglo-Canadians, however, affiliation was rather less complete than in England or in the United States. In many ways Jews developed into a third national group in Canada—English speakers with institutions similar and parallel to those of Anglo-Canadians.

The ambivalence with which they were greeted in Canada under-standably aroused among Jews a sense of insecurity and nervousness regarding their status. In turn, some felt a

> racial obligation . . . to take a personal and active interest in all new arrivals in order to prevent . . . the occurrence of anything that could be twisted into an imputation on the record of Jewish citizenship.[129]

Insecurity led many to turn inward. These devoted their energies to strengthening the Jewish community. Some opted out of Canada by embracing Jewish nationalism, that is, Zionism. For some, insecurity led to self-abnegation bordering on self-contempt. One of the main reasons for opening the Baron de Hirsch School was that Jewish children were ashamed to enter the Protestant schools before they had mastered English. In 1914, when Rabbi Abramowitz became an army chaplain, he discov-ered that Jews were enlisting under false names and lying about their religion, afraid that their Jewishness might expose them to ridicule. As late as 1917 Mortimer B. Davis, Mark Workman, and others opposed the candidacy of Samuel W. Jacobs for Parliament, on the grounds that Jews should remain inconspicuous in Canada.[130]

American Jews at the time found their Canadian coreligionists self-effacing and even cowardly. In 1897 the *Reform Advocate* was puzzled by the fawning excitement of Montreal Jews when the lieutenant gov-ernor of Quebec appeared at a session of the convention of the Central Conference of American Rabbis in that city. From the paper's admittedly "American point of view," it was hard to understand why the lieutenant governor should have been praised, "because he for the first time attended a Jewish house of worship." To the *Advocate*'s correspondent it seemed "entirely too servile" for Jews to "give . . . a reward to a man because he 'condescends' to visit for once a synagogue."[131] Some years later another correspondent for the same paper was amazed to find that, although Montreal Jews had prospered financially, they were careful to do nothing "to make themselves loom large in the eyes of the rest of the population." The writer found the Montrealers "the most isolated and most negligible quantity for their numbers and their intrinsic importance" of any Jewish community he had ever visited. It surprised the American to see Montreal Jews "most singularly devoid of all power," eschewing political office at every level. It seemed to him as if there were no "Canadian Jews, only . . . Jews living in Canada." The contrast with the United States was particularly striking.[132]

JEWISH CONSULS

Samuel Nordheimer, Toronto (Germany)

The author's collection

Andrew Cohen Joseph, Quebec (Belgium)

The author's collection

Maxwell Goldstein, Montreal (Austria-Hungary)

Samuel Gintzburger, Vancouver (Switzerland)

One way in which certain Canadian Jews sought status is symptomatic of their situation. The list of those who became foreign consuls is not short. The Jews who represented Francophone Europe in Canada have already been mentioned. Other countries were represented by Jews in these years, as well: David A. Ansell was Mexican consul in Montreal; A. Boronow served as Danish consul there and was succeeded by another Jew, Herman A. Wolff; Maxwell Goldstein served for a time as consul in Montreal for both Germany and Austria-Hungary. Consulships were generally unpaid or minimally paid positions, but the post conferred status on its holder. Ironically, then, one of the few ways for a Jew to acquire high standing in the general community during these years was by becoming an officer of a foreign power. Yet, although these offices imparted status to individual Jews, as noted earlier, they reinforced the sense of Jews as foreigners, an image further strengthened by Jews' adherence to Zionism.[133]

The relative insecurity of Canadian Jews and the ambiguousness of their status help explain the relatively small scale of Jewish immigration to the Dominion. Naturally far fewer Jews immigrated to Canada than to the United States during the period under review (perhaps seventy-five thousand as compared with about three million). Canada itself had a much smaller population than its southern neighbor; and its economic absorptive capacity was more limited. But even proportionately, far fewer Jews entered Canada than the United States. In 1914 Jews represented close to 3 percent of the American population; in Canada they accounted for about 1 percent. There were as many Jews in the greater Boston area in 1914 as there were in all of Canada. Official immigration policy, the harsh climate, limited economic opportunities, among other factors, influenced the number of Jewish immigrants. It is likely, however, that Jews' awareness of Canadian ambivalence regarding them weighed even more heavily. Given the opportunity for full equality in the United States and to a somewhat lesser degree in England, Jews understandably exhibited some reluctance to become a third solitude in Canada.

CHAPTER SEVEN

Poſtſcript:

"Plus ça change, plus c'est la même chose?"

"A Minor Land of Promise"

Whatever obstacles they encountered on the path to integration during the period under review, Canadian Jews and others still felt—and not without reason—that Jews were better accepted in Canada than in most other countries of the world. They certainly were beginning to feel at home in Anglo-Canada. It must be remembered, after all, that Jews of the nineteenth and early twentieth century lived with vivid personal memories of Russian and Romanian poverty and persecution. As a result, they tended to downplay the relatively mild and polite discrimination they met in Anglo-Canada and in other English-speaking countries, perhaps even to expect it as a fact of Jewish life. On the other hand, French-Canadian antisemitism—because it evoked memories of continental Europe, because it sometimes called for the total exclusion of Jews from Canada, because it was often not polite, although it was usually not violent—appeared menacing and unacceptable.

To a significant degree in the period before World War I, Jews entered into the life of Anglo-Canada, following, for the most part, the occupational patterns and life styles of Anglo-Canadians. They learned to speak their language and participated in their cultural life; like WASP Canadians they maintained strong ties with England and the United States. Also like many gentile Anglo-Canadians, Jews had poor relationships with French Canada and its European motherland. Indeed, if not all was easy for Jews within Anglo-Canada, in comparison with French Canada (and certainly in comparison with eastern Europe) it had become, as the London *Jewish Chronicle* asserted in 1907, "a minor land of promise."[1]

After the turn of the century Jews were less well integrated into Canada than they had been earlier, when their numbers had been negligible; and they began to experience considerable antisemitism in many quarters, especially in Anglo-Canada, where it had not been evident before. To a degree, however, they understood their difficulties to be related to their immigrant status; most expected that the future, like the past, held the promise of fuller acceptance for the acculturated.[2] Acutely aware of French-Canadian hostility, Jews had nonetheless learned that they could live with it as long as Anglo-Canadians controlled the country. Some in the immediate pre-World War I years sensed that the affinity of Anglo-Canadians for Judaism and their consequent acceptance of Jews might be waning. Not many realized—or were willing to admit—however, that the future might hold out less promise than had the past. In part, their perceptions were colored by the desperate need to find a home more secure than the Europe they had left.

In 1897 when Canadian Jewry centered in Montreal was becoming nervous about mounting French-Canadian antisemitism, one of their responses was to found a journal to combat racist propaganda. They established the English-language Canadian *Jewish Times* and chose a philo-Semitic Anglo-Canadian gentile, Carroll Ryan, to head it. The French were probably thought to be beyond repair; there seemed little point in appealing to them in their language.[3] One hoped, however, that Anglo-Canadians were open to reason and could be immunized against a serious outbreak of the antisemitic disease. And, at the very least, Jews themselves could read the periodical, exploring and reinforcing their own identity. The founding of the *Jewish Times* exemplified Jews' condition during the period under review—excluded from French Canada and wishing to be part of Anglo-Canada. But they were preparing themselves, perhaps without being altogether aware of it, for the eventuality of remaining outside of both.

The 1920s and Beyond—Toward Integration

Although the years after 1914 fall beyond the scope of the present study, a few words are in order. For one thing, events in the interwar period and, to a degree, in the post–World War II era, as well, have reflected the trends and patterns of the earlier, formative years. But even more, it is the present situation of which events described in the previous pages are prologue. Within the Jewish community the period between the wars was a time of slow growth and consolidation, marked by the founding of new institutions and the development of older ones. As had been the case in the period under review, the institutions established in the 1920s and 1930s represented a response both to the growing needs of the Jewish community and to the exclusion of Jews from both French and Anglo-Canada. Mount Sinai Hospital, which evolved out of the old Toronto Jewish Dispensary in the early 1920s, and the Jewish General Hospital of Montreal, opened in 1934, are cases in point. They were established not only to care for the ill, a traditional Jewish concern, but also to provide a training ground for Jewish interns, who were not admitted into hospitals under non-Jewish auspices. The year the Montreal hospital opened actually saw French-Canadian interns in that city go on strike because of the appointment of a Jewish intern at Notre Dame Hospital. The strike ended only after Dr. Rabinovitch resigned his internship.[4] The Canadian Jewish Congress also represented a response to both impetuses. Established in 1919 and reorganized in 1934, the national Congress was meant to coordinate Jewish communal activities but also to enable Canadian Jewry to speak with one voice to gentiles on matters of deep concern to Jews, especially antisemitism. In the United States, where somewhat fuller integration into the general society was possible, and where ethnic separatism has, until recently, been frowned upon, no national organization like the Congress has ever come into being.

The 1920s and 1930s saw the increasing acculturation and integration of Canadian Jews. As the eastern Europeans became Anglicized, they were better accepted as part of the Anglo-Canadian scene. In French Canada there were generally "good communications in day-to-day dealings" between French Canadians and Jews.[5] But this was also a period in which the antisemitic attitudes and behavior of French and Anglo-Canadians, already evident in the latter years of the period under review, became more pronounced. In the early 1920s the question of Sunday observance arose once more in French Canada, stirring up animosity against Jews and culminating in repeal of the local-option legislation that had allowed Saturday Sabbath observers to work on Sundays. In the early 1930s, as noted previously, French Canadians embarked on a campaign to boycott Jewish merchants under the slogan, "Achat chez nous!" ("Buy from us!")[6] From the mid-twenties the federal government vigorously pursued a policy of discouraging Jewish immigration. In general, Jews found it harder and harder to immigrate to the Dominion, for, although Canada's laws seemed less restrictive than those of the United States or Great Britain, Canadian legislation allowed extensive freedom of administrative action, as noted previously; and it was through such means that the exclusion of Jews was achieved.[7]

Although the movement of people to and from Canada, the United States, and Britain slowed to a trickle by the end of the 1920s, the institutional ties of Canadian Jews to their coreligionists in the other two countries continued to develop; and echoes of European events continued to be heard in Canada. Zionism in these years drew Canadians rather closer to the mother country, which held the mandate for Palestine under League of Nations auspices and thus responsibility for Jewish settlement there. Canadian Jews such as the wealthy playboy, Ben Dunkelman, found it easy to be "both a Zionist and a loyal British subject."[8] As Ottawa department store magnate and Zionist leader Archibald Freiman put it, Britain and the Jews were "partners in . . . [the Zionist] enterprise."[9] With the rise of Hitler, European influence began to be felt more strongly and less benignly in Canada, now more from Germany and Italy than from England or France. As before, European ideas blended easily with indigenous Canadian currents of thought. The relationship of Canadian fascist movements to Jews in the 1930s has been amply chronicled elsewhere.[10] It will suffice to note here that although, for the most part, these movements remained outside the mainstream of Canadian politics, they caused Jews a great deal of discomfort by helping to swell the tide of antisemitism connected in part with the Great Depression—especially in French Canada. It is characteristic of the atmosphere in the country that as late as 1941, when the Department of National War Service issued a propaganda pamphlet promoting Canadian unity, Watson Kirkconnell's *Canadians All,* it was deemed desirable to omit the section on Jews from the French-language version, *Canadiens tous.* Although Canadian fascism either withered or was suppressed when war broke out, and although Nazi Germany, a country synonymous with the hatred of Jews, was the enemy, antisemitism remained widespread and deep-rooted in Canada. Probably the most significant aspect of Canadian antisemitism in the Hitler period was the government's refusal to open the country's doors to Jewish refugees. In part because of the vehement opposition of French Canadians, Canada's immigration policy was considerably harsher in the 1930s and 1940s than that of other countries in the Western world.[11]

As earlier, the rejection of Jews in the interwar years propelled them toward more intense Zionism, especially in the 1930s, when Palestine appeared to be a more likely haven than Canada for persecuted Jews. When Zionist leaders, such as Yitzhak Ben-Zvi and Arthur Ruppin, visited Canada in these years, they were delighted by the vigor of Canadian Zionism, although it is unlikely that they were altogether aware of the causes.[12] On a visit to Winnipeg in 1926 Ben-Zvi found a flourishing Po'alei Zion Youth Organization there. Its only other active chapter in North America at the time was in the giant Jewish community of New York City.[13] Although few of the scarce Palestine immigration certificates were allotted to Canadians in the 1920s and 1930s, a number of Zionists from the Dominion did succeed in settling there, including Dov Yosef (Bernard Joseph) and John Lewis Michaels from Montreal, and journalist Molly Lyons (Bar David) and the son of Rabbi Marcus Berner from the West.[14]

Contemporary Canadians understood well the connection between enthusiasm for Zionism and their own country's atmosphere and policies. One of the stores targeted by the fascists for boycott in the 1930s was that of Archibald Freiman. In late 1935 Freiman brought a libel suit against Jean Tissot, the man who had spearheaded the campaign against his concern. Although Tissot, a former police detective, was convicted, he became a hero to many antisemites and was actually vindicated by the trial judge and by much of the French-Canadian press, including Montreal's *Le Devoir*. At the height of the affair Tissot ran for the federal Parliament in an Ottawa riding and received some 20 percent of the votes. Later he became chief of police in Rouyn, Quebec.[15] Freiman was "shocked and frightened" at the events, suffering a "sickening feeling of loss that such deep prejudice could be found" in Canada.[16] In his 1935 presidential address to the convention of the Zionist Organization of Canada, Freiman urged the delegates to respond to the formation in their "own country [of] Nazi groups" by increasing their efforts on behalf of Zionism. His own experiences and the anti-Jewish agitation in many places around the country had resulted, Freiman asserted, in there being more "sympathy for the cause of Zionism" among Canadian Jews than ever before.[17] At the same convention the Honorable Arthur Roebuck, then attorney general of Ontario and a member of the provincial legislature representing a largely Jewish riding in Toronto, was "greeted with thunderous applause" when he told the delegates that he looked

> forward to the time when our economic conditions will be less severe than they are today and when we may open wide the gates, throw down the restrictions and make of Canada a Mecca [!] for all the oppressed peoples of the world.[18]

Although not in Roebuck's case, it can be assumed that some of the gentile political support for Zionism was at least partly motivated, as it had been earlier, by the determination to keep Jews out of Canada. In 1934 Prime Minister R. B. Bennett opened the annual United Palestine Appeal fund drive with a coast-to-coast radio broadcast in which he reiterated the belief that the Balfour Declaration and the conquest of Palestine by the British represented the beginning of the fulfillment of biblical prophecies. At the same time, Bennett opposed the admission into Canada of Jewish refugees from Nazi Germany, ostensibly out of fear of stirring up antisemitism.[19] In the 1940s, Zionism, by then concerned explicitly with the question of Jewish statehood, came into sharp conflict with British policy; the Canadian government under Prime Minister Mackenzie King and his successor, Louis St. Laurent, distanced itself from the movement, while maintaining the barriers to Jewish immigration to Canada.[20] (The conflict between Britain and the Zionists served to push Canadian Jewry closer to the United States, which seemed more receptive to the goals of Zionism than Britain. In fact, the struggles of the late 1940s almost completely severed the old ties to the mother country.)[21]

In the post–World War II years attitudes to Jews and other previously "non-preferred" groups altered radically in Canada, in part because of a new cosmopolitanism and internationalism born of the wartime experience, in part because the reviving economy needed more laborers, and for many other reasons. The change was marked by a new willingness to admit immigrants of various backgrounds; and, in fact, Canadian Jewry grew by 50 percent between 1945 and 1961, mostly because of immigration.[22] The changed attitudes were evident not only in Anglo-Canada, but also in French Canada, where the "Quiet Revolution" of the 1950s and 1960s largely effected the transformation of Quebec into a secular, industrial society, French in language and culture, but in many ways indistinguishable from the rest of North America. No longer were Jews an anomaly in Quebec or elsewhere in Canada because of their urban way of life. All over the country the older conceptions of Canada as a Christian country and a bi-national or bi-racial society receded. There arose, instead, a new vision of Canada as an ethnic mosaic, bi-lingual but multi-cultural. The mosaic theory of society was a Canadian version of "cultural pluralism," first articulated in North America in the early years of the present century by the American-Jewish social thinker and Zionist Horace Kallen, among others. It gained popular acceptance simultaneously in Canada and the United States, largely in response to the new ethnic assertiveness of blacks and French Canadians. (As noted previously, some French-Canadian writers came to refer to themselves as "white niggers," in order to stress the similarities in the situations of the two groups).[23]

The mosaic concept at last accorded Jews and Judaism a legitimate place in Canadian society. Jewish political achievements in recent years are a sign of this new legitimacy. In 1969 Herb Gray became the first Jew appointed to the federal cabinet; three years later David Barrett of British Columbia became the first Jew to be elected a provincial premier. Since that time Jews have occupied the posts of chief justice of the Supreme Court of Canada, federal minister of defense, ambassador to Washington and to the United Nations, leader of the opposition in Ontario, the country's most populous province, and leader of the national New Democratic Party. In other areas, as well, Jews have penetrated Anglo-Canadian institutions once largely the preserve of WASPs: the boards of governors of McGill University and the University of Toronto as early as 1964; the presidency of other institutions of higher learning, such as York University, Ryerson Polytechnical Institute, and the Ontario Institute for Studies in Education in Toronto and the University of Alberta, later; the presidency of the Canadian Bar Association in 1976. Another sign of the acceptability of Jews is a rate of intermarriage approaching that of the United States. Particularly noteworthy in Quebec is the prevalence of intermarriage between French Canadians and Jews of North African origin in recent years.[24] This new legitimacy of Judaism in Canada can be seen in the public funding in Alberta since 1967 and in Quebec since 1968 of Jewish parochial schools. Thus ethnic pluralism has meant the breakdown of the old bi-national, bi-religious conceptions of Canada, which had served to keep Jews on the periphery of Canadian life; and it has facilitated their integration into the mainstream.

Multi-culturalism, the social concomitant of ethnic pluralism, has served to strengthen Jewish communal life in Canada. Government funding, available to support a variety of projects since the 1960s, has provided a major stimulus for the development of Jewish culture.[25] One of the most significant by-products of multiculturalism has been the extraordinary number of Jewish children enrolled in all-day Jewish schools in Montreal, Toronto, Winnipeg, and some of the smaller centers, a percentage far greater than in most other Diaspora communities.[26] At the same time, then, ethnic pluralism and multiculturalism both support greater tolerance and integration into the mainstream and promote ethnic separatism. Whether their long-term effect on the Jewish community will be to weaken it or to strengthen it cannot yet be foreseen.

A measure of Jews' new sense of belonging in Canada is the changed character of Canadian Zionism and of the government's attitudes toward Israel. Since the 1950s the Canadian government has overcome some of the coolness of the Mackenzie King and St. Laurent years; and no longer does anyone seriously harbor hopes of using Israel to deflect potential Jewish immigrants away from Canada or to encourage the emigration of Canadian Jews. Canada has sold arms to Israel; and although the federal government has been unwilling to take action against the anti-Israel Arab economic boycott, Ontario did so in 1978. The federal government has supported the establishment of a chair in Canadian Studies at the Hebrew University in Jerusalem, one of only a few outside of Canada. Canada has been rather supportive of Israel in international forums (much more so than Britain or France, although less so than the United States), despite the fact that Jews do not have "the kind of financial power [in Canada] that can break a political party. Unlike the Jews in the United States [moreover,] they are not numerous enough to have [decisive] political influence [in any province]."[27]

Since the founding of Israel support for the state has been virtually universal among Canadian Jews, who maintain an extraordinarily high per-capita level of financial contributions to Israeli causes. On the other hand, post-World War II Zionism has lost much of its earlier force and immediacy. Relatively few Canadian Jews today seriously consider settling in Israel, although more since 1967 than earlier.[28] As was not the case in the early days of Canadian Zionism, very few Canadians today think the day might come when conditions for Jews in Canada will make it necessary to seek refuge in the Jewish homeland. The Zionist movement has surrendered almost all of its national, representative functions to the Canadian Jewish Congress.[29] And for the most part Zionism in Canada today is a philanthropic endeavor, much as it has always been for American Zionists, a sign that Canadian Jews now feel as much at home in their country as Americans do in theirs.[30] The shift is also clear evidence of the ongoing American influence on Canadian Jews.

Whereas Zionism has become less of a generative force in Canadian-Jewish life, the Canadian Jewish Congress, especially through its local affiliates, has become much more important over the years. The Congress was successful, even in the anti-establishment era of the 1960s and beyond, in attracting younger Jews to its ranks, unlike establishment Jewish organizations in America and Britain. A recent president of the Congress, Irwin Cotler, was the youngest person ever to serve in that post; and his election was made possible by the support of the younger elements in the organization. The Congress is perhaps the outstanding illustration of Jews' functioning within the ethnic mosaic, rather than on the fringes of Canadian society, as an autonomous group with certain national characteristics parellel to those of French and Anglo-Canadians and people of other origins, at the same time English-speaking and mostly Anglo-Canadian by culture.[31]

The 1920s and Beyond—Toward Isolation

Although the behavior of Anglo-Canadians as well as attitudinal survey data indicate that their willingness to accept Jews today has increased considerably since the period under review in this study, progress has not been steady, nor is the change universal.[32] In the 1950s, for example, McGill University, since the days of Abraham De Sola a symbol of Jewish acceptance in Anglo-Canada, was imposing quotas on the number of Jewish students and faculty; more recently those restrictions were removed. Antisemitism cloaked as anti-Israel sentiment has surfaced in Anglo-Canada in the last few years, as it has elsewhere.[33] And in 1985 dramatic trials of a high school teacher in Alberta, who had been teaching that the Holocaust had never occurred, and a publicist and distributor of anti-Jewish materials in Ontario highlighted the existence of pockets of virulent anti-Jewish sentiment in the country.

Doubts regarding the acceptance of Jews have arisen especially with regard to French Canada. One recent essay makes the claim that today antisemitism in Quebec "compares favourably with that in Europe and is no worse than in other Canadian provinces or the American states."[34] Another writer has asserted that "in the present climate of Quebec, . . . antisemitism is no longer an issue."[35] Evidence of the new climate is found in the rate of intermarriage between Jews and French Canadians mentioned earlier, in the appointment of a Jew as provincial minister of justice by the new Liberal premier elected in 1985, and in other developments. Although several large business firms have shifted their headquarters to Ontario in the last decade because of French Canadian nationalist demands that French be the language of the working place in Quebec, some of Montreal's English-speaking Jewish elite remain committed to maintaining their commercial and industrial activities there. As Mitzi Dobrin, head of the huge Steinberg's/Miracle Mart supermarket chain, recently put it, they believe that the "political and social" climate in Quebec "has improved" greatly since the period under review here; and they intend to stay.[36] The organized Jewish community in Montreal has also exhibited a degree of confidence regarding the future. In 1983 the Bialik High School announced plans to erect a new $4.5 million building, while the Saidye Bronfman cultural center unveiled a major expansion scheme in 1986.

These changes and signs of confidence notwithstanding, there are indications, with regard to tension between Anglo and French Canadians and with regard to the place of Jews, that French Canada is not an altogether different place from what it was during the period under discussion. A review of some recent events is instructive. Poll data show that antisemitism remains at an appreciably higher level everywhere in Canada than in the United States. Attitudes toward Jews and Israel are, moreover, measurably more negative in French Canada than in Anglo-Canada.[37] Furthermore, whereas French Canadians accept multicultur-alism for Canada as a whole, they have not accepted it as applicable to French-Canadian society itself. These attitudes have been manifested in highly dramatic ways. Between 1963 and 1969 the quiet of Quebec's "Quiet Revolution" was shattered by violence on a number of occasions. In October 1970, two kidnappings heightened the sense of growing crisis. The Quebec Liberation Front (FLQ) seized a British consular official in Montreal and the Quebec minister of labor and immigration. The minister, later found murdered, was taken following an unsuccessful attempt to kidnap the Israeli trade attaché in Montreal. These events precipitated the invoking by the federal government of the War Measures Act, which was replaced in December 1970 by the Public Order Bill. The latter, which outlawed the FLQ, remained in force until April 1971. Such tough measures, just short of martial law, brought the violence to a halt.

They did not, however, put an end to the growing sentiment for

Quebec independence. In November 1976, the separatists succeeded in electing a government in Quebec, headed by René Lévesque. The Parti Québécois was reelected in 1981. In power, the separatists pursued a policy of French-Canadian nationalism: first, the "francization" of Quebec life (that is, making French the overwhelming cultural and linguistic influence), to be followed, many of them hoped, by the independence of Quebec. "Sovereignty association," a euphemism for independence, was turned down by the Quebec electorate in a referendum in May 1980, although it received some 40 percent of the votes; and the Parti Québécois was defeated in elections held in late 1985. Francization, however, a policy initiated long before the ascension to power of the Parti Québécois, is probably irreversible in most areas of Quebec life.

These developments had special consequences for Jews, as was recognized early on by Jews and non-Jews. The approximately 40 percent of the Canadian-Jewish community who were Holocaust survivors or their descendants were, on the whole, "highly allergic to the growing spirit of nationalism," sensing a "philosophy which would tolerate discrimination against non-French-Canadian groups." The descendants of Jews long settled in Canada sensed in the new nationalism echoes of "the virulent antisemitism of fascist-nationalist movements in French Canada before World War II."[38] When the Parti Québécois came to power, Jews were "brutally shocked," according to the director general of Montreal's Jewish Community Research Institute.[39]

Statements by prominent Quebec nationalists over the years did little to allay Jews' fears. A few examples must suffice. In 1965 René Lévesque, then an influential provincial cabinet minister in the Liberal government of Premier Jean Lesage, accused Jews of gravitating to "where the strength lay," that is, to the Anglophone community in Quebec and in Canada as a whole.[40] He seemed to take no account of the historical reality that it had been virtually impossible for Jews to integrate into the French-Canadian community in earlier eras; for that matter, he also disregarded the racial and religious exclusivity of contemporary French-Canadian nationalism, noted by others.[41] A few years later, Claude Ryan, then editor of *Le Devoir* and later to become for a time head of the Quebec Liberal Party, made a similar accusation in an address to the annual meeting of the Christian-Jewish Dialogue in Montreal. On that occasion Ryan noted that "very few French Canadians . . . maintain friendly private relations with Jews," that most of them look upon the individual Jew as "first and above all a money-maker . . . who will do practically anything in order to make a fast dollar," that a majority of them feel

Jews have been born to "suffer and be persecuted," because they killed Jesus, and that most believe Jews care little "for morality." Although Ryan mostly dissociated himself from such views, he urged Jews to reform their religion and to ally themselves with the legitimate nationalist aspirations of French Canadians.[42] During the debate over the War Measures Act in the House of Commons the next year, the "anti-Jewish" character of the FLQ was noted by a government spokesman.[43] In 1973 Michel Chartrand, a French-Canadian trade-union leader once involved with the FLQ, told the convention of the Federation of Canadian Arab Societies that he felt the "Jewish people in Quebec" enjoyed "more privileges than any other minority in the world." Chartrand expressed the hope that they would not "poison the air of this country any further."[44] In February 1978, over a year after the Parti Québécois had come to power, a Montreal journal, *Ici Québec,* the publisher of which was president of the Montreal branch of the party, printed a long article written by the journal's editor-in-chief attacking Zionism as "racism." Although Premier Lévesque denounced the piece as "lousy, . . . reeking of prejudice," it reinforced in the minds of the country's Jews the feeling that separatism was inimical to their interests. In 1982 an official delegation of the Palestine Liberation Organization was invited to participate in the convention of the Parti Québécois.[45]

Occasionally even federal government officials uttered pronouncements that unnerved Jews. In November 1973, just after the Yom Kippur War, Pierre Brisson of the Department of Manpower and Immigration asserted in a Cairo newspaper interview that Jewish capital controlled Canada's foreign policy. (He was subsequently dismissed from his post.) During the election campaign of 1979, Pierre Trudeau, longtime prime minister and soon to be prime minister again, the M.P. for a Montreal riding that was the most heavily Jewish of any in the country and a person generally very friendly to Jews and to Israel, asserted publicly that Jews were themselves exciting antisemitism in the country with their demands for government policies favorable to Israel and for legislation to outlaw the Arab economic boycott of Israel.[46]

Politics has hardly been the only arena to witness anti-Jewish sentiment in French Canada in recent years. The growing secularization and urbanization of Quebec notwithstanding, the old literary and cultural stereotypes of Jews as rich exploiters, as the embodiment of moral and spiritual degeneracy retain some of their currency. Jews continue to serve as symbols of radical evil—albeit in secularized form—for many French-Canadian writers, most of them sympathetic to separatism. Promiment novelists Gabrielle Roy and Roch Carrier have written in this vein.[47] So, too, has Raoul Roy, who, in his *Lettre aux Juifs de Montréal* (1979), offered Jews a choice between "assimilation and emigration to Israel."[48] More recently controversy has been raging over Yves Beauchemin's novel, *Le Matou,* the villain of which appears to many to exemplify the old, anti-Jewish stereotypes of nineteenth- and early-twentieth-century French and French-Canadian literature. The book was serialized in the mass circulation *La Presse* in 1981; it received the literary prize of the Montreal Urban Community a year later and has been a best seller in France as well as in Quebec; it has now been made into a movie.[49] Yet another controversy of the 1980s has involved *Le Devoir* and two Jewish journalists. An editorial in the Montreal daily accused the newspapermen of "defaming" Quebec in an article they had published in the *Jerusalem Post.* The Jewish community leadership in Montreal became so nervous over the issue that the Canadian Jewish Congress issued a statement of "profound regret'" that an article portraying a "false" image of Quebec's Jews had been written. The Congress statement evoked memories of responses to earlier threats. The journalists sued *Le Devoir* for its refusal to correct errors made in translating their article and for printing the piece without permission. Almost four years after the start of the affair, *Le Devoir* issued an apology and agreed to an out-of-court settlement. One of the Jewish newspapermen emigrated to the United States in the wake of the storm.[50]

Jews' anxieties in French Canada in recent years have stemmed not only from the pronouncements of political and cultural leaders but also from the policies pursued by the Parti Québécois governments between 1977 and 1985 and by previous governments in Quebec. Policies that concern Jews relate to language, education, community control, and economics. Here, too, a few examples must suffice.

Partly because of their traditional connections with the English-speaking world, partly because of their small number (which serves to enhance the importance of those connections), and partly because of the history of French-Canadian–Jewish conflict, Quebec Jews have been even more uncomfortable with francization and the move away from bilingualism than other Anglophone Quebeckers. Especially disquieting were several provincial laws: Bill 63 (1969), which established the watchdog Office de la Langue Française; Bill 22 (1974), the Official Language Act, which established the primacy of French in schools and in places of work; and Bill 101 (1977), which essentially made French the official language of Quebec to the exclusion of English. Few Jews went as far as journalist

Stanley Cohen, who asserted in 1977 that for Jews switching to French would be "cultural and religious suicide."[51] Most agreed on the need to be bilingual in Quebec and to provide services in French in Jewish institutions.[52] Most, however, probably regretted the changing times that made these innovations necessary.

The issue of education is intimately connected to the language question. Successive governments in Quebec have understood that the path to francization leads through the schools. Instruction in English for the children of Anglophone Quebeckers has not been an issue. The right of newcomers to have their children educated in English (which would eventually augment the Anglophone community) was challenged, however, and, finally, restricted. This was a particular blow to the Jewish community, much of which is of immigrant origin, and which has depended on immigration to maintain its numbers and some of its essential services.[53] (The constitutionality of this bill has recently been questioned.) Montreal's Jewish schools have experienced a particular problem. In 1973 pressure began to mount for linking school subsidies, enjoyed by the Jewish schools since 1968, to the francization of the schools. The Parti Québécois made linkage government policy; and schools had to alter their curricula substantially in order to provide in-depth education in Hebrew, French, and English.

The question of community control over institutions has been less contentious and, in fact, not an issue unique to Quebec. As once private or communal institutions have received more and more government funding, there has been a demand that they be opened to all citizens. At issue are the Jewish hospital and several social service agencies in Montreal. Jews feared that when these institutions became integrated into the provincial systems, the Jewish community would lose control, and special services required by Jews would no longer be available. Despite initial anxieties these developments have not so far materialized.

Potentially, at least, contemporary French-Canadian nationalism has particular economic consequences for Jews. Economic nationalism has meant the desire to wrest control of the Quebec economy from "foreigners," that is, from non-French Canadians. Jews, the quintessential outsiders in traditional Quebec, have been primary targets of such efforts in the past, as in the "Achat chez nous!" campaign mentioned previously. Many fear that too little has changed in this area of life. As Claude Ryan put it in 1969, Jews still appear to French Canadians to "enjoy . . . a superior economic position" and, thus, to deserve a measure of discrimination.[54] Civil service jobs in Quebec and often government contracts are assumed by many not to be earmarked for "outsiders" under the francization program, giving Jews concern for their economic well-being. And there is concern that an independent Quebec would nationalize much of the business and industrial sector.[55] As early as 1967 the *Canadian Jewish Chronicle Review* talked of a flight of Jewish capital from Quebec. When the author of the article was interviewed on national television, an outcry arose in the French-Canadian press. Eventually the journal felt constrained to publish an "official statement" expressing confidence in Quebec. The statement did little except to underscore Jews' fear of speaking out.[56] Just before the Quebec election of 1976, Charles Bronfman, one of the country's most prominent and wealthy Jews, threatened to take his giant Seagram's liquor conglomerate out of Quebec should the Parti Québécois come to power. Subsequently he withdrew the threat. He also withdrew his candidacy for the presidency of the Canadian Jewish Congress, so that the Jewish community would not be tainted by his impolitic statements.[57] Once again Jews' fears about their position in Quebec were publicly underlined. In November 1982, the existence of a Quebec government file on minority leaders came to light, lending credence to fears of discrimination against them. Denials that the list had ever "been used to make decisions on provincial contracts, grants, appointments, or other benefits" aroused suspicions that it had, indeed, been so used.[58]

All these developments have led to growing and continuing concern about the future among most Jews of French Canada. As a committee report of Montreal's Allied Jewish Community Services (AJCS) put it in 1982, Jews in French Canada "are living under considerable economic and socio-political stress, and . . . are beset by a general apprehension about the future."[59] Another observer has spoken of an "attitude of hopelessness" among Quebec Jews.[60] And, as noted at the outset of this study, there has been a large-scale exodus of Jews from the province. As in the past, Quebec Jews have headed mostly for destinations in Anglo-Canada and the United States. In recent years the American sun belt has been particularly popular among departing Quebeckers, including a not inconsiderable number of French Canadians. In the mid-1960s there were three Jewish communities in Quebec: Sherbrooke, Quebec, and Montreal. By 1984 the Sherbrooke community had closed its synagogue; and Quebec had rented out the sanctuary of its synagogue to a theater. The 1981 census showed a drop of almost 12 percent in the Jewish population of Quebec in just ten years. Many believe the drop to have been even greater, since some of the émigrés maintain a mailing address in Quebec and were probably counted as residents by the census takers.[61] Jewish organizations have begun to follow their membership to Ontario.[62]

Predictions have been made that an even larger number of Jews will leave Quebec in the future. A 1977 survey indicated that 45 percent of the province's Jewish university students who were in their last year of study expected to emigrate. Among non-Jewish students the figure was only 12 percent.[63] Five years later the AJCS was anticipating the emigration of one-third of each year's graduating class and the drop of Montreal's Jewish population to between eighty and ninety thousand by 1987.[64] The exodus of young people is reflected in the rapidly rising average age of the Montreal Jewish population.[65] A 1970s Jewish-Canadian joke illustrates the pessimism felt by many Jews in Quebec:

> QUESTION: How does a smart Jew from Quebec talk to a stupid Jew from Quebec?
> ANSWER: Long distance.

Equally telling is a resolution circulated at the 1970 convention of the Federated Zionist Organizations of Canada by the Student Zionists. The resolution called, on the one hand, for the support of the national liberation of French Canada and, on the other, for the organization of the mass emigration of Canadian Jews to Israel. The resolution was not adopted.[66] As noted earlier, however, as many as 80 percent of Montreal's Jews, including Francophones, have said they would probably leave the province of Quebec should it become independent of Canada.[67] Although the direst predictions have not come true, and although emigration may now slow further since the 1985 defeat of the separatists at the polls, it seems unlikely that the trend of recent decades will be halted altogether or reversed.

Looking Ahead

The condition of Canadian Jewry in recent years, then, is apparently much different from what it was during the period reviewed in this study. Many political and social barriers have fallen in both French and Anglo-Canada. Jews and Judaism are no longer outsiders; they are part of the Canadian mosaic. And in more than a formal sense, they occupy a legitimate place in Canadian society. The improved climate, as well as longer residence in Canada, have led to increased assimilation. Only a very small number of Canadian Jews any longer considers itself Yiddish-speaking. Many Jews intermarry; and religious practice seems to be declining significantly.[68] On the other hand, the Jewish community is in many ways stronger than ever before. In most areas of the country it is no longer under siege by antisemitism. It has developed a larger measure of national autonomy and independence from foreign communities than it has ever had. Certainly the old British connections of Canadian Jews are broken, the participation of Canadian Jews in a Commonwealth Jewish Conference in 1985 and the recent renewal of British ties by Toronto's Holy Blossom Temple in hiring Rabbi Dow Marmur of London notwithstanding.

An examination of other aspects of contemporary Canadian-Jewish life, however, makes clear that the changes have not affected all Canadian Jews nor all areas of Jewish life. In many ways, in fact, the old French proverb, "Plus ça change, plus c'est la même chose" ("The more things change, the more they remain the same"), still obtains. Moreover, the recent changes have brought about a deterioration of the Jewish position in some respects. Jews continue to be better accepted in Anglo-Canada than in French Canada, for example. Considerable hostility toward Jews is still openly manifested in Quebec, although the rhetoric is somewhat different from what it was in the past, now more anti-Israel than religious in thrust. And Arab countries are now the main foreign source of antisemitism, rather than France or Germany. The Montreal Jewish community has remained remarkably cohesive and geographically concentrated; but it is aging rapidly. Jews still socialize largely within their own group, many even doing business primarily with other Jews.[69] Multi-culturalism is not, at present, a feature of French-Canadian society. The diminishing size of the Montreal Jewish community means an even greater tilt toward Anglo-Canada on the part of Canadian Jews than in the past. And the notion that Montreal Jews could serve as a bridge between French and Anglo-Canadians has ceased to have any credibility.[70] The connections with the United States and with American Jewry remain in place and in some ways have grown stronger over the years, reinforcing still further Canadian Jews' sense of belonging to the English-speaking world. If one leg of the Jewish North Atlantic Triangle is now much weaker than before, the other two are stronger and more firmly joined together. In the country at large, then, the changes are striking. They have had a major impact on Jewish life and appear to be permanent. With regard to French Canada, continuity with the past seems much in evidence, pointing the way to serious decline. Canadian Jewry, as a whole, is today uniquely vigorous among Diaspora communities, with brighter prospects than most others. Despite their long history, their tradition of leadership in Canada, and their significant achievements, however, the Jews of French Canada cannot fully share the optimism about the future.

Notes

Chapter 1

1. Louis Rosenberg, *A Gazetteer of Jewish Communities in Canada Showing the Jewish Population in the Cities, Towns, and Villages in the Census Years, 1851–1951,* Canadian Jewish Population Studies: Canadian Jewish Communities Series 7 (Montreal, n.d.).

2. Bernard Baskin, "Canada," *American Jewish Year Book,* 1978, p. 277. For one of the few examples of enthusiastic endorsement of the Parti Québécois by a Jew, see Paul Unterberg, "The Jews in Quebec: Two Views," *Jewish Dialog,* spring 1970. Unterberg was an unsuccessful Parti Québécois candidate for the Quebec National Assembly in a Montreal riding populated heavily by Jews.

3. Morton Weinfeld, "The Jews of Quebec: Perceived Antisemitism, Segregation, and Emigration," *The Journal of Jewish Sociology* 22 (June 1980): 13. See also the alarmist views of Milton Winston, "The Jews in Quebec: Two Views," *Jewish Dialog,* spring 1970; and David Weiss, "Is There a Future For the Montreal Jewish Community?" *Journal of Jewish Communal Service* (September 1979): 28–34.

4. See Colman Romalis, "The Attitudes of the Montreal Jewish Community Toward French-Canadian Nationalism and Separation" (Master's thesis, McGill University, 1967), p. 81; Stuart E. Rosenberg, "French Separatism: Its Implications for Canadian Jewry," *American Jewish Year Book,* 1972, pp. 410–12.

5. Ruth R. Wisse and Irwin Cotler, "Quebec's Jews: Caught in the Middle," *Commentary,* September 1977, p. 55.

6. Romalis, "Attitudes," p. 52.

7. See "Statistical Tables on Languages Spoken by Jews and Other Ethnic Groups According to Census Statistics, 1931–1951," Bronfman Collection of Jewish Canadiana, Jewish Public Library, Montreal; Stuart E. Rosenberg, "Separatism," p. 418.

8. See, for example, A. M. Klein, *The Rocking Chair* (Toronto, 1948) and Mordecai Richler, *The Apprenticeship of Duddy Kravitz* (Montreal, 1959).

9. For Jewish expressions of such a view, see, for example, the statement of Rabbi E. S. Triester, as quoted in the *Canadian Jewish News,* 30 June 1977; and *Canada-Israel Friendship,* eds. Shira Herzog Bessin and David Kaufman (Toronto, 1979), pp. 97–98. For analogous statements by French Canadians, see Stuart E. Rosenberg, "Separatism," pp. 415–16; speech of Premier René Lévesque to the Biennial Plenary of the Canadian Jewish Congress, Montreal, June 1977; and " 'Quebec, like Israel, is fighting for survival,' " *Canadian Jewish News,* 18 May 1977.

10. See, among many sources, Raymond Beaugrand Champagne, as quoted in *L'Arche,* January 1977, p. 22; Yves Taschereau, "La Floride aux Québécois," *L'Actualité,* December 1976; Harold M. Waller, *The Canadian Jewish Community: A National Perspective* (Jerusalem and Philadelphia, 1977), p. 22; Victor Teboul, *Mythe et Images du Juif au Québec* (Montreal, 1977); "Jews Protest Anti-Zionist Quebec Article," Toronto *Star,* 8 March 1978; "Is Separatist Body Condoning Anti-Zionism?" *Canadian Jewish News,* 17 March 1978.

11. For a survey of antisemitic manifestations in Anglo-Canada in the early 1970s, see Melvin Fenson, "Canada," *American Jewish Year Book,* 1974–75, pp. 345–48. See also Robert Fulford, "Is the Unfashionable Anti-Semitism Becoming Fashionable Again?" *Canadian Jewish News,* 27 November 1980.

12. See, for example, "Quebec Jews Are Reassured by Lévesque," *Canadian Jewish News,* 4 February 1977.

13. See Stuart E. Rosenberg, "Separatism," pp. 407–10; Wisse and Cotler, "Middle," p. 57.

Chapter 2

1. There seems to have been a settlement of Jews in Nova Scotia for some years before the British conquest of New France. That community, if indeed it can be called a community, was short-lived and left no traces other than a few tombstones. Consequently, Aaron Hart is herein considered to have been the founder of Canadian Jewry. Hart and his compatriots have been referred to as "army officers" or "commissary officers." (See, for example, Martin Wolff, "The Jews of Canada," *American Jewish Year Book,* 5686 (1925–26), p. 4; and E. C. Woodley, *The House of Joseph in the Life of Quebec* (Quebec, [1946]), p. 13. It is more likely, however, that they were sutlers, private contractors, who supplied the armies, following them in their progress.

2. *The Form of Prayer, which was Performed at the Jews Synagogue in the City of New York On Thursday, Oct. 23, 1760. Being the Day appointed by Proclamation for a General Thanksgiving to Almighty God for the Reducing of Canada to His Majesty's Dominions. Composed by D. R. Joseph Yesurun Pinto in the Hebrew Language, and Translated into English by a Friend of Truth,* cited by David Rome, *The Early Jewish Presence in Canada: A Booklover's Ramble Through Jewish Canadiana* (Montreal, 1971), p. 5.

3. Abraham De Sola, *Biography of David Aaron De Sola* (Philadelphia, 5624 [1864], pp. 3–7; George Maclean Rose, ed., *A Cyclopedia of Canadian Biography,* 2d ser. (Toronto, 1888), p. 98; Lloyd P. Gartner, *The Jewish Immigrant in England, 1870–1914* (Detroit, 1960), pp. 13, 38–40; and many other sources.

4. As quoted in "The Emigration of Russian Jews to England," *Jewish Chronicle,* 6 January 1888.

5. See, for example, "English-speaking Jews" [Hebrew], *Hasman,* 5 November 1909. All translations herein are the author's unless otherwise noted.

6. Vivian David Lipman, *Social History of the Jews in England, 1850–1950* (London, 1954), p. 111; "The Emigration of Russian Jews."

7. As quoted in "Thanksgiving Messages from Montreal Clergymen," Montreal *Daily Herald,* 23 November 1901.

8. "The Coronation in England" [Hebrew], 30 Sivan, 1911. Compare also Maurice Samuel, *Little Did I Know* (New York, 1963), pp. 91–100.

9. See Charles H. L. Emanuel, *A Century and a Half of Jewish History: Extracted from the Minute Books of the London Committee of Deputies of the British Jews* (London, 1910), p. 157. For Jewish reactions to these developments, see among other sources "Abroad" [Hebrew], *Hamelitz,* 10 Nisan 1887; "From Jewish Life Abroad" [Hebrew], *Hasman,* 12 August 1909.

10. Meir Berlin, *Mi-Volozhin ad Yerushalayim* [Hebrew], vol 2 (Tel Aviv, 1940), p. 41; see also pp. 42–44.

11. Lipman, *Social History,* pp. 46–47. A different approach is taken by Robert A. Huttenback, "The Patrician Jew and the British Ethos in the Nineteenth and Twentieth Centuries," *Jewish Social Studies* 40 (winter 1978): 49–62.

12. Lipman, *Social History,* p. 37.

13. Ibid., p. 83.

14. M. Edmund Gordon, "Political and Legal Aspects of Jewish History in Canada" (unpublished paper, Montreal, 1959), p. 1; Cecil Roth, *A History of the Jews in England,* 3d ed. (Oxford, 1964), pp. 243–44; Isaiah Berlin, "Benjamin Disraeli, Karl Marx, and the Search for Identity," *Midstream,* August–September 1970, p. 39.

15. *Jewish Chronicle,* 28 April 1876, 5 May 1876; G. F. Abbott, *Israel in Europe* (London, 1907), p. 323; Arthur Brodey, "Political and Civil Status of the Jews in Canada" (Rabbi and Master's thesis, Jewish Institute of Religion, 1933), p. 14; Cecil Roth, *Essays and Portraits in Anglo-Jewish History* (Philadelphia, 1962), p. 277.

16. Abraham De Sola, "The Righteous Man," sermon preached on Sabbath Noah 5625, November 1864, in McGill University, Montreal, Archives, De Sola Papers (hereafter referred to as ADSP).

17. As quoted in Abbott, *Israel,* p. 385.

18. Compare, "Lord Beaconsfield," *Jewish Chronicle,* 18 August 1876; Abraham Gilam, "Anglo-Jewish Attitudes Toward Benjamin Disraeli During the Era of Emancipation," *Jewish Social Studies* 42 (summer–fall 1980): 313–22; Isaiah Berlin, "Disraeli," pp. 29–49.

19. "Sir Rufus Isaacs Becomes Lord Chief Justice" [Yiddish], *Keneder odler,* 30 October 1913.

20. "Farewell Address," Canadian *Jewish Times,* 28 February 1902.

21. Quoted in "Governor-General Makes Strong Zionist Plea," *Canadian Zionist,* May 1936. See also "Lord Tweedsmuir Expresses Unabated Interest in Zionism," *Canadian Zionist,* December 1936.

22. Roth, *History,* pp. 258–59, and many other sources.

23. As quoted in Montagu Frank Modder, *The Jew in the Literature of England* (New York and Philadelphia, 1960), p. 94.

24. Minute Books of Temple Emanu-El, Montreal, 20 April, 9 December 1894; Emanuel, *Century,* p. 48; S. Dubnow, *History of the Jews in Russia and Poland,* trans. Israel Friedlander, vol. 2 (Philadelphia, 1916), pp. 63, 288–92.

25. See "Public Meeting at the Mansion House," *Jewish Chronicle,* 3 February 1882; *Hamelitz* [Hebrew], 4 Shvat 1882; Moritz Ellinger, Hebrew Emigrant Aid Society of the United States, *Report* (New York, 1882), p. 2; "The Next Step," *Jewish Chronicle,* 20 January 1882; "England's View," *Jewish Chronicle,* 27 January 1882; Benjamin G. Sack, *History of the Jews in Canada,* trans. Ralph Novek (Montreal, 1965), pp. 193–95;

A. J. Arnold, "Inside Canada: The Role of the Jews in the Opening of the West," *Pioneer Woman,* February–March 1969, p. 22.

26. "Montreal," *The American Israelite,* 3 June 1881.

27. "The Persecution of Jews in Russia," Montreal *Gazette,* 21 January 1882; "Jewish Persecution in Russia," Montreal *Gazette,* 18 March 1882; "Montreal, Canada," New York *Jewish Messenger,* 24 March 1882; "Aid for Russian Refugees," Montreal *Gazette,* 15 May 1882; "Jewish Relief," Montreal *Daily Witness,* 23 May 1882; "A Plea for the Jew," "The Jew as a Menace to Russian Bureaucracy," "Jewish Emigration," Montreal *Star,* 21 November 1905; "Help for the Jews," Montreal *Daily Witness,* 21 November 1905; "Russian Atrocities," Canadian *Jewish Times,* 1 December 1905; "Sympathy With the Jews," Montreal *Gazette,* 2 July 1906; "The Beiliss Case Goes to the Jury," Montreal *Daily Mail,* 10 November 1913; "Abroad" [Hebrew], *Ha-Zefirah,* 7 Adar Sheni 1913; "Pope Sends Information Against Franiatis" [Yiddish], *Keneder odler,* 27 October 1913; "Our Jewish Immigration" [Yiddish], *Keneder odler,* 8 August 1915; Stephen A. Speisman, *The Jews of Toronto: A History to 1937* (Toronto, 1979), p. 124.

28. Untitled editorial, *The Week,* 22 August 1890.

29. M. Ravitch, "Jews and Peasants in Russia," *The Week,* 20 February 1891.

30. "Politics Knoweth Not Righteousness" [Yiddish], *Keneder odler,* 10 June 1908.

31. "England and Russia," *Jewish Chronicle,* 5 April 1907. See also "The Anglo-Russian Convention," *Jewish Chronicle,* 6 September 1907; "King Edward Appeals for the Jews" [Yiddish], *Keneder odler,* 28 June 1908.

32. Canadian *Jewish Times,* 3 August 1900; Abbott, *Israel,* p. 384; "King Edward VII" [Yiddish], *Keneder odler,* 9 May 1910; John A. Garrard, *The English and Immigration, 1880–1910* (London, 1971), pp. 16–17.

33. Dean Milman's popular poem, "The Fall of Jerusalem" (1820) and his widely read *History of the Jews* (1830) represented the beginnings of English literary expression of concern with Jews. Other writers with greater talents followed. See Norman Bentwich, "Anglo-Jewish Travellers to Palestine in the Nineteenth Century," The Jewish Historical Society of England *Miscellanies* 4 (1942): 9, 12.

34. Emma Lazarus, *The Dance of Death* (New York, 1882), dedication page.

35. "Literary Notices," *New Dominion Monthly,* June 1876; excerpts, June, December 1876.

36. Charles Freshman, *The Jews and the Israelites* (Toronto, 1870), pp. 453–54; Manitoba *Free Press* quoted in Samuel Joseph, *History of the Baron de Hirsch Fund* (n.p., 1935), p. 362. On Hellmuth, see Owsley Robert Rowley, *The Anglican Episcopate of Canada and Newfoundland* (Milwaukee, 1928), pp. 53–54.

37. Address to Montreal Zionist meeting, quoted in "Governor-General Makes Strong Zionist Plea," *Canadian Zionist,* May 1936. The governor-general's remarks, although made at a later date, may be understood as reflecting gentile opinion of the period under review, as well. Tweedsmuir, himself, had been an active supporter of Zionism for years before he came to Canada. Moreover, in 1936 the British government was backing away from its commitments to the Jewish national home, and the king's representative had every political reason to speak differently. Apparently, however, he spoke from the heart, expressing sentiments with which many non-Jewish Canadians had long agreed.

38. Mark Wischnitzer, *To Dwell in Safety* (Philadelphia, 1948), pp. 14–15, 55–56; Isaiah Berlin, "Disraeli," p. 40.

39. Bentwich, "Travellers," pp. 11–12; V. D. Lipman, "The Age of Emancipation, 1815–1880," in *Three Centuries of Anglo-Jewish History,* ed. V. D. Lipman (Cambridge, 1961), pp. 92–94.

40. Ismar Elbogen, *A Century of Jewish Life* (Philadelphia, 1945), p. 275; Nahum

Sokolow, *History of Zionism, 1600–1918,* vol. 2, (New York, 1969), pp. xliv–xlvi; Huttenback, "Patrician Jew," pp. 49–62. Sokolow's book was first published in 1919.

41. S. Talpis, letter [Hebrew], *Hamelitz,* 26 Kislev 1903; "Palestine as an English Colony" [Hebrew], *Ha-Zefirah,* 25 Sivan 1912; Walter Laqueur, *A History of Zionism* (London, 1972), pp. 120–29.

42. A. B. Aylesworth, Dominion minister of justice, quoted in *Report* of the Proceedings of the Convention of the Federation of Zionist Societies of Canada, 1907.

43. Quoted in London *Jewish Chronicle,* 30 August 1907. See also Montreal *Daily Witness,* 10 December 1898; Minute Books of Holy Blossom Temple, Toronto, 7 May 1899; *Hamelitz,* 10 Iyyar 1900; Atlanta *Jewish Sentiment,* 9 March 1900, 23 February 1901; Canadian *Jewish Times* 20 December 1901, 13 July 1906; *Jewish Chronicle,* 31 January 1902; *Report* of the Proceedings of the Convention of the Federation of Zionist Societies of Canada, 1907; Speisman, *Toronto,* pp. 202–03.

44. W[illiam] Evans Gordon, *The Alien Immigrant* (London, 1903), p. 12. See also Garrard, *The English,* pp. 23–24.

45. As quoted in Garrard, *The English,* p. 142.

46. "The Anti-Jewish Riots in Wales," Canadian *Jewish Times,* 25 August 1911. See also Naphtali Herz Imber, "Letters from London" [Hebrew], *Ha-Zefirah,* 5 Tishri 1888; "A Retrospect of 5663," *Jewish Year Book,* 5664 [1904], p. 427; "Riots and Signs of Antisemitism in England" [Hebrew], *Ha-Zefirah,* 3 Elul 1911; Garrard, *The English,* pp. 20, 71; Geoffrey Alderman, "The Jew as Scapegoat? The Settlement and Reception of Jews in South Wales before 1914," The Jewish Historical Society of England *Transactions* 25 and *Miscellanies* 11 (1979): pp. 62–70.

47. Joseph Pennell, *The Jew at Home* (London, 1892), passim; "The Alien Babe," *Jewish Chronicle,* 6 December 1907; Garrard, *The English,* pp. 17–20, 38–39; Yosef Gorni, "Beatrice Webb's Views on Judaism and Zionism," *Jewish Social Studies* 40 (spring 1978): 95–116.

48. Lucien Wolf, "The Queen's Jewry," in *Essays in Jewish History* (London, 1934), p. 339. The essay was originally published many years earlier.

49. Letter, *Jewish Chronicle,* 11 May 1894.

50. See, for example, "A Pitiable Record," Canadian *Jewish Times,* 3 June 1904.

51. "The Future of Alien Immigration," *Jewish Chronicle,* 23 March 1906.

52. "The Condition of Fellow Jews Abroad," [Hebrew], *Hasman,* 9 Shvat 1905. See also Lipman, *Social History,* pp. 134–44.

53. Abbott, *Israel,* p. 452. See also various issues of *The Week* and Goldwin Smith's earlier publication, *The Bystander,* also published in Toronto.

54. See, for example, "The Jews in Palestine," *The Bystander,* March 1880; personal letter to Jonas Rosenfeld, Dallas, Texas, 12 October 1908, in *A Selection from Goldwin Smith's Correspondence,* ed. Arnold Haultain (Toronto, n.d.), p. 505; Lipman, *Social History,* p. 141; Aharon Aharonson, *Yoman* [Hebrew], ed. Yoram Efrati (Tel Aviv, 1970), p. 362, 2 December 1917.

55. As quoted in "Gladstone and the Jews," *The American Hebrew,* 28 February 1890.

56. "Inaugural Address to the Fourth Zionist Congress," quoted in Sokolow, *Zionism,* vol. 2, p. xliv.

57. Thomas Stirson Jarvis, *Letters from East Longitudes* (Toronto, 1875), p. 71. See also J. Bell Forsyth [A Canadian], *A Few Months in the East; or, A Glimpse of the Red, the Dead, and the Black Seas* (Quebec, 1861), p. 13.

58. Compare Isidore G. Ascher, *Voices from the Hearth* (Montreal, 1863); John Douglas Borthwick, *The Harp of Canaan,* 2d ed., rev. and imp. (Montreal, 1871); Mrs. Alexander (Mary Ellen) Ross, *The Legend of the Holy Stone* (Montreal, 1878) and *The Wreck of the*

White Bear, East Indiaman, 2 vols. (Montreal, 1870); Carroll Ryan, *Songs of a Wanderer* (Ottawa, 1867), and *Poems, Songs, Ballads* (Montreal, 1903); and many other works.

59. [I. J.] Benjamin, *Three Years in America, 1859–1862,* trans. Charles Reznikoff, vol. 3 (Philadelphia, 1956), p. 231.

60. See Harold Fisch, *The Dual Image* (New York, 1971), passim; Abbott, *Israel,* pp. 301–28; and Huttenback, "Patrician Jew," pp. 49–62.

61. Jarvis, *Longitudes,* p. 71.

62. Ross, *The Legend,* pp. 265–66.

63. [Richard Brothers], *A Revealed Knowledge of the Prophecies and Times* (London, 1794), p. 54.

64. Richard S. Lambert, *For the Time Is at Hand* (London, [1947]), passim.

65. Cecil Roth, *The Nephew of the Almighty* (London, 1933), pp. 49–50.

66. Brothers, *Prophecies,* p. 54.

67. "Editorial Comments," *Jewish Chronicle,* 16 June 1876.

68. "The Lost Ten Tribes," *Jewish Chronicle,* 21 January 1876.

69. Ibid.

70. Lambert, *Time,* pp. 28–29.

71. Henry Wentworth Monk, *A Simple Interpretation of the Revelation Together with Three Lectures Lately Delivered in Canada and the United States,* 2d ed. (London, [1858?]); Lambert, *Time,* pp. 55, 64–65, 96–98, 106–16.

72. "Sir Ellsworth Flavelle Opens Palestine Exhibit," *Canadian Zionist,* June 1947.

73. Lambert, *Time,* pp. 118–39, 150–57.

74. W. H. Poole, *Anglo-Israel in Nine Lectures* (Toronto, [1890?]), pp. 14–15.

75. "Christianity and Judaism," *The Bystander,* April 1881, pp. 214–18; Goldwin Smith, "The Jewish Question," *The Nineteenth Century,* October 1881, p. 494; Poole, *Anglo-Israel,* pp. i–vii, 686; "Anglo-Israel; or, the Saxon Race Proved to Be the Lost Ten Tribes," *The Dominion Illustrated,* 1 March 1890, p. 143; "The Anglo-Israel Theory: Are the British the Lost Ten Tribes?" Canadian *Jewish Times,* 24 May 1901; *Encyclopedia of Religion and Ethics* (1908), s.v. "Anglo-Israelitism," by Albert M. Hyamson.

76. James S. Woodsworth, *Strangers Within Our Gates* (Toronto, 1909), p. 159. See also "Jews the Mirror of the World" [Yiddish], *Keneder odler,* 27 April 1910; "Minister Preaches Tolerance" [Yiddish], *Keneder odler,* 3 January 1909.

77. *The Fourth Book of Lessons for the Use of Schools* (Montreal, 1845), pp. 215–21.

78. *The Old Testament Vindicated as Christianity's Foundation-Stone* (Toronto, 1898), p. 92; see also p. 50.

79. The sources that may be cited are many. Adolphus Mordecai Hart, in his *History of the Valley of the Mississippi* (Cincinnati, 1853), pictured "the Canadian colonist . . . as unchanged as ever . . . with his Bible in one hand and his axe in the other" (pp. 13–14). The historian grandson of Aaron Hart felt that it had been the spirit of Protestantism and the Hebrew Bible that had conquered Canada. Gentiles said the same. Thomas Talbot, in *The Hebrews at Home* (Montreal, 1874), a popular work on the ways and customs of the ancient Hebrews, accepted them as "our forefathers" (p. 12). Writers such as Charles Heavysege dealt extensively with themes from the Hebrew Bible. (See, for example, his "Saul," a drama in fifteen acts published in 1857 and 1869; "Jephthah's Daughter," a poem written in 1865; and his "Sonnets: Jezebel," written two years later.) See also introduction to *The Book of Psalms Translated out of the Original Hebrew* (Toronto, 1851), pp. vi, viii; Sir J. William Dawson, *Egypt and Syria* (London, 1885), and idem, *Nature and the Bible* (New York, 1875); "From the Jewish World" [Hebrew], *Hayehoody,* 23 May 1901; Richard Allen, "The Social Gospel and the Reform Tradition in Canada, 1880–1925," *Canadian Historical Review* 49 (December 1968): 388–89; Rome, *Ramble,* pp. 56–57.

80. "Canada," *Jewish Chronicle,* 16 April 1909; Jan Goeb, "The Maritimes," *Viewpoints* (winter/spring 1973): 16.

81. Arthur Ruppin, *The Jews of To-day,* trans. Margery Bentwich (New York, 1913), p. 117.

82. See Norman Macdonald, *Canada: Immigration and Colonization, 1841–1903* (Toronto, 1966), passim.

83. *Hamelitz* [Hebrew], 8 Nisan 1882.

84. Lucien Wolf, "Old Anglo-Jewish Families," in *Essays,* pp. 223–24. This essay was originally published in the London *Jewish Chronicle* in 1886.

85. Oscar Douglas Skelton, *Life and Letters of Sir Wilfrid Laurier,* vol. 1 (Toronto, 1965), p. 108. See also "Should the Jews Be Emancipated?" *Jewish Chronicle,* 2 May 1845; Kalman Schulmann, *Mosdei Eretz* [Hebrew] (Vilna, 1871), p. 153; "The Year 1910 Among Jews Abroad" [Hebrew], *Hasman,* 11 January 1911; L. Loydald, "Die Juden in der nordamerikanerischen Ein- und Auswanderungstatistik, 1910–1911," *Zeitschrift für Demographie und Statistik der Juden,* 8 (November 1912): 162–66; *Lovell's Historic Report of the Census of Montreal* (Montreal, 1891), p. 21.

86. "The Exact Details of the Operations of the Jewish Colonization Association During the Past Year" [Hebrew], *Hasman,* 13 August 1909.

87. Aaron Nirenberg, "Letters from Canada" [Hebrew], *Ha-Zefirah,* 27 Shvat 1913.

88. See, among other places, *Hamelitz* [Hebrew], 24 Av 1882; Joseph Elijah Bernstein, "Montreal (America)" [Hebrew], *Hamelitz,* 2 Heshvan 1883; Zalman Engelman, "Montreal, Canada" [Hebrew], *Hamelitz,* 9 Iyyar 1886; "In the Jewish World" [Hebrew], *Ha-Zefirah,* 29 Iyyar 1886; "Our Far-Flung Brethren" [Hebrew], *Ha-Zefirah,* 8 Tishri 1888; Alexander Harkavy, letter [Hebrew], *Ha-Zefirah,* 4 Adar 1888; André Siegfried, *The Race Question in Canada,* trans. Eveleigh Nash (New York, 1907), p. 253; C. A. Magrath, *Canada's Growth and Some Problems Affecting It* (Ottawa, 1910), p. 55; Wischnitzer, *Safety,* p. 90: Macdonald, *Canada,* pp. 115–16, 205–06. For a description of the hospitality of Canadian Jews to newcomers in comparison to American standoffishness, see Jonathan Sarna, "Jewish Immigration to North America: The Canadian Experience (1870–1900)," *The Jewish Journal of Sociology* 18 (June 1976): 33. Sarna offers a generous view of the Canadian welcome.

89. "Report of the Jewish Emigrants' Information Board," *Jewish Chronicle,* 16 March 1906.

90. "Announcement" [Hebrew], *Hamelitz,* 5 Nisan 1903; "Jewish Emigrants' Information Society," *Jewish Chronicle,* 8 January 1904; "Emigrants in Canada," *Jewish Chronicle,* 2 September 1904; Gartner, *Immigrant,* p. 36; Macdonald, *Canada,* p. 134.

91. See, for example, advertisements of Hamburg-America Line, *Hamelitz,* 1892. See also William George Smith, *A Study in Canadian Immigration* (Toronto, 1920), p. 56; and chapter 3 herein.

92. See, among other places, Tahkemoni [pseud.], "London" [Hebrew], *Ha-Zefirah,* 12 Tishri 1886; Zalman Engelman, "Montreal, Canada" [Hebrew], *Hamelitz,* 11 Tammuz 1887: J. L. Slosberg, "Letters from Our Correspondents" [Hebrew], *Ha-Zefirah,* 26 Elul 1888; *Hayehoody* [Hebrew], 9 March 1899; "Jottings" [Hebrew], *Hamelitz,* 7 Kislev 1901; S. Talpis, letter [Hebrew], *Hamelitz,* 26 Kislev 1903; *Vichtige Fragen un Richtige Antworten* [Yiddish] (Winnipeg, [1913]); Aaron Nirenberg, "Letters from Canada" [Hebrew], *Ha-Zefirah,* 27 Shvat 1913; Herbert Brown Ames, *The City Below the Hill,* 2d ed. (Toronto and Buffalo, 1972), pp. 46, 112.

93. "Our Race in the Colonies," 15 August 1902. See also *Jewish Year Book,* 1902–03, pp. ix, 282; "Jews and Colonial Enterprise," *Jewish Chronicle,* 19 April 1907.

94. "Lands of Refuge," *Jewish Chronicle,* 6 January 1904.

95. "5664," *Jewish Chronicle,* 9 September 1904.

96. "A Retrospect of 5665," *Jewish Year Book,* 1905–06, p. 455.

97. "The Growing Jewish Community of Canada," *Jewish Chronicle,* 3 June 1904. Compare also Carl Berger, *The Sense of Power* (Toronto and Buffalo, 1970), p. 149.

98. "Canada as a Refuge," *Jewish Chronicle,* 19 January 1906.

99. "The Year 5667," *Jewish Chronicle,"* 6 September 1907.

100. W. Schorr, "The Meeting of the Reform Rabbis in Montreal" [Hebrew], *Hamelitz,* 8 Elul 1897.

101. Samuel Talpis, "Abroad" [Hebrew], *Hamelitz,* 28 Kislev 1899.

102. Letter from Abraham Levin [Hebrew] of Cleveland, formerly of Winnipeg, to Yitzchak Ben Zvi, New York, 25 Adar 5677 (1917), in Ben Zvi Institute, Jerusalem, Archives, File 1/1/3/14.

103. Compare Magrath, *Growth,* p. 55, and other sources.

104. "Roumanian Transmigrants in London," *Jewish Chronicle,* 22 November 1907; "Foreign News," *The Reform Advocate,* 4 April 1908; "Jews' Temporary Shelter," *Jewish Chronicle,* 8 January 1909; Magrath, *Growth,* p. 36; W. S. Shepperson, *British Emigration to North America* (Minneapolis, 1957), pp. 243–46, 257–59; Helen I. Cowan, *British Emigration to British North America* (Toronto, 1961), pp. 185, 288; Louis Rosenberg, "The Earliest Jewish Settlers in Canada, Facts vs. Myths," in *Canadian Jewish Reference Book and Directory, 1963,* comp. Eli Gottesman (Montreal, 1963), pp. 12–13; Joseph R. Rosenbloom, *A Biographical Dictionary of Early American Jews* ([Lexington, Kentucky], n.d.), p. 79; *Canada: An Encyclopedia* (1899), s.v. "Historical Sketch of the Jews of Canada," by A. Lazarus; *Who's Who and Why* (Toronto, 1915–16), p. 957; "The Late Hyman Miller," in *The Jew in Canada,* ed. Arthur Daniel Hart (Toronto and Montreal, 1926), p. 336; Raymond Arthur Davies, *Printed Jewish Canadiana* (Montreal, 1955), p. 6; Solomon Frank, *Two Centuries in the Life of a Synagogue* (n.p., n.d.), p. 89; and various documents in Canadian Jewish Congress, Montreal, Archives, Hart Family Papers.

105. See Louis Rosenberg, *A Gazetteer of Jewish Communities in Canada Showing the Jewish Population in the Cities, Towns, and Villages in Canada in the Census Years, 1851–1951.* Canadian Jewish Population Studies: Canadian Jewish Communities Series 7 (Montreal, n.d.), pp. 38–41; and idem, "Two Centuries of Jewish Life in Canada, 1760–1960," *American Jewish Year Book,* 1961, p. 33.

106. Louis Rosenberg, *Canada's Jews* (Montreal, 1939), p. 341. See also, S. J. Birnbaum, "The History of the Jews in Toronto," Canadian *Jewish Times,* 20 December 1912; "The Late Jacob Hirsch," in Arthur Hart, *The Jew,* p. 97; Hirsch Wolofsky, *Journey of My Life* (Montreal, 1945), p. 3; Rowland Tappan Berthoff, *British Immigrants in Industrial America* (Cambridge, Massachusetts, 1953), p. 2; A. I. Willinsky, *A Doctor's Memoirs* (Toronto, 1960), p. 3; Cowan, *British Emigration,* p. 218; Bernard Figler, *Rabbi Dr. Herman Abramowitz, Lazarus Cohen, Lyon Cohen* (Ottawa, 1968), p. 102; Ludwik Kos-Rabcewicz-Zublowski, *The Poles in Canada* (Ottawa and Montreal, 1968), passim; A. R. Rollin, "Russo-Jewish Immigrants in England Before 1881," Jewish Historical Society of England *Transactions* 21 (1968): pp. 202–13.

107. "Jewish Emigration," *Jewish Chronicle,* 28 May 1875.

108. Joseph Jacobs, *Studies in Jewish Statistics* (London, 1891), pp. 18, 21; V. D. Lipman, *A Century of Social Service, 1859–1959* (London, 1959), p. 25; Simon Belkin, *Through Narrow Gates* (Montreal, 1966), pp. 14–15; Lipman, *Social History,* p. 78; Macdonald, *Canada,* p. 92.

109. "After 1848 as . . . canal and railroad transportation across England improved, Liverpool shipping merchants began to promote European emigrant trade." (Cowan, *British Emigration,* p. 218) In later years many of the routes from the Continent to North America and specifically to Canada were by way of England. Libau was the chief Russian port of emigration; and most lines stopping there sailed to England. Of the eight shipping lines advertising in *Lovell's Historic Report of the [1891] Census of Montreal,* only one

sailed directly from the Continent to Canada. The other seven set out from England. In 1903 ten lines sailed from Montreal to the British Isles, but only four from Montreal to the Continent. Compare also Evans Gordon, *Immigrant,* pp. 98–100; *Montreal* (Montreal, [1903]), p. 8; "Sir Wilfred [sic] Laurier and Jewish Colonisation," *Jewish Chronicle,* 3 May 1907; "A. Rhinewine, Toronto," in Arthur Hart, *The Jew,* p. 418; Gartner, *Immigrant,* pp. 170–71; Meilech Schiff, "Lost Boryslaw," *Jewish Dialog,* summer 1977.

110. The Baron de Hirsch Institute, Montreal, *Annual Report,* 1903, p. 5.

111. See, for example, "Renewed Roumanian Emigration Through London," *Jewish Chronicle,* 13 March 1908; Wolofsky, *Journey,* p. 3; Jacob Leib Becker, *Derzeilungen un Zichroinos* [Yiddish] (Montreal, 1956), pp. 183, 257. London *Standard* and *St. James Gazette* quoted in "The British Empire and the Roumanian Jews," *Jewish Chronicle,* 26 September 1902.

112. Macdonald, *Canada,* pp. 93–94, 136, 253–56; Shepperson, *Emigration,* p. 120.

113. "Liverpool Board of Guardians," *Jewish Chronicle,* 22 June 1877.

114. "Jews' Emigration Society," *Jewish Chronicle,* 20 May 1909; "YWHA," in Arthur Hart, *The Jew,* p. 444; Jacob Neusner, "The Role of English Jews in the Development of American Jewish Life, 1775–1850," *YIVO Annual of Jewish Social Science* 12 (1958–59): 150; Shepperson, *Emigration,* p. 131; Goeb, "The Maritimes," p. 13.

115. Compare Lipman, *Social Service,* pp. 276–85.

116. See letters of David A. Ansell, president of the Baron de Hirsch Institute, to Alfred L. Cohen, London, 29 October 1902, Mr. M. Stephany, Board of Guardians for the Relief of the Jewish Poor, London, 19 November 1903, and Chairman of the Board of Guardians, London, 22 December 1903, in Letterbook of the Baron de Hirsch Institute—the Young Men's Hebrew Benevolent Society, Montreal, Jewish Public Library, Montreal, Archives (hereafter referred to as LBBDHI); The Baron de Hirsch Institute, Montreal, *Annual Report* [vol. 6]; "Canada as a Settlement for the Jews," *Jewish Chronicle,* 12 August 1904; "Baron de Hirsch Loose Leaf Book," Jewish Public Library, Montreal, Archives, 28 December 1906 (hereafter referred to as LLB); Lipman, *A Century,* pp. 99, 139.

117. Lyon Cohen, "Recollections and Reminiscences, 1881–1891," *The Jewish Daily Eagle Centennial Jubilee Edition,* 8 July 1932, p. 49.

118. Joseph, *History,* passim.

119. Jewish Colonization Association, *Rapport[s] de l'Administration Centrale au Conseil d'Administration;* "The Jewish Colonization Association," *Jewish Chronicle,* 25 October 1907; "Jewish Colonial Association [sic]," Canadian *Jewish Times,* 6 July 1900; Israel Hoffer, "Recollections and Reminiscences," *Saskatchewan History* 5 (winter 1952): 28; Sack, *History,* pp. 220–21. On assisted Jewish immigration to Canada from England see also Sarna, "Jewish Immigration," p. 32.

120. Belkin, *Gates,* p. 78; Miriam Rothschild, *Dear Lord Rothschild* (Philadelphia and London, 1983), p. 19.

121. Anonymous sources, quoted in Cowan, *British Emigration,* p. 203; "Immigration Restrictions," Canadian *Jewish Times,* 29 May 1908.

122. "First Annual Meeting of the Montreal Hebrew Philanthropic Society," *The Occident and American Jewish Advocate,* October 1848, pp. 268–70. See also Cowan, *British Emigration,* pp. 99, 203; Macdonald, *Canada,* pp. 65–66; and Kenneth Duncan "Irish Famine Immigration and the Social Structure of Canada West," in *Studies in Canadian Social History,* ed. Michiel Horn and Ronald Sabourin (Toronto, 1974), pp. 140–63.

123. Abraham De Sola, personal letter to D. Samuel, n.d., in ADSP.

124. Macdonald, *Canada,* p. 95.

125. *The Canadian Annual Review* (1908): p. 118.

126. Lipman, *A Century,* pp. 276–85; William George Smith, *Study,* pp. 70–71.

127. See David A. Ansell, personal letter to Mr. Cohen, London, 23 December 1903,

in LBBDHI; "Emigration to Canada," *Jewish Chronicle,* 14 October 1904; "From the Colonies," *Jewish Chronicle,* 25 October 1907; and many other sources.

128. "Jews are Agriculturists," 22 September 1893. See also "Emigrants and Immigrants," *Jewish Chronicle,* 27 April 1894.

129. Louis Rosenberg, "The Story of Edenbridge," in Bronfman Collection of Jewish Canadiana, Jewish Public Library, Montreal, Louis Rosenberg File; *R[ural] M[unicipality] of Willow Creek, No. 458, Jubilee Year, 1912–1962* (n.p., n.d.), p. 53; Hoffer, "Recollections," passim; William George Smith, *Study,* p. 67.

130. Berthoff, *British Immigrants,* p. 136.

131. "J. S. Leo, Montreal," in Arthur Hart, *The Jew,* p. 315; John Simons, ed., *Who's Who in American Jewry,* vol. 3 (New York, 1938–39), p. 956.

132. Arthur Hart, *The Jew,* pp. 225, 395; Patty Tennenhouse, "My Grandfather and His Girl," in *The Israelite Press Centennial Issue* (Winnipeg, 1967), p. 12.

133. Rosenbloom, *Dictionary,* p. 79; "The Late Mrs. Montefiore Joseph," in Arthur Hart, *The Jew,* p. 251; "Rev. Meldola De Sola," New York *Hebrew Standard,* 12 January 1894; and many other places.

134. "The Jewish Ministry," *Jewish Chronicle,* 16 October 1846.

135. See "Sephardim Congregation," *Jewish Chronicle,* 5 September 1845; Henry Morais, *Eminent Israelites of the Nineteenth Century* (Philadelphia, 1880), p. 102; Albert M. Hyamson, *The Sephardim of England* (London, 1951), pp. 304–05; Michael Goulston, "The Status of the Anglo-Jewish Rabbinate, 1840–1914," *The Jewish Journal of Sociology* 10 (June 1968): 57, 63–64.

136. Abraham Hart, Jr., personal letter to Benjamin Hart, London, 13 December 1838, in "Transcripts of Documents and Letters," *Canadian Jewish Archives* 1 (June 1956): 2; Minutes of the Spanish and Portuguese Synagogue, Shearith Israel, Montreal (hereafter referred to as MSP), 17 November 1839, 17 February 1847; "History of the Jewish Communal Bodies of Montreal," Canadian *Jewish Times,* 11 December 1899; Benjamin G. Sack, "A Suit at Law Involving the First Jewish Minister in Canada," *Publications of the American Jewish Historical Society* 31 (1928): 181–86; Hyamson, *The Sephardim,* p. 341.

137. "The Late Dr. De Sola," Montreal *Gazette,* 7 June 1882.

138. See Rose, *Cyclopedia,* p. 98; and various letters in ADSP.

139. MSP, 21 May 1862, 31 August 1862; Carroll Ryan, "Jews in Canada," Baltimore *Jewish Comment,* 7 December 1900; Lazarus, "Historical Sketch"; "From the Jewish Quarter" [Hebrew], *Hayehoody,* 30 May 1901; Canadian *Jewish Times,* 15 March 1901; E. N. Adler, "Visit to the Jewish Colony at Hirsch, Saskatchewan, Canada," *Jewish Chronicle,* 27 December 1907; "From the Colonies," *Jewish Chronicle,* 6 March 1908; *Who's Who and Why* (Toronto, 1919–20), p. 762; "Rabbi Solomon Jacobs," Toronto *Globe,* 7 August 1920; "Rabbi H. J. Samuels, B.A., Winnipeg," in Arthur Hart, *The Jew,* p. 126; W. Stewart Wallace, comp., *The Dictionary of Canadian Biography* (Toronto, 1926), pp. 178–79; Rowley, *Anglican Episcopate,* pp. 53–54; *CCAR Yearbook,* 1936, p. 252; Speisman, *Toronto,* pp. 44–55, 131–41, 314–15. Compare also Meir Berlin, *Mi-Volozhin,* vol. 2, pp. 41–44.

140. The Baron de Hirsch Institute, Montreal, *Annual Report,* 1892, p. 8; "Jewish Benevolent," Montreal *Gazette,* 3 November 1897.

141. "L'Hon. M. Samuel au Montefiore Club," Montreal *La Patrie,* 10 October 1913; "Jewish Girls' Club, Toronto," in Arthur Hart, *The Jew,* p. 269; letter of Sir John A. Macdonald to Arthur W. Hart, 11 January 1888, quoted in Sack, *History,* p. 200; "Guest and Host at Baron de Hirsch Institute," Montreal *Daily Mail,* 10 October 1913; Louis Rosenberg, *Jews,* p. 210.

142. See, among other places, MSP, 29 March 1863; Arthur Weir, ed., *Montreal Illustrated, 1894* (Montreal, 1894), p. 354; Carroll Ryan, "Jews in Canada," Baltimore

Jewish Comment, 7 December 1900; "The Late Mrs. David Moss," Canadian *Jewish Times,* 15 January 1904; "Canada," *Jewish Chronicle,* 10 March 1905; S. J. Birnbaum, "The History of the Jews in Toronto," Canadian *Jewish Times,* 20 December 1912; [Clarence I. De Sola?], *History of the Corporation of Spanish and Portuguese Jews of Montreal, Canada* (Montreal, 1918), pp. 45–46; Arthur Hart, *The Jew,* pp. 93–95, 369, 371; Leo Heaps, *The Rebel in the House* (London, 1970), p. 162.

143. Extracts of the Minutes of the Board of Directors, Baron de Hirsch Institute (hereafter referred to as Extracts), in Archives, Jewish Public Library, Montreal, 30 December 1888, 19 October 1908; "From the Colonies," *Jewish Chronicle,* 3 May 1907; "Immigration and Emigration Figures," *Jewish Chronicle,* 31 January 1908.

144. See, for example, *Jewish Chronicle,* 27 January 1893; "Marriage of the Chief Rabbi's Daughter to Mr. Alfred Eicholz," *Jewish Chronicle,* 28 June 1895; "Local," Canadian *Jewish Times,* 4 May 1906; "The Lord's Day Observance Bill in Canada," *Jewish Chronicle,* 13 July 1906; "Sir Wilfred [sic] Laurier and Jewish Colonisation," *Jewish Chronicle,* 3 May 1907; Sigmund Samuel, *In Return* (Toronto, 1963), pp. 106–19.

145. "Mr. Herman Landau on Canada and the Jews," *Jewish Chronicle,* 19 January 1906; "A. C. M. De Sola, M.A., B.C.L., Montreal," in Arthur Hart, *The Jew,* p. 385; *Who's Who and Why* (Toronto, 1915–16), p. 1003; John Murray Gibbon, *Canadian Mosaic* (Toronto, 1938), p. 407.

146. Henry J. Morgan, ed., *The Canadian Men and Women of the Time* (Toronto, 1912), pp. 321–22. See also Henry J. Morgan, *Bibliotheca Canadensis* (Ottawa, 1867), pp. 12–13; "Notes," London *Jewish World,* 9 August 1895; "Madame Pauline Donalda," in Arthur Hart, *The Jew,* p. 531; Hyman Edelstein, "Canada's First Jewish Poet," Toronto *Jewish Standard,* October 1951.

147. *The Canada Directory,* 1851, p. 241; *The Canada Directory,* 1857–58, p. 377; Weir, *Montreal,* pp. 231, 254, 324; Montreal *Star,* 29 November 1898; *Lovell's Montreal Directory,* 1911–1912, p. 1036; *Who's Who and Why* (1919–20), p. 836; "Prothonotary's Register, 1832–1890," in Gottesman, *Directory,* p. 159; Sigmund Samuel, *In Return,* pp. 10–26, 89–95.

148. "Death of Mr. Samuel Benjamin," Montreal *Daily Witness,* 22 March 1893; "The Late Mr. John E. Moss," Canadian *Jewish Times,* 20 June 1902.

149. "Canadian Jewry," London *Jewish World,* 17 February 1899.

150. Compare Goulston, "Rabbinate," pp. 61–62; Neusner, "English Jews," pp. 137–47; Cecil Roth, "The Chief Rabbinate of England," in *Essays in Honour of the Very Rev. Dr. J. H. Hertz,* ed. I. Epstein, E. Levine, and C. Roth (London, 1942), pp. 378–79; S. Gaon, "Some Aspects of the Relations between Shaar Hashamayim of London and Shearith Israel of New York," in *Migration and Settlement: Proceedings of the Anglo-American Jewish Historical Conference* (London, 1971), pp. 3–5; Speisman, *Toronto,* p. 30. See also letter of Chief Rabbi N. M. Adler, London, to the president of the Victoria, B. C. congregation, 11 February 5623 (1863) in minutes of Congregation Emanu-El, Victoria, 29 June 1863.

151. Siegfried, *Race,* p. 258.

152. "The Late Rabbi S. Jacobs," in Arthur Hart, *The Jew,* p. 108.

153. Lazarus, "Historical Sketch." See also "Montreal, Canada," New York *Jewish Messenger,* 7 February 1890.

154. Rev. D. Piza, letter to Rev. David Meldola, London, 19 March 1844, in ADSP; "By-Laws of the Corporation of the Portuguese Jews of Montreal," 1857; Abraham De Sola, ed. and rev., *The Form of Prayer According to the Custom of the Spanish and Portuguese Jews,* 6 vols. (Philadelphia, 1878), title page; Roth, "Rabbinate," p. 377; Speisman, *Toronto,* p. 30.

155. "By-Laws of the Corporation of German and Polish Jews of Montreal," 1886.

156. MSP, 3 April 1892.

157. The Baron de Hirsch Institute, Montreal, *Annual Report,* 1900, p. 8. See also Michael Brown, "The Beginnings of Reform Judaism in Canada," *Jewish Social Studies* 34 (October 1972): 322–42.

158. MSP, 26 Elul 5539 (1779).

159. Abraham De Sola, personal letter to David A. Ansell, 21 February 1873, in ADSP.

160. As quoted in Frank, *Two Centuries,* pp. 43–44.

161. Ibid., p. 59.

162. MSP, 15 June 1854; receipts for amounts sent to Montefiore in ADSP; Belkin, *Gates,* p. 60. See also "English, German and Polish Congregation Subscription List, 1885," in Canadian Jewish Congress, Montreal, Archives, Shaar Hashomayim File; "Appendix to the Privy Council Order No. 622, 4 April 1887, giving lien on Moosomin settlers' houses to Mansion House Committee in London," in Bronfman Collection of Jewish Canadiana, Jewish Public Library, Montreal, Scrapbook on Jewish Farming; David A. Ansell, president, Baron de Hirsch Institute, letter to Alfred Cohen, London, 7 March 1902, in LBBDHI; Lawrence M. Lande, comp. and ed., *Montefiore Club* ([Montreal], 1955), p. 3; Hyamson, *The Sephardim,* p. 384.

163. London *Jewish World,* 24 January 1894, 29 November 1895; *The American Israelite,* 8 August 1895. See also Jewish Public Library, Montreal, Archives, Meldola De Sola Scrapbook.

164. Theodor Herzl, *The Complete Diaries,* ed. Raphael Patai, vol. 3 (New York and London, 1960), pp. 939–40, 25 April 1900.

165. "Lodge of Joppa," *Jewish Chronicle,* 17 March 1876; MSP, 22 October 1898; Raphael Patai, ed., *Encyclopedia of Zionism and Israel,* vol. 1 (New York, 1971), p. 175.

166. "Toronto Branch, Anglo-Jewish Association [Draft] Report for General Meeting Held Sunday, April 19, 1896," Bronfman Collection of Jewish Canadiana, Jewish Public Library, Montreal, Anglo-Jewish Association File.

167. "Anglo-Jewish Association," Canadian *Jewish Times,* 4 April 1913.

168. "Anglo-Jewish Association," *Jewish Chronicle,* 19 October 1877; *Lovell's Montreal Directory,* 1884–1891 (Moise Schwob); "Anglo-Jewish Association," Canadian *Jewish Times,* 4 April 1913; Arthur Hart, *The Jew,* pp. 444, 455. See also, Speisman, *Toronto,* pp. 57–59, 70. Speisman incorrectly dates the beginning of the Anglo-Jewish Association branch in Montreal.

169. W. H. Baker, letter of condolence to Major H. Marks, Brigade Staff Secretary, Jewish Lads' Brigade, London, 28 April 1904, in LBBDHI. See also "Death of Colonel Goldsmid," *Jewish Chronicle,* 1 April 1904; "The Lads' Brigade," Baltimore *Jewish Comment,* 12 August 1904; Gartner, *Immigrant,* p. 174.

170. "Jewish Lads' Brigade, Montreal Companies," Canadian *Jewish Times,* 11 December 1899; *Jewish Year Book,* 5663 (1902–03), p. 185; "Colonial and Foreign News," *Jewish Chronicle,* 21 October 1904; "Foreign and Colonial News," *Jewish Chronicle,* 11 May 1906; Louis Rasminsky, ed., *Hadassah Jubilee* ([Toronto, 1928]), p. 98.

171. W. H. Baker, "Principal's Report," 30 May 1904, in LBBDHI.

172. LBBDHI, 15 June 1903.

173. Abraham Joseph, diary, 5 August 1837, Public Archives of Canada, Ottawa, File MG-24I61; MSP, 26 November 1862, 17 March 1884, 20 April 1884; "Sir Moses Montefiore," unidentified newspaper clipping, Bronfman Collection of Jewish Canadiana, Jewish Public Library, Montreal, Montefiore Club File; Speisman, *Toronto,* p. 56; Arthur A. Chiel, *Jewish Experiences in Early Manitoba* (Winnipeg, 1955), pp. 22–27.

174. MSP, 4 November 1855, 15 August 1858; Benjamin Cohen, letter to D. A. Ansell, 22 November 1900, in LLB; Extracts, 30 June 1907; Sack, *History,* p. 166.

175. "Britain's Honored Dead," Montreal *Gazette,* 18 January 1892; "Our Dead Queen," Montreal *Daily Witness,* 4 February 1901; MSP, 7 May 1910.

176. Donald Creighton, *Canada's First Century* (Toronto, 1970), pp. 90–91.

177. Berger, *Power,* p. 217.

178. Ibid., p. 152. See also John Porter, *The Measure of Canadian Society* (n.p., 1979), p. 153.

179. *A History of Canada for the Use of Schools* (Toronto, 1876), as quoted in Berger, *Power,* p. 112.

180. Siegfried, *Race,* p. 275.

181. Ibid.

182. As quoted in "Welcomed to Montreal," Montreal *Star,* 7 July 1897.

183. See Berger, *Power,* pp. 116–17; Siegfried, *Race,* p. 106; Joseph Schull, *Laurier* (Toronto, 1966), pp. 186, 539.

184. Meldola De Sola, "Sermon—at the Laying of the Cornerstone of the New Stanley Street Synagogue of the Montreal Spanish and Portuguese Congregation, 'Shearith Israel'," 22 September 1887, in ADSP.

185. Zvi Hirsch Masliansky, *Kitvei Masliansky* [Hebrew] vol. 3 (New York, 1929), pp. 220–21. See also "British Freedom Is Appreciated," Montreal *Star,* 9 December 1901.

186. See Robert Craig Brown, *Canada's National Policy, 1883–1900* (Princeton, 1964), pp. 278–80; Norman Penlington, *Canada and Imperialism* (Toronto and Buffalo, 1965), pp. 34–38, 57.

187. See Joseph Levitt, *Henri Bourassa and the Golden Calf* (Ottawa, 1969), pp. 6, 15–16; Penlington, *Imperialism,* pp. 188, 241, 246–47.

188. See Gideon Shimoni, *Jews and Zionism: The South African Experience (1910–1967)* (Capetown, 1980), pp. 61–70.

189. "The Shame of Canada," broadside, Montreal, March 1900; Canadian *Jewish Times,* 13 April 1900. For a brief discussion of Jewish interests in the war, see Rothschild, *Rothschild,* pp. 80–85.

190. "The Zion Cadets Are Among the Smartest of Montreal's Junior Soldiers," Montreal *Daily Herald,* 28 December 1901. See also, "Parade d'Eglise," Montreal *La Presse,* 30 October 1899; "La Parade Militaire," Montreal *La Patrie,* 30 October 1899; "Voice of the Pulpit on the Transvaal War," Montreal *Star,"* 30 October 1899; Berger, *Power,* p. 7.

191. As quoted in "Champion of the Rights of Man," Montreal *Daily Herald,* 9 December 1901.

192. "Rabbi Ashinsky on British Supremacy," Canadian *Jewish Times,* 17 August 1900.

193. Capt. Barker of "C" Company, First Canadian Contingent, quoted in "The Shame of Canada." See also, Bram De Sola, "Beheaded Words," Montreal *Daily Witness,* 24 November 1899; "Winnipeg Jews and the Canadian Patriotic Fund," Canadian *Jewish Times,* 30 March 1900; "Briefs" [Hebrew], *Hamelitz,* 28 Kislev 1901; Berger, *Power,* pp. 254–57; Zvi Cohen, ed., *Canadian Jewry: Prominent Jews of Canada* (Toronto, 1933), p. 296.

194. Robert Craig Brown, *Policy,* p. 19; Berger, *Power,* p. 38.

195. David A. Ansell, *Welding the Links of Union* (n.p., 1886). See also H. Abramowitz and Lawrence Cohen, "Schedule of Material in the Ansell Collection," Bronfman Collection of Jewish Canadiana, Jewish Public Library, Montreal, Ansell File.

196. "Imperial Defense [Conference] Finishes Its Work" [Yiddish], *Keneder odler,* 20 August 1909.

197. See Lande, *Montefiore Club,* pp. 4–5.

198. As quoted in "Current Events," *Queen's Quarterly* 5 (July 1897): 85.

199. As quoted in Skelton, *Letters,* vol. 1, p. 128.

200. [William Lyon Mackenzie King], "The Jewish Population," Toronto *Mail and Empire,* 25 September 1897.

201. "The Late Louis Aronson," Canadian *Jewish Times*, 29 March 1901.

202. Quoted in William Henry Atherton, *Montreal from 1535 to 1914*, vol. 3 (Montreal, 1914), p. 227.

203. Michael Hirsch, "Memories of Four Score Years," Montreal *Gazette*, 5 February 1944; Sigmund Samuel, *In Return*, passim.

204. Meldola De Sola [Briton], letter, "The Marriage Question," Monteal *Daily Witness*, 19 January 1901.

205. "The Duke and Duchess of Cornwall and York," Canadian *Jewish Times*, 29 March 1901. See also "Toronto, Canada," New York *Jewish Messenger*, 27 May 1887; Weir, *Montreal*, pp. 220–21; "Alderman Samuel Rosenthal," Canadian *Jewish Times*, 17 January 1902; *Montreal Board of Trade Souvenir*, 1914–15, p. 52; Jewish Public Library, Montreal, Archives, Joseph S. Leo File; Evelyn Kallen, *Spanning the Generations* (Don Mills, Ontario, 1977), pp. 37–40 and the sources cited there. Kallen indicates mistakenly that the British affiliations of Canadian Jewry ended in 1880.

206. "Canada," London *Jewish World*, 14 August 1896.

207. M. Ginsburg, "The King George Sick Benefit Association in the Last Fifteen Years," *Souvenir: King George Sick Benefit Association of Montreal* (Montreal, 1946), p. 1. See also Canadian *Jewish Times*, 13 September 1903; Meir Fox, "The Jewish Mutual Aid Movement in the United States and Canada," in Russian-Polish Hebrew Sick Benefit Association *Jubilee Book* ([Montreal], 1937), p. 7.

208. "Hebrew Men of England Congregation, Spadina Avenue, Toronto," in Arthur Hart, *The Jew*, p. 141.

209. *The House of Nordheimer* ([Toronto, 1903]), pp. 16–17.

210. A. Harkavy, "Our Distant Brothers, the Jews of Canada" [Hebrew], *Ha-Zefirah*, 3 Adar 1888. Compare *The Jewish Encyclopedia* (1901–1906), s.v. "Canada" by C.[larence] I. D.[e] S.[ola]; and Frank, *Two Centuries*, passim. See also Michael Brown, "The Empire's Best Known Jew and Little Known Jewry," in *Community and the Individual*, eds. Ronald S. Aigen and Gershon D. Hundert (Philadelphia, 1986), pp. 156–70.

211. Berger, *Power*, p. 89.

212. R. P. Joyal, O.M.I., "Sermon," in Le Congrès de la Jeunesse à Québec, *Rapport Officiel*, 1910, p. 92. See also Berger, *Power*, pp. 87–89.

213. *Additional Papers Concerning the Province of Quebeck: being an Appendix to the book, entitled An Account of the Proceedings of the British and Other Protestant Inhabitants of the Province of Quebeck in North America, in order to obtain a House of Assembly in that Province* (London, 1776), cited in Rome, *Ramble*, pp. 5–6.

214. "Deaths Abroad," *The European Magazine and London Review*, March 1801.

Chapter 3

1. Charles Freshman, *The Autobiography of the Reverend Charles Freshman* (Toronto, 1868), p. 50.

2. Compare Meir Berlin, *Mi-Volozhin ad Yerushalayim* [Hebrew], vol. 1 (Tel Aviv, 1940), p. 37.

3. Alexander Levy of Montreal, quoted in New York *Herald*, 5 December 1858. See also, "The Mortara Case," *New York Times*, 6 December 1858; New York *Jewish Messenger*, 10 December 1858.

4. See Cyrus Adler and Aaron Margalith, *With Firmness in the Right* (New York, 1946), pp. 3–4, 20, 23, 261–70; Bertram Wallace Korn, *The American Reaction to the Mortara Case: 1858–1859* (Cincinnati, 1957), passim; André Chouraqui, *Cent Ans d'Histoire: L'Alliance Israélite Universelle et la Renaissance Juive Contemporaine (1860–1960)* (Paris, 1965), p. 100; and many other sources. Interestingly, Chouraqui, a French patriot

and an enthusiastic apologist for the Alliance Israélite Universelle, admits that in Romania, "only the Americans successfully exercised any influence."

It should be noted with regard to the Russian-American treaty, that the ostensible reason for renunciation was Russian discrimination against American Jews seeking to trade or travel in Russia. Unquestionably, however, popular support for revoking the treaty came from people who abhorred Russian treatment of Jews in general.

5. Compare Perry Miller, *The New England Mind,* vol. 2 (Cambridge, Massachusetts, 1953), passim; and other sources.

6. Henry Wentworth Monk, *A Simple Interpretation of the Revelation Together with Three Lectures Lately Delivered in Canada and the United States,* 2d ed. (London, [1858?]), passim.

7. See Henry Feingold, *Zion in America* (New York, 1974), p. 198; and many other sources.

8. See Anita Libman Lebeson, *Pilgrim People* (New York, 1950), pp. 193–94.

9. Compare among other sources, "Where from and Where to?" [Hebrew], *Hamelitz,* 5 Sivan 1882; "We Have Reached Great Heights in America" [Yiddish], *Keneder odler,* 24 February 1903; Henry Adams, *The Education of Henry Adams* (n.p., 1907); Claris Edwin Silcox and Galen M. Fisher, *Catholics, Jews, and Protestants* (New York and London, 1934), pp. 16–17; Naomi W. Cohen, "Antisemitism in the Gilded Age: The Jewish View," *Jewish Social Studies* 41 (summer–fall 1979): 187–89, and the sources cited there.

10. *Israelite Press, Winnipeg: The 100th Anniversary Souvenir* (Winnipeg, 1932), p. 16.

11. "History of the Jews in the United States" [Hebrew], *Ha-Zefirah,* 27 Nisan 1888.

12. Sigmund Samuel, *In Return* (Toronto, 1963), p. 6.

13. 10 July 1846.

14. Sir Moses Montefiore, personal letter to Rabbi Abraham De Sola, Montreal, February 1872, in McGill University Archives, Montreal, De Sola Papers (hereafter referred to as ADSP). Compare also W. S. Shepperson, *British Emigration to North America* (Minneapolis, 1957), pp. 6–7.

15. Quoted in "The Hebrew in America," *American Jews' Annual,* 1892–93.

16. Abraham Joseph, diary, 25 December 1837, Public Archives of Canada, Ottawa, File MG-24I61.

17. See S. F. Wise and Robert Craig Brown, *Canada Views the United States* (Toronto, 1967), pp. 8–9, 20, 26, 39, 48, 80, 83, 98. Compare also Robert T. Mullen, "Plutocracy and the Social Crisis," *The Week,* 5 October 1894; "The Article 'Canada' in the *Jewish Encyclopedia,*" *Canadian Jewish Times,* 16 January 1903.

18. "Canadian-American Trade" [Yiddish], *Keneder odler,* 12 August 1909. See also "The Relationship Between Canada and the United States" [Yiddish], *Keneder odler,* 20 May 1910; V.-E. Beaupré, address, in Le Congrès de la Jeunesse à Québec, *Rapport Officiel,* 1910, pp. 6–25; Allen Smith, "Introduction," to Samuel E. Moffett, *The Americanization of Canada* (Toronto and Buffalo, 1957), p. xxiv; Wise and Brown, *Views,* pp. 95–96; Robert Craig Brown, *Canada's National Policy, 1883–1900* (Princeton, 1964), pp. 278–80; Norman Penlington, *Canada and Imperialism* (Toronto and Buffalo, 1965), pp. 34–45, 57.

19. "Socialism Among Jews in Montreal," *Canadian Jewish Times,* 4 May 1906. See also "The Strong Word" [Yiddish], *Keneder odler,* 23 October 1910; Abraham De Sola, personal letter to Alexander Miller, 1873, in ADSP.

20. Quoted in "Mr. Harris Vineberg on the New York Ghetto," *Canadian Jewish Times,* 28 March 1902.

21. Compare Donald Avery, "The Radical Alien and the Winnipeg General Strike of 1919," in *The West and the Nation,* eds. Carl Berger and Ramsay Cook (Toronto, 1976), pp. 209–31.

22. Smith, "Introduction," p. xi. See also Elizabeth Wallace, *Goldwin Smith: Victorian Liberal* (Toronto, 1957), pp. 20–39; Carl Berger, *The Sense of Power* (Toronto and Buffalo, 1970), p. 76; W. L. Morton, *The Canadian Identity,* 2d ed. (Toronto and Buffalo, 1972), pp. 62–63.

23. Wise and Brown, *Views,* p. 17.

24. As quoted in "Congress," Montreal *Gazette,* 12 January 1872. See Wise and Brown, *Views,* pp. 29–32, 46–47, 55–58, 70, 127, for similar views expressed by De Sola's gentile Canadian contemporaries. See also John Bartlet Brebner, *North Atlantic Triangle* (Toronto, 1970), p. 185.

25. Adolphus Mordecai Hart [Hampden], *The Impending Crisis* (New York, 1855), p. 4.

26. Mary Ellen Ross, *The Legend of the Holy Stone* (Montreal, 1878), p. 245.

27. "The Hebrews of New York," Montreal *Star,* 15 October 1887.

28. A. V. Spada, *The Italians in Canada* (Ottawa and Montreal, 1969), p. 91. See also Mark Wischnitzer, *To Dwell in Safety* (Philadelphia, 1948), p. 99; Mordecai Richler, *The Street* (London, 1971), pp. 19–20.

29. Compare Moshe Cryshtall, letter [Hebrew], *Ha-Zefirah,* 1 Elul 1887; Joseph Elijah Bernstein, letter [Hebrew], *Hamelitz,* 7 Iyyar 1884; "Abroad" [Hebrew], *Hamelitz,* 8 Heshvan 1883; Wischnitzer, *Safety,* p. 149; B. G. Kayfetz, "Immigrant Reaction as Reflected in Jewish Literature," undated manuscript, Bronfman Collection of Jewish Canadiana, Jewish Public Library, Montreal, Kayfetz File.

30. "Colonial and Foreign News," *Jewish Chronicle,* 8 June 1906. See also "Letters from Our Correspondents" [Hebrew], *Ha-Zefirah,* 11 Av 1888; S. Talpis, "Abroad" [Hebrew], *Hamelitz,* 28 Kislev 1899.

31. Letter quoted in Zosa Szajkowski, "The European Attitudes to East European Jewish Immigration (1881–93)," *Publications of the American Jewish Historical Society* (hereafter referred to as *PAJHS*) 41 (1951): 154–55.

32. Compare "Toronto: The Congregation," *Jewish Chronicle,* 26 September 1862; Norman Macdonald, *Canada: Immigration and Colonization, 1841–1903* (Toronto, 1966), p. 77.

33. See, for example, Aharon Yehudah Leib Horowitz, *Rumania ve-America,* vol. 2 [Hebrew] (Berlin, 1874), pp. 55, 63; advertisements of Hamburg-America Line, *Hamelitz,* 1892; "Mr. Herman Landau on Canada and the Jews," *Jewish Chronicle,* 19 January 1906; Macdonald, *Immigration,* p. 27.

34. Compare also "Brief Jottings" [Hebrew], *Hamelitz,* 7 Kislev 1901; "Abroad" [Hebrew], *Ha-Zefirah,* 9 Nisan 1911.

35. "Canada as a Land of Immigration" [Hebrew], *Ha-Zefirah,* 12 Av 1913.

36. As quoted in "My Views on Philanthropy," *North American Review,* July 1891.

37. Marcus Lee Hansen and John Bartlet Brebner, *The Mingling of the Canadian and American Peoples* (New Haven, 1940), p. 214.

38. Canada, Royal Commission on Bilingualism and Biculturalism, *The Cultural Contribution of the Other Ethnic Groups,* Report, Book 4 (1969), pp. 18–20; Hansen and Brebner, *Mingling,* p. 182.

39. Ottawa *Free Press,* 1 June 1911, as quoted in *The Canadian Annual Review,* 1911, p. 396.

40. David A. Ansell, president, Baron de Hirsch Institute, letter to president, Jewish Colonization Association, Paris, 5 June 1903, in Letterbook of the Baron de Hirsch Institute–Young Men's Hebrew Benevolent Society (hereafter referred to as LBBDHI).

41. "The Jews of Winnipeg," Winnipeg *Telegram,* as quoted in Baltimore *Jewish Comment,* 25 August 1901.

42. Hansen and Brebner, *Mingling,* pp. 214, 246–47; Leon E. Truesdell, *The Ca-*

nadian-Born in the United States (New Haven, 1943), pp. 6, 16; R. H. Coats and M. C. Maclean, *The American-Born in Canada* (Toronto, 1943), p. 24; Moffett, *Americanization,* pp. 11, 13.

43. See Brebner, *Triangle,* pp. 212, 233; Joseph Kage, *With Faith and Thanksgiving* (Montreal, 1962), p. 12; and other places; John Douglas Borthwick, *Montreal History and Gazetteer* (Montreal, 1892), p. 424.

44. Unidentified newspaper clipping, 1890, in Jewish Public Library, Montreal, Archives, Meldola De Sola Papers; "Canadian Jews in the Medical and Dental Professions" and "The Late Abraham Pinto Joseph," in *The Jew in Canada,* ed. Arthur Daniel Hart (Toronto and Montreal, 1926), pp. 410, 430; Hamilton *Herald,* 23 April 1904.

45. Baron de Hirsch Institute, Montreal, *Annual Report,* 1892, p. 4.

46. Minutes of the Spanish and Portuguese Synagogue, Montreal, 3 September 1855 (hereafter referred to as MSP); "St. Paul, Minnesota," New York *Jewish Messenger,* 15 February 1884; Extracts from the Minutes of the Board of Directors of the Young Men's Hebrew Benevolent Society, 30 May 1885, 14 June 1886, and 31 October 1886, (hereafter referred to as Extracts); Carroll Ryan, "Letter from Canada," Baltimore *Jewish Comment,* 15 November 1901; Edmund Scheuer, "Reminiscences of Canadian Jewry," appended to Arthur Brodey, "Political and Civil Status of the Jews in Canada" (Rabbi and Master's thesis, Jewish Institute of Religion, 1933), pp. 357–58.

47. W. H. Baker, secretary, Baron de Hirsch Institute, letter to editor, Montreal *Star,* 5 May 1905, in LBBDHI; Extracts, 1 August 1907. See also William Evans Gordon, *The Alien Immigrant* (London, 1903), p. 210.

48. See, for example, *American Israelite,* 7 November 1901, 9 January 1902; Coats and Maclean, *American-Born,* p. 45.

49. Reuben Brainin, *Kol Kitvei Reuben Mordecai Brainin* [Hebrew], vol. 3 (New York, 1940), passim. See also *Ha-Zefirah* [Hebrew], 27 Shvat 1902.

50. Sigmund Samuel, *In Return,* pp. 27–28; letter of Benjamin Hart, Philadelphia, to Ezekiel Hart, New York, 22 November 1793, in McGill University, Montreal, McCord Museum, Early Hart Papers, File 15.

51. "Rabbis in Session," Montreal *Star,* 7 July 1897; "Dr. L. J. Solway, B.A., M.B., M.R.C.P., Toronto," in Arthur Hart, *The Jew,* p. 415; Raymond Douville, *Aaron Hart* [French] (Trois Rivières, 1938), p. 103; Louis Rosenberg, "The Earliest Jewish Settlers in Canada: Facts vs. Myths," in *Canadian Jewish Reference Book and Directory, 1963,* comp. Eli Gottesman (Montreal, 1963), p. 140.

52. "Nathaniel S. Fineberg, M.A., B.C.L., Montreal," in Arthur Hart, *The Jew,* p. 217; Ethel Vineberg, *The History of the National Council of Jewish Women of Canada* (Montreal, 1967), p. 84; Berger, *Power,* pp. 43–48.

53. See Zvi Cohen, ed., *Canadian Jewry: Prominent Jews of Canada* (Toronto, 1933), pp. 116, 118; "Dr. J. J. Lavine, Toronto," in Arthur Hart, *The Jew,* p. 425; Ross Hamilton, ed., *Prominent Men of Canada, 1931–32* (Montreal, 1932), p. 422. See also David Eisen, *Diary of a Medical Student* (Toronto, 1974), pp. 104–26.

54. Alexander Harkavy, "Our Distant Brethren" [Hebrew], *Ha-Zefirah,* 17 Sivan 1888; "A. C. Cohen, Vancouver," in Arthur Hart, *The Jew,* p. 346; Hamilton, *Prominent Men,* p. 537; Louis Rosenberg, *Canada's Jews* (Montreal, 1939), p. 136; Coats and Maclean, *American-Born,* pp. 24, 56; Truesdell, *Canadian-Born,* p. 6.

55. Abraham Joseph, diary, 30 November 1844, Public Archives of Canada, Ottawa, File MG-24I61; "A Half-Hour in Canada," Toronto *Globe,* 27 April 1889. See also Harold Martin Troper, *Only Farmers Need Apply* (Toronto, 1972), pp. 41–42.

56. "At Montreal," New York *Jewish Messenger,* 30 September 1882.

57. *American Jews' Annual,* 1893, pp. 85–86.

58. "A Critic Criticised," Canadian *Jewish Times,* 28 October 1898.

59. See, for example, "Jews in Canada," Baltimore *Jewish Comment,* 7 December 1900.

60. "Letter from Canada," Baltimore *Jewish Comment,* 3 May 1901.

61. See "Is Canada a Land for Jewish Immigration?" [Yiddish], *Keneder odler,* 5 July 1908; "The *Warheit* Bluffs" [Yiddish], *Keneder odler,* 21 October 1910.

62. "Current Topics," *Reform Advocate,* 7 August 1897.

63. Carroll Ryan, "Letter from Canada," Baltimore *Jewish Comment,* 3 May 1901.

64. As quoted in Bernard Figler, *Rabbi Dr. Herman Abramowitz, Lazarus Cohen, Lyon Cohen* (Ottawa, 1968), p. 89.

65. See "At Montreal," New York *Jewish Messenger,* 30 September 1892; Robert Craig Brown, *Policy,* pp. 182–83, 238; Morton, *Identity,* pp . 59–60.

66. "The Canadian West," as quoted in Troper, *Farmers,* p. 87.

67. "Letter from Canada," Baltimore *Jewish Comment,* 3 May 1901.

68. Howard Angus Kennedy, *New Canada and the New Canadians* (London, 1907), pp. 53–54.

69. See, among other sources, "Letters from Our Correspondents" [Hebrew], *Ha-Zefirah,* 11 Av 1888; *Who's Who and Why* (Toronto, 1920), p. 1324; "C. Benjamin, Calgary," in Arthur Hart, *The Jew,* p. 366; *Israelite Press Souvenir,* pp. 14, 54–58; Hansen and Brebner, *Mingling,* pp. 191–92; Abe L. Plotkin, *Struggle for Justice* (New York, 1960), pp. 29–32; Donald Creighton, *Canada's First Century* (Toronto, 1970), p. 104; Troper, *Farmers,* pp. 41–42; Macdonald, *Canada* p. 36.

70. Liebmann Hersch, "International Migration of the Jews," in *International Migrations,* ed. Walter Wilcox, vol. 2 (New York, 1931), p. 477.

71. See, for example, "Montreal," *American Israelite,* 20 July 1883; *Canada: An Encyclopedia* (1898–1900), s.v. "Historical Sketch of the Jews of Canada," by Abraham Lazarus; "The Montefiore Club," Canadian *Jewish Times,* 5 October 1906; Arthur Hart, *The Jew,* pp. 152, 368, 386, 406, 422, 429; *Who's Who and Why* (Toronto, 1916), p. 566; Hamilton, *Prominent Men,* pp. 120, 507; Zvi Cohen, *Prominent Jews,* pp. 64, 66, 95; Coats and Maclean, *American-Born,* p. 136; A. I. Willinsky, *A Doctor's Memoirs* (Toronto, 1960), p. 4; and many other sources.

72. Carroll Ryan, "Review of Canadian Conditions," Baltimore *Jewish Comment,* 6 February 1903.

73. "First Annual Meeting of the Montreal Hebrew Philanthropic Society," *The Occident and American Jewish Advocate,* October 1848, pp. 268–70; D. A. Ansell, "Reminiscences of the Young Men's Hebrew Benevolent Society, etc., etc.," in Canadian Jewish Congress, Montreal, Archives, Ansell Papers; Extracts, 31 October 1885; "Milton Blackstone, Toronto," in Arthur Hart, *The Jew,* p. 528. On Canadians' views of conditions in Canada compared to those in the United States, see J. T. Copp, "The Condition of the Working Class in Montreal, 1897–1920," in *Studies in Canadian Social History,* eds. Michiel Horn and Ronald Sabourin (Toronto, 1974), pp. 189–212.

74. George M. Price, "The Russian Jews in America," trans. Leo Shpall, *PAJHS* 48 (1958): 42. See also Simon Belkin, *Through Narrow Gates* (Montreal, 1966), p. 26.

75. David Bressler, "Distribution," in *The Russian Jew in the United States,* ed. Charles S. Bernheimer (Philadelphia, 1905), p. 367.

76. Samuel Joseph, *History of the Baron de Hirsch Fund* (n.p., 1935), p. 204; Mark Wischnitzer, *Visas to Freedom* (Cleveland, 1956), pp. 65–66.

77. "Abraham Blumenthal, Montreal," in Arthur Hart, *The Jew,* p. 363; Hamilton, *Prominent Men,* p. 349; Zvi Cohen, *Prominent Jews,* p. 88; Brebner, *Triangle,* p. 212; Ben Dunkelman, *Dual Allegiance* (Toronto, 1976), pp. 7–8.

78. See, for example, "Isaac Rubenstein, Sault-Ste. Marie," in Arthur Hart, *The Jew,* p. 152.

79. Rebecca Gratz, personal letter to her sister-in-law, Ann Boswell Gratz, 5 May 1854, in *Letters of Rebecca Gratz,* ed. David Philipson (Philadelphia, 1929), pp. 394–95; N. Taylor Phillips, "Clarence I. De Sola," *PAJHS* 28 (1922): 271; "A. M. Vineberg," in Arthur Hart, *The Jew,* p. 523; Joseph R. Rosenbloom, *A Biographical Dictionary of Early American Jews* (Lexington, Kentucky, n.d.), p. 154; Figler, *Abramowitz,* p. 68.

80. Baron de Hirsch Institute Loose Leaf Book (hereafter referred to as LLB), 28 December 1906.

81. "The Jewish Divorce Question," unidentified newspaper clipping, 24 August 1894, in Jewish Public Library, Montreal, Archives, Meldola De Sola Scrapbook (hereafter referred to as MDSB); "She is Coming from Philadelphia to Arrest Her Husband" [Yiddish], *Keneder odler,* 8 July 1908; Baron de Hirsch Institute, Montreal, *Annual Report,* 1913, pp. 8–9. See also Reena Sigman Friedman, " 'Send Me My Husband Who Is in New York City': Husband Desertion in the American-Jewish Immigrant Community, 1900–1926," *Jewish Social Studies* 44 (winter 1982): 1–18.

82. "Montreal, Canada" [Hebrew], 20 Av 1884. See also Carroll Ryan, "Jewish Immigration to Canada," Baltimore *Jewish Comment,* 20 May 1904; Michael N. Dobkowski, *The Tarnished Dream* (Westport, Conn., 1979), pp. 52–53.

83. See "A Golden Wedding," *The American Hebrew,* 20 October 1893; S. J. Birnbaum, "The History of the Jews in Toronto," Canadian *Jewish Times,* 24 January 1913.

84. Hansen and Brebner, *Mingling,* pp. 78–79. See also Rosenbloom, *Dictionary,* pp. 111–12.

85. Benjamin G. Sack, "When Did David S. Franks Last Leave Canada?" *PAJHS* 31 (1928): 234; Rosenbloom, *Dictionary,* pp. 89–90; Irving A. Katz, *The Beth El Story: Jews in Michigan Before 1850* (Detroit, 1955), pp. 35–36; Richard Morris, "The Jews, Minorities and Dissent in the American Revolution," in *Migration and Settlement: Proceedings of the Anglo-American Jewish Historical Conference* (London, 1971), pp. 153–54, 156; Doris M. Judah, "Genealogy of the Judah Family" (typescript, no date) in McGill University, Montreal, McCord Museum, Judah papers.

86. Hansen and Brebner, *Mingling,* p. 148.

87. Ansell, "Reminiscences."

88. Rebecca Gratz, personal letter to her brother, Benjamin Gratz, 15 April 1863, in Philipson, *Letters,* pp. 436–37.

89. See S. J. Birnbaum, "Toronto"; will (15 November 1864) and probate documents (30 August 1865) of Rachel Barnett Davega, Municipal Archives, Montreal.

90. Adolphus Mordecai Hart [Hampden], *The Political State and Condition of Her Majesty's Protestant Subjects in the Province of Quebec (Since Confederation)* (Toronto, 1871), p. 54; Zvi Cohen, *Prominent Jews,* pp. 200–01; Brebner, *Triangle,* pp. 165–66; Raymond Arthur Davies, *Printed Jewish Canadiana, 1685–1900* (Montreal, 1955), p. 24; David and Tamar De Sola Pool, *An Old Faith in the New World* (New York, 1955), p. 333; Fredrick L. Hitchcock, *History of Scranton* (New York, 1914), p. 148.

91. Rebecca Gratz, personal letter to her brother, Benjamin Gratz, 15 April 1863, in Philipson, *Letters,* pp. 436–37. See also *Encyclopedia Judaica* (1971), s.v. "Raphall, Morris J."

92. E. N. Adler, "Visit to the Jewish Colony at Hirsch, Saskatchewan, Canada," London *Jewish Chronicle,* 27 December 1907; Hansen and Brebner, *Mingling,* pp. 76–77; Brebner, *Triangle,* p. 133; Moffett, *Americanization,* pp. 52–73.

93. Lazarus, "Sketch."

94. See I. G. Ascher, personal letter to president, Young Man's Hebrew Benevolent Society, 31 August 1890, in Extracts; "The Death of Mrs. A. De Sola, Montreal *Daily Witness,* 13 May 1898; Montreal *Star,* 19 June 1902; "Canadian Jews in the Medical and Dental Professions," in Arthur Hart, *The Jew,* p. 410.

95. Abraham Joseph, diary, October 1844 to February 1845, Public Archives of

Canada, Ottawa, File MG-24I61; Rebecca Gratz, personal letters to her sister-in-law, Ann Boswell Gratz, 3 September 1851, 5 May 1854, 15 September 1848, 22 April 1849, 7 May 1852, 27 January 1863, and to Benjamin Gratz, 2 January 1848, in Philipson, *Letters,* pp. 342–43, 350–52, 358–59, 377–79, 382–84, 394–95, 433–34; Abraham De Sola, various personal letters to Jane Belais and to Henry Pereira Mendes, invitation to the silver wedding anniversary reception of Mr. and Mrs. William Cane, Plattsburg, 21 October 1872, and undated invitation to a social evening from Rebecca Gratz, all in ADSP.

96. Coats and Maclean, *American-Born,* pp. 43–44. See also Moffett, *Americanization,* p. 67.

97. Figler, *Abramowitz,* pp. 169–70; unidentified newspaper clippings, Jewish Public Library, Montreal, Archives, Meldola De Sola Papers; N. Taylor Phillips, "De Sola," p. 272.

98. Compare Montreal *Star,* 3 July 1907; and herein, chapter 2.

99. See Moffett, *Americanization,* pp. 79–81, 84–85.

100. Hansen and Brebner, *Mingling,* pp. 241–42; Moffett, *Americanization,* pp. 107–10; William F. Ryan, "The Church's Contribution to Progress, 1896–1914," in *One Church, Two Nations?,* eds. Philip LeBlanc and Arnold Edinborough (Don Mills, Ontario, 1968), pp. 85–87.

101. Letters of Aaron Hart, Three Rivers, to Ezekiel Hart, New York, 24 December 1789, and 20 December 1793, McGill University, Montreal, McCord Museum, Early Hart papers, Files 10, 16; Samuel David, diary, 1800–1806, Public Archives of Canada, Ottawa, MG-24I13; MSP, 12 October 1856. See also Arthur Weir, ed., *Montreal Illustrated, 1894* (Montreal, 1894), p. 248; "The Late Mr. Baruch Bloomfield," Canadian *Jewish Times,* 17 January 1902; "Jew from New York a Prisoner" [Yiddish], *Keneder odler,* 17 October 1910; *Dominion of Canada and Newfoundland Gazetteer and Classified Directory,* 1915, p. 1358, and other such directories; Israel Hoffer, "Recollections and Reminiscences," *Saskatchewan History* 5 (1952): 32; Sigmund Samuel, *In Return,* pp. 55–56, 70–79.

102. Hamilton, *Prominent Men,* p. 359; Zvi Cohen, *Prominent Jews,* pp. 151, 230; *The Vision and Understanding of a Man* (Montreal, 1951), p. 11.

103. "Jewish Bakers Still Out," Montreal *Gazette,* 31 May 1906; *Canadian Annual Review,* 1908, pp. 113–15; A. Suffrin, "Reminiscences in the History of Local No. 115," *Thirty-fifth Jubilee Journal of the Montreal Bakers' Union, Local 115* (Montreal, 1938); Jacob Leib Becker, *Derzeilungen un Zichroines* [Yiddish] (Montreal, 1956), pp. 254–55; Joseph Levitt, *Henri Bourassa and the Golden Calf* (Ottawa, 1969), p. 13; Moffett, *Americanization,* p. 93; and many other sources.

104. Abraham Rhinewine, "The Jewish Labour Movement in Canada," in Arthur Hart, *The Jew,* p. 460; Elias Tcherikower, *The Early Jewish Labor Movement in the United States,* trans. and rev. Aaron Antonovsky (New York, 1961), pp. 330–31; David Rome, comp. and ed., *Early Documents on the Canadian Jewish Congress, 1914–1921, Canadian Jewish Archives,* n.s., no. 1 (Montreal, 1974), p. 44; interview with Arnold Rose, Toronto, regarding the activities of his father, a former union organizer, 11 December 1974; Stephen A. Speisman, *The Jews of Toronto: A History to 1937* (Toronto, 1977), pp. 192–93.

105. Cyrus MacMillan, *McGill and Its Story, 1821–1921* (London, 1921), pp. 195–96.

106. Compare Adolphus Mordecai Hart, *History of the Valley of the Mississippi* (Cincinnati, 1853); idem, *Life in the Far West* (Cincinnati, 1860); idem, *The Impending Crisis* (New York, 1855); idem, *The Political State.* See also Henry J. Morgan, *Bibliotheca Canadensis* (Ottawa, 1867), pp. 12–13; "Adolphus Mordecai Hart," Bronfman Collection of Jewish Canadiana, Jewish Public Library, Montreal, Adolphus Mordecai Hart File; Hyman Edelstein, "Canada's First Jewish Poet," Toronto *Jewish Standard,* October 1951;

David Rome, *The Early Jewish Presence in Canada: A Booklover's Ramble Through Jewish Canadiana* (Montreal, 1971), pp. 10–12.

107. Letters of J. Gardner, Montreal, to James Fields of Ticknor and Fields, Boston, 2 July 1868, and of Willett J. Hyatt, Secretary of the Athaeneum Bureau of Literature, New York, to Abraham De Sola, 9 March 1880, in ADSP.

108. Sir Moses Montefiore, personal letter to Abraham De Sola, February 1872, in ADSP; New York, *Jewish Messenger,* 12 January 1872.

109. "Canada," *Jewish Chronicle,* 26 February 1909; Robert Craig Brown, *Policy,* pp. 244–55.

110. See "American Jewish Historical Society," New York *Jewish Messenger,* 31 December 1897; "Proposed American Jewish Historical Exhibition," Baltimore *Jewish Comment,* 5 July 1901; *Who's Who and Why,* 1915–16, pp. 532–33.

111. Moffett, *Americanization,* p. 63.

112. Spada, *Italians;* Joseph M. Kirschbaum, *Slovaks in Canada* (Toronto, 1967), p. 287.

113. See Meldola De Sola [Old Timer], "Re-introduction of Orthodoxy in Forty-Fourth Street," New York *Hebrew Standard,* 21 December 1891; "Rag Journalism," New York *Hebrew Standard,* 10 March 1899; Lazarus, "Sketch," p. 150; Meldola De Sola, "The Future of Judaism in America," New York *Herald,* 26 November 1905.

114. Hirsch Wolofsky, *Journey of My Life* (Montreal, 1929), p. 218. Speisman, *Toronto,* p. 236.

115. Augustus Bridle, "The Drama of the 'Ward'," *The Canadian Magazine,* November 1909, p. 6; Olivar Asselin, "The Jews in Montreal," *The Canadian Century,* 16 September 1911; I. Rabinovitch, "Yiddish Theater in Montreal," *Canadian Yewish Year-Book,* 1940–41, p. 167; "The Jewish Theater in Montreal" [Yiddish], *Keneder odler,* 8 August 1915; Arthur Chiel, *The Jews in Manitoba* (Toronto, 1961), pp. 118–19; Speisman, *Toronto,* 236–39.

116. See Newton Bosworth, ed., *Hochelaga Depicta: The Early History and Present State of the City and Island of Montreal* (Montreal, 1839), passim, on the early churches and synagogue of the city. For a discussion of the full range of exchanges between Canada and the United States in the religious sphere during the period under review, see Robert T. Handy, *A History of the Churches in the United States and Canada* (Oxford, 1976), pp. 132–35, 232, 346–51, 362.

117. Carroll Ryan, "Letter from Canada," Baltimore *Jewish Comment,* 1 February 1901; Leo M. Schapp, "Judaism in Western Canada," London *Jewish Chronicle,* 8 May 1905; Sch[muel] N. Gottlieb, *Oholei Shem* [Hebrew] (Pinsk, 1912), pp. 293, 300; "The Holy Blossom Toronto Hebrew Congregation," in Arthur Hart, *The Jew,* pp. 105–07; Zvi Cohen, *Prominent Jews,* pp. 203–04.

118. MSP, 24 August 1846, 17 February 1847, 19 May 1847, 2 June 1847, 7 March 1852, 2 June 1861, 31 January 1907, 13 November 1907; "History of the Jewish Communal Bodies of Montreal," Canadian *Jewish Times,* 11 December 1899; "The Late Abraham Kirschberg," Canadian *Jewish Times,* 15 August 1902.

119. "Montreal, Canada," New York *Jewish Messenger,* 21 October 1881; "Montreal," *American Israelite,* 24 October 1901; "Rabbi Herman Abramowitz," Canadian *Jewish Times,* 9 October 1902; "Biographical Sketches of Rabbis and Cantors Officiating in the United States," *American Jewish Year Book,* 1903–04, p. 67; Figler, *Abramowitz,* passim; and many other places.

120. "Beth Midrash Hagodal Chevra Shaas," Canadian *Jewish Times,* 11 April 1902; Irwin A. Swiss and H. Norman Shoop, *Rabbi Aaron M. Ashinsky* (Pittsburgh, 1935), passim; "Rabbi A. M. Ashinsky, a Zionist Leader, 87," *New York Times,* 3 April 1954; Speisman, *Toronto,* pp. 222–24, 233; Harry Gutkin, *Journey Into Our Heritage* (Toronto, 1980), p. 125.

121. New York *Jewish Messenger,* 20 April 1875; "Biographical Sketches," p. 64; Birnbaum, "Toronto," 20 December 1912; Speisman, *Toronto,* pp. 25–27; on Wittenberg, see also Selig Adler and Thomas E. Connolly, *From Ararat to Suburbia* (Philadelphia, 1960), p. 199. Speisman says that Goldberg came to Toronto from Buffalo.

122. See "Canada," *Jewish Chronicle,* 27 May 1904; "Nathan Gordon" [Yiddish], *Keneder odler* 12 January 1909; William Henry Atherton, *Montreal from 1535 to 1914,* vol. 3 (Montreal, 1914), pp. 283–84; "Nathan Gordon, M.A., B.C.L., Montreal," in Arthur Hart, *The Jew,* p. 125; Michael Brown, "The Beginnings of Reform Judaism in Canada," *Jewish Social Studies* 34 (1972): 323–24; Speisman, *Toronto,* pp. 51–54.

123. See, among other sources, A. Eliasson, "Abroad" [Hebrew], *Hamelitz,* 18 Nisan 1897; Michael Brown, "Beginnings," passim.

124. MSP, 28 April 1850, 26 February 1852; Benjamin G. Sack, "A Suit at Law Involving the First Jewish Minister in Canada," *PAJHS* 31 (1928): 181–86; Pool, *Old Faith,* p. 431.

125. Bertram Jonas, "Refugees from the Jewish Pulpit," *Canadian Jewish Chronicle,* 18 October 1935, pp. 5, 16.

126. Benjamin Joseph, Berthier, Lower Canada, circumcision certificate, 2 November 1811, in ADSP; MSP, various entries; Speisman, *Toronto,* pp. 26–27.

127. Minutes of the Spanish and Portuguese Synagogue, New York (hereafter cited as SPNY), 6 June 1882; "Consecration of a Montreal Synagogue," *American Hebrew,* 5 September 1890; "Montreal," New York *Jewish Messenger,* 23 September 1892; "Tomorrow's Anniversary," Montreal *Star,* 29 December 1893; Minute Books of Temple Emanu-El, Montreal (hereafter referred to as MTEE), 3 March 1896, 12 September 1897; *CCAR Yearbook,* 1897, pp. vi–xiii; "A Denver Rabbi Taken to Account," Montreal *Daily Herald,* 10 July 1897; MSP, 15 September 1897; "Abroad" [Hebrew], *Hamelitz,* 10 Av 1898; Carroll Ryan, "Jews in Canada," Baltimore *Jewish Comment,* 7 December 1900; "Montreal, Canada," *American Israelite,* 26 December 1901; "Noted Jewish Scholar Visiting City," Canadian *Jewish Times,* 17 February 1911; "The Shaar Hashomayim Synagogue, Montreal," in Arthur Hart, *The Jew,* p. 93.

128. Abraham De Sola, personal letter to Rev. J. L. Meyer, 26 December 1871, and other documents in ADSP; unidentified newspaper clipping, "An Israelitish Wedding," 1878, and unidentified newspaper clipping, "Married," n.d., in MDSB; "Congregation Shearith Israel," New York *Jewish Messenger,* 15 March 1889; "Congregation Shearith Israel," New York *Jewish Messenger,* 23 May 1892; The Jewish Sabbath Observance Association, *Report,* 1894; "Congregation Zichron Ephraim," *American Hebrew,* 4 January 1895; SPNY, 26 May 1896; "Nineteenth Street Temple," New York *Jewish Messenger,* 8 January 1897; "Congregation Shearith Israel," New York *Jewish Messenger,* 21 May 1897; "New York," *American Israelite,* 24 November 1898; "Call to Orthodox Jews," New York *Sun,* 7 January 1902; *Jewish Year Book,* 5663 (1903), p. 282; MSP, 29 November 1906.

129. Freshman, *Autobiography,* p. 120.

130. "Religious Riot in Toronto," Canadian *Jewish Times,* 23 June 1911; Speisman, *Toronto,* pp. 131, 137, 314.

131. "An Interesting Bread Story," Montreal *Daily Herald,* 19 January 1892.

132. MSP, 23 September 1856; various letters and documents in ADSP; SPNY, 11 June 1882; "Montreal, Canada," New York *Jewish Messenger,* 5 October 1888; Meldola De Sola [A Well-Known Israelite], letter, Montreal *Daily Herald,* 19 January 1892; "A Venerable Book," Montreal *Daily Witness,* 24 April 1893; *CCAR Yearbook,* 1897–98, p. xxviii; "Montreal," New York *Jewish Messenger,* 16 June 1899; Pool, *Old Faith,* p. 115; Chiel, *Manitoba,* p. 69; Speisman, *Toronto,* p. 29.

133. MSP, 12 September 1853; Speisman, *Toronto* pp. 108–09.

134. SPNY, 6 May 1885, 1 July 1885, 2 June 1887; MSP, 3 April 1892; MTEE, 7 January 1892; Chiel, *Manitoba,* pp. 130–31.

135. As quoted in Figler, *Abramowitz,* pp. 89–90.

136. Figler, *Abramowitz,* p. 12; Speisman, *Toronto,* pp. 181–82.

137. SPNY, 7 January 1886; Meldola De Sola, "Orthodox Organization," New York *Hebrew Standard,* 17 February 1893; Clarence I. De Sola [An Orthodox Layman], "Orthodox Union," New York *Hebrew Standard,* 3 March 1898; *Jewish Year Book,* 5663 (1903), p. 282.

138. See *CCAR Yearbook,* 1897–98; Michael Brown, "Beginnings," p. 323.

139. See J. S. Woodsworth, *My Neighbor,* 2d ed. (Toronto, 1913), pp. 52, 72–73; *The YM-YWHA Beacon Dedication Issue,* 1950, p. 2; *Jewish Year Book,* 1914, pp. 141–49; Richard Allen, "The Social Gospel and the Reform Tradition in Canada, 1880–1925," *Canadian Historical Review* 44 (1968): passim; Handy, *Churches,* pp. 299–303; Speisman, *Toronto,* pp. 182, 313.

140. Brainin, *Kitvei,* vol. 3, p. 262; Evelyn Miller, "The Montreal Jewish Public Library," *Congress Bulletin,* November 1973, p. 13.

141. Louis Lewis and David Dainow, "Report on the Visit to New York Charities," Montreal, 1914, p. 2. See also David Rubin, "Letters from Canada" [Hebrew], *Ha-Ibri,* 23 March 1917, pp. 9–10.

142. "History of the Federation of Jewish Philanthropies of Montreal," in Arthur Hart, *The Jew,* p. 196; Speisman, *Toronto,* pp. 145–57, 259–68.

143. See *Keneder odler,* 1907–14; Handy, *Churches,* pp. 365–72.

144. "The Conference," *The American Hebrew,* 9 June 1882; *Proceedings* of the Conference of Hebrew Emigrant Aid Societies and Auxiliary Committees, New York, 1882, pp. 6–7; Gilbert Osofsky, "The Hebrew Emigrant Aid Society of the United States (1881–1883)," *PAJHS* 49 (1960): 176.

145. "The Conference," *The American Hebrew,* 9 June 1882; Wischnitzer, *Visas,* p. 62.

146. Benjamin G. Sack, *History of the Jews in Canada,* trans. Ralph Novek (Montreal, 1965), pp. 220–21; Leonard G. Robinson, "Agricultural Activities of Jews in America," *American Jewish Year Book,* 1912–13, p. 54; Chiel, *Manitoba,* p. 53.

147. Zvi Hirsch Masliansky, *Kitvei Masliansky* [Hebrew], vol. 3 (New York, 1929), p. 221; Eliahu Zev Halevi Lewin-Epstein, *Zichronotai* [Hebrew] (Tel Aviv, 5692 [1932]), pp. 280–85; Leon Goldman, "History of Zionism in Canada," in Arthur Hart, *The Jew,* p. 291; "The Zionist Organization of Canada," *Canadian Jewish Year-Book,* 1939–40, p. 292; Bernard J. Sandler, "The Jews of America and the Settlement of Palestine, 1908–1934: Efforts and Achievements" (Ph.D. diss., Bar Ilan University, Ramat Gan, Israel, 1978), pp. 62, 114, 192–96; Marnin Feinstein, *American Zionism 1884–1904* (New York, 1965), pp. 80–93.

148. *American Jewish Year Book,* 1907–08, pp. 44–46; "Poalei Zionists Meet," Montreal *Daily Witness,* 19 October 1910; Brainin, *Kitvei,* vol. 3, p. 265; Moe Levitt, "The Federation of Young Judea of Canada," in Arthur Hart, *The Jew,* p. 289; Louis Rosenberg, "Chronology of Canadian Jewish History," *Canadian Jewish Chronicle,* 30 October 1959, p. 25; Baruch Zuckerman, *Zichroines* [Yiddish] (New York, 1962), pp. 331–35; Rome, *Early Documents,* p. 12.

149. See *The American Hebrew,* 6 January 1899; Masliansky, *Kitvei,* vol. 3, p. 218.

150. Compare Zuckerman, *Zichroines,* pp. 275–77, 329–30; and Jacob Zipper, *Leyzer Zuker Gedenkbuch* (Montreal, 1968), passim.

151. Aaron Hart, certificate of acceptance, Worshipfull Trinity Lodge No. 4, New York, 10 June 1760, in McGill University, Montreal, McCord Museum, Early Hart papers, file 68; various letters in ADSP; N. W. Goldstein, "Die jüdischen Brüder Orden

in den Vereinigten-Staaten," *Zeitschrift für Demographie und Statistik der Juden* 8 (1912): p. 30; Douville, *Hart,* p. 49; Louis Rosenberg, "Two Centuries of Jewish Life in Canada, 1760–1960," *American Jewish Year Book,* 1961, p. 40; Kage, *Thanksgiving,* p. 49; Speisman, *Toronto,* pp. 107–08.

152. "Montreal," New York *Jewish Messenger,* 5 May 1899; Nathan Phillips, "The B'nai B'rith in Canada," in Arthur Hart, *The Jew,* p. 433; Maxwell H. Tucker, "Montreal B'nai B'rith in Retrospect," *Canadian Jewish Chronicle,* 25 May 1934, p. 3; Rosenberg, "Settlers," p. 189.

153. Nathan Phillips, "B'nai B'rith," pp. 433–37.

154. "History of the Jewish Communal Bodies of Montreal," Canadian *Jewish Times,* 11 December 1899; *American Jewish Year Book,* 1900–01, p. 132; "A Grandiose Plan" [Yiddish], *Keneder odler,* 9 November 1910; "The Workmen's Circle," *Canadian Jewish Year-Book,* 1939–40, pp. 280–81; *Pride of Israel Golden Jubilee* (Toronto, 1955); Rome, *Early Documents,* p. 47; Speisman, *Toronto,* p. 109.

155. See Meldola De Sola, *Jewish Ministers?* (New York, 1905), p. 27; "An Interesting Episode," New York *Hebrew Standard,* 27 November 1896; Meldola De Sola [Maccabeus], "The Lady of the Torah," *American Hebrew,* 9 February 1900; Meldola De Sola [Yehudi], "The Latest Chutzpah," New York *Hebrew Standard,* 9 February 1900; "Jewish Women Organize," Montreal *Star,* 30 August 1896; "Jewish Women's Council," Montreal *Star,* 21 October 1896; "Canada," *Jewish Chronicle,* 6 March 1908.

156. *American Jewish Year Book* 1907–08, pp. 90–94; Bernard Figler and David Rome, *The H. M. Caiserman Book* (Montreal, 1962), p. 82.

157. *Upsilon Chapter of Zeta Beta Tau, 1913–1923: A History* (Montreal, 1923); Figler, *Abramowitz,* p. 68.

158. Moffett, *Americanization,* p. 88.

159. André Siegfried, *The Race Question in Canada,* trans. Eveleigh Nash (New York, 1907), p. 126.

160. Isaac Landman [Ben Sirach], "Canadian Jews and Judaism," *American Israelite,* 21 November 1901.

161. "Canadian Jewry," *The Jewish World,* 17 February 1899.

162. Quoted in Montreal *Daily Witness,* 16 September 1901. See also "Special Prayers in City Churches," Montreal *Star,* 9 September 1901.

163. See, for example, "The Battle Against the American Trusts," 8 July 1908; "The Strike in Philadelphia," 10 March 1910; "True and False Partisans," 17 June 1908, all in Yiddish in *Keneder odler.*

164. "Today is Thanksgiving Day," 31 October 1910. See also "Lincoln's Birthday," 11 February 1909, both in Yiddish in *Keneder odler.*

165. "Montreal," New York *Jewish Messenger,* 14 October 1892.

166. See, for example, Canadian *Jewish Times,* 15 December 1905; Meldola De Sola, "The Future of Judaism in America," New York *Herald,* 26 November 1905.

167. "Canada," London *Jewish Chronicle,* 17 March 1893.

168. See, for example, "The Woodbine Agricultural School," Canadian *Jewish Times,* 30 September 1898; "The Jewish Theater in New York" [Yiddish], *Keneder odler,* 13 January 1909; "The Comrades' Mire" [Yiddish], on the New York Yiddish press, *Keneder odler,* 4 November 1910.

169. See Morris, "Minorities."

170. Brebner, *Triangle,* pp. 269–73; Penlington, *Imperialism,* p. 3; Scheuer, "Reminiscences," pp. 357–58; various letters in ADSP; C[harles] Freshman, *The Jews and the Israelites* (Toronto, 1870), p. viii; LLB, 7 June 1901; A. Segal, "Mi-Canada" [Hebrew], *He-Ahdut,* 14 Adar and 24 Teveth 5673 [1913].

171. Shepperson, *Emigration,* p. 242.

172. Birnbaum, "Toronto," 29 November 1912; *History of the Corporation of Spanish*

and Portuguese Jews of Montreal, Canada (Montreal, 1918), p. 11; "The Late J. P. Davies," in Arthur Hart, *The Jew,* p. 561; David Rome, *The First Two Years* (Montreal, 1942), pp. 15–16; Jacob Neusner, "The Role of English Jews in the Development of American Jewish Life, 1775–1850," *YIVO Annual of Jewish Social Science* 12 (1958–59): 135; Rosenberg, "Settlers," p. 139; Sigmund Samuel, *In Return,* pp. 6–10; Lloyd P. Gartner, "North Atlantic Jewry," in *Migration and Settlement,* pp. 118–19; and many other places including chapters 2 and 3 of this work.

173. Wlad. W. Kaplun-Kogan, "Die jüdische Auswanderung der Neuzeit," *Zeitschrift für Demographie und Statistik der Juden* 8 (1912): 171.

174. Borthwick, *Gazetteer,* p. 26; "David, Aaron Hart, M.D.," *Dominion Annual Register and Review,* 1882.

175. *Canadian Jewish Times,* 23 November 1900, 7 June 1901, 26 April 1901; J. William Dawson, *Fifty Years of Work in Canada* (London and Edinburgh, 1901), pp. 145–61, 165, 173, 307–08.

176. Mordecai Yahalomstein, untitled article [Hebrew], *Hamelitz,* 3 Av 1882; "English and American Jews," *Jewish Chronicle,* 10 June 1904; "England and America: the Interchange of Ideas," *Jewish Chronicle,* 17 June 1904; "Die jüdischen Ordensbrüderschaften in England," *Zeitschrift für Demographie und Statistik der Juden* 8 (1912): 149–50; John A. Garrard, *The English and Immigration, 1880–1910* (London, 1971), pp. 169–70.

177. John Gwynne Timothy, "The Evolution of Protestant Nationalism," in LeBlanc and Edinborough, *One Church,* pp. 31–36; Handy, *Churches,* p. 362.

178. "By-Laws of the Corporation of the Portugueses Jews of Montreal," 1857.

179. *Canadian Jewish Times,* 29 November 1912; 6 December 1912; 20 December 1912; 3 January 1913; 10 January 1913; 24 January 1913; 14 February 1913; 14 March 1913.

180. Lloyd G. Reynolds, *The British Immigrant: His Social and Economic Adjustment in Canada* (Toronto, 1935), p. 121; Coats and Maclean, *American-Born,* pp. 160–61. Compare also Michael Katz, *The People of Hamilton: Canada West* (Cambridge, 1975), p. 67. Katz argues convincingly that being English-born (and also a member of the Church of England) was a key to power in mid-nineteenth-century Hamilton.

181. As quoted in Rowland Tappan Berthoff, *British Immigrants in Industrial America* (Cambridge, Mass., 1953), pp. 132–33. See also Brebner, *Triangle,* pp. 241–42.

182. Siegfried, *Race,* pp. 96–99.

183. Montreal *Daily Witness,* 18 February 1898. See also Penlington, *Imperialism,* p. 106; Timothy, "Evolution," pp. 41–44.

184. See Berger, *Power,* pp. 171–72.

185. Lazarus, "Sketch."

186. Various letters in MDSB.

Chapter 4

1. Compare among other sources, *Ha-Zefirah* [Hebrew], 1 Shvat 1887; "Jews and the Entente Cordiale," London *Jewish Chronicle,* 11 August 1905; Paula Hyman, *From Dreyfus to Vichy* (New York, 1979), pp. 40–41.

2. Benjamin G. Sack, *History of the Jews in Canada,* trans. Ralph Novek (Montreal, 1965), pp. 13–21; Zosa Szajkowski, *Jews and the French Revolutions of 1789, 1830, and 1848* (New York, 1971), p. 97.

3. S[imon] Dubnow, *History of the Jews in Russia and Poland,* trans. Israel Friedlander, vol. 1 (Philadelphia, 1916), pp. 298–99; Szajkowski, *Revolutions,* pp. 97, 482–87; Hyman, *Dreyfus,* p. 12.

4. See François Delpech, "La Révolution et l'Empire," in *Histoire des Juifs en France,* ed. Bernhard Blumenkranz (Toulouse, 1972), pp. 269–71; Hyman, *Dreyfus,* p. 3; and other sources. On the United States and Great Britain, see chapters 2 and 3 in this work.

5. Szajkowski, *Revolutions,* p. 481.

6. Hyman, *Dreyfus,* pp. 19, 12.

7. Charles Freshman, *The Jews and the Israelites* (Toronto, 1870), p. 430.

8. See, for example, "How Roman Catholic Priests Delude the Laity," London *Jewish Chronicle,* 21 March 1862.

9. Adolphus Mordecai Hart [Hampden], *The Political State and Condition of Her Majesty's Protestant Subjects in the Province of Quebec (Since Confederation)* (Toronto, 1871), p. 30.

For a comparison of the Catholic and Protestant approaches to society, see Ernst Simon, "Are We Still Jews?" in *Prakim Be-Yahadut* [Hebrew], eds. Ezra Spicehandler and Jacob Petuchowski (Jerusalem and Cincinnati, n.d.), pp. 250–78; and Arthur Silver, "Some Sources of Anti-Semitism in Quebec," *Jewish Dialog,* summer 1971, pp. 6–15. Simon also discusses the Jewish approach.

It may be noted that Jews at the turn of the century assumed that Catholic willingness to compromise in places where they were in the minority amounted to little more than hypocrisy. Compare "Jews and Catholics," Baltimore *Jewish Comment,* 25 January 1907.

10. Compare Silver, "Sources." Silver fails to explain why Jews became such a potent symbol of financial power in Quebec, where they obviously exercised relatively little power, in fact.

11. "The Mortara Case," *New York Times,* 6 December 1858.

12. Quoted in "The Mortara Abduction," New York *Herald,* 5 December 1858.

13. Bertram Wallace Korn, *The American Reaction to the Mortara Case: 1858–1859* (Cincinnati, 1957), p. 137.

14. "The League of St. Sebastian," *Jewish Chronicle,* 18 February 1876.

15. "The Jews in the Papal States," *Jewish Chronicle,* 28 November 1862.

16. "The Pope and the Jews," New York *Jewish Messenger,* 2 September 1892.

17. "The Pope and the Jews," *American Israelite,* 14 November 1901. See Also *La Vérité,* August 1883; "Abroad" [Hebrew], *Hamelitz,* 5 Adar 1895; W[illiam] Evans Gordon, *The Alien Immigrant* (London, 1903), p. 157; Ismar Elbogen, *A Century of Jewish Life* (Philadelphia, 1945), pp. 155–59; André Chouraqui, *Cent Ans d'Histoire: l'Alliance Israélite Universelle et la Renaissance Juive Contemporaine (1860–1960)* (Paris, 1965), p. 138.

18. Two contemporary descriptions of the events are "A Catholic Newspaper and the Massacre," *Jewish Chronicle,* 6 July 1906; and "The Priest Franiatis, a Vaudeville Actor" [Yiddish], *Keneder odler,* 4 November 1913.

19. See "Ireland and the Jews," *Jewish Chronicle,* 4 August 1893; "Letters from England" [Hebrew], *Hamelitz,* 10 Shvat 1904; "Trouble in Limerick," *Jewish Chronicle,* 8 April 1904; "A Review of the Year 5664," *Jewish Comment,* 9 September 1904; G[eorge] F[rederick] Abbott, *Israel in Europe* (London, 1907), p. 471.

20. "The Approaching Session of Parliament," 4 February 1876. See also "Abroad" [Hebrew], *Hamelitz,* 17 Iyyar 1887; *Hayehoody* [Hebrew], for the years 1900 and 1901.

21. "The Catholic Movement in France and the Jews," *Jewish Chronicle,* 28 April 1876. See also Szajkowski, *Revolutions,* pp. 420, 478–82.

22. As quoted in Charles C. Lehrmann, *The Jewish Element in French Literature,* trans. George Klin (Rutherford, New Jersey, 1971), pp. 203–04; see also p. 200.

23. Anna Krakowski, introduction to Moses Debré, *The Image of the Jew in French Literature from 1800 to 1908,* trans. Gertrude Hirschler (New York, 1970), p. 6. See also

Henry H. Weinberg, "The Image of the Jew in Late Nineteenth Century French Literature," *Jewish Social Studies* 45 (summer-fall 1983): 241–50.

24. Debré, *Literature,* pp. 11–14, 65–66, 86; Hyman, *Dreyfus,* p. 12.

25. As quoted in Krakowski, "Introduction," pp. 3–4.

26. Ibid., p. 5; Michael Marrus, *The Politics of Assimilation* (Oxford, 1971), p. 76; Weinberg, "Image," pp. 245–47.

27. Gustav Karpeles, *Jews and Judaism in the Nineteenth Century* (Philadelphia, 1905), p. 31; Chouraqui, *Cent Ans,* p. 17; Elie Kedourie, *Arabic Political Memoirs and Other Studies* (London, 1974), p. 77. Chouraqui attempts to whitewash France's actions by emphasizing the allegedly crucial role of Adolphe Crémieux in ending the crisis.

28. "Jewish Chronicle Abroad" [Hebrew], *Hasman,* 5 Elul 1905. See also "The Jewish Question in France," Montreal *Gazette,* 25 January 1898; "French Methods in Algeria," *Jewish Comment,* 21 July 1899; Kedourie, *Memoirs,* p. 77.

29. As quoted in Marrus, *Politics,* p. 158.

30. Arnold White, *The Modern Jew* (London, 1899), p. 114.

31. Benjamin Sulte, *Pages d'Histoire du Canada* (Montreal, 1891), p. 432; "Socialism and Anti-Semitism," Canadian *Jewish Times,* 4 May 1900. See also "Yet Another French Loan to Russia" [Hebrew], *Hasman,* 6 Shvat 1906.

32. "The Echo of the Pogroms Abroad" [Hebrew], *Hasman,* 10 Tammuz 1906. See also, Dubnow, *History,* vol. 2, p. 408; Marrus, *Politics,* pp. 54, 155–57; Hyman, *Dreyfus,* pp. 38–39.

33. Quoted in Marrus, *Politics,* p. 170. See also A. Bennett, "The Queen's University Bill," Canadian *Jewish Times,* 17 June 1912.

34. Hyman, *Dreyfus,* p. 65.

35. "Abroad" [Hebrew], *Hamelitz,* 16 Adar Sheni 1883; "The Jewish Population of France and Immigration, *Jewish Chronicle,* 24 February 1905; "Immigrant Riots in Paris" [Hebrew], *Hasman,* 2 Shvat 1906; "The Immigrant Problem in Paris," *Jewish Chronicle,* 13 April 1906; Marrus, *Politics,* p. 159; Chouraqui, *Cent Ans,* p. 136. Chouraqui says, "The persecuted Jews of central and eastern Europe found in France the asylum they sought." As a generalization, nothing could be farther from the truth in the period under review.

36. Marrus, *Politics,* p. 29.

37. "Abroad" [Hebrew], *Hamelitz,* 27 Teveth 1895; Anatole Leroy-Beaulieu, *Israel Among the Nations* (New York, 1895), pp. xix–xx.

38. "The Dreyfus Case" [Hebrew], *Hamelitz,* 10 Teveth 1894; "France on Trial," New York *Jewish Messenger,* 11 February 1898; "The International Observer" [Hebrew], *Hayehoody,* 23 February 1899; Gustav Gottheil, "The Bearing of the Dreyfus Case on the Zionist Movement," *Jewish Comment,* 23 June 1899; "Foreign Events," *American Israelite,* 3 December 1908; and many other sources.

39. Among many other sources, see "Abroad" [Hebrew], *Hamelitz,* 4 Nisan 1883; "The Sacrifice of Isaac" [Hebrew], *Ha-Zefirah,* 27 Nisan 1886; "Jewish News" [Hebrew], *Ha-Zefirah,* 27 Tammuz 1887; "Drumont" [Hebrew], *Hamelitz,* 20 Teveth 1887; "And Now in France," *American Hebrew,* 7 February 1890; "Abroad" [Hebrew], *Hamelitz,* 22 Tammuz 1892; "A New St. Bartholomew," Montreal *Daily Witness,* 26 February 1898; M. Seligsohn, "Jewish Affairs in France," *Jewish Comment,* 22 March 1901; *Hasman* [Hebrew] 24 Tammuz, 1903; "The Municipal Elections in France and the Jewish Question," London *Jewish Chronicle,* 22 April 1904; "Jewish Chronicle Abroad" [Hebrew], *Hasman,* 7 Nisan 1906; "Socialists Shout: 'Down With the Jews!'" [Yiddish], *Keneder odler,* 16 November 1910; "The Spread of Antisemitism in France" [Hebrew], *Ha-Zefirah,* 2 Teveth 1911.

40. "Abroad" [Hebrew], *Hamelitz,* 6 Teveth 1903.

41. Ahad Ha-Am, "Slavery in Freedom," in *Selected Essays,* trans. Leon Simon (Philadelphia, 1912), pp. 179, 182. The essay first appeared in Hebrew in *Hamelitz* in 1891. See also the essay, "A New Savior," pp. 242–52. That essay first appeared in Hebrew in 1901.

42. "Abroad" [Hebrew], *Hamelitz,* 6 Teveth 1903.

43. "Foreign Events," *American Israelite,* 19 November 1908.

44. Quoted in Marrus, *Politics,* p. 54. See also "Letter from Paris," *Ha-Magid* [Hebrew], 26 February 1903; Hyman, *Dreyfus,* p. 119.

45. Marrus, *Politics,* p. 239. See also Kedourie, *Memoirs,* pp. 78–79, 263–64; Chouraqui, *Cent Ans,* pp. 196–200; Hyman, *Dreyfus,* p. 119.

46. "Another French Scandal," Canadian *Jewish Times,* 16 January 1903. See also C. Edmond Chartier, "Le Ralliement du Juin, 1912," *Revue Canadienne* 8 (December 1911): 482.

47. Gerald E. Hart, *The Fall of New France* (Montreal, 1888), pp. 63–64.

48. White, *Modern Jew,* pp. vii–viii.

49. "Ex-Royal Degenerate," Canadian *Jewish Times,* 30 March 1900.

50. See Charles S. Spencer, "The Alliance Israélite Universelle of France and Anglo-Jewry," *AJA Quarterly,* July 1960, pp. 13–20; Kedourie, *Memoirs,* pp. 76–77.

51. Szajkowski, *Revolutions,* pp. 100–01; idem, "Some Facts Regarding Alsatian Jews in America," *YIVO Bleter* 20 (September–December 1942): 314.

52. Marrus, *Politics,* p. 34.

53. François-Xavier Garneau, *History of Canada,* trans. Andrew Bell, vol. 2 (Montreal, 1862), pp. 495–96.

54. See, for example, "Dans la Youpinstrass," *l'Etudiant,* 8 November 1912.

55. Gilles Marcotte, "Le Romancier Canadien Français et son Juif," in *Juifs et Canadiens,* ed. Naim Kattan (Montreal, 1967), p. 64.

56. See Joseph Tassé, "Droits Politiques des Juifs en Canada," *Revue Canadienne* 7 (June 1870): 413–17.

57. Pierre Joseph Olivier Chauveau, *Charles Guérin,* 2d ed. (1900), pp. 205, 216.

58. "The Attack on Mme. Bernhardt," Canadian *Jewish Times,* 15 December 1905; Marcotte, "Romancier," p. 63.

59. "Sur Qui Compter?" 7 January 1905. See also "Une Franc-Maçonnerie Negre," *La Croix,* 10 December 1904.

60. See, for example, L.-C. Farly, "La Question Juive," in Le Congrès de la Jeunesse à Québec, *Rapport Officiel,* 1908, pp. 118–33; and Olivar Asselin, "The Jews in Montreal," *The Canadian Century,* 16 September 1911. Compare also Hugh MacLennan, *Two Solitudes* (Toronto, 1945), pp. 223–25.

61. 'La "Libre Parole," ' *La Libre Parole Illustrée,* 5 September 1896.

62. Ibid.

63. See "Grenier Is Free," Montreal *Star,* 18 November 1897.

64. "The Revolution in Russia," *La Croix,* 18 February 1905; "Canada," *Jewish Chronicle,* 5 March 1909; Edouard Drumont, "The French Elections," *Le Devoir,* 13 April 1910; "A l'Oeuvre," 22 February 1912, "A travers le monde," 21 March 1912, Isaac, fils d'Abraham, circoncis [pseud.], "Dans la Youpinstrass," 8 November 1912, "Nos Cousins de France," 10 January 1913, all in *l'Etudiant;* Arthur Brodey, "Political and Civil Status of the Jews in Canada" (Rabbi and Master's thesis, Jewish Institute of Religion, 1933), p. 138.

65. O[mer] H[éroux], "Carl Lueger," 12 March 1910; "Pour la défense des églises," 12 March 1910.

66. "A Guttersnipe Journalist," Canadian *Jewish Times,* 31 January 1902; "L. G. Robillard, the Anti-Jew and Swindler," Canadian *Jewish Times,* 28 February 1902; "Purim

and the Haman of Canada," *American Israelite,* 14 March 1902; Isaac Landman, "Canadian Jews and Judaism," *American Israelite,* 20 February 1902; Carroll Ryan, "Letter from Canada," Baltimore *Jewish Comment,* 26 May 1902; "Abroad" [Hebrew], *Hamelitz,* 18 Adar Sheni 1902.

67. "Imported Mischief Makers," Canadian *Jewish Times,* 3 January 1902.

68. Ibid.

69. "Capt. Chartrand's Libellous Attack on the Jews," Canadian *Jewish Times,* 12 August 1904; "Le Programme Juif," *La Vérité,* 5 March 1898; "The Press Against the Antisemitic League" [Yiddish], *Keneder odler,* 6 July 1908; William David Kenneth Kernaghan, "Freedom of Religion in the Province of Quebec with Particular Reference to the Jews, Jehovah's Witnesses, and Church-State Relations, 1930–1960" (Ph.D. diss., Duke University, 1966), p. 45.

70. See, for example, "L'Eglise et les Juifs," 5 February 1898; and "Zola-Dreyfus," 5 March 1898; both in *La Vérité.* See also David Rome, *Clouds in the Thirties,* vol. 3 (Montreal, 1977), p. 74.

71. "Le Scandale Dreyfus," 18 November 1897; "L'Exil du Capitaine Dreyfus," 20 November 1897; "L'Exil du Capitaine Dreyfus," 27 November 1897; "Autour de Dreyfus," 30 November 1897; "L'Affaire Dreyfus," 1 December 1897, all in *La Patrie.*

72. "L'Affaire Dreyfus," *La Patrie,* 3 December 1897.

73. "L'Affaire Dreyfus," 24 December 1897; see also "l'Affaire Dreyfus, un article de Rochefort," 9 December 1897, both in *La Patrie.*

74. "Le Verdict de Rennes," *La Patrie,* 11 September 1899.

75. See, for example, "L'Affaire Dreyfus," *La Presse,* 31 January 1898; and all issues in November 1913.

76. Léon Provancher, *De Québec à Jérusalem* (Quebec, 1884), pp. 244–45.

77. J. F. C. Delaplanche, *Le Pèlerin de Terre Sainte* (Quebec, 1887), p. 106.

78. Jean François Dupuis, *Rome et Jérusalem* (Quebec, 1894), pp. 400–01.

79. Henri Cimon, *Au Vieux Pays,* 3d ed. (Montreal, 1917), pp. 184–85.

80. Ibid., p. 165.

81. Frédéric de Ghyvelde, *Album de Terre Sainte* (Quebec, 1905), p. 13.

82. Ibid., pp. 175–76.

83. Ibid., p. 175.

84. Ibid., pp. 341–42.

85. "An Open Attack," Canadian *Jewish Times,* 3 November 1908.

86. Quebec *Le Soleil,* as quoted in "The Black Choir" [Yiddish], *Keneder odler,* 5 April 1910. See also "Wants a Special Tax on Jews" [Yiddish], *Keneder odler,* 5 May 1910; "l'Immigration," *Le Devoir,* 17 March 1910.

87. Catholics were not alone in thinking of Nathan as part of a Jewish-socialist-Freemason conspiracy to destroy the Christian world. Sir Gerald Lowther, British ambassador to Turkey in 1910, thought the Jewish mayor part of a conspiracy of Jews, Freemasons, socialists, and Young Turks aimed at Great Britain. See letter of Lowther, 29 May 1910, Constantinople, to Sir Charles Hardinge, permanent undersecretary of state for foreign affairs, London, in Kedourie, *Memoirs,* pp. 249–61. Lowther's views were not usual in the English-speaking world.

88. See untitled editorial, Montreal *Daily Witness,* 11 October 1910; "Catholic Protest Meeting Against Mayor Nathan" [Yiddish], *Keneder odler,* 12 October 1910; "Le Conseil Censure le Maire Ernesto Nathan," Montreal *La Presse,* 12 October 1910.

89. "The Pope Sends Thanks," *Daily Witness,* 19 October 1910.

90. "Le Discours du Maire de Rome," *La Presse,* 10 November 1910; "Mayor Nathan Makes Reply," *Daily Witness,* 11 November 1910.

91. "Catholics to Make Protest," *Daily Witness,* 11 October 1910.

92. "Mayor Guerin" [Yiddish], *Keneder odler,* 16 October 1910.

93. Quoted in "Catholics to Make Protest," *Daily Witness*, 11 October 1910.

94. See, for example, untitled editorial, *Daily Witness*, 11 October 1910; "Censure the Mayor of Rome," *Daily Witness*, 18 October 1910; "Catholic Mass Meeting Sunday" [Yiddish], *Keneder odler*, 14 October 1910; "Rabbi Abramowitz and *l'Action Sociale*" [Yiddish] *Keneder odler*, 20 November 1910.

95. "L'Anti-pape du Rome," *La Presse*, 13 October 1910.

96. "Une protestation nécessaire," *Le Devoir*, 12 October 1910.

97. "Catholic Mass Meeting Sunday" [Yiddish], *Keneder odler*, 14 October 1910.

98. Untitled editorial, *Daily Witness*, 15 October 1910.

99. "Latest Portrait of Mayor of Rome," Montreal *Star*, 17 November 1910.

100. "Montréal Contre les Insultes de Nathan," *Le Devoir*, 17 October 1910; "Great Crowd on Champs de Mars," Montreal *Gazette*, 17 October 1910; "Protestations Contre les Insultes du maire de Rome à la Chrétienté," *La Patrie*, 17 October 1910; "La Protestation des Catholiques de Montréal," *La Presse*, 17 October 1910; "A Catholic Gathering Makes Protest," Montreal *Star*, 17 October 1910; "Censured Mayor Nathan," *Daily Witness*, 17 October 1910; "Council Approves the Protest Resolution" [Yiddish], *Keneder odler*, 20 October 1910.

101. "Antisemitic Demonstration also in Quebec" [Yiddish], *Keneder odler*, 24 October 1910.

102. "Sympathy Cables to Mayor Nathan" [Yiddish], *Keneder odler*, 24 October 1910.

103. "l'Insulteur du Pape est conspué," 29 October 1910.

104. "A Protest and a Quarrel," *Daily Witness*, 17 October 1910; "Protestations Contre les Insultes du maire de Rome à la Chrétienté," *La Patrie*, 17 October 1910.

105. "Frenchman Warns the Jews" [Yiddish], *Keneder odler*, 1 November 1910; A. Segal, "Mi-Canada" [Hebrew], *He-Ahdut*, 24 Teveth 5673 [1913].

106. Archbishop Bruchési, letter to David A. Ansell, Montreal, 15 November 1905, in Letterbook of the Baron de Hirsch Institute–The Young Men's Hebrew Benevolent Society, Montreal (hereafter cited as LBBDHI).

107. Untitled editorial, *True Witness*, 10 January 1894; "Jewish Immigration," *True Witness*, 22 August 1894; "H'nucca," *True Witness*, 14 December 1887. See also "A Plea for the Jew," "The Jew as a Menace to Russian Bureaucracy," and "Jewish Emigration," Montreal *Star*, 14 January 1904: "Christians Join With Hebrews," Montreal *Star*, 21 November 1905; "Help for the Jews," *Daily Witness*, 21 November 1905; "Russian Atrocities," Canadian *Jewish Times*, 1 December 1905; Laurent-Olivier David, letter to David A. Ansell, Montreal, 17 November 1905, in LBBDHI; Jewish Public Library, Montreal, Archives, Baron de Hirsch Loose Leaf Book, 28 December 1906; "Sympathy With the Jews," Montreal *Gazette*, 2 July 1906; "Our Jewish Immigration in Canada" [Yiddish], *Keneder odler*, 8 August 1915.

108. Farly, "Question," p. 119.

109. Ibid., p. 120.

110. Ibid., p. 121.

111. Ibid., p. 118.

112. Ibid., p. 122.

113. Ibid., p. 124.

114. Ibid., p. 131.

115. "Young Catholics Against the Jews" [Yiddish], *Keneder odler*, 6 July 1909.

116. Antonio Huot, *La Question Juive* (Quebec, 1914); Provancher, *Jérusalem*, pp. 114–15; "Anti-Semitic Newspaper Against Blood Libel Protests" [Yiddish], *Keneder odler*, 26 October 1913; "La Fin du Procès de Beiliss," *La Patrie*, 10 November 1913; "French-Canadian Nationalist Attacks the Jews" [Yiddish], *Keneder odler*, 27 October 1913; *American Jewish Year Book*, 1914–15, p. 179; Rome, *Clouds*, 3, pp. 72–73.

117. See Canadian *Jewish Times,* 10 August 1906; "Stones Thrown in Jewish Windows" [Yiddish], *Keneder odler,* 22 June 1908; "Frenchman Stabs a Jewish Boy" [Yiddish], *Keneder odler,* 1 July 1908; "A Deplorable Incident," Canadian *Jewish Times,* 27 August 1909; "Anti-semitism in Canada" [Hebrew], *Hasman,* 5 November 1909; "Jews Demand Police Protection" [Yiddish], *Keneder odler,* 15 November 1910; "The Kiev Trial," Montreal *Gazette,* 11 November 1913; "Anti-Semitic Trial to Begin in Quebec Court" [Yiddish], *Keneder odler,* 7 November 1913; "The Trial of the Talmud" [Hebrew], *Ha-Zefirah,* 27 Tishri 1913; "The Quebec Trial" [Yiddish], *Keneder odler,* 26 October 1913; "Jugement Dans la Cour Supérieure en Appel: Benjamin Ortenberg vs. Joseph Edouard Plamondon et René Leduc, Défendeurs," 28 December 1914, in Bronfman Collection of Jewish Canadiana, Jewish Public Library, Montreal, Plamondon File; Hirsch Wolofsky, *Journey of My Life* (Montreal, 1945), pp. 57–60; W. E. Greening, "Guilty as Charged," *The ADL Bulletin,* April 1964; Bernard Figler, *Sam Jacobs: Member of Parliament,* 2d ed. (Ottawa, 1970), pp. 23–29.

118. "Abroad" [Hebrew], *Ha-Zefirah,* 18 Kislev 1913.

119. André Siegfried, *The Race Question in Canada* (New York, 1907), p. 11.

120. Ibid., pp. 20, 19.

121. See Kernaghan, "Freedom," pp. 22–24; and Siegfried, *Race,* p. 11.

122. Siegfried, *Race,* p. 3. See also *Canadian Annual Review,* 1912, p. 425; Claris Edwin Silcox and Galen M. Fisher, *Catholics, Jews, and Protestants* (New York and London, 1934), p. 96; Ramsay Cook, *Canada and the French-Canadian Question* (Toronto, 1966), p. 13; Norman Macdonald, *Canada: Immigration and Colonization, 1841–1903* (Toronto, 1966), pp. 22–23.

123. Louis Hémon, *Maria Chapdelaine,* trans. W. H. Blake (Toronto, 1978), p. 49.

124. Laurier La Pierre, "The Clergy and the Quiet Revolution," in *One Church, Two Nations?,* eds. Philip LeBlanc and Arnold Edinborough (Don Mills, Ontario, 1968), p. 76. See also Rome, *Clouds,* vol. 3, p. 74.

125. Compare, for example, Charles Lindsey, *Rome in Canada* (Toronto, 1872).

126. As quoted in "The Black Choir." On the role of Jews in deflecting French-Canadian anti-English sentiment, see Everett Cherrington Hughes, *French Canada in Transition* (Chicago, 1943), pp. 217–18.

127. *Ten Commandments of the Roman Catholic Church humbly inscribed for the consideration of the Roman Catholics of Ireland, Canada and the United States.*

128. Charles Freshman, *The Autobiography of the Rev. Charles Freshman* (Toronto, 1868), p. 62.

129. "The Expiry of Catholicism" [Yiddish], *Keneder odler,* 8 August 1909. See also *Hayehoody* [Hebrew], for the years, 1900–01; "Abroad" [Hebrew], *Hamelitz,* 17 Iyyar 1887.

130. See *The Reform Advocate,* 26 June 1897.

131. Isaac Landman [Ben Sirach], "Canadian Jews and Judaism," *American Israelite,* 21 November 1901.

132. Abraham Rhinewine, *Canada: Ihr Geschichte un Entwicklung* [Yiddish] (Toronto, 1923), p. 33.

133. Montreal *Daily Herald,* 2 March 1895.

134. Hémon, *Maria Chapdelaine,* p. 29. Hémon's novel, which was first published in French in 1914, is generally regarded as the quintessential statement of French Canadian consciousness at the beginning of the present century. Interestingly in regard to the present study, Hémon, a Frenchman, lived only a short time in French Canada. He correctly saw French Canada as very close in spirit to the peasantry of his native France.

For a more recent consideration of Canadian attitudes toward Americans and Jews, see Edgar Z. Friedenberg, "Changing Canadian Attitudes Toward American Immigrants," in *The Canadian Ethnic Mosaic,* ed. Leo Driedger (Toronto, 1978), pp. 135–46. Compare also Margaret Atwood, *Surfacing* (Toronto, 1972).

135. "Anti-Semite Always Anti-British," Canadian *Jewish Times,* 17 January 1902. See also "A Roman Catholic View of Russia," Canadian *Jewish Times,* 21 October 1904; "Anti-Semitic Hatred," Canadian *Jewish Times,* 15 December 1905; "Mr. Henri Bourassa and the Russian Atrocities," Canadian *Jewish Times,* 23 March 1906.

136. Leon E. Truesdell, *The Canadian-Born in the United States* (New Haven, 1943), p. 43. See also Arthur Weir, ed., *Montreal Illustrated, 1894* (Montreal, 1894), p. 169; John A. Cooper, ed., *Men of Canada* (Montreal and Toronto, 1901–02), p. 242; *Who's Who and Why* (Toronto, 1915–16), p. 625.

137. Macdonald, *Canada,* pp. 102–03.

138. C. A. Magrath, *Canada's Growth and Some Problems Affecting It* (Ottawa, 1910), p. 78; Henri Bunle, "Migratory Movements Between France and Foreign Lands," in *International Migrations,* ed. Walter Wilcox, vol. 2 (New York, 1931), p. 206; Macdonald, *Canada,* pp. 99–100.

139. *Lovell's Montreal Directory,* 1870–71, p. 429; Baron de Hirsch Institute, Montreal, *Annual Report,* 1891, p. 17; "Prothonotary's Register, 1832–92," in *Canadian Jewish Reference Book and Directory,* comp. Eli Gottesman (Montreal, 1963), pp. 158–60; Asselin, "Jews," p. 14; *Le Canada et la France, 1886–1911* (Montreal, [1911]), p. 243; Ross Hamilton, ed., *Prominent Men of Canada, 1931–32* (Montreal, 1932), p. 338; Scheuer, "Reminiscences," p. 357; Louis Rosenberg, *Canada's Jews* (Montreal, 1939), p. 78; Solomon Frank, *Two Centuries in the Life of a Synagogue* (n.p., n.d.), pp. 78–79; Louis Rosenberg, "Chronology of Canadian Jewish History," *Canadian Jewish Chronicle,* 30 October 1959; Arthur A. Chiel, *The Jews in Manitoba* (Toronto, 1961), p. 24.

140. "Beth Hamidrash Hagodal Chevra Shaas," Canadian *Jewish Times,* 11 April 1902; "Jewish Journalists and Writers in Canada" [Yiddish], *Keneder odler,* 6 August 1915; Arthur Daniel Hart, *The Jew in Canada* (Toronto and Montreal, 1926), pp. 107, 320; *History of the Corporation of Spanish and Portuguese Jews of Montreal, Canada* (Montreal, 1918), p. 49.

141. *Archives Israélites,* May 1842, 15 June 1872; *l'Univers Israélite,* September 1862; Siegfried, *Race,* p. 326; "Obsèques de Feu M. Hirtz," *La Patrie,* 21 November 1910; "Death of Mr. Jules Hirtz," Montreal *Daily Witness,* 18 November 1910; Nahum Slousch, *Voyage aux Etats Unis; au Canada; et à l'Exposition de Panama* (Thouers, 1916), p. 14; N[arcisse] Leven, *Cinquante Ans d'Histoire de l'Alliance Israélite Universelle (1860–1910),* vol. 2 (Paris, 1920), pp. 466, 470–72; Joseph Levitt, *Henri Bourassa and the Golden Calf* (Ottawa, 1969), pp. 38–39; Szajkowski, "Facts."

142. Joseph Elijah Bernstein, "The Jews in Canada" [Hebrew], *Hamelitz,* 11 Iyyar 1884; "Short Notes" [Hebrew], *Hamelitz,* 14 Kislev 1901; "Abroad" [Hebrew], *Hamelitz,* 18 Adar Sheni 1902; Halitvack [pseud.], "Canada" *Jewish Chronicle,* 8 May 1908; "Canada," *Jewish Chronicle,* 5 March 1909; "Antisemitism in Canada" [Hebrew], *Hasman,* 5 November 1909; "Retrospect of 1909," *Jewish Year Book,* 1910, p. xxi; "Retrospect of 1910," *Jewish Year Book,* 1911, p. xxvii; "The Talmud Judged" [Hebrew], *Ha-Zefirah,* 27 Tishri 1913.

143. Arthur Hart, *The Jew,* pp. 530–31; Zvi Cohen, ed., *Canadian Jewry: Prominent Jews of Canada* (Toronto, 1933), p. 274.

144. "Mr. Jesse Joseph, Montreal," London *Jewish Chronicle,* 18 March 1904; "Le capital français et le Canada," *Le Devoir,* 2 February 1910; *Who's Who and Why,* 1916, p. 68.

145. *Lovell's Montreal Directory,* 1879–80, p. 710; *The Dominion Annual Register and Review,* 1886, p. 275; "Mr. Jesse Joseph, Montreal," London *Jewish Chronicle,* 18 March

1904; "Canada," *Jewish Chronicle,* 3 March 1905; "Canada," *Jewish Chronicle,* 10 March 1905; *Who's Who and Why,* 1916, p. 618; Arthur Hart, *The Jew,* p. 254.

146. Leon Goldman, "History of Zionism in Canada," in Arthur Hart, *The Jew,* p. 291; Herman Abramowitz, "Samuel William Jacobs," *American Jewish Year Book,* 5700 (1939–40), p. 107; Louis Rosenberg, "Two Centuries of Jewish Life in Canada, 1760–1960," *American Jewish Year Book,* 1961, p. 40.

147. Adolphus Solomons, personal letters to Abraham De Sola, Montreal, 1871–72, in McGill University, Montreal, Archives, De Sola Papers (hereafter referred to as ADSP); Bernard H. Conn, "Adolphus S. Solomons," Bronfman Collection of Jewish Canadiana, Jewish Public Library, Montreal, Adolphus S. Solomons File; Zosa Szajkowski, "The Alliance Israélite Universelle in the United States," *Publications of the American Jewish Historical Society* 39 (June 1950); Chouraqui, *Cent Ans,* pp. 423–32.

148. H[annaniah] M[eir] Caiserman, "Edmund Scheuer: Grand Old Man of Toronto Jewry," *Canadian Jewish Year-Book,* 1940, p. 123.

149. Letters of Is[idore] Loeb, Secretary of the Central Committee of the Alliance Israélite Universelle, Paris, to J[acob] H. Joseph, 18 April 1876, and J[acob] H. Joseph to Meldola De Sola, April 1876, in ADSP; Behar quoted in Szajkowski, "Alliance," p. 395.

150. Chouraqui, *Cents Ans,* p. 432.

151. Baron de Hirsch Institute, Montreal, *Annual Report,* 1893, p. 7.

152. Leven, *Cinquante Ans,* vol. 2, pp. 465–69.

153. S[imon] Belkin, "Jewish Colonization in Canada," in Arthur Hart, *The Jew,* p. 483; Chiel, *Manitoba,* p. 165.

154. See Baron de Hirsch Institute, Montreal, *Annual Report,* 1892, p. 46; ibid., 1902, pp. 4, 7; ibid., 1904, p. 16; ibid., 1910, p. 10; *Rapport de l'Administration Centrale au Conseil d'Administration,* Jewish Colonization Association, Paris, 1908, p. 66; *Le Baron Maurice de Hirsch et la Jewish Colonization Association* (Paris, [1931]), pp. 23–30.

155. David A. Ansell, letter to A. L. Cohen, London, 29 October 1902, in LBBDHI. See also letter of A. L. Cohen, London, to David A. Ansell, Montreal, 6 November 1902, in LBBDHI; Baron de Hirsch Institute, Montreal, *Annual Report,* 1907, p. 8.

156. Jewish Colonization Association, Paris, *Rapport de l'Administration Centrale au Conseil d'Administration,* 1910, pp. vii–viii.

157. See Baron de Hirsch Institute, Montreal, *Annual Report,* 1900, p. 8; ibid., 1907, p. 8; "JCA," London *Jewish Chronicle,* 7 July 1905; Extracts of the Minutes of the Board of Directors of the Young Men's Hebrew Benevolent Society–Baron de Hirsch Institute, Montreal, Jewish Public Library, Montreal, Archives, 4 December 1906, 25 August 1907; Jewish Colonization Association, Paris, *Rapport de l'Administration Centrale au Conseil d'Administration,* 1908, pp. 9–10; ibid., 1910, pp. 68–69; Belkin, "Colonization," pp. 483–88; Bernard Figler, *Rabbi Dr. Herman Abramowitz, Lazarus Cohen, Lyon Cohen* (Ottawa, 1968), p. 12.

158. See various letters in LBBDHI; Jewish Colonization Association, Paris, *Rapport de l'Administration Centrale au Conseil d'Administration,* 1905, p. 58; ibid., 1910, p. 66; ibid., 1912, p. 102.

159. "Abroad" [Hebrew], *Ha-Zefirah,* 8 Tammuz 1911; Slousch, *Voyage,* p. 13; Szajkowski, "Facts," pp. 314–15, 317, 319; Bertram Korn, *The Early Jews of New Orleans* (Waltham, Mass., 1969), passim.

160. Macdonald, *Canada,* p. 102. See also Hughes, *Transition,* p. 85. Information regarding Jules Rueff comes from the Victoria *Colonist,* 19 March 1861, 1 September 1875. It was brought to the author's attention by Mr. David Rome, Canadian Jewish Congress Archives, Montreal.

161. A[lexander] Harkavy, "Letters of Our Correspondents" [Hebrew], *Ha-Zefirah,*

26 Sivan 1888; Henry J. Morgan, ed., *The Canadian Men and Women of the Time* (Toronto, 1898), p. 453; "Coup d'Oeil Retrospectif," *La Croix,* September 1904, p. 3; *Lovell's Montreal Directory,* 1905–06, p. 1055; "Funerailles de M. Jules Hertz," *La Presse,* 21 November 1910; "Echo Judiciare d'une Assemblée," *La Presse,* 3 November 1913; Benjamin G. Sack, "History of the Jews in Canada," in Arthur Hart, *The Jew,* p. 76; David Rome, *The Early Jewish Presence in Canada: A Booklover's Ramble Through Jewish Canadiana* (Montreal, 1971), pp. 67b–67d.

162. "Mort Subite de M. Jules Hirtz," *La Patrie,* 18 November 1910; "Funerailles de M. Jules Hertz," *La Presse,* 21 November 1910; "Obsèques de Feu M. Hirtz," *La Patrie,* 21 November 1910; "Death of Mr. Jules Hirtz," Montreal *Daily Witness,* 18 November 1910; "M. Jules Hirtz Meurt Ce Matin," *La Presse,* 18 November 1910; advertisement in *Keneder odler,* 17 October 1910.

163. *Lovell's Montreal Directory,* 1879–80, pp. 326, 752.

164. Arthur Hart, *The Jew,* pp. 107, 237; Hamilton, *Prominent Men,* pp. 248–49, 338; herein, n. 160; Victoria *Colonist,* 1 September 1875.

165. "Mort Subite"; Szajkowski, "Facts," p. 314; Macdonald, *Canada,* p. 116.

166. *Le Canada et La France,* p. 26.

167. John Murray Gibbon, *Canadian Mosaic* (Toronto, 1938), pp. 205–06; Conrad Langlois, "Montréal Anglicise les Juifs Nord-Africains Réfugies au Québec par Milliers Pour y Parler Français," in *Studies and Documents on Immigration and Integration in Canada,* ed. Joseph Kage (Montreal, 1965), pp. 4–6; Naomi Moldofsky, "The Economic Adjustment of North African Jewish Immigrants in Montreal" (Ph.D. diss., McGill University, 1968), p. 194.

Chapter 5

1. Compare Lloyd G. Reynolds, *The British Immigrant: His Social and Economic Adjustment in Canada* (Toronto, 1935), p. 107; Kathleen Jenkins, *Montreal* (Garden City, New York, 1966), p. 511; Naomi Moldofsky, "The Economic Adjustment of North African Jewish Immigrants in Montreal" (Ph.D. diss., McGill University, 1968), pp. 100–01.

2. Louis Rosenberg, *Canada's Jews* (Montreal, 1939), p. 258.

3. Leon E. Truesdell, *The Canadian-Born in the United States* (New Haven, 1943), p. 193. See also Joseph M. Kirschbaum, *Slovaks in Canada* (Toronto, 1967), pp. 322–23; Royal Commission on Bilingualism and Biculturalism, Report, Book 4, *The Cultural Contribution of the Other Ethnic Groups* (Ottawa, 1969), pp. 118–19.

4. "Statistical Tables on Languages Spoken by Jews and Other Ethnic Groups According to Census Statistics, 1931–1951," Bronfman Collection of Jewish Canadiana, Jewish Public Library, Montreal, Tables 3, 7.

5. See, for example, Naim Kattan, "Jews and French Canadians," in *One Church, Two Nations?,* eds. Philip LeBlanc and Arnold Edinborough (Don Mills, Ontario, 1968), p. 105.

6. "The Jews in Canada" [Hebrew], *Ha-Zefirah,* 17 Sivan 1888.

7. Arthur Ruppin, *The Jews of To-day,* trans. Margery Bentwich (New York, 1913), pp. 117–18.

8. "The Jews in Canada (North America)" [Hebrew], *Hamelitz,* 7 Iyyar 1884.

9. Minutes of the Spanish and Portuguese Synagogue, Montreal (hereafter cited as MSP), 15 September 1887; "Politics To-Day," Montreal *Daily Witness,* 22 October 1900.

10. "By-laws of De Sola Lodge No. 89, A.J.O.K.S.B.," 1875.

11. M. L. Zack, "Montreal, Canada" [Hebrew], *Hasman,* 8 Tammuz 1905. See also A[aron] Nirenberg, "In Canada" [Hebrew], *Ha-Zefirah,* 8 Shvat 1914.

12. Baron de Hirsch Institute, Montreal, *Annual Report*, 1910, p. 15. See also Evelyn Miller, "The Montreal Jewish Public Library," *Congress Bulletin*, November 1973, p. 13; A. Segal, "Mi-Canada" [Hebrew], *He-Ahdut*, 14 Adar Rishon 5673 [1913].

13. "The Jewish Public Library of Montreal," *Canadian Jewish Year-Book*, 1939–40, pp. 308–10; *Keneder odler*, 19 February 1909.

14. Olivar Asselin, "The Jews in Montreal," *The Canadian Century*, 16 September 1911, p. 15.

15. Jean-C. Falardeau, "Role et importance de L'Eglise au Canada français," in *La Société Canadienne-Française*, ed. Marcel Rioux (Montreal, 1971), p. 356.

16. André Siegfried, *The Race Question in Canada*, trans. Eveleigh Nash (New York, 1907), p. 22.

17. Baron de Hirsch Institute, Montreal, *Annual Report*, 1902, p. 10, 1905, p. 25, 1910, p. 15; J. M. Salkind, letter, *Jewish Chronicle*, 5 February 1909; Louis Rosenberg, *Jews*, p. 321; "Statistical Tables," Table 12.

18. See "For Fair Play," Montreal *Daily Herald*, 6 October 1910; Ramsay Cook, *Canada and the French-Canadian Question* (Toronto, 1966), pp. 35–36; Mason Wade, *The French Canadians, 1760–1967*. vol. 2, rev. ed. (Toronto, 1968), pp. 636–37.

19. Compare *The Canadian Annual Review*, 1912, pp. 424–25.

20. See A. Gordon Darroch and Michael D. Ornstein, "Ethnicity and Occupational Structure in Canada in 1871: The Vertical Mosaic in Historical Perspective," *The Canadian Historical Review* 61 (September 1980): 313–15.

21. William George Smith, *A Study in Canadian Immigration* (Toronto, 1920), p. 37. See also Darroch and Ornstein, "Ethnicity," p. 318; Truesdell, *Canadian-Born*, p. 15; Cook, *Question*, p. 34. As recently as 1971, although 98 percent of French Canadians were Canadian born, only 79 percent of Anglo-Canadians were. (Werner Cohn, "English and French Canadian Public Opinion on Jews and Israel: Some Poll Data," *Canadian Ethnic Studies* 11 [1979]: 32.)

22. Joseph Kage, *With Faith and Thanksgiving* (Montreal, 1962), p. 9; and many other sources.

23. Arthur Brodey, "Political and Civil Status of the Jews in Canada" (Rabbi and Master's thesis, Jewish Institute of Religion, 1933), pp. 292–96; Norman Macdonald, *Canada: Immigration and Colonization, 1841–1903* (Toronto, 1966), pp. 102–07; Truesdell, *Canadian-Born*, p. 43.

24. "The Wrongs of Immigration," New York *Jewish Messenger*, 29 September 1875.

25. See, for example, the statements of John Howe, quoted in S. F. Wise and Robert Craig Brown, *Canada Views the United States* (Toronto, 1967), p. 24.

26. Louis Rosenberg, "Studies in Canadian Jewish Statistics," Bronfman Collection of Jewish Canadiana, Jewish Public Library, Montreal, Louis Rosenberg File, 18 March 1926; idem *Jews*, p. 73.

27. See Arthur Weir, ed., *Montreal Illustrated 1894* (Montreal, 1894), p. 253; S[imon] Belkin, "Jewish Colonization in Canada," in *The Jew in Canada*, ed. Arthur Daniel Hart (Toronto and Montreal, 1926), p. 485; Belkin, *Through Narrow Gates* (Montreal, 1966), p. 25.

28. Baron de Hirsch Institute, Montreal, *Annual Report*, 1891–1914, passim; ibid., 1908, p. 8; Frederick William Terrill, *A Chronology of Montreal and of Canada from A.D. 1752 to A.D. 1893* (Montreal, 1893), pp. 357, 412; "Jewish Colonization Association," *Jewish Chronicle*, 6 July 1906; "Canada," *Jewish Chronicle*, 18 January 1907; "Jewish Colonization Association," *Jewish Chronicle*, 4 October 1907; Jewish Colonization Association, Paris, *Rapport de l'Administration Centrale au Conseil d'Administration* (hereafter, *Rapport*), 1908; Extracts of the Minutes of the Board of Directors of the Young Men's Hebrew Benevolent Society–Baron de Hirsch Institute, Montreal (hereafter, Extracts), 19 January 1908; *The One Hundredth Anniversary Souvenir of Jewish Emancipation in*

Canada and the Fiftieth Anniversary of the Jew in the West, 1832–1932 (Winnipeg, 1932), p. 14.

29. "The Late Jesse Joseph," Canadian *Jewish Times,* 26 February 1904; L. Homfray Irving, *Officers of British Forces in Canada During the War of 1812–15* (Welland, Ontario, 1908), pp. 6, 129, 139, 157, 165, 170, 172, 174, 192, 211; "Dr. D. A. Hart, Montreal," in Arthur Hart, *The Jew,* p. 411; Lyon Cohen, "Recollections and Reminiscences, 1881–1897," *The Jewish Daily Eagle Centennial Jubilee Edition,* 8 July 1932, pp. 48–49; Everett Cherrington Hughes, *French Canada in Transition* (Chicago, 1943), pp. 17–19; Bernard Figler, *Louis Fitch, Q.C.* (Ottawa, 1968), p. 10.

30. See Baron de Hirsch Institute, Montreal, *Annual Report,* 1892–1914, passim; Louis Rosenberg, *Jews,* pp. 308–10.

31. Louis Rosenberg, *Growth and Change in the Distribution of the Jewish Population of Montreal,* Jewish Population Studies: vol. 1, no. 4 (Montreal, 1955), pp. 37–45; Judith Seidel, "The Development and Social Adjustment of the Jewish Community in Montreal" (Master's thesis, McGill University, 1939), pp. 107–30.

32. See Reynolds, *Adjustment,* pp. 77, 279; Kirschbaum, *Slovaks,* p. xii; A. V. Spada, *The Italians in Canada* (Ottawa and Montreal, 1969), p. 250; Nathan Keyfitz, "Développements démographiques au Québec," in Rioux, *Société,* p. 229.

33. Compare Sigmund Samuel, *In Return* (Toronto, 1963), pp. 70–74.

34. Stewart Crysdale, "Upheaval and Integration," in LeBlanc and Edinborough, *One Church,* p. 133.

35. See, among other sources, MSP, 23 September 1856; H. Lockman, personal letter to Rabbi Abraham De Sola, Arnprior, Ontario, 6 November 1869, in McGill University Archives, Montreal, Abraham De Sola Papers (hereafter, ADSP); L. Cohen, personal letter to Rabbi Abraham De Sola, Toronto, 18 April 1871, in ADSP; Bernard Figler, *Sam Jacobs, Member of Parliament,* 2d ed. (Ottawa, 1970), p. 3; Stephen A. Speisman, *The Jews of Toronto* (Toronto, 1979), p. 29.

36. "Hamilton, Canada," New York *Jewish Messenger,* 17 June 1881; "Hamilton, Canada," *Jewish Messenger,* 13 September 1882; "Quebec," *Jewish Messenger,* 27 July 1888; "Toronto," Canadian *Jewish Times,* 4 May 1906; "A Jewish Wedding," Cornwall, Ontario *Standard,* 5 May 1893.

37. Baron de Hirsch Institute, Montreal, *Annual Report,* 1892, p. 15; unsigned letter to Lazarus Cohen, Hirsch, North West Territories, 19 Teveth 5654 (1894), in Bronfman Collection of Jewish Canadiana, Jewish Public Library, Montreal, Scrapbook on Jewish Farming; "An Interesting Episode," New York *Hebrew Standard,* 27 November 1896; *Canada: An Encyclopedia* (1898–1900), s.v. "Historical Sketch of the Jews of Canada," by Abraham Lazarus; Jewish Public Library, Montreal, Archives, Baron de Hirsch Loose Leaf Book (hereafter, LLB), 23 June 1899; Meldola De Sola [Maccabeus], "The Lady of the Torah"; *The American Hebrew,* 9 February 1900; Meldola De Sola [Yehudi], "The Latest Chutzpah," *Hebrew Standard,* 9 February 1900; "Briefs" [Hebrew], *Hamelitz,* 7 Kislev 1901; E[lkan] N[athan] Adler, "Visit to the Jewish Colony at Hirsch, Saskatchewan, Canada," *Jewish Chronicle,* 27 December 1907; *Jewish Year Book,* 1910, p. 227; *Rapport,* 1912, p. 101; Belkin, "Colonization," pp. 483–85; Bernard Figler, *Rabbi Dr. Herman Abramowitz, Lazarus Cohen, Lyon Cohen* (Ottawa, 1968), pp. 12, 99.

38. See Federation of Zionist Societies of Canada, *Report of the Proceedings of the Convention,* 1907; Leon Goldman, "History of Zionism in Canada," in Arthur Hart, *The Jew,* p. 292.

39. See untitled article, *Jewish Chronicle,* 31 January 1902; "Federation of Zionist Societies in Canada," Canadian *Jewish Times,* 13 July 1906; "Canada," *Jewish Chronicle,* 10 January 1908; "Canada," *Jewish Chronicle,* 15 May 1908; "Canada," *Jewish Chronicle,* 26 February 1909; Irwin A. Swiss and H. Norman Shoop, *Rabbi Aaron M. Ashinsky* (Pittsburgh, 1935), pp. 25–26.

40. "Briefs" [Hebrew], *Hamelitz,* 14 Kislev 1907. In the 1940s the Zionist movement still served such a unifying function, especially in the outlying areas. See Aron Horowitz, *Striking Roots* (Oakville, Ontario, 1979), pp. 97–98.

41. Compare "The Zionist Movement," *Jewish Chronicle,* 19 July 1907.

42. Reynolds, *Adjustment,* p. 90. For data regarding the period just beyond that under review, see John Porter, *The Vertical Mosaic* (Toronto, 1965), pp. 80–82, 84–85, 90, 101, and sources cited there.

43. See Cook, *Question,* p. 129; and Jacques Dofny and Marcel Rioux, "Les classes sociales au Canada français," in Rioux, *Société,* p. 317. The theory originated with the French-Canadian historian Michel Brunet.

44. William Henry Atherton, *Old Montreal in the Early Days of British Canada* (Montreal, 1925).

45. See *The Canada Directory,* 1851, p. 241, and 1857–58, p. 377; *Lovell's Montreal Directory,* 1870–71, p. 429; "Moise Schwob, Montreal," in Arthur Hart, *The Jew,* p. 207; Kage, *Faith,* p. 12; Sigmund Samuel, *In Return,* pp. 14–26, 89–105; "Prothonotary's Register, 1832–1890," in *Canadian Jewish Reference Book and Directory,* comp. Eli Gottesman (Montreal, 1963), p. 159.

46. John Douglas Borthwick, *Montreal History and Gazetteer* (Montreal, 1892), pp. 471–72; Terrill, *Chronology,* p. 83; Benjamin G. Sack, "History of the Jews in Canada," in Arthur Hart, *The Jew,* pp. 24–25; E. C. Woodley, *The House of Joseph in the Life of Quebec* (Quebec, 1946), pp. 44–46; Speisman, *Toronto,* p. 16; *The House of Nordheimer* ([Toronto, 1903]), p. 16.

47. See Borthwick, *Gazetteer,* pp. 471–72; Terrill, *Chronology,* p. 113; *The Jewish Encyclopedia* (1905), s.v. "Joseph"; "The Late Sigisimund Mohr," and "L. Wolfe," in Arthur Hart, *The Jew,* pp. 356, 427; Joseph Kage, "Jewish Immigration and Immigrant Aid Effort," in Bronfman Collection of Jewish Canadiana, Jewish Public Library, Montreal, Joseph Kage File; Louis Rosenberg, *Jews,* pp. 206–08; *History of the Corporation of Spanish and Portuguese Jews of Montreal, Canada* (Montreal, 1918), pp. 51–52.

48. See "The Late Lewis Alexander Hart, M.A., B.C.L." and "Dr. D. A. Hart, Montreal," in Arthur Hart, *The Jew,* pp. 376, 411; M. Edmund Gordon, "Political and Legal Aspects of Jewish History in Canada," in Bronfman Collection of Jewish Canadiana, Jewish Public Library, Montreal, M. Edmund Gordon File; Solomon Frank, *Two Centuries in the Life of a Synagogue* (n.p., n.d.), pp. 79–80; Oscar Douglas Skelton, *Life and Letters of Sir Wilfrid Laurier,* vol. 1 (Toronto, 1965), pp. 42–43.

49. See Reynolds, *Adjustment,* p. 95; Macdonald, *Canada,* p. 127; Joseph Levitt, *Henri Bourassa and the Golden Calf* (Ottawa, 1969), p. 124; Albert Faucher and Maurice Lamontagne, "L'histoire du Développement Industriel au Québec," in Rioux, *Société,* passim; Porter, *Mosaic,* pp. 94–95.

50. See W. H. Baker, personal letter to S. Blaicklock, Montreal, 3 January 1905, in Baron de Hirsch Institute, Jewish Public Library, Montreal, Archives, Letter Book (hereafter, LBBDHI); *Rapport,* 1908, p. 179, 1910, p. 65; *Lovell's Montreal Directory,* 1905–1906, 1911–1912, passim; *Dominion of Canada and Newfoundland Gazetteer and Classified Business Directory,* 1915, passim; Herbert Brown Ames, *The City Below the Hill* (Toronto and Buffalo, 1972), p. 95; Reynolds, *Adjustment,* pp. 93–94, 107; Rosenberg, *Jews,* pp. 373–86; Seidel, "Development," pp. 18–19; Bernard Shane, "Labourers and Builders," *Canadian Jewish Year-Book,* 1940–41, p. 198; Vivian David Lipman, *Social History of the Jews in England, 1850–1950* (London, 1954), p. 115; Lloyd P. Gartner, *The Jewish Immigrant in England, 1870–1914* (Detroit, 1960), pp. 274ff.; Joseph Kage, *The Dynamics of Economic Adjustment of Canadian Jewry: A Historical Review* (Montreal, 1970), pp. 16, 19; John A. Garrard, *The English and Immigration, 1880–1910* (London, 1971), passim.

51. Compare "Bourassa Barks" [Yiddish], *Keneder odler,* 27 April 1910; Joseph Schull, *Laurier* (Toronto, 1966), p. 113.

52. See A[lexander] Harkavy, "The Jews in Canada" [Hebrew], *Ha-Zefirah,* 4 Adar 1888; *Lovell's Business and Professional Directory of All Cities, Towns, and Banking Villages in Canada,* 1896, passim.

53. See, for example, "Les Finances d'Israel," *La Libre Parole Illustrée,* 19 September 1896.

54. See, for example, Benjamin Sulte, *Pages d'Histoire du Canada* (Montreal, 1891), p. 404.

55. Compare Gabriel Glazer, "French-Canadian Nationalism and the Jews," *In the Dispersion,* winter 1964–65, p. 36; William David Kenneth Kernaghan, "Freedom of Religion in the Province of Quebec with Particular Reference to the Jews, Jehovah's Witnesses, and Church-State Relations, 1930–1960" (Ph.D. diss., Duke University, 1966), p. 48.

56. See Baron de Hirsch Institute, Montreal, *Annual Report,* 1892, p. 4; "The Early Closing Law" [Yiddish], *Keneder odler,* 8 August 1909; Hughes, *Transition,* p. 135; Kernaghan, "Freedom," pp. 30–45; Lita-Rose Betcherman, *The Swastika and the Maple Leaf* (Toronto, 1975), pp. 4, 7, 23, 33.

57. See, among other sources, "Cigar Making," Montreal *Gazette,* 6 June 1882; *Lovell's Historic Report of the Census of Montreal* (Montreal, 1891), pp. 93, 97, 118; Weir, *Montreal,* pp. 111, 179, 256, 292–93, 299; *Lovell's Business and Professional Directory,* p. 613; Lazarus, "Sketch," passim; Ernest J. Chambers, *The Book of Canada* (Montreal and Toronto, 1904), pp. 167, 378, 380; *Lovell's Montreal Directory,* 1905–06, pp. 1063, 1279, 1456, 1911–12, p. 1433; Asselin, "Jews," p. 15; William Henry Atherton, *Montreal from 1535 to 1914,* vol. 3 (Montreal, 1914), pp. 375–76; *Dominion of Canada and Newfoundland Gazetteer and Classified Business Directory,* 1915, pp. 1363–66, 1423–24; *History of the Corporation of Spanish and Portuguese Jews,* pp. 51–52; "Mr. Louis Lewis Becomes Manager I.C.A. Committee," *Canadian Jewish Chronicle,* 6 October 1916; "Mark Workman, Montreal," in Arthur Hart, *The Jew,* p. 338; John Murray Gibbon, *Canadian Mosaic* (Toronto, 1938), p. 406; Louis Rosenberg, *Jews,* pp. 206–08, 214–15; idem., "Chronology of Canadian Jewish History," *Canadian Jewish Chronicle,* 30 October 1959; Woodley, *House,* p. 50; *The Jewish Daily Eagle Centennial Jubilee Edition,* 8 July 1932, p. 44; Levitt, *Bourassa,* pp. 35–36; Wade, *Canadians,* vol. 2, pp. 9–10; Kage, *Dynamics,* p. 29.

58. "Abraham Joseph" and "The Social Life of the Jews in Canada," in Arthur Hart, *The Jew,* pp. 332, 431–32; Irving Katz, *The Beth-El Story: Jews in Michigan Before 1850* (Detroit, 1955), pp. 32–34.

59. Hugh W. Becket, *The Montreal Snow Shoe Club: Its History and Record* (Montreal, 1882), pp. 334, 503, 517–18; *Lovell's Montreal Directory,* 1889–90, p. 823; *Montreal* (Montreal, [1903]), p. 64; "Montefiore Joseph, Quebec" and "Dr. J. Rubin, Montreal," in Arthur Hart, *The Jew,* pp. 340, 423; Raymond Arthur Davies, *Printed Jewish Canadiana, 1685–1900* (Montreal, 1955), p. 51.

60. See, among other sources, *Lovell's Historic Report,* p. 61; Baron de Hirsch Institute, Montreal, *Annual Report,* 1892, p. 7, 1905, p. 30, 1907, p. 14, 1910, p. 2; "The Home for Incurables Fair," Montreal *Daily Witness,* 4 March 1893; Julia Drummond, personal letter to Rev. Meldola De Sola, Montreal, 21 April 1894, in Jewish Public Library, Montreal, Archives, Meldola De Sola Papers; "Notre Dame Hospital Kermesse," Montreal *Star,* 28 September 1895; "Will Be Held in October," Montreal *Gazette,* 18 December 1895; "The General Hospital," Montreal *Star,* 11 November 1897; "Montreal," *American Israelite,* 9 January 1902; "Montreal General Hospital," *Canadian Jewish Times,* 29 December 1905; LLB, 28 December 1906; "Montreal Maternity Hospital," *Canadian Jewish Times,* 2 November 1906; Atherton, *Montreal,* vol. 3, pp. 11–12, 624–25; *The Montreal Board of Trade Souvenir,* 1914–15, pp. 76, 92; "Israel S. Goldenstein, Montreal," in Arthur Hart, *The Jew,* p. 90; Zvi Cohen, ed., *Canadian Jewry: Prominent Jews of Canada* (Toronto, 1933), p. 258.

61. Owen Dawson, *My Story of the Boys' Farm at Shawbridge* (n.p., 1952), p. 27.

62. See Meldola De Sola [Humanity], "Treatment of Horses," Montreal *Star,* 16 April 1892; "Our Dumb Friends," Montreal *Daily Witness,* 20 January 1893; H[ananiah] M[eir] Caiserman, "Builders of Canadian Jewry," *Canadian Jewish Year-Book,* 1939, pp. 132–39; Dawson, *Shawbridge,* p. 27; *Who's Who and Why,* 1919–20, p. 762.

63. See, among other sources, Weir, *Montreal,* p. 234; "Women's National Council," Montreal *Gazette,* 15 February 1894; "Montreal," *The American Hebrew,* 14 December 1894; "The Council of Women," Montreal *Star,* 22 January 1897; [William Lyon Mackenzie King?], "The Jewish Population," Toronto *Mail and Empire,* 25 September 1897; *Who's Who and Why 1915–1916* (Toronto, 1916), p. 70; "Mrs. Martin Wolff (Irene Rachel Joseph), Montreal," and "Imperial Order Daughters of the Empire," in Arthur Hart, *The Jew,* pp. 249, 250; Woodley, *House,* p. 56; Edward C. Joseph, "Quebec's Contribution to Canadian Life," in Gottesman, *Directory,* p. 309.

64. See Weir, *Montreal,* p. 281; "Gershom De Sola Died Yesterday," Montreal *Daily Herald,* 18 March 1902; "The Late Mr. Gershom De Sola," Canadian *Jewish Times,* 28 March 1902; "The Late Simon Silverman," Canadian *Jewish Times,* 26 February 1904; *The Vision and Understanding of a Man* ([Montreal, 1954]), p. 11.

65. Jenkins, *Montreal,* p. 512.

66. MSP, 11 March 1856; invitation in H[erman] Abramowitz and Lawrence Cohen, "Schedule of Material in the Ansell Collection," Bronfman Collection of Jewish Canadiana, Jewish Public Library, Montreal, Ansell File; invitation in Jewish Public Library, Montreal, Archives, Meldola De Sola Scrapbook; Montreal *Metropolitan,* 26 January 1895; Benjamin Sulte, "La Maison Hart," *Le Monde Illustré,* 11 March 1893; "History of the Jewish Communal Bodies," Canadian *Jewish Times,* 11 December 1899; Woodley, *House,* pp. 33–43; Louis Rosenberg, "The Earliest Jewish Settlers in Canada: Facts vs. Myths," in Gottesman, *Directory,* pp. 142–43; and other sources.

67. Alexander Levy, as quoted in "The Mortara Abduction," New York *Herald,* 5 December 1858. See also various documents in ADSP; George Maclean Rose, ed., *A Cyclopedia of Canadian Biography,* 2d ser. (Toronto, 1888), p. 275; Sulte, "Maison," p. 542; Ludwik Kos-Rabcewicz-Zubkowski, *The Poles in Canada* (Ottawa and Montreal, 1968), pp. 10–18, 31–47, 54–76; Spada, *Italians,* pp. 172–73; and chapter 4 of this work.

68. *Proceedings at the Annual Meeting of the Natural History Society of Montreal,* 1874, p. 25; "David, Dr. Aaron Hart," *The Dominion Annual Register and Review,* 1882; Borthwick, *Gazetteer,* p. 478; Spencer Ervin, *The Political and Ecclesiastical History of the Anglican Church of Canada* (Ambler, Pennsylvania, 1967), p. 85.

69. "The Late Dr. De Sola," Montreal *Gazette,* 7 June 1882.

70. Among other sources, see MSP, 1847–82; Henry J. Morgan, *Bibliotheca Canadensis* (Ottawa, 1867), p. 104; Henry Samuel Morais, *Eminent Israelites of the Nineteenth Century* (Philadelphia, 1880), pp. 53–57; Atherton, *Montreal,* vol. 3, p. 73.

Although a number of contemporary sources mention Abraham De Sola's work on the cosmography of Peritsal (i.e., Farissol), this writer has been unable to locate the work.

71. As quoted in Cyrus MacMillan, *McGill and Its Story* (London, 1921), p. 80.

72. Compare Brodey, "Status," pp. 207–08.

73. See Ervin, *Anglican Church,* p. 85; Speisman, *Toronto,* p. 15.

74. Abraham De Sola, personal letter to Alexander Levy, president of the Spanish and Portuguese Congregation, Montreal, 4 May 1858, in ADSP.

75. Morgan, *Bibliotheca,* p. 104.

76. Mary Ellen Ross, *The Legend of the Holy Stone* (Montreal, 1878), p. 241.

77. Rose, *Cyclopedia,* p. 100.

78. Compare *l'Univers Israélite,* September 1862; Skelton, *Letters,* vol. 1, pp. 21–23. ADSP and the Scrapbooks of the Rev. Meldola De Sola in the Archives of the Jewish Public Library, Montreal, offer no evidence of any contact.

79. *Lovell's Montreal Directory,* 1889–90, p. 823; Somerville Free Lectures, Programme, 1890 season, in Jewish Public Library, Montreal, Archives, Meldola De Sola Papers; Gerald E. Hart, *The Quebec Act, 1774* (Montreal, 1891), p. 1; "The House Next Door" [Yiddish], *Keneder odler,* 16 October 1910; Davies, *Canadiana,* pp. 26–28; Speisman, *Toronto,* p. 34; "J. S. Leo, Montreal," in Arthur Hart, *The Jew,* p. 315. Reuven Brainin, *Kol Kitvei Reuven ben Mordecai Brainin* [Hebrew], vol. 3 (New York, 1940), p. 305.

80. See, among other sources, "The Hebrew Graduates of McGill," Montreal *Star,* 8 July 1880; "Jewish Lecturer at McGill" [Yiddish], *Keneder odler,* 12 January 1909; "The McGill Oriental Society" [Yiddish], *Keneder odler,* 18 March 1910; "Retrospect of 1910," *Jewish Year Book,* 1911, p. xxvii.

81. Siegfried, *Race,* p. 94.

82. See ibid., p. 89; in *l'Etudiant,* the student newspaper of Laval University, see "A l'Oeuvre," 22 February 1912, "A travers le monde," 21 March 1912, Isaac, fils d'Abraham, circoncis [pseud.], "Dans la Youpinstrass," 8 November 1912, "Nos cousins de France," 12 January 1913.

83. See *Jewish Year Book* 1911, p. 393; "Sir Mortimer B. Davis, Montreal," in Arthur Hart, *The Jew,* p. 337; Cohen, *Prominent Jews,* pp. 47, 164; Caiserman, "Builders," p. 133.

84. *Montreal Business Sketches* (Montreal, 1865), p. 160. See also MSP, 11 March 1856.

85. MSP, 4 April 1854, 9 July 1854; Minute Books of Temple Emanu-El, Montreal, 31 December 1882, and intermittently to 28 October 1890.

86. Borthwick, *Gazetteer,* p. 26.

87. Raymond Douville, *Aaron Hart* [French] (Trois Rivières, 1938), pp. 184–92; Joseph R. Rosenbloom, *A Biographical Dictionary of Early American Jews* ([Lexington, Kentucky], n.d.), p. 165.

88. See Charles Freshman, *The Autobiography of the Rev. Charles Freshman* (Toronto, 1868), pp. 67, 73.

89. George Barnard, personal letter to Rabbi Abraham De Sola, Montreal, 27 March 1850, in ADSP.

90. Douville, *Hart,* p. 30.

91. See "Communal Bodies," p. 6; Louis Rosenberg, "Earliest," pp. 2, 140; Rosenbloom, *Dictionary,* pp. 74–75, 162; Schull, *Laurier,* pp. 37–38; Denis Vaugeois, *Les Juifs et la Nouvelle France* (Trois Rivières, 1968), p. 39; and other sources.

92. E. Z. Massicotte, "Le Rameau Catholique des 'Joseph'," *Le Bulletin des Recherches Historiques* 40 (December 1934): 751–56.

93. See "Marchand, Louis," *The Dominion Annual Register and Review,* 1880–1881; Léon Trépanier, "Un Montréalais du siècle dernier: l'immigrant juif Louis Marchand," *Les Cahiers des Dix* 30 (1965): pp. 131–48.

94. Siegfried, *Race,* p. 23.

95. Meldola De Sola, *Jewish Ministers?* ([New York], 1905), p. 31; Louis Rosenberg, *Jews,* p. 114.

96. See, among other sources, Claris Edwin Silcox and Galen M. Fisher, *Catholics, Jews, and Protestants* (New York and London, 1934), pp. 250, 287; Louis Rosenberg, *Jews,* pp. 118, 350; Malcolm H. Stern, comp., *Americans of Jewish Descent* (Cincinnati, 1960), p. 44. Olivar Asselin, "The Jews in Montreal," *The Canadian Century,* 16 September 1911, p. 19.

97. See Frank, *Two Centuries,* pp. 47–50; Gordon, "Aspects," p. 2; Camille Bertrand, *Histoire de Montréal,* vol. 2 (Montreal, 1942), p. 28.

98. See Rosenberg, "Two Centuries," p. 30.

99. See M[arcus] M. Sperber, "Legislation in Canada Affecting Jews," in Arthur Hart, *The Jew,* p. 461.

100. See, for example, Joseph Tassé, "Droits Politiques des Juifs en Canada," *Revue*

Canadienne 7 (June 1870): 407–25; Julius J. Price, "Proceedings Relating to the Expulsion of Ezekiel Hart from the House of Assembly of Lower Canada," *Publications of the American Jewish Historical Society* 23 (1915): 43–53; Benjamin G. Sack, *History of the Jews in Canada,* trans. Ralph Novek (Montreal, 1965), pp. 81–92; Jean-Pierre Wallot, "Les Canadiens français et les Juifs (1808–1809)," in *Juifs et Canadiens,* ed. Naim Kattan (Montreal, 1967), pp. 111–12. The most recent popular treatment of the affair is that of Erna Paris in *Jews: An Account of Their Experience in Canada* (Toronto, 1980), pp. 23–26.

101. Ezekiel Hart, Three Rivers, letter to Messrs. Jonas Phillips and Sons, 26 May 1808, McGill University, Montreal, McCord Museum, Early Hart Papers, File 63. See also Viscount Castlereagh, letters to Sir James Craig, as quoted in Wallot, "Canadiens," pp. 115, 120.

102. See Tassé, "Droits," p. 407; Sulte, *Pages,* p. 419.

103. *Histoire du Canada,* 8th ed., vol. 7 (Montreal, 1945), pp. 74–75.

104. Ezekiel Hart, Three Rivers, letter to Messrs. Jonas Phillips and Sons, 26 May 1808, McGill University, Montreal, McCord Museum, Early Hart Papers, File 63; François-Xavier Garneau, *History of Canada,* trans. Andrew Bell, vol. 2 (Montreal, 1862), p. 252, n.

105. Samuel B. Hart, petition to the Provincial Parliament of Lower Canada, 31 January 1831, in McGill University, Montreal, McCord Museum, Early Hart Papers. See also Sperber, "Legislation," p. 461.

106. Abraham Joseph, diary, 24–25 June, 5, 16 August, 11 November 1837, Public Archives of Canada, Ottawa, File MG24I61; Wade, *Canadians,* vol. 1, p. 190. See also Fernand Ouellet, "Les Insurrections de 1837–38," in *Studies in Canadian Social History,* ed. Michiel Horn and Ronald Sabourin (Toronto, 1974), p. 409.

107. Abraham Joseph, diary, 19, 27 November, 3, 31, December 1837, 15 April 1838, Public Archives of Canada, Ottawa, File MG-24I61; letter (copy) of Benjamin Hart, Liverpool, to Lord John Russell, Secretary of State for the Colonies, [London], 14 July 1840, in McGill University, Montreal, McCord Museum, Gerald E. Hart Papers, File 31. See also "The Jew in the Military Life of Canada," in Arthur Hart, *The Jew,* pp. 503–04; Sulte, "Hart," p. 542; Gérald Malchelosse, "Les Juifs dans l'histoire Canadienne," *Les Cahiers des Dix* 4 (1939): 182–83; Jonathan D. Sarna, "The Canadian Connection of an American Jew: The Case of Mordecai M. Noah," Canadian Jewish Historical Society *Journal* 3 (fall 1979): 122–23, 128, and the sources cited there.

108. Letter of Sir John A. Macdonald to David A. Ansell, Montreal, 6 February 1891, in Abramowitz and Cohen, "Schedule."

109. Letter of Sir John A. Macdonald to Col. A[rthur] W[ellington] Hart, 11 June 1888, quoted in Gibbon, *Mosaic,* p. 402; undated autobiographical note of Gerald E. Hart, typescript, McGill University, Montreal, McCord Museum, Gerald E. Hart Papers, File 31. Compare also John Murray Gibbon, "The Hebrews and Canada," *Canadian Jewish Year-Book,* 1940–41, pp. 108–18; Sir John A Macdonald, letter to Sir Alexander T. Galt, Canadian high commissioner in London, 23 March 1882, in Public Archives of Canada, Ottawa, Macdonald Papers, 82, p. 31999; Sir John A. Macdonald, letters to David A. Ansell, cited in Abramowitz and Cohen, "Schedule"; "The Late Henry Nathan," in Arthur Hart, *The Jew,* p. 371; Sack, *History,* p. 169.

110. J[acob] H. Joseph, personal letter to David A. Ansell, Paris, 20 December [1873], in Canadian Jewish Congress, Montreal, Archives, Ansell Papers.

111. F. W. A. Osborne, secretary of the Protestant Defense Alliance, letter to Rabbi Abraham De Sola, Montreal, 24 March 1877, in ADSP; "May It Herald Victory," Montreal *Gazette,* 13 April 1893; "Montreal," New York *Hebrew Standard,* 16 June 1893; *Inauguration of Montreal's Monument to the Late Right Hon. Sir John Macdonald, G.C.B.* (n.p., 1895); "Montreal," *Jewish Messenger,* 14 June 1895; *The Montreal Board of Trade*

Souvenir, 1914–15, p. 70; unidentified newspaper clipping, 1943, Canadian Jewish Congress, Montreal, Archives, Joseph S. Leo Papers.

112. *Canadian Jewish Year-Book,* 1940–41, p. 218. See also "Welcomed to Montreal," Montreal *Star,* 7 July 1897; Tony Cashman, *Abraham Cristall* ([Edmonton, 1963]), pp. 10–11; Figler, *Abramowitz,* pp. 144–49; "Why We Are Not Supporting the Jewish Candidate" [Yiddish], *Keneder odler,* 9 June 1908; "The Elections," Canadian *Jewish Times,* 23 October 1908; A[haron] Nirenberg, "Immigration Restrictions in Canada" [Hebrew], *Ha-Zefirah,* 9 Adar Sheni 1913.

113. See Herman Abramowitz, "Samuel William Jacobs," in *American Jewish Year Book,* 5700 (1939–40), p. 101; Irving Abella and Harold Troper, " 'The Line Must Be Drawn Somewhere': Canada and the Jewish Refugees, 1933–39," *Canadian Historical Review* 11 (June 1979); Speisman, *Toronto,* pp. 245–55; A. Segal, "Mi-Canada" [Hebrew], *He-Ahdut,* 24 Teveth 5673 [1913]; Gerald E. Hart, notes, typescript, no date, McGill University, Montreal, McCord Museum, Gerald. E. Hart Papers, File 31.

114. J[ames] S. Woodsworth, *My Neighbor,* 2d ed. (Toronto, 1913), p. 168.

115. *History of the Valley of the Mississippi* (Cincinnati, 1853), pp. 13–14. Compare also *The Fourth Book of Lessons for the Use of Schools* (Montreal, 1845), pp. 215–21; Thomas Talbot, *The Hebrews at Home* (Montreal, 1874), p. 12.

116. Woodsworth, *Neighbor,* pp. 19, 169. See also Charles Heavysege, "Saul," a drama in fifteen acts (1857, 1869), "Jephthah's Daughter," a poem (1865), and "Sonnets: Jezebel" (1867), all cited in David Rome, *The Early Jewish Presence in Canada: A Booklover's Ramble Through Jewish Canadiana* (Montreal, 1971), p. 3; Porter, *Mosaic,* pp. 88–103.

117. In "Letter from Canada," Baltimore *Jewish Comment,* 2 August 1901. See also *Lovell's Historic Report,* p. 21.

118. Samuel David, journal, Public Archives of Canada, Ottawa, File MG24I13; Abraham Joseph, diary, 2 February 1847, and other places, Public Archives of Canada, Ottawa, File MG-24I61; Woodsworth, *Neighbor,* p. 168.

119. As quoted in "Montreal," *Jewish Messenger,* 28 June 1901. See also Nathan Phillips, *Mayor of All the People* (Toronto and Montreal, 1967), p. 20.

120. "The Jews in Canada" [Hebrew], *Ha-Zefirah,* 4 Adar 1888.

121. See A. Eliasson, "Abroad" [Hebrew], *Hamelitz,* 18 Nisan 1897; "Temple Emanu-El of Montreal," *American Israelite,* 21 November 1907.

122. "Temple Emanu-El," *Daily Witness,* 18 September 1911. See also "Temple Emanu-El," Montreal *Star,* 24 November 1893; Michael Brown, "The Beginnings of Reform Judaism in Canada," *Jewish Social Studies* 34 (October 1972): passim.

123. "Montreal, Canada," *Jewish Messenger,* 28 July 1882; Hamilton *Herald,* 23 April 1904.

124. Aaron Nirenberg, "Letters from Canada" [Hebrew], *Ha-Zefirah,* 27 Shvat 1913.

125. Carroll Ryan, "Letter from Canada," *Jewish Comment,* 15 November 1901. See also Samuel Talpis, "Abroad" [Hebrew], *Hamelitz,* 28 Kislev 1899.

126. See Sigmund Samuel, *In Return,* p. 107; Michael Brown, "Beginnings," passim; Speisman, *Toronto,* passim.

127. See Canadian *Jewish Times,* 4 December 1903; W. H. Baker, letters to Herbert Brown Ames and Lyon Cohen, Montreal, 28 November 1904, in LBBDHI; Baron de Hirsch Institute, Montreal, *Annual Report,* 1905, p. 4; Charles S. Bernheimer, "Conclusions," in *The Russian Jew in the United States,* ed. Charles S. Bernheimer (Philadelphia, 1905), p. 409; *Y.M.-Y.W.H.A. Beacon Dedication Issue,* 1950, p. 5; Lawrence M. Lande, ed. and comp., *Montefiore Club* ([Montreal], 1955), pp. 14–15, 37–38. Boas quoted in Minute Books of Temple Emanu-El, Montreal, 18 September 1904.

128. Garneau, *History,* vol. 2, p. 491.

129. Adolphus Mordecai Hart [Hampden], *The Political State and Condition of Her*

Majesty's Protestant Subjects in the Province of Quebec (Since Confederation) (Toronto, 1871), p. 71; see also p. 47.

130. John McMullen, *History of Canada from Its First Discovery to the Present Time* (1855), pp. 385–86, as quoted in Carl Berger, *The Sense of Power* (Toronto and Buffalo, 1970), p. 112.

131. Reynolds, *Adjustments,* p. 182.

132. C. A. Magrath, *Canada's Growth and Some Problems Affecting It* (Ottawa, 1910), pp. 149–50.

133. Siegfried, *Race,* p. 101; see also pp. 118–19; Hughes, *Transition,* p. 82; P. F. W. Rutherford, introduction to Ames, *City,* p. xiv.

134. See Elizabeth H. Armstrong, *The Crisis of Quebec, 1914–18* (New York, 1937), p. 13.

135. Rebecca Gratz, personal letter to Ann Boswell Gratz describing the life of her newly married niece, 25 June 1848, in *Letters of Rebecca Gratz,* ed. David Philipson (Philadelphia, 1929), pp. 347–49.

136. Abraham De Sola, *The Sanatory Institutions of the Hebrews* (Montreal, 1861), p. 34, n.

137. Adolphus Mordecai Hart, *Political State,* pp. 5, 12.

138. Ibid., p. 29; Gerald E. Hart, undated notes, probably from the turn of the century, handwritten, in McGill University, Montreal, McCord Museum, Gerald E. Hart Papers, File 31.

139. See Berger, *Power,* pp. 231–32.

140. Compare Watson Kirkconnell, "Canada, a Multi-National State," *Canadian Jewish Year-Book,* 1940–41, pp. 97–101; and other sources.

141. Jenkins, *Montreal,* p. 511.

142. See Siegfried, *Race,* pp. 116, 249–50.

143. Cook, *Question,* p. 13; see also p. 185.

144. Siegfried, *Race,* p. 3. See also *The Canadian Annual Review,* 1909, p. 233; Kirkconnell, "Multi-National," p. 100.

145. Carroll Ryan, "Letter from Canada," *Jewish Comment,* 2 August 1901. Compare also Kirkconnell, "Multi-National," p. 100.

146. Magrath, *Growth,* p. 167. See also J. R. Conn, "Immigration," *Queen's Quarterly* 8 (October 1900): 123.

147. Howard Angus Kennedy, *New Canada and the New Canadians* (London, 1907), pp. 258–59; Woodsworth, *Neighbor,* pp. 338–39.

148. "Jews in the Schools," Montreal *Daily Witness,* 12 February 1898.

149. See, for example, "The *Witness* on the Jews" [Yiddish], *Keneder odler,* 4 May 1910; Becky Kahn, as quoted in Cyril Edel Leonoff, *Wapella Farm Settlement* ([Winnipeg], 1972), p. 19.

150. Compare Silcox and Fisher, *Catholics,* pp. 34–37.

151. Canadian *Jewish Times,* 8 April 1904.

152. Borthwick, *Gazetteer,* pp. 465–80; Israel Zangwill, *The Mantle of Elijah* (Toronto, 1900); *Jewish Year Book,* 5663 (1902–03), p. 282.

153. J. Bell Forsyth [A Canadian], *A Few Months in the East; or, A Glimpse of the Red, the Dead, and the Black Seas* (Quebec, 1861), p. 80.

154. Ross, *Legend,* p. 449.

155. "The Jews and Palestine," *The Canada Farmers' Sun,* 22 November 1892. See also S. E. D. Shortt, "Social Change and Political Crisis in Rural Ontario: The Patrons of Industry, 1889–1896," in *Oliver Mowat's Ontario,* ed. Donald Swainson (Toronto, 1979), pp. 210–35.

After 1896, with the dissolution of The Patrons of Industry in Ontario, *The Canada*

Farmers' Sun came under the control of Goldwin Smith, and support for Jews ceased.

156. "The Jew in North America," in *World Wide Evangelization* (New York, 1902), p. 419. See also "Relieving the Destitute," Montreal *Gazette,* 3 February 1892; "The Newspapers Say It Was an Antisemitic Attack" [Yiddish], *Keneder odler,* 24 August 1909; "The Beiliss Case Goes to the Jury," Montreal *Daily Mail,* 10 November 1913; J. T. M. Anderson, *The Education of the New Canadians* (London and Toronto, 1918), p. 86; and many other sources, especially in the English-language daily press of Montreal between 1896 and 1914.

157. "English, German and Polish Congregation Subscription List," in Canadian Jewish Congress, Montreal, Archives, Shaar Ha-shomayim Papers.

158. "A Library," Canadian *Jewish Times,* 8 November 1901. See also Baron de Hirsch Institute, Montreal, *Annual Report,* 1892–1914; "Montreal, Canada," *The American Hebrew,* 8 December 1901; "The YMHA Library, Montreal," in Arthur Hart, *The Jew,* p. 442; Speisman, *Toronto,* p. 124.

159. Saul Hayes, "Antisemitism in Canada," *The Facts,* May 1949, p. 3.

160. "Un Peu Fort!" *La Libre Parole Illustrée,* 10 October 1896.

161. See, herein, chapter 4; and also "The Jew in the Canadian Press" [Yiddish], *Keneder odler,* 2 February 1909.

162. See, for example, R. P. Hyacinthe, "L'église des Juifs dans son rapport avec l'église des Chrétiens," *L'Echo de la France,* April 1869, pp. 348–49; "Tribune Libre," *l'Etudiant,* 15 November 1912.

163. Asselin, "Jews," p. 4.

164. Untitled editorial, Canadian *Jewish Times,* 15 March 1901. See also Carroll Ryan, "Letter from Canada," *Jewish Comment,* 3 May 1901.

165. See, among other sources, "Un Juif Condamné," *La Patrie,* 12 November 1897; "On Arrête Un Syndic Juif En Sa Synagogue," *La Presse,* 24 November 1913; "Letter to the Editor," Canadian *Jewish Times,* 2 October 1912; Speisman, *Toronto,* pp. 119–20.

166. Asselin, "Jews," p. 18.

167. "Canada," *Jewish Chronicle,* 11 January 1907. See also R[obert] H. Coats and M. C. Maclean, *The American-Born in Canada* (Toronto, 1943), p. 136; and other sources.

Chapter 6

1. Hamilton (Ontario) *Herald* 10 January 1931; Benjamin G. Sack, *History of the Jews in Canada,* trans. Ralph Novek (Montreal, 1965), pp. 50–51, 153–54, 172–73; Stephen A. Speisman, *The Jews of Toronto* (Toronto, 1979), pp. 16–34.

2. *The Young Men's Hebrew Benevolent Society of Montreal* (Montreal, 1872); David A. Ansell, letter to S[amuel] Davis, president of the Spanish and Portuguese Synagogue, Montreal, 13 October 1874, in Jewish Public Library, Montreal, Archives, Documents Relating to the Young Men's Hebrew Benevolent Society and Other Institutions, microfilm; Speisman, *Toronto,* p. 56. See also chapter 3 herein.

3. See, for example, John Murray Gibbon, *Canadian Mosaic* (Toronto, 1938), p. 400.

4. Compare the listings in *Lovell's Montreal Directory,* 1828–70.

5. *Lovell's Historic Report of the Census of Montreal* (Montreal, 1891), pp. 78–79. Compare also C[harles] A[rchibald] Price, "Immigration and Group Settlement," in *The Cultural Integration of Immigrants,* ed. Wilfred Borrie (Paris, 1959), pp. 278–85.

6. See "The Jewish Times," Canadian *Jewish Times,* 20 December 1897; "Jewish Journalists and Writers in Canada" [Yiddish], *Keneder odler,* 6 August 1915; "The Jewish Press in Canada" [Yiddish], *Keneder odler,* 8 August 1915; Arthur Daniel Hart, *The Jew in Canada* (Montreal and Toronto, 1926), pp. 209–16; Joseph Kage, *With Faith and*

Thanksgiving (Montreal, 1962), pp. 48–49; and Evelyn Miller, "The Montreal Jewish Public Library," *Congress Bulletin,* November 1973, p. 13.

7. Joseph Elijah Bernstein, "Montreal (Canada, North America)" [Hebrew], *Ha-melitz,* 9 Marheshvan 1883; S.[amuel] Tchernovitz, *B'nai Moshe u-Tekufatam* [Hebrew] (Warsaw, 1914), p. 93; Nahum Sokolow, *History of Zionism,* vol. 2 repr. (New York, 1969), pp. lvii, 355; Leon Goldman, "History of Zionism in Canada," in Arthur Hart, *The Jew,* p. 292; Louis Rasminsky, ed., *Hadassah Jubilee* ([Toronto, 1928]), pp. 83–84; Bernard Figler, "History of the Zionist Ideal in Canada," in *Canadian Jewish Reference Book and Directory,* comp. Eli Gottesman (Montreal, 1965), pp. 88–95.

8. *Hamelitz* [Hebrew], 10 Iyyar 1900; Goldman, "Zionism," p. 296; Irwin A. Swiss and H. Norman Shoop, *Rabbi Aaron M. Ashinsky* (Pittsburgh, 1935), p. 9; *New York Times,* 3 April 1954; Speisman, *Toronto,* pp. 202–03; A. Segal, "Mi-Canada" [Hebrew], *He-Ahdut,* 24 Teveth 5673 [1913].

9. Minute Books of Holy Blossom Temple, Toronto (hereafter, HBT), 7 May 1899; Atlanta *Jewish Sentiment,* 9 March 1900; Rasminsky, *Hadassah,* pp. 97, 102; Goldman, "Zionism," p. 292; Edmund Scheuer, "Reminiscences of Canadian Jewry," appended to Arthur Brodey, "Political and Civil Status of the Jews in Canada" (Rabbi and Master's thesis, Jewish Institute of Religion, 1933). For a different view, see Speisman, *Toronto,* pp. 200–05.

10. See Minute Books of Temple Emanu-El, Montreal (hereafter, MTEE), for the period 1897–1907; London *Jewish Chronicle,* 26 February 1909; *Keneder odler* [Yiddish], 18 March 1910; *Canadian Zionist,* April 1934, January 1938, February 1938; Michael Brown, "The Beginnings of Reform Judaism in Canada," *Jewish Social Studies* 34 (October 1972).

11. *The American Hebrew,* 3 March 1898; Canadian *Jewish Times,* 18 March 1898, 7 November 1902; Sokolow, *Zionism,* vol. 2, p. 355; *History of the Corporation of Spanish and Portuguese Jews of Montreal, Canada* (Montreal, 1918), p. 50; Zvi Hirsch Masliansky, *Kitvei Masliansky* [Hebrew] vol. 3 (New York, 1929), pp. 220–22; Swiss and Shoop, *Ashinsky,* pp. 24–25; *Canadian Zionist,* 1 February 1941; H. M. Caiserman, *Two Canadian Personalities* (Montreal, 1948), p. 6; Abel Selick, ed., *History of the B'nai B'rith in Eastern Canada* (Toronto, 1964), pp. 55–64.

12. See *Jewish Sentiment,* 24 November 1899; *Jewish Chronicle,* 19 July 1901; *Hamelitz,* 10 Iyyar 1900; Canadian *Jewish Times,* 20 December 1901, 13 July 1906; *Report* of the Proceedings of the Convention of the Federation of Zionist Societies of Canada, 1907; Sokolow, *Zionism,* vol. 2, p. xliv.

13. Newton Bosworth, ed., *Hochelaga Depicta* (Montreal, 1839), p. 210. On the "high value placed on ethnic separateness in Canada," see John Porter, *The Vertical Mosaic* (Toronto, 1965), p. 71.

14. "The Jews in Canada (North America)" [Hebrew], *Hamelitz,* 11 Iyyar 1884.

15. "The Strong Word" [Yiddish], *Keneder odler,* 23 October 1910. See also "Anti-Semitism in Business" [Yiddish], *Keneder odler,* 23 July 1909; *Dominion of Canada and Newfoundland Gazetteer and Classified Business Directory,* 1915, pp. 1288–90, 1363–66, 1423–24; Brodey, "Status," p. 209; Rosalynd Gold, "Occupational Selection and Adjustment in the Jewish Group in Montreal with Special Reference to the Medical Profession" (Master's thesis, McGill University, 1942), p. 147; A[braham] I. Willinsky, *A Doctor's Memoirs* (Toronto, 1960), pp. 18–27; Gabriel Glazer, "French Canadian Nationalism and the Jews," *In the Dispersion* 4 (winter 1964–65): 33–38.

16. See André Siegfried, *The Race Question in Canada,* trans. Eveleigh Nash (New York, 1907), pp. 20–21; Lloyd G. Reynolds, *The British Immigrant: His Social and Economic Adjustment in Canada* (Toronto, 1935), pp. 129–40.

17. MTEE, 17 February 1896.

18. MTEE, 26 December 1882, 5 May 1884, 5 April 1886, 18 April 1886, 8 July 1886, 6 November 1887, 7 January 1892, 21 October 1892, 19 September 1897, 31 March 1908, 14 February 1910.

19. MTEE, 9 June 1909.

20. David Ajnhorn, *Fon Berlin biz San Francisco* [Yiddish] (Warsaw, 1930), p. 101.

21. As quoted in "Superior of the Sulpicians Received by City Council," Montreal *Daily Witness,* 10 November 1910.

22. Siegfried, *Race,* p. 77. See also p. 78; untitled editorial, Canadian *Jewish Times,* 10 May 1901.

23. See "The Registrarship," Canadian *Jewish Times,* 15 February 1901.

24. See, for example, "Past Year's Achievements Examined from Many Different Points of View," Montreal *Star,* 18 December 1897.

25. Peter Wiernik, *History of the Jews in America* (New York, 1912), p. 385.

26. J[ames] S. Woodsworth, *My Neighbor,* 2d ed. (Toronto, 1913), p. 327. See also idem, *Strangers Within Our Gates* (Toronto, 1909), pp. 344–45; untitled editorial, *Daily Witness,* 15 January 1898.

27. Claris Silcox and Galen M. Fisher, *Catholics, Jews, and Protestants* (New York and London, 1934), p. 277; Speisman, *Toronto,* pp. 131–34.

28. "Week of Prayer," *Daily Witness,* 3 January 1898. See also Joseph Elijah Bernstein, "Montreal (Canada)" [Hebrew], *Hamelitz,* 14 Tishri 1884; Meldola De Sola [Israelite], "Formerly a Rabbi," Montreal *Daily Herald,* 7 April 1896; "The Winning of Israel," *Daily Witness,* 17 November 1897.

29. Carroll Ryan, "Review of Canadian Conditions," Baltimore *Jewish Comment,* 6 February 1903.

30. "The Proposed Zionist Institute in Toronto," Canadian *Jewish Times,* 4 April 1913. See also W. Drysdale, "Montreal Jewish Mission," *Daily Witness,* 12 February 1898; Carroll Ryan, "Letter from Canada," *Jewish Comment,* 3 May 1901; J[Ignatius] T[imothy] Trebitsch-Lincoln, *The Autobiography of an Adventurer* (London, 1931), passim.

31. J. R. Dobson, as quoted in "The Jews Are Hard to Bite" [Yiddish], *Keneder odler,* 10 November 1910.

32. See Canadian *Jewish Times,* 18 March 1898; "Israel's Past, Present, and Future," *Daily Witness,* 7 April 1898; "Converting the Jew," Montreal *Gazette,* 8 April 1898; "Rabbi De Sola May Invoke the Law," Montreal *Daily Herald,* 30 December 1898; "The Conversionists," Canadian *Jewish Times,* 19 January 1900; Extracts of the Minutes of the Board of Directors of the Young Men's Hebrew Benevolent Society–Baron de Hirsch Institute, Montreal (hereafter, Extracts), 27 October 1907; Arthur Hart, *The Jew,* p. 268; Speisman, *Toronto,* pp. 133–34.

33. Lewis A. Hart, *A Jewish Reply to Christian Evangelists,*(New York, 1906), p. vii.

34. Ibid., p. 209.

35. As quoted in "The Jewish Mission Has Big Programme," Montreal *Star,* 11 November 1910.

36. See Louis Rosenberg, *Jewish Children in the Protestant Schools of Greater Montreal in the Period from 1878 to 1958,* Research Papers: Series E., no. 1 (Montreal, 1959), p. 6; "Jews Are 40 Percent of the Protestant School Population" [Yiddish], *Keneder odler,* 18 March 1910; *The Canadian Annual Review,* 1914, p. 505.

37. Compare Arthur R. M. Lower, *Canadians in the Making* (Toronto, 1958), pp. 373–83; David Rome, *Clouds in the Thirties,* vol. 2 (Montreal, 1977), p. 47.

38. See, among other sources, J. William Dawson, *Fifty Years of Work in Canada* (London and Edinburgh, 1901), p. 123; "Only French and English Are Supposed to Live in Peace" [Yiddish], *Keneder odler,* 20 November 1910; Ramsay Cook, *Canada and the French-Canadian Question* (Toronto, 1966), pp. 51, 147, 173–74.

39. See, among many sources, John Porter, *The Measure of Canadian Society* (n.p., 1979), pp. 103–62.

40. See, for example, "Zionism and Canada," London *Jewish World,* 9 December 1898; "The Zionist Movement," *Daily Witness,* 14 December 1898; Meldola De Sola, "Zionism: A Sermon Delivered in the Spanish and Portuguese Synagogue, Montreal, on the Seventh Day of Passover 5660 [1900]," in McGill University, Montreal, Archives, Abraham De Sola Papers (hereafter, ADSP); Bernard M. Kaplan, *The Origin and Goal of Zionism* (Montreal, 1901), pp. 4–5; "Russian Atrocities," Canadian *Jewish Times,* 1 December 1905; "The Zionist Movement," *Jewish Chronicle,* 19 July 1907; Federation of Zionist Societies of Canada, *Report* of the Proceedings of the Convention, 1907.

41. Letter, *Hamelitz,* 9 Marheshvan 1883.

42. Meldola De Sola, "Zionism."

43. See, for example, Bernstein, letter, *Hamelitz* [Hebrew], 9 Marheshvan 1883; Hyman Edelstein, "The Idol Corpse," Canadian *Jewish Times,* 4 July 1913; idem, *From Judean Vineyards* (Montreal, 1914), passim.

44. See "In the Military Because of Zionism" [Yiddish], *Keneder odler,* 7 July 1909; "Letters to the Editor" [Yiddish], *Keneder odler,* 20 November 1910; A. B. Bennett, "The Jew in Canada: A Reply," *The Canadian Forum,* May 1934, pp. 306–08; *Canadian Zionist,* 2 May 1941, 30 December 1946; Yitzhak Ben Zvi, *Po'alei Zion Ba-Aliyah Ha-Shniyah* [Hebrew] (Tel Aviv, 1958), p. 32.

45. Walter Laqueur, *A History of Zionism* (London, 1972), p. 162.

46. Quoted in Palestine *Post,* 6 May 1925. See also A. Segal, "Mi-Canada."

47. P. F. W. Rutherford, introduction to Herbert Brown Ames, *The City Below the Hill* (Toronto and Buffalo, 1972), p. viii. See also "The Latest Development," Montreal *Gazette,* 24 April 1889; "The Manitoba School Question," *Daily Witness,* 29 November 1892; B. A. T. DeMontigny, "Les Ecoles Séparées," *Revue Canadienne* 29 (October–November 1893): 600–05, 671–79; J[ames] R. Conn, "Immigration," *Queen's Quarterly* 8 (October 1900): 122–23; Henri Bourassa, *Great Britain and Canada* (Montreal, 1901), p. 45; "L'Historique de la Question des Ecoles," *La Croix,* 24 December 1904; J.-E. Monette, "L'Appel au Peuple," *Le Devoir,* 11 February 1910; "The Death of King Edward and the Jews" [Yiddish], *Keneder odler,* 10 May 1910; "Finds One Defect in Canadian Town, Tells Mr. Samuel," Montreal *Daily Mail,* 10 October 1913; Lionel Groulx, "Les vingt ans de l'A.C.J.C.," *l'Action française,* June 1924, pp. 360–62; Siegfried, *Race,* pp. 1–2; Oscar Douglas Skelton, *Life and Letters of Sir Wilfrid Laurier,* vol. 1, 2d ed. (Toronto, 1965), p. 96; Elizabeth H. Armstrong, *The Crisis of Quebec* (New York, 1937), pp. 22–24; T.-Damien Bouchard, "Climbing the Hill," *Le Haut Parleur,* 26 July 1952, p. 6; William Petersen, "The Ideological Background to Canada's Immigration," in *Canadian Society,* eds. Bernard Blishen et al. (Toronto, 1961), p. 72; Norman Penlington, *Canada and Imperialism* (Toronto and Buffalo, 1965), p. 6; Joseph Schull, *Laurier* (Toronto, 1966), pp. 507–09, 540; Cook, *Question,* p. 145; idem, "Protestant Lion, Catholic Lamb," in *One Church, Two Nations?,* eds. Philip LeBlanc and Arnold Edinborough (Don Mills, Ontario, 1968), p. 6; Lower, *Making,* p. 373.

48. Compare Everett Cherrington Hughes, *French Canada in Transition* (Chicago, 1943), pp. 123, 218–19; Porter, *Mosaic,* p. 67.

49. Hughes, *Transition,* pp. 217–18.

50. "The Jews in Canada" [Hebrew], *Ha-Zefirah* 4 Adar 1888. See also "Anti-Jap Legislation," Montreal *Gazette,* 25 July 1902; Simon Belkin, *Through Narrow Gates* (Montreal, 1966), p. 9.

51. Sigmund Samuel, *In Return* (Toronto, 1963), p. 125.

52. As quoted in "The Jews of Winnipeg," *Jewish Comment,* 26 August 1901.

53. "The Jew in North America," in *World Wide Evangelization* (New York, 1902), pp. 420–21.

54. C. A. Magrath, *Canada's Growth and Some Problems Affecting It* (Ottawa, 1910), pp. 96–104. Compare also William George Smith, *A Study in Canadian Immigration* (Toronto, 1920), pp. 183–85. Recent studies (1968–75) have shown that anti-Jewish sentiment continues to be more prevalent in Canada than in the United States and in French Canada than in English Canada. See Werner Cohn, "English and French Canadian Public Opinion on Jews and Israel: Some Poll Data," *Canadian Ethnic Studies* 11 (February 1979): 31–48.

55. Augustus Bridle, "The Drama of the 'Ward'," *The Canadian Magazine,* November 1909. See also "Canada," *Jewish Chronicle,* 13 October 1905; Reynolds, *Adjustment,* pp. 143–44; Rowland Tappan Berthoff, *British Immigrants in Industrial America* (Cambridge, 1953), p. 133; Carl Berger, *The Sense of Power* (Toronto and Buffalo, 1970), pp. 116–19.

56. "The Jews in Palestine," *The Bystander,* March 1880, p. 156.

57. Ibid.; "Christianity and Judaism," *The Bystander,* April 1881, pp. 216–17.

58. Olivar Asselin, "The Jews in Montreal," *The Canadian Century,* 16 September 1911, pp. 14–15.

59. See "Anti-Semitism in Business" [Yiddish], *Keneder odler,* 23 July 1909.

60. See, among many sources, Carroll Ryan, "This Month in Canada," *Jewish Comment,* 6 November 1903; "Wholesale Disfranchisement," Montreal *Gazette,* 29 January 1904; Extracts, 28 February 1908; "Canada," *Jewish Chronicle,* 5 March 1909; "La Question juive devant les tribunaux," *Le Devoir,* 9 February 1910; Canadian *Jewish Times,* April–July 1913; A[aron] Nirenberg, "Canada" [Hebrew], *Ha-Zefirah,* 23 Av 1913; "Treatment of Jews on Canadian Pacific Ships" [Hebrew], *Ha- Zefirah,* 25 Nisan 1914; Brodey, "Status," p. 218; Willinsky, *Memoirs,* pp. 18–27.

61. See Ames, *City,* p. 75

62. Compare "Dr. Bryce and Jewish Immigration," Canadian *Jewish Times,* 7 October 1904; Mark Wischnitzer, *To Dwell in Safety* (Philadelphia, 1948), p. 131.

63. Compare "A New Danger," Canadian *Jewish Times,* 17 August 1900; Norman Macdonald, *Canada: Immigration and Colonization, 1841–1903* (Toronto, 1966), pp. 109–10.

64. Y. L. Schlossberg, "Letters of Our Correspondents" [Hebrew], *Ha-Zefirah,* 26 Elul 1888.

65. "Labor Congress Demands Total Exclusion of Asiatics from Canada," *Daily Witness,* 24 September 1913.

66. "Garment Workers Out on Strike," Toronto *Globe,* 8 September 1900; Belkin, *Gates,* p. 8; Macdonald, *Canada,* pp. 141–42.

67. See "Notre Programme," *La Vérité,* 14 July 1881; Hughes, *Transition,* pp. 23–24; Cook, *Question,* pp. 85–86; William F. Ryan, "The Church's Contribution to Progress," in LeBlanc and Edinborough, *One Church,* pp. 90–92; Paul-André Linteau, "Georges Pelletier et les questions économiques (1910–1929)," *Revue d'Histoire de l'Amérique Française* 23 (March 1970): passim; Joseph Levitt, *Henri Bourassa and the Golden Calf* (Ottawa, 1969), pp. 67–70.

68. See Woodsworth, *Neighbor,* pp. 89–91. See also Rutherford, "Introduction," p. vii; Stewart Crysdale, "Upheaval and Integration," in LeBlanc and Edinborough, *One Church,* pp. 134–35.

69. Berger, *Power,* pp. 195, 177.

70. Magrath, *Growth,* p. 90. See also Carroll Ryan, "Letter from Canada," *Jewish Comment,* 2 August 1901.

71. See "Canada and Immigration," *Jewish Comment,* 16 August 1901; Carroll Ryan, "Canadian Immigration Problems," *Jewish Comment,* 24 July 1903; *The Canadian Annual Review,* 1908, p. 116; Marcus Lee Hansen and John Bartlet Brebner, *The Mingling of the Canadian and American Peoples* (New Haven, 1940), p. 225; Harold Martin Troper, *Only Farmers Need Apply* (Toronto, 1972), p. 7.

72. Letter, 26 December 1891, quoted in Belkin, *Gates*, pp. 61–62.

73. Quoted in "Jewish Colonisation," *Jewish Chronicle*, 3 May 1907. See also "A New Land of Promise," Montreal *Gazette*, 24 May 1892; "Canada Against the Immigrants" [Hebrew], *Hasman*, 1 August 1909.

74. See *The Dominion Annual Register and Review*, 1882, p. 81; A. J. Arnold, "Inside Canada: The Role of the Jews in Opening the West," *Pioneer Woman*, February–March 1969, p. 22.

75. *Official Report* of the Debates of the House of Commons of the Dominion of Canada, 25 April 1895, pp. 241–65. Canadian government representative quoted in "Jewish Immigration into Canada and New Zealand," *Jewish Chronicle*, 16 August 1907.

76. "A Word in Season," Canadian *Jewish Times*, 17 August 1900; "A Question of Degree," Montreal *Gazette*, 3 July 1902; Woodsworth, *Strangers*, pp. 155–58.

77. Quoted in *Report* of the Superintendent of Immigration, Department of the Interior, 1906, p. 83. See also *Report*, 1907, pp. 85–89.

78. See Mark Samuel and Lewis A. Hart, letter to "Sir," 8 January 1884, in Bronfman Collection of Jewish Canadiana, Jewish Public Library, Montreal, Scrapbook on Jewish Farming, Louis Rosenberg File; Meldola De Sola, "Jewish Agriculturists," *Daily Witness*, undated clipping in Jewish Public Library, Montreal, Archives, Meldola De Sola Scrapbook; *Rapport de l'Administration Centrale au Conseil d'Administration*, Jewish Colonization Association, Paris, (hereafter, *Rapport*), 1910, p. 67; Swiss and Shoop, *Ashinsky*, p. 27.

79. James Mavor, "Note on the Ethnical Affinities of the Present Inhabitants of Canada," in *Handbook of Canada* (Toronto, 1897), pp. 129–30.

80. See Reynolds, *Adjustment*, p. 15; Silcox and Fisher, *Catholics*, p. 108; A. V. Spada, *The Italians in Canada* (Ottawa and Montreal, 1969), p. 137.

81. See Elizabeth Wallace, *Goldwin Smith: Victorian Liberal* (Toronto, 1957), p. 184.

82. Goldwin Smith, letter to Sir Robert Collins, 24 March 1907, in *A Selection from Goldwin Smith's Correspondence*, ed. Arnold Haultain (Toronto, n.d.), p. 379; "Current Events and Opinions," *The Week*, December 1890.

83. "The Germans and the Jews," *The Bystander*, August 1880. See also "The New York *Sun* and the Jew Question," *The Bystander*, February 1881.

84. Goldwin Smith, letter to Jonas A. Rosenfeld, Dallas, Texas, 12 October 1908, in Haultain, *Correspondence*, p. 505. See also "Dr. Adler on Dr. Smith," Montreal *Gazette*, 10 November 1881; Hermann Adler, "Recent Phases of Judaeophobia," *Nineteenth Century*, December 1881; Goldwin Smith, "The Jewish Question," *Nineteenth Century*, October 1881.

85. "The Jews and Palestine," *The Bystander*, March 1880.

86. "Christianity and Judaism," *The Bystander*, April 1881.

87. Ibid. See also Michael N. Dobkowski, *The Tarnished Dream* (Westport, Conn., 1979), pp. 31–32, 97–98.

88. "The Most Eminent of Canadians," *Jewish Comment*, 12 October 1906.

89. Samuel E. Dawson, *The Prose Writers of Canada* (Montreal, 1901), p. 27. See also Speisman, *Toronto*, p. 64.

90. "Immigration Restrictions," Canadian *Jewish Times*, 29 May 1908.

91. See the columns of the *Keneder odler* betwen 1907 and 1914, and especially, "The Immigration Bill in the House of Commons" [Yiddish], 23 March 1910.

92. See, for example, Louis Rosenberg, *Canada's Jews* (Montreal, 1939), p. 126.

93. *Annual Report*, Baron de Hirsch Institute, Montreal, 1900, p. 4. See also Smith, *Study*, pp. 56–60, 72–73; Reynolds, *Adjustment*, p. 299.

94. Bourassa quoted in Mason Wade, *The French Canadians, 1760–1967*, vol. 1, rev. ed. (Toronto, 1968), p. 546.

95. "Jewish Chronicle Abroad" [Hebrew], *Hasman*, 1 October 1908.

96. "Canada Against the Immigrants" [Hebrew], *Hasman*, 1 August 1909. See also

"Canada's Half-Open Door," *Jewish Chronicle*, 27 March 1908; Reynolds, *Adjustment*, p. 100.
    97. Troper, *Farmers*, p. 23.
    98. *Rapport*, 1911, pp. 182–83.
    99. A[aron] Nirenberg, "Immigration Restriction in Canada" [Hebrew], *Ha-Zefirah*, 9 Adar Sheni 1913.
    100. *Rapport*, 1912, p. 99. See also Smith, *Study*, p. 95; Robert England, *The Central European Immigrant in Canada* (Toronto, 1929), p. 21; Belkin, *Gates*, p. 9.
    101. M. J. Finkelstein et al., Winnipeg, letter to Baron de Hirsch Institute, Montreal, and other correspondence, in *Early Documents on the Canadian Jewish Congress, 1914–21, Canadian Jewish Archives*, vol. 1, comp. and ed. David Rome, n.s., (Montreal, 1974), pp. 10–16; *American Jewish Year Book*, 1914–15, p. 179; Louis Rosenberg, *Jews*, p. 125; Belkin, *Gates*, p. 10.
    102. Minutes of the Spanish and Portuguese Synagogue, Montreal (hereafter, MSP), 8 November 1874, 3 December 1876, 27 January 1878, 26 May 1881, 23 July 1882, 15 April 1883, 25 January 1885; *Jewish Chronicle*, 4 August 1876; Secretary, Protestant Board of School Commissioners, letter, to President, Spanish and Portuguese Synagogue, Montreal, 19 June 1882, in Jewish Public Library, Montreal, Archives, Documents Relating to the Young Men's Hebrew Benevolent Society and Other Institutions; New York *Jewish Messenger*, 18 July 1884; "A l'Honorable Secrétaire Provincial Re Taxe Scolaire Juive, Cité de Montréal," memorial of the Young Men's Hebrew Benevolent Society, Montreal, n.d; Maxwell Goldstein, "The Status of the Jew in the Public Schools of Canada," in Arthur Hart, *The Jew*, pp. 497–98; "Tax-Supported Jewish School in Montreal in the 1890s," *Congress Bulletin*, February 1953, p. 5; Louis-Philippe Audet, *Histoire du Conseil de l'Instruction Publique de la Province de Québec, 1856–1964* (Montreal, 1964), pp. 108–09.
    103. "A Splendid Entertainment," Montreal *Daily Herald*, 3 March 1885; "A l'Honorable Secrétaire," MSP, 6 May 1891; Baron de Hirsch Institute, Montreal, *Annual Report*, 1892, pp. 5–6, 25–31; untitled editorial, Montreal *Gazette*, 18 May 1892; "Hebrew School Taxes," Montreal *Star*, 19 May 1892; "The Jewish School Tax," Montreal *Star*, 23 May 1892; "The Spanish and Portuguese Schools," Montreal *Gazette*, 29 June 1893; "Canada," *Jewish Chronicle*, 28 September 1894; "Montreal," *Jewish Messenger*, 28 June 1895; "Tax-Supported Jewish Schools"; *Baron de Hirsch Institute, 1863–1963* (n.p., n.d.), p. 16; Belkin, *Gates*, p. 39.
    104. "Montreal," *Jewish Messenger*, 21 September 1894; Protestant Board of School Commissioners for Montreal, *Financial Statement and Statistics of Attendance*, 1894–95, p. 7; "Education in Quebec," Montreal *Gazette*, 3 November 1897; "The Jews and Public Schools," Montreal *Star*, 15 February 1898; Lewis A. Hart, "Jewish Children in the Schools," *Daily Witness*, 19 March 1898; "Our Protestant Schools," *Daily Witness*, 8 October 1898; untitled editorial, Canadian *Jewish Times*, 6 July 1900; Carroll Ryan, "Letter from Canada," *Jewish Comment*, 1 February 1901; "Discrimination Against Jewish Pupils in the Protestant Schools," Canadian *Jewish Times*, 5 July 1901; "The School Question," Canadian *Jewish Times*, 2 August 1901; "The Question of Scholarships in the Public Schools," Canadian *Jewish Times*, 6 December 1901; "Jewish Pupils in Protestant Schools," Canadian *Jewish Times*, 20 December 1901; Carroll Ryan, "Letter from Canada," *Jewish Comment*, 14 February 1902; "The School Commissioners and Jewish Pupils," Canadian *Jewish Times*, 11 April 1902; Isaac Landman, "Canadian Jews and Judaism," *American Israelite*, 1 May 1902; S[amuel] Talpis, "Montreal" [Hebrew], *Hamelitz*, 19 Adar 1903; *The Jewish Encyclopedia* (1901–06), s.v. "Montreal"; "Jews and the Schools," Canadian *Jewish Times*, 18 December 1903; Martin Wolff, "The Jews of Canada," *American Jewish Year Book*, 5686 (1925–26); Leon Crestohl, *The Jewish School Problem in Quebec* ([Montreal, 1926]); Silcox and Fisher, *Catholics*, pp. 70, 193–95; Rosenberg, *Jews*, pp. 268–

70; Audet, *Histoire,* pp. 108–10; Solomon Frank, *Two Centuries in the Life of a Synagogue* (n.p., n.d.), pp. 90–91.

105. See Elson I. Rexford, *Manual of the School Law and Regulations of the Province of Quebec,* rev. ed. (Montreal, 1895), p. 55; *The Canadian Annual Review,* 1903, p. 133; S[amuel] T[alpis], "Letter from Canada" [Hebrew], *Hamelitz,* 21 Sivan 1903; "Protestant School Commissioners Opposed to Justice," Canadian *Jewish Times,* 23 April 1909; *American Jewish Year Book,* 1913–14, p. 284; Elson I. Rexford, *Our Educational Problem: The Jewish Population and the Protestant Schools* (Montreal, 1924?); Arthur Hart, *The Jew,* p. 464; C[harles] B[ruce] Sissons, *Church and State in Canadian Education* (Toronto, 1959), pp. 148–53; William David Kenneth Kernaghan, "'Freedom of Religion in the Province of Quebec with Particular Reference to the Jews, Jehovah's Witnesses, and Church-State Relations" (Ph.D. diss., Duke University, 1966), p. 36.

106. Levitt, *Bourassa,* p. 86. See also Hughes, *Transition,* pp. 106–21.

107. Siegfried, *Race,* p. 79. See also "Canada," *Jewish Chronicle,* 16 April 1909; Brodey, "Status," p. 109.

108. As quoted in Rexford, *Problem,* p. 20.

109. See "Ministers Demand Separate School for Jews" [Yiddish], *Keneder odler,* 12 April 1910; Rexford, *Problem,* pp. 27–28; Brodey, "Status," p. 110. See also Speisman, *Toronto,* pp. 64, 67, 320.

110. See Landman, "Canadian"; W. H. Baker, letter to Mr. Hutchison, 28 April 1904, in Baron de Hirsch Institute–Young Men's Hebrew Benevolent Society, Montreal, Letterbook; "The Baron de Hirsch Institute," Canadian *Jewish Times,* 1 December 1905; "A Jewish School Board" [Yiddish], *Keneder odler,* 26 April 1910; Asselin, "Jews," p. 15; "Finds One Defect in Canadian Town, Tells Mr. Samuel," Montreal *Daily Mail,* 10 October 1913; Rexford, *Problem,* pp. 33–35; Lavy M. Becker and Louis Rosenberg, "Jewish Education in Montreal," *Jewish Education* (winter-spring 1950–51); Bernard Figler, *Rabbi Dr. Herman Abramowitz, Lazarus Cohen, Lyon Cohen* (Ottawa, 1968), pp. 119–20.

111. Compare *La Vérité,* 6 October 1881; Samuel Talpis, "Abroad" [Hebrew] *Hamelitz,* 11 Sivan 1900; "Roman Catholic Teachers," Montreal *Gazette,* 11 July 1901; S[amuel] T[alpis], "Letters from Canada" [Hebrew], *Hamelitz,* 19 Adar 1903; Siegfried, *Race,* p. 3; Rexford, *Problem,* pp. 7, 40; Naim Kattan, "Minorités et Majorités au Canada," in Gottesman, *Directory,* p. 108; S[ydney] F. Wise and Robert Craig Brown, *Canada Views the United States* (Toronto, 1967), p. 118.

112. Compare Frank Stock, "Jewish-Protestant Discontent in Montreal Schools," Bronfman Collection of Jewish Canadiana, Jewish Public Library, Montreal; A. Segal, "Mi-Canada."

113. "Montreal, Canada," *Jewish Messenger,* 29 July 1887. See also John Mordy, "Wholesale Sabbath Desecration," *Daily Witness,* 14 December 1887.

114. Untitled editorial, *Daily Witness,* 15 February 1898.

115. See, for example, "Montreal" [Hebrew], *Hayehoody,* 13 June 1901; "Abroad" [Hebrew], *Hamelitz,* 27 Tishri 1901.

116. Carroll Ryan, "Jewish Immigration to Canada," *Jewish Comment,* 20 May 1904.

117. See Meldola De Sola, "Address to Sir Wilfred [sic] Laurier and the Hon. Mr. Fitzpatrick in Support of Memorial presented by Jewish deputation against the Lord's Day Bill at Ottawa, March 15, 1906," in McGill University Archives, Montreal, De Sola Papers; "Sunday Observance Bill," Canadian *Jewish Times,* 20 April 1906; "The Lord's Day Observance Bill in Canada," *Jewish Chronicle,* 13 July 1906; Charles H. L. Emanuel, *A Century and a Half of Jewish History, Extracted from the Minute Books of the London Committee of Deputies of the British Jews* (London, 1910), pp. 85, 100–01.

118. See "Mr. Bourassa Again," Canadian *Jewish Times,* 29 June 1906; Canada, House of Commons, *Debates,* 20 June 1906, pp. 5636–37.

119. "Jew Is an Anachronism in Our Modern Society," Toronto *World,* 19 March 1906.

120. "Methodists and the Lord's Day," Canadian *Jewish Times,* 15 June 1906.

121. "The Sunday Observance Law," Canadian *Jewish Times,* 13 July 1906.

122. Quoted in "Jew Is an Anachronism."

123. See "The Sunday Observance Bill," Canadian *Jewish Times,* 4 May 1906; "The Lord's Day Bill," Montreal *Gazette,* 9 June 1906; "The Lord's Day Bill," Montreal *Gazette,* 21 June 1906; "The Sunday Work Bill," Montreal *Gazette,* 22 June 1906; "A Curious Discrimination," Montreal *Gazette,* 29 June 1906; "The Lord's Day Bill," Montreal *Gazette,* 2 July 1906; "The Lord's Day Bill," Montreal *Gazette,* 7 July 1906; "The Lord's Day Observance Bill in Canada," *Jewish Chronicle,* 13 July 1906; "L'Observance du Dimanche," Montreal *La Patrie,* 13 July 1906; "The Sunday Observance Legislation," Canadian *Jewish Times,* 23 July 1906; Baron de Hirsch Institute, Montreal, *Annual Report,* 1907, pp. 11–12; Emanuel, *Century,* p. 171; "Our Jewish Immigration in Canada" [Yiddish], *Keneder odler,* 8 August 1915; Wallace, *Smith,* pp. 180–82; *Baron de Hirsch Institute,* p. 24; Levitt, *Bourassa,* p. 104.

124. See "The Lord's Day Bill," Montreal *Gazette,* 2 June 1906; "Jewish Chronicle Abroad" [Hebrew], *Hasman,* 13 Av 1906; "Canada," *Jewish Chronicle,* 10 January 1908; *American Jewish Year Book,* 5672 (1911–12), p. 147; "Review of Lord's Day Act may bring Sunday opening," *Canadian Jewish News,* 27 January 1977.

125. "Ministers Begin Campaign Against Jews" [Yiddish], *Keneder odler,* 20 April 1910. See also "Canada," *Jewish Chronicle,* 6 March 1908; "Canada," *Jewish Chronicle,* 22 May 1908; "The Victory of the Ministers Over the Jews" [Yiddish], *Keneder odler,* 22 April 1910.

126. As quoted by Herman Abramowitz, "Samuel William Jacobs," *American Jewish Year Book,* 5700 (1939–40), p. 108.

127. See A. Bennett, "The Queen's University Bill," Canadian *Jewish Times,* 7 June 1912; Berger, *Power,* pp. 30–31.

128. See Abramowitz, "Jacobs"; *Keneder odler* [Yiddish], all during the year 1912; M[arcus] M. Sperber, "The Queen's University Bill," Canadian *Jewish Times,* 22 March 1912; "Protest Against the Queen's College Bill," Canadian *Jewish Times,* 22 March 1912; *Who's Who and Why, 1919–20* (Toronto, 1920), p. 458; Bernard Figler, *Sam Jacobs: Member of Parliament,* 2d ed. (Ottawa, 1970), p. 30.

129. Carroll Ryan, "Jewish Affairs in Canada," *Jewish Comment,* 25 March 1902. See also J. L. Schlossberg, "Letters of Our Correspondents" [Hebrew], *Ha-Zefirah,* 26 Elul 1888.

130. Harris Vineberg, as quoted in Belkin, *Gates,* p. 39; see also p. 93; Figler, *Abramowitz,* p. 45.

131. "Conference of American Rabbis," *Reform Advocate,* 10 July 1897.

132. Halitvack [pseud.], "The Jews of Montreal," *Reform Advocate,* 28 March 1908.

133. See, herein, chapter 4; Arthur Weir, ed., *Montreal Illustrated, 1894* (Montreal, 1894), p. 299; John A. Cooper, ed., *Men of Canada* (Montreal and Toronto, 1901–02), p. 86; *Jewish Year Book,* 1911, p. 376.

Chapter 7

1. "The Year 5667," *Jewish Chronicle,* 6 September 1907.

2. See, for example, "Anti-Semitism and Its Cure," Canadian *Jewish Times,* 25 April 1902.

3. A sign of change in recent years is the sponsorship of a French-language journal,

Jonathan, by the Canada-Israel Committee. *Jonathan* aims to inform French Canadians about aspects of Israeli life.

4. See William David Kenneth Kernaghan, "Freedom of Religion in the Province of Quebec with Particular Reference to the Jews, Jehovah's Witnesses, and Church-State Relations, 1930–1960," (Ph.D. thesis, Duke University, 1966), pp. 101–03; Stephen A. Speisman, *The Jews of Toronto* (Toronto, 1979), pp. 306–08.

5. Lita-Rose Betcherman, *The Swastika and the Maple Leaf* (Toronto, 1975), p. 5.

6. See Kernaghan, "Freedom," pp. 84–88; Betcherman, *Swastika,* p. 23; David Rome, *Clouds in the Thirties,* vol. 2 (Montreal, 1977), pp. 1–38.

7. See Select Standing Committee on Agriculture and Colonization, *Report,* in official report of the *Debates* of the House of Commons of the Dominion of Canada, 8 June 1928, pp. 76ff.; Norman Macdonald, *Canada: Immigration and Colonization, 1841–1903* (Toronto, 1966); William Peters, *Planned Migration* (Berkeley, 1955); Harold Troper, *Only Farmers Need Apply* (Toronto, 1972).

8. Ben Dunkelman, *Dual Allegiance* (Scarborough, Ontario, 1978), p. 13. In later years Dunkelman shed his playboy character and achieved notable success in the Canadian and Israeli armies and as a businessman in Canada.

9. Quoted in *Canadian Zionist,* May 1934. See also "The Jubilee Forest," *Canadian Zionist,* November 1935; and *Canadian Jewish Year-Book,* 1941, p. 254.

10. See, for example, Kernaghan, "Freedom"; Betcherman, *Swastika;* Rome, *Clouds.* See also David Lewis, *The Good Fight: Political Memoirs, 1901–1958* (Toronto, 1981), pp. 342–43.

11. See Irving Abella and Harold Troper, *None Is Too Many: Canada and the Jews of Europe, 1933–1948* (Toronto, 1982); Lewis, *Fight,* p. 344.

12. See, among other sources, Yitzhak Ben-Zvi, Winnipeg, letter to Rahel Yanait, 1 March 1926, in Ben-Zvi Archives, Yad Ben-Zvi, Jerusalem, File 1/4/16/36; Arthur Ruppin, letter to his wife, 27 December 1922, in *Pirqei Hayyai,* vol. 3 [Hebrew] (Tel Aviv, 1968), pp. 49–50.

13. Yitzhak Ben-Zvi, "Mi-Ma'arav Shemesh," *Davar,* 7 July 1926.

14. See *Canadian Zionist,* March 1934, February 1935, December 1935, May 1938, 12 February 1941, 2 May 1941, 30 December 1946, November 1947, March 1957; Molly Lyons Bar David, *My Promised Land* (New York, 1953), pp. 2–25.

15. Rome, *Clouds,* vol. 2, pp. 82–85; Betcherman, *Swastika,* pp. 40–45, 91.

16. Quoted in Lawrence Freiman, *Don't Fall off the Rocking Horse* (Toronto, 1978), pp. 49–51, 56.

17. Archibald Freiman, "Three Years of Achievements," *Canadian Zionist,* February 1935. See also Michael Brown, "The Americanization of Canadian Zionism," in *Contemporary Jewry: Studies in Honor of Moshe Davis,* ed. Geoffrey Wigoder (Jerusalem, 1984), pp. 129–58.

18. Quoted in *Canadian Zionist,* February 1935.

19. *Canadian Zionist,* June 1934. See also Zachariah Kay, *Canada and Palestine* (Jerusalem, 1978), p. 107.

20. See David Bercuson, *Canada and the Birth of Israel* (Toronto, 1985), passim.

21. See, for example, Dunkelman, *Allegiance,* p. 119; Lewis, *Fight,* pp. 338–42; *Canadian Zionist,* 30 December 1946, March 1947, April 1947, September 1947, September 1967.

22. Compare Harold Waller, *The Canadian Jewish Community: A National Perspective* (Jerusalem and Philadelphia, 1977), p. 5.

23. See, for example, Pierre Vallières, *Nègres Blancs d'Amérique* (Montreal, 1968).

24. Morton Weinfeld, "Intermarriage: Agony and Adaptation," and Jean-Claude Lasry, "A Francophone Diaspora," both in *The Canadian Jewish Mosaic,* eds. M. Weinfeld, W. Shaffir, and I. Cotler (Toronto, 1981), pp. 231–32, 369.

25. For example, the project for cataloguing and photographing Canadian synagogues and the book, _Treasures of a People,_ by Sheldon Levitt, Lynn Milstone, and Sidney T. Tenenbaum (Toronto, 1985); and the volume by Weinfeld, et al., _Canadian Jewish Mosaic._

26. See Yaacov Glickman, "Jewish Education: Success or Failure?" in Weinfeld et al., _Canadian Jewish Mosaic,_ pp. 113–28.

27. Peter Desbarats, _The State of Quebec_ (Toronto and Montreal, 1965), p. 70. For a discussion of anti-Israel sentiment in the Canadian Senate, see Senator Nathan Nurgitz, "A Senator Responds," _Middle East Focus,_ September 1985.

28. See, among other sources, _Canadian Zionist,_ April 1955, June 1955, September 1972, September 1973, November–December 1973; Harold Waller, "Canada," in _Zionism in Transition,_ ed. Moshe Davis (New York, 1980), pp. 111–20.

29. Waller, "Canada."

30. Compare Leon Kronitz, "Zionism: Creator of a State, Guardian of a People," _Canadian Zionist,_ November 1972.

31. Compare Waller, _Perspective,_ pp. 11–16; Charles Lazarus, "The Jewish Fact and the Referendum," Toronto _Globe and Mail,_ 14 May 1980; Charles Liebman, "The Modern Mind," _Midstream,_ April 1981.

32. See Arnold Ages, "Antisemitism: The Uneasy Calm," in Weinfeld et al., _Canadian Jewish Mosaic,_ pp. 383–96.

33. One of the most outspoken anti-Israel and sometimes anti-Jewish periodicals in Canada was for many years _The United Church Observer,_ organ of one of the country's largest churches. In November 1970, Premier Golda Meir of Israel was very roughly handled during an interview on the CBC, the country's public, English-language television network. These were not altogether isolated phenomena.

34. Harold M. Waller and Morton Weinfeld, "The Jews of Quebec and 'Le Fait Français'," in Weinfeld et al., _Canadian Jewish Mosaic,_ p. 424.

35. Gerald Clark, _Montreal: The New Cité_ (Toronto, 1982), p. 163.

36. Quoted in ibid., pp. 153–54.

37. Werner Cohn, "English and French Canadian Public Opinion on Jews and Israel: Some Poll Data," _Canadian Ethnic Studies_ 11 (1979): 35–48; "Exodus 1977: Why Younger Jews are Leaving Montreal," Toronto _Globe and Mail,_ 17 September 1977; Ruth R. Wisse and Irwin Cotler, "Quebec Jews Caught in the Middle," _Commentary,_ September 1977. Although the authors later claimed that their implied comparison of Nazism and Quebec nationalism had been wrongly quoted, the editors of _Commentary_ denied it (October 1977).

38. Desbarats, _State,_ p. 62. See also Morton Weinfeld, "Le milieu juif contemporain du Québec," in _Juifs et réalités juives au Québec,_ eds. Pierre Anctil and Gary Caldwell (Quebec, 1984), pp. 72–85; Dominique Clift and Sheila McLeod Arnopolous, _Le Fait Anglais au Québec_ (Montreal, 1979), pp. 182ff.

39. Michael Yarosky, "The Jewish Community of Quebec Province: Bridging the Past and the Present," _Journal of Jewish Communal Service_ (September 1977): 19.

40. Quoted in Desbarats, _State,_ p. 63. See also the speech of Lévesque to a Toronto Jewish audience in December 1971, as reported in Stuart E. Rosenberg, "French Separatism and Its Implications for Canadian Jewry," _American Jewish Year Book,_ 1972, p. 409, and in W. Gunther Plaut, _Unfinished Business_ (Toronto, 1981), pp. 251–52.

41. For example, Desbarats, _State,_ pp. 178–82; and Joseph Kage, "The Jew Within the Context of Canadian Pluralism," _Viewpoints,_ October 1969, pp. 27–31.

42. Ryan, "A French Canadian Looks at the Jews," _Viewpoints,_ October 1969, pp. 5–14. The article is a shortened version of the talk given by Ryan in February 1969, at Loyola College in Montreal to the annual meeting of the Christian-Jewish Dialogue, sponsored by the B'nai B'rith.

43. Jean Marchand, then federal minister of regional economic expansion, cited by Michael M. Solomon, "Canada," *American Jewish Year Book*, 1971, p. 275.

44. Quoted in Melvin Fenson, "Canada," *American Jewish Year Book*, 1974–75, p. 321.

45. On the *Ici Québec* incident, see "Jews Protest Anti-Zionist Quebec Article," Toronto *Star*, 8 March 1978; Bernard Baskin, "Canada," *American Jewish Year Book*, 1980, p. 177.

46. Concise reports of these incidents can be found in Bernard Baskin, "Canada," *American Jewish Year Book*, 1976, p. 257, and 1981, p. 185. See also Plaut, *Business*, p. 277.

47. Gabrielle Roy, *Alexandre Chenevert* (Montreal, 1955), *Ces enfants de ma vie* (Ottawa, 1977), and other works; Roch Carrier, *La Guerre, Yes Sir!*, trans. Sheila Fischman (Toronto, 1970).

48. Raoul Roy, *Lettre aux Juifs de Montréal* (Montreal, 1979), p. 211.

49. See Janice Arnold, "Best-selling Quebec Novel Prompts Controversy," *Canadian Jewish News*, 17 October 1985, for a summary of the *Le Matou* affair to date.

50. Shloime Perel and Henry Srebrnik, "Signs of the Times," *Jerusalem Post Magazine*, 22 January 1982; *Le Devoir*, 17–18 February 1982, 17 December 1985; *Canadian Jewish News*, 23 January 1986.

51. Quoted in "Quebec Jews Face Fact that Migrants Won't be Replaced," Toronto *Globe and Mail*, 19 September 1977.

52. Compare "Report on the French Fact," by a special committee of Montreal's Allied Jewish Community Services, September 1970; Jack Kantrowitz, "Jews in the New Quebec: Where Do We Go From Here?" *Viewpoints*, spring 1979, p. 7; "Jews and Québécois: Coming to Terms," *Canadian Jewish News*, 18 October 1979.

53. Compare Baskin, "Canada," *American Jewish Year Book*, 1976, p. 254; Fenson, "Canada," *American Jewish Year Book*, 1974–75, p. 321; Janice Arnold, "English Instruction Still Hard to Obtain in Quebec," *Canadian Jewish News*, 17 March 1983.

54. Ryan, "French Canadian Looks," p. 7.

55. Compare Jacob Ziegel, "The Place of Minorities in Developing Quebec," *Viewpoints*, October 1969, p. 25; Desbarats, *State*, pp. 106–08; Yarosky, "Bridging," p. 25; Weinfeld, "Milieu," p. 76.

56. *Canadian Jewish Chronicle Review*, 6 October 1967; Ben Kayfetz, "Canada," *American Jewish Year Book*, 1968, p. 390.

57. See Plaut, *Unfinished Business*, p. 333, and other sources.

58. "Quebec Orders Secret Ethnic File Destroyed," Toronto *Star*, 3 November 1982.

59. "Toward a New Consensus," the Preliminary Report of the Long Range Planning Committee of the Allied Jewish Community Services, Montreal, August 1982, p. 1.

60. Joseph Baumholz, "Quebec Jewry's Future," *Viewpoints*, May 1983, p. 7.

61. *Update from the 1981 Census* (Ottawa: Statistics Canada, 26 April 1983) reports a drop in the Jewish population of Quebec from 115,990 in 1971 to 102,355 in 1981. See, among other sources, "Exodus from Quebec City," *Maclean's*, 30 January 1984; "Young Jews Fleeing Quebec, Lawyer Says," and "Anglophone Class of '71: 31% have left Quebec," Toronto *Star*, 28 February and 28 March 1978; "Exodus, 1977," Toronto *Globe and Mail*.

62. Compare Shlomo Perel, "Quebec's Nationalist Movement and the Future of its Jews," *Israel Horizons*, April 1977, pp. 26–27.

63. Survey reported in Michael Solomon, "Canada," *American Jewish Year Book*, 1971, p. 277.

64. Survey by George Kantrowitz, research director of the Allied Jewish Community Services, Montreal, reported by Bernard Baskin in "Canada," *American Jewish Year Book*, 1982, p. 180; "Toward a New Consensus," p. 17.

65. Leo Davids, "Canadian Jewry: Some Recent Census Findings," *American Jewish Year Book,* 1985, Table I, p. 194.

66. Milton Winston, "The Jews of Quebec: Two Views," *Jewish Dialog,* spring 1970.

67. Clark, *Montreal,* p. 161.

68. Census *Update,* p. 7; Weinfeld, "Intermarriage," p. 369; survey of religious behavior by Paul Bain, cited by Baskin in "Canada," *American Jewish Year Book,* 1980, p. 179.

69. Compare Wisse and Cotler, "Middle"; and Morton Weinfeld, "The Jews of Quebec: Perceived Antisemitism, Segregation, and Emigration," *The Jewish Journal of Sociology* 22 (June 1980): 5–20.

70. See L. Rosenberg, "Changes in the Geographical Distribution of the Jewish Population of Metropolitan Montreal in the Decennial Periods from 1901 to 1961 and the Estimated Possible Changes during the Period from 1961 to 1971," *Research Papers,* Series A, 1 December 1966; Waller, *Perspective,* pp. 3–7; Paul Bain, unpublished materials relating to demography and the geographical distribution of Canadian Jews. See also Mortimer Schiff, "Separatism in Quebec," *Midstream,* March 1965, pp. 69–78.

Selected Bibliography

Manuscripts and Unpublished Materials

Abramowitz, H[erman], and Lawrence Cohen. "Schedule of Material in the Ansell Collection." Jewish Public Library, Montreal. Bronfman Collection of Jewish Canadiana.

"Adolphus Mordecai Hart (April 11, 1811–March 23, 1879)." Jewish Public Library, Montreal. Bronfman Collection of Jewish Canadiana.

Ansell, D[avid] A[braham]. "Reminiscences of the Young Men's Hebrew Benevolent Society, etc., etc." Jewish Public Library, Montreal. Bronfman Collection of Jewish Canadiana.

Anshe Sholom Congregation, Hamilton, Ontario. Minute Books of the Congregation, 1882–1914.

Bain, Paul. Manuscript materials relating to the demography of Canadian Jews, given to the author.

"Baron de Hirsch Institute and Hebrew Benevolent Society, Montreal, Charter and By-Laws." 1966.

Ben Zvi Institute, Jerusalem. Archives. Miscellaneous documents pertaining to Canada.

Brodey, Arthur. "Political and Civil Status of the Jews in Canada." Rabbi and Master's thesis, Jewish Institute of Religion, 1933.

"By-Laws of the Corporation of the Portuguese Jews of Montreal." 1857.

"By-Laws of De Sola Lodge No. 89, A[ncient] J[ewish] O[rder] K[esher] S[hel] B[arzel]." 1875.

Canadian Jewish Congress, Montreal. Archives. D[avid] A[braham] Ansell file.

Canadian Jewish Congress, Montreal. Archives. N. Friedman file.

Canadian Jewish Congress, Montreal. Archives. Hart family file.

Canadian Jewish Congress, Montreal. Archives. Shaar Hashomayim Congregation Minute Books and papers.

Conn, Bernard H. "Adolphus S. Solomons." Jewish Public Library, Montreal. Bronfman Collection of Jewish Canadiana.

David, Samuel. Journal, 1800–1806. Public Archives of Canada, Ottawa. File MG-24I13.

Gold, Roslyn. "Occupational Selection and Adjustment of the Jewish Group in Montreal with Special Reference to the Medical Profession." Master's thesis, McGill University, 1942.

Gordon, M. Edmund. "Political and Legal Aspects of Jewish History in Canada." Jewish Public Library, Montreal. Bronfman Collection of Jewish Canadiana.

Holy Blossom Temple, Toronto. Minute Books of the Congregation.

Jacobs, Solomon. "Who Is Behind the Times? A sermon." Jewish Public Library, Montreal. Bronfman Collection of Jewish Canadiana.

Jewish Public Library, Montreal. Archives. Baron de Hirsch Loose Leaf Book.

Jewish Public Library, Montreal. Archives. Meldola De Sola papers.

Jewish Public Library, Montreal. Archives. Meldola De Sola Scrapbook.

Jewish Public Library, Montreal. Archives. Documents relating to the Young Men's Hebrew Benevolent Society and other institutions.

Jewish Public Library, Montreal. Archives. Extracts of the Minutes of the Board of Directors of the Young Men's Hebrew Benevolent Society—Baron de Hirsch Institute.

Jewish Public Library, Montreal. Archives. Joseph S. Leo file.

Jewish Public Library, Montreal. Archives. Letterbook of the Baron de Hirsch Institute—Young Men's Hebrew Benevolent Society.

Jewish Public Library, Montreal. Bronfman Collection of Jewish Canadiana. Judah file.

Jewish Public Library, Montreal. Bronfman Collection of Jewish Canadiana. William Raphael file.

Jewish Public Library, Montreal. Bronfman Collection of Jewish Canadiana. Scrapbook on Jewish farming.

Joseph, Abraham. Diary. Public Archives of Canada, Ottawa. File MG-24I61.

Judah, Doris M. "Genealogy of the Judah Family." McGill University, Montreal. McCord Museum. Judah papers.

"Jugement Dans La Cour Supérieure en Appel. Benjamin Ortenberg, demandeur vs. Joseph Edouard Plamondon et René Leduc, défendeurs." 28 December 1914. Jewish Public Library, Montreal. Bronfman Collection of Jewish Canadiana.

Kage, Joseph. "Jewish Immigration and Immigrant Aid Effort, 1760–1959." Jewish Public Library. Montreal. Bronfman Collection of Jewish Canadiana.

Kayfetz, B[enjamin] G. "Immigrant Reaction as Reflected in Jewish Literature." Jewish Public Library, Montreal. Bronfman Collection of Jewish Canadiana.

Kernaghan, William David Kenneth. "Freedom of Religion in the Province of Quebec with Particular Reference to the Jews, Jehovah's Witnesses, and Church-State Relations, 1930–1960." Ph.D. diss., Duke University, 1966.

Lewis, Louis, and David Dainow. "Report on the Visit to New York Charities." 1914. Jewish Public Library, Montreal. Archives.

McGill University, Montreal. Archives. De Sola papers.

McGill University, Montreal. McCord Museum. Early Hart papers.

McGill University, Montreal. McCord Museum. Gerald E. Hart papers.

Miller, Mrs. Emmanuel. "Abraham de Sola Papers, a Guide to the Microfilm."

Moldofsky, Naomi. "The Economic Adjustment of North African Jewish Immigrants in Montreal." Ph.D. diss., McGill University, 1968.

Municipal Archives, Montreal. Will and probate documents of Rachel Barrett Davega, 15 November 1864, 30 August 1865.

Public Archives of Canada, Ottawa. Sir John A. Macdonald papers. File 82.

"Report on the French Fact" by Allied Jewish Community Services Special Committee. Montreal. September 1970.

Romalis, Coleman. "The Attitudes of the Montreal Jewish Community Towards French Canadian Nationalism and Separatism." Master's thesis, McGill University, 1967.

Rosenberg, Louis. "The Story of Edenbridge." Jewish Public Library, Montreal. Bronfman Collection of Jewish Canadiana.

———. "Studies in Canadian Jewish Statistics." Jewish Public Library, Montreal. Bronfman Collection of Jewish Canadiana.

Sandler, Bernard J. "The Jews of America and the Settlement of Palestine, 1908–1934: Efforts and Achievements." Ph.D. diss., Bar Ilan University, Israel, 1978.

Seidel, Judith. "The Development and Social Adjustment of the Jewish Community in Montreal." Master's thesis, McGill University, 1939.

Spanish and Portuguese Synagogue (Shearith Israel Congregation). New York, New York. Minutes of the Meetings of the Board of Trustees.

Spanish and Portuguese Synagogue (Shearith Israel Congregation). Montreal. Minutes and papers.

Stock, Frank. "Jewish-Protestant Discontent in Montreal Schools." Jewish Public Library, Montreal. Bronfman Collection of Jewish Canadiana.

Temple Emanu-El, Montreal. Minute Books.

"Toronto Branch Anglo-Jewish Association [Draft] Report for General Meeting Held Sunday, April 19th, 1896." Jewish Public Library, Montreal. Bronfman Collection of Jewish Canadiana.

"Toward a New Consensus." Preliminary Report of the Long Range Planning Committee of the Allied Jewish Community Services. Montreal. August 1982.

Weiss, David. "One Hundred Years of Communal Services: A Brief Overview of the Baron de Hirsch Institute of Montreal." Jewish Public Library, Montreal. Bronfman Collection of Jewish Canadiana.

Newspapers and Periodicals

American Hebrew (New York). 1879–1914.

American Israelite (Cincinnati). 1854–1914.

American Jewish Year Book (Philadelphia). 1899–1986.

American Jews' Annual (Cincinnati). 1884–1896.

Annual Report of the Baron de Hirsch Institute (Montreal). 1892–1914.

Archives Israélites (Paris). 1840–1885.

Bystander (Toronto). 1880–1883; 1889–1890.

Canada Directory (Montreal). 1851; 1857–1858.

Canada Farmers' Sun (London, Ontario). 22 November 1892.

Canada Today (London, England). 1906–1916.

Canadian Annual Review (Toronto). 1902–1914.

Canadian Jewish Archives (Montreal). 1955–1962.

Canadian Jewish Chronicle (Montreal). 1914–1960.

Canadian Jewish Chronicle Review (Montreal). 6 October 1967.

Canadian Jewish News (Toronto). 1975–1982.

Canadian Jewish Outlook (Toronto). 1963–1975.

Canadian *Jewish Times* (Montreal). 1897–1914.

Canadian Jewish Year-Book (Montreal). 1939–1941.

Canadian Zionist (Montreal). 1934–1950.

CCAR Yearbook (Cincinnati). 1890–1914.

Colonist (Victoria). 1 September 1875.

Congrès de la Jeunesse à Québec: Rapport Officiel (Montreal). 1907–1914.

Congressional Globe (Washington, D.C.). 1872.

Croix (Montreal). 1893–1895; 1903–1908.

Croix (Quebec). 1903–1905.

Cultivateur (Montreal). 1893–1906.

Daily Herald (Montreal). 1820–1914.

Daily Mail (Montreal). 1912–1914.

Daily Transcript and Commercial Advertiser (Montreal). 1836–1865.

Daily Witness (Montreal). 1862–1914.

Davar (Tel Aviv). 7 July 1926.

Devoir (Montreal). 1910–1914; 17–18 February 1982; 17 December 1985.

Dominion Annual Register and Review (Toronto). 1878–1886.

Dominion of Canada and Newfoundland Gazetteer and Classified Business Directory (Toronto). 1915.

Etudiant (Montreal). 1911–1915.

European Magazine and London Review (London, England). March 1801.

Financial Statements and Statistics of Attendance, Protestant Board of School Commissioners (Montreal). 1895–1914.

Gazette (Montreal). 1825–1914.

Globe (Toronto). 1860–1914.

Globe and Mail (Toronto). 17, 19 September 1977, 14 May 1980.

Herald (Hamilton). 1904.

Herald (New York). 1858, 1905.

Ha-Ibri (Berlin and New York). 1910–1921.

Ha-Magid (Lyck). 1856–1891; 1893–1903.

Hamelitz (Warsaw). 1860–1904.

Hasman (Warsaw). 1903–1914.

Hayehoody (London, England). 1897–1913.

Ha-Zefirah (St. Petersburg). 1874–1914.

He-Ahdut (Jerusalem). 1912–1913.

Hebrew Standard (New York). 1882–1914.

Jewish Chronicle (London, England). 1841–1914.

Jewish Comment (Baltimore). 1897–1914.

Jewish Messenger (New York). 1857–1902.

Jewish Sabbath Observance Association Report (New York). 1895–1910.

Jewish Sentiment (Atlanta). 1900–1905.

Jewish World (London, England). 1873–1914.

Jewish Year Book (London, England). 1897–1914.

Journal des Trois Rivières (Trois Rivières). 1865–1891.

Keneder odler (Montreal). 1907–1920.

Libre Parole Illustrée (Montreal). 1896.

Lovell's Business and Professional Directory of All Cities, Towns, and Banking Villages in Canada (Montreal). 1851, 1857–58, 1896.

Lovell's Montreal Directory (Montreal). 1842–1914.

Mail and Empire (Toronto). 25 September 1897.

Metropolitan (Montreal). 26 January 1895.

Montreal Board of Trade Souvenir. 1914–1915.

National Council of Jewish Women, Montreal Section Yearbook. 1917.

New York Times. 1858–1954.

Occident and American Jewish Advocate (Philadelphia). 1843–1868.

Official Report of the Debates of the House of Commons of the Dominion of Canada (Ottawa). 1882, 1905, 1906, 1908, 1912, 1928.

Opinion Publique (Montreal). 1870–1883.

Patrie (Montreal). 1878–1914.

Post (Jerusalem). 6 May 1925; 22 January 1982.

Presse (Montreal). 1884–1914.

Proceedings of the Annual Meeting of the Natural History Society of Montreal. 1861–1883.

Public Archives of Canada Annual Report (Ottawa). 1883–1905.

Rapport de l'Administration Centrale au Conseil d'Administration—Jewish Colonization Association (Paris). 1896–1914.

Reform Advocate (Chicago). 1893–1902.

Report of the Proceedings of the Convention of the Federation of Zionist Societies of Canada (Montreal). 1907.

Report of the Superintendent of Immigration, Department of the Interior (Ottawa). 1897–1914.

Standard (Cornwall, Ontario). 5 May 1893.

Star (Montreal). 1869–1914.

Star (Toronto). 28 February, 8, 28 March 1978; 3 November 1982.

True Witness (Montreal). 1885–1910.

Univers Israélite (Paris). 1844–1903.

Vérité (Quebec). 1881–1914.

Viewpoints (Montreal and Toronto). 1969–1986.

Week (Toronto). 1883–1896.

World (Toronto). 1880–1914.

Zeitschrift für Demographie und Statistik der Juden (Berlin). 1905–1914.

Printed Memoirs and Letters

Aharonson, Aharon. *Yoman* [Hebrew]. Edited by Yoram Efrati. Tel Aviv, 1970.

Ajnhorn, David. *Fon Berlin biz San Francisco* [Yiddish]. Warsaw, 1930.

Bar-David, Molly Lyons. *My Promised Land.* New York, 1953.

Becker, Jacob Leib. *Derzeilungen un Zichroinos* [Yiddish]. Montreal, 1956.

Benjamin, [I.J.]. *Three Years in America.* Translated by Charles Reznikoff. 2 vols. Philadelphia, 1956.

Berlin, Meir. *Mi-Volozhin ad Yerushalayim* [Hebrew]. 2 vols. Tel Aviv, 1940.

Brainin, Reuben. *Kol Kitvei Reuven ben Mordecai Brainin* [Hebrew]. 3 vols. New York, 1940.

Burnfield, George. *Voices from the Orient.* Toronto, 1884.

Cimon, Henri. *Aux Vieux Pays.* 3d ed. Montreal, 1917.

Dawson, Owen. *My Story of the Boys' Farm at Shawbridge.* N.p., 1952.

Dawson, William. *Fifty Years of Work in Canada.* London and Edinburgh, 1901.

De Ghyvelde, Frédéric. *Album de Terre Sainte.* Quebec, 1905.

Delaplanche, J.F.C. *Le Pèlerin de Terre Sainte.* Quebec, 1887.

De Sola, Abraham. *Biography of David Aaron De Sola.* Philadelphia, 5624 [1864].

Dunkelman, Ben. *Dual Allegiance.* Toronto, 1976.

Dupuis, J[ean] F[rançois]. *Rome et Jérusalem.* Quebec, 1894.

The Echo. Rocanville, Saskatchewan, 1964.

Eisen, David. *Diary of a Medical Student.* Toronto, 1974.

Emard, J. M. *Souvenirs d'un Voyage en Terre Sainte.* Montreal, 1884.

Forsyth, J. Bell [A Canadian]. *A Few Months in the East; or, A Glimpse of the Red, the Dead, and the Black Seas*. Quebec, 1861.

Freiman, Lawrence. *Don't Fall off the Rocking Horse*. Toronto, 1978.

Freshman, Charles. *The Autobiography of the Rev. Charles Freshman*. Toronto, 1868.

Frank, Solomon, Rabbi emeritus, Spanish and Portuguese Synagogue, Montreal. Interview, 28 July 1973.

Golden Jubilee Souvenir Book. Montreal, 1957.

Gompers, Samuel. *Seventy Years of Life and Labor*. 2 vols. New York, 1967.

Haultain, Arnold, ed. *A Selection from Goldwin Smith's Correspondence*. Toronto, n.d.

Heaps, Leo. *The Rebel in the House*. London, 1970.

Henry, Alexander. *Travels and Adventures in Canada and the Indian Territory Between the Years 1760 and 1776*. New York, 1809.

Hoffer, Clara, and F. H. Kahn. *Land of Hope*. Saskatoon, 1960.

Hoffer, Israel. "Recollections and Reminiscences." *Saskatchewan History* 5 (winter 1952): 28–32.

Jarvis, Thomas Stirson. *Letters from East Longitudes*. Toronto, 1875.

Jubilee Book. [Montreal], 1937.

Kinglake, Alex[ander] Wm. *Eöthen; or, Traces of Travel*. Toronto, 1871.

L'archevêque, Jos.-A. *Vers la Terre-Sainte*. Montreal, 1911.

Lazaron, Anita de Sola. *De Sola Odyssey*. Richmond, Virginia, 1966.

Leonoff, Cyril Edel. *Wapella Farm Settlement*. [Winnipeg], 1972.

Lewin-Epstein, Eliyyahu Ze'ev Halevi. *Zikhronotai* [Hebrew]. Tel Aviv, 5692 [1932].

Lewis, David. *The Good Fight: Political Memoirs, 1909–1958*. Toronto, 1981.

Lisitzky, Ephraim E. *In the Grip of Crosscurrents*. Translated by Moshe Kohn and Jacob Sloan. New York, 1959.

McAdam, J. [Captain "Mac"]. *Canada: The Country, its People, Religions, Politics, Rulers, and its Apparent Future*. Montreal, 1882.

Masliansky, Zvi Hirsch. *Kitvei Masliansky* [Hebrew]. 3 vols. New York, 1929.

Medres, I. *Montreal fon Nechten* [Yiddish]. Montreal, 1947.

Philipson, David, ed. *Letters of Rebecca Gratz*. Philadelphia, 1929.

Phillips, Nathan. *Mayor of All the People*. Toronto and Montreal, 1967.

Plaut, W. Gunther. *Unfinished Business*. Toronto, 1981.

Plotkin, Abe L. *Struggle for Justice*. New York, 1960.

Pride of Israel Golden Jubilee. Toronto, 1955.

Provancher, Léon. *De Québec à Jérusalem*. Quebec, 1884.

Rhinewine, Abraham. *Looking Back a Century*. Toronto, 1932.

Rose, Arnold, Toronto businessman. Interview, 11 December 1974.

Ruppin, Arthur. *Pirkei Hayyai* [Hebrew]. 3 vols. Tel Aviv, 1968.

R[ural] M[unicipality] of Willow Creek No. 458 Jubilee Year, 1912–1962. N.p., n.d.

Samuel, Maurice. *Little Did I Know*. New York, 1963.

Samuel, Sigmund. *In Return*. Toronto, 1963.

Sansom, Joseph. *Travels in Lower Canada*. London, 1820.

Scheuer, Edmund. "Reminiscences of Canadian Jewry." Appended to Brodey, Arthur. "Political and Civil Status of the Jews in Canada." Rabbi and Master's thesis, Jewish Institute of Religion, 1933.

Schiff, Meilech. "Lost Boryslaw." *Jewish Dialog*. Summer 1977.

Skelton, Oscar Douglas. *Life and Letters of Sir Wilfrid Laurier*. 2 vols. Toronto, 1965.

Slousch, Nahum. *Voyage aux Etats-Unis; au Canada; et à l'Exposition de Panama*. Thouars, 1916.

Souvenir Journal Dedicated to Rabbi Hirsch Cohen. Montreal, 1940.

Thirty-fifth Jubilee Journal of the Montreal Bakers' Union, Local 115 . [Montreal], 1938.

Trebitsch-Lincoln, J. [Ignatius] T. *The Autobiography of an Adventurer*. London, 1931.

Willinsky, A[braham] I. *A Doctor's Memoirs.* Toronto, 1960.
Wolofsky, H[irsch]. *Journey of My Life.* Montreal, 1945.
Zipper, Jacob, ed. *Leiser Zucker Gedenkbuch* [Yiddish]. Montreal, 1968.
Zuckerman, Baruch. *Zichroinos* [Yiddish]. New York, 1962.

Printed Sources Contemporaneous with the Study

BOOKS AND PAMPHLETS

Abbott, G[eorge] F[rederick]. *Israel in Europe.* London, 1907 .
Anderson, J. T. M. *The Education of the New Canadians.* London and Toronto, 1918.
Ames, Herbert Brown. *The City Below the Hill.* repr. Toronto and Buffalo, 1972.
Ascher, Isidore G. *Voices from the Hearth.* Montreal, 1863.
Atherton, William Henry. *Montreal from 1535 to 1914.* 3 vols. Montreal, 1914.
Beaumont, [J. W.]. *Judea for the Jews.* London, Ontario, and Toronto, 1876.
Becket, Hugh W. *The Montreal Snow Shoe Club: Its History and Record.* Montreal, 1882.
Bernheimer, Charles S., ed. *The Russian Jew in the United States.* Philadelphia, 1905.
Bevis Marks Records. 3 vols. London, 1973.
The Book of Psalms translated out of the original Hebrew. Toronto, 1851.
Borthwick, John Douglas. *The Harp of Canaan.* 2d ed. Montreal, 1871.
———. *Montreal History and Gazetteer.* Montreal, 1892.
Bosworth, Newton, ed. *Hochelaga Depicta: The Early History and Present State of the City and Island of Montreal.* Montreal, 1839.
Bourassa, Henri. *Great Britain and Canada.* Montreal, 1901.
[Brothers, Richard]. *A Revealed Knowledge of the Prophecies and Times.* London, 1794.
Cahan, Abraham. *Historia fun di Fereinigte Shtaaten* [Yiddish]. 2 vols. New York, 1912.
Le Canada et la France. Montreal, [1911].
The Canadian Biographical Dictionary and Portrait Gallery of Eminent and Self-Made Men. Chicago, New York, and Toronto, 1881.
Carrel, Frank, and Louis Feiczwicz, comps. and eds. *The Quebec Tercentenary Commemorative History.* Quebec, 1908.
Chambers, Ernest J. *The Book of Canada.* Montreal and Toronto, 1904.
Chauveau, Pierre Joseph Olivier. *Charles Guérin.* Montreal, 1846–54.
Cochrane, William, ed. *Men of Canada; or, Success by Example.* 5 vols. Brantford, Ontario, 1891–96.
Consecration of the Jewish Synagogue, Richmond Street, Toronto, Canada. New York, 1876.
Cooper, John A., ed. *Men of Canada.* Montreal and Toronto, 1901–02.
Cornish, George A. *Cyclopaedia of Methodism in Canada.* Toronto and Halifax, 1881.
Cunningham, W[illiam]. *Alien Immigrants to England.* London, 1897.
Daly, Charles P. *The Settlement of the Jews in North America.* New York, 1893.
Dawson, J. William. *Egypt and Syria.* London, 1885.
———. *Nature and the Bible.* New York, 1875.
Dawson, Samuel E. *The Prose Writers of Canada.* Montreal, 1901.
Debré, Moses. *The Image of the Jew in French Literature from 1800 to 1908.* Translated by Gertrude Hirschler. New York, 1970.
De Brumath, A. Leblond. *Guide de Montréal et de Ses Environs.* Montreal, 1861.
De Sola, Abraham, ed. and rev. *The Form of Prayers According to the Custom of the Spanish and Portuguese Jews.* 6 vols. Philadelphia, 5638 [1878].
———. *The Sanatory Institutions of the Hebrews.* Montreal, 1861.
———. *Valedictory Address to the Graduates in Arts of the University of McGill College.* Montreal, 1864.

De Sola, Abraham, and Jacques J. Lyons. *A Jewish Calendar for Fifty Years.* Montreal, 5614 [1854].

De Sola, Meldola. *The Duty of Orthodox Congregations: A Sermon Preached at Staten Island, New York, Tebeth 23d, 5648* [1888]. N.p., n.d.

———. *Jewish Ministers?* [New York], 1905.

———. *Zionism: Sermon Delivered in the Spanish and Portuguese Synagogue, Montreal, on the Seventh Day of Passover 5660.* N.p., 5660 [1900].

Dewart, Edward Hartley, ed. *Selections from Canadian Poets.* Montreal, 1864.

Edelstein, Hyman. *Canadian Lyrics and Other Poems.* Toronto, 1916.

———. *From Judean Vineyards.* Montreal, 1914.

———. *Mordecai Krechtz the Independent Jew.* Montreal, n.d.

Ellinger, Moritz. *Hebrew Emigrant Aid Society of the United States Report.* New York, 1882.

Emanuel, Charles H. L. *A Century and a Half of Jewish History: Extracted from the Minute Books of the London Committee of Deputies of the British Jews.* London, 1910.

Evans-Gordon, W[illiam]. *The Alien Immigrant.* London, 1903.

Fourth Book of Lessons for the Use of Schools. Montreal, 1845.

Frederic, Harold. *The New Exodus.* London, 1892.

Freshman, C[harles]. *The Jews and the Israelites.* Toronto, 1870.

Garneau, François-Xavier. *Histoire du Canada.* 9 vols. 8th ed. Montreal, 1944–46.

———. *History of Canada.* 2 vols. Translated by Andrew Bell. Montreal, 1862.

Ginzburg, Asher [Ahad Ha-Am]. *Selected Essays.* Translated by Leon Simon. Philadelphia, 1912.

Gottlieb, Sch[muel] N. *Oholei-Shem* [Hebrew]. Pinsk, 1912.

Handbook of Canada. Toronto, 1897.

Harkavy, Alexander. *Compendium of Mathematical, Physical, and Political Geography* [Yiddish]. 2 vols. New York, 1911.

Hart, Adolphus M. *History of the Valley of the Mississippi.* Cincinnati, 1853.

———. [Hampden]. *The Impending Crisis.* New York, 1855.

———. *The Political State and Condition of Her Majesty's Protestant Subjects in the Province of Quebec (Since Confederation).* Toronto, 1871.

Hart, Gerald E. *The Fall of New France.* Montreal, 1888.

———. *The Quebec Act 1774.* Montreal, 1891.

Hart, Lewis A. *A Jewish Reply to Christian Evangelists.* New York, 1906.

Hémon, Louis. *Maria Chapdelaine.* Translated by W. H. Blake. Toronto, 1978 (originally published, 1914).

Herzl, Theodor. *The Complete Diaries.* 5 vols. Edited by Raphael Patai. New York and London, 1960.

Horowitz, Aharon Yehudah Leib. *Romania ve-America* [Hebrew]. Berlin, 1874.

The House of Nordheimer. [Toronto, 1903].

Howlett, Thomas Rosling. *Anglo-Israel and the Jewish Problem.* Philadelphia, 1892.

Huot, Antonio. *La Question Juive.* Quebec, 1914.

Inauguration of Montreal's Monument to the Late Right Hon. Sir John Macdonald, G.C.B. N.p., 1895.

Irving, L. Homfray. *Officers of British Forces in Canada During the War of 1812–15.* Welland, Ontario, 1908

Jacobs, Joseph. *Studies in Jewish Statistics.* London, 1891.

Jewish Encyclopedia. 12 vols. 1901–1906. S.v. "Canada," "De Sola," "Montreal." by Clarence I. De Sola.

Joseph, Samuel. *Jewish Immigration to the United States from 1881 to 1910.* repr. New York, 1967.

Kaplan, Bernard M. *Miriam the Prophetess.* Montreal, 1901.

————. *The Origin and Goal of Zionism.* Montreal, 1901.

Kaplun-Kogan, Wlad. W. *Die jüdischen Wanderbewegungen in den neuesten Zeit (1881– 1914).* Bonn am Rhine, 1919.

Karpeles, Gustav. *Jews and Judaism in the Nineteenth Century.* Philadelphia, 1905.

Kennedy, Howard Angus. *New Canada and the New Canadians.* London, 1907.

Lazarus, Emma. *The Dance of Death and Other Poems.* New York, 1882.

Leroy-Beaulieu, Anatole. *Israel Among the Nations.* London, 1895.

Leven, N[arcisse]. *Cinquante ans d'histoire de l'Alliance Israélite Universelle (1860–1910).* 2 vols. Paris, 1911, 1920.

Lighthall, W[illiam] D[ouw]. *Montreal After 250 Years.* Montreal, 1892.

Lindsey, Charles. *Rome in Canada.* Toronto, 1877.

Lovell's Historic Report of the Census of Montreal. Montreal, 1891.

Magrath, C. A. *Canada's Growth and Some Problems Affecting It.* Ottawa, 1910.

Moffett, Samuel E. *The Americanization of Canada.* repr. Toronto and Buffalo, 1972.

Monk, Henry Wentworth. *The Restoration of Judah and Israel: A Simple Interpretation of the Revelation together with Three Lectures Lately Delivered in Canada and the United States.* 2d ed. London, [1858?].

Montreal. Montreal, [1903].

Montreal Business Sketches. Montreal, 1865.

Morais, Henry Samuel. *Eminent Israelites of the Nineteenth Century.* Philadelphia, 1880.

Morgan, Henry J. *Bibliotheca Canadensis.* repr. Detroit, 1968.

————. ed. *The Canadian Men and Women of the Time.* Toronto, 1898, 1912.

Myers, E[manuel] M[oses]. *The Centurial: A Jewish Calendar for One Hundred Years.* New York, 1901.

Pennell, Joseph. *The Jew at Home.* London, 1892.

Phillips, Samuel G., ed. *The Canadian Methodist Pulpit.* Toronto, 1875.

Poole, W[illiam] H. *Anglo-Israel in Nine Lectures.* Toronto, [1882?].

Proceedings of the Conference of Hebrew Emigrant Aid Societies and Auxiliary Committees, New York, June 4th, 1882. New York, 1882.

Provancher, Léon, and Frédéric de Ghyvelde. *Le Chemin de la croix à Jérusalem.* Quebec, 1882.

Raisin, Max. *Toledot Ha-Yehudim be-America* [Hebrew]. Warsaw, 1902.

Rexford, Elson I., preparer. *Manual of the School Law and Regulations of the Province of Quebec.* rev. ed. Montreal, 1895.

Rose, George Maclean, ed. *A Cyclopedia of Canadian Biography.* 1st ser. and 2d ser. Toronto, 1886, 1888.

Ross, Mrs. Alexander (Mary Ellen). *The Wreck of the White Bear, East Indiaman.* 2 vols. Montreal, 1870.

————. *The Legend of the Holy Stone.* Montreal, 1878.

Ruppin, Arthur. *The Jews of To-day.* Translated by Margery Bentwich. New York, 1913.

Russell, C[yril], and H. S. Lewis. *The Jew in London.* London, 1900.

Ryan, Carroll. *Songs of a Wanderer.* Ottawa, 1867.

————. *Poems, Songs, Ballads.* Montreal, 1903.

Sandham, Alfred. *Ville-Marie or, Sketches of Montreal, Past and Present.* Montreal, 1870.

Schulmann, Kalman. *Mosdei Eretz* [Hebrew]. 10 vols. Vilna, 1871–77.

Siegfried, André. *The Race Question in Canada.* Translated by Eveleigh Nash. New York, 1907.

Smith, William George. *A Study in Canadian Immigration.* Toronto, 1920.

Sokolow, Nahum. *History of Zionism, 1600–1918.* repr. New York, 1969.

Stenographisches Protokoll der Verhandlungen des IV, Zionisten Congresses in London 13 . . 14 . . 15 . . und 16, August 1900. Vienna, 1900.

Steuart, John A. *The Hebrew.* Toronto, 1903.

Sulte, Benjamin. *Pages d'Histoire du Canada*. Montreal, 1891.
Talbot, Thomas. *The Hebrews at Home*. Montreal, 1874.
Tchernowitz, S[amuel]. *B'nei Moshe u-Tekufatam* [Hebrew]. Warsaw, 1914.
Terrill, Fred'k Wm. *A Chronology of Montreal and of Canada from A.D. 1752 to A.D. 1893.* Montreal, 1893.
Vichtige Fragen un Richtige Antworten [Yiddish]. Winnipeg, [1913].
Weir, Arthur, ed. *Montreal Illustrated*. Montreal, 1894.
Weiss, Louis. *Some Burning Questions*. Toronto, 1905.
White, Arnold. *The Modern Jew*. London, 1899.
Who's Who and Why. Toronto, 1916, 1920.
Wiernik, Peter. *History of the Jews in America*. New York, 1912.
Wightman, F. A. *Our Canadian Heritage*. Toronto, 1905.
Wolf, Lucien. *Essays in Jewish History*. London, 1934.
Woodsworth, J[ames] S. *Strangers Within Our Gates*. Toronto, 1909.
———. *My Neighbor*. 2d ed. Toronto, 1913.
Workman, George Coulson. *The Old Testament Vindicated as Christianity's Foundation Stone*. Toronto, 1898.
The Young Men's Hebrew Benevolent Society of Montreal. Montreal, 1872.

ARTICLES

Adler, Hermann. "Recent Phases of Judaeophobia." *The Nineteenth Century,* December 1881.
"Anglo-Israel; or, the Saxon Race Proved to Be the Lost Ten Tribes." *Dominion Illustrated,* 1 March 1890.
Asselin, Olivar. "The Jews in Montreal." *The Canadian Century,* 16 September 1911.
"Biographical Sketches of Rabbis and Cantors Officiating in the United States." *American Jewish Year Book,* 1903.
Birnbaum, S. J. "The History of the Jews in Toronto." Canadian *Jewish Times,* 29 November 1912, 6 December 1912, 20 December 1912, 3 January 1913, 10 January 1913, 24 January 1913, 14 February 1913, 14 March 1913.
Bridle, Augustus. "The Drama of the Ward." *The Canadian Magazine,* November 1909.
Bruce, Herbert A. "Our Heritage of Tolerance." In *Our Heritage and Other Addresses.* By Herbert A. Bruce. Toronto, 1934.
Bruchési, Jean. "Lettres d'un Exile (1843–1845)." *Les Cahiers des Dix* 17 (1952): 103–135.
Canada: An Encyclopedia. 1898–1900. S. v. "Historical Sketch of the Jews of Canada." By A[braham] Lazarus.
Chartier, C. Edmond. "l'A.C.J.C. à Sherbrooke." *Revue Canadienne* 10 n.s. (October 1912): 313–18.
Conn, J[ames] R. "Immigration." *Queen's Quarterly* 8 (October 1900): 117–31.
Corré, Alan D., comp. "The Record Book of the Reverend Jacob Raphael Cohen." *American Jewish Historical Quarterly* 59 (December 1969): 23–82.
Coté, Stanislas. "Nos Jeunes Gens." *Revue Canadienne* 5 (May 1883): 321–31.
De Hirsch, Maurice. "My Views on Philanthropy." *North American Review,* July 1891.
De Montigny, B. A. T. "Les Ecoles Séparées." *Revue Canadienne* 29 (October, November 1893): 600–05, 671–79.
Encyclopaedia of Religion and Ethics. 1900. S.v. "Anglo-Israelism." By Albert M. Hyamson.
Farly, L.-C. "La Question Juive." *Le Congrès de la Jeunesse à Québec: Rapport Officiel,* 1908.
Friedenwald, Herbert. "Jews Mentioned in the Journal of the Continental Congress." *Publications of the American Jewish Historical Society* 1 (1893): 65–89.

Goldstein, N. W. "Die jüdische Bevölkerung Kanadas." *Zeitschrift für Demographie und Statistik der Juden* 5 (July 1909): 97–103.

Groulx, Lionel. "La jeunesse canadienne-française." *Revue Canadienne* 8 n.s. (October 1911): 291–300.

Hyacinthe, R. P. "De la lutte entre la lettre et l'esprit dans l'église des Juifs." *L'Echo de la France,* April 1869.

———. "L'église des Juifs dans son rapport avec l'église des Chrétiens." *L'Echo de la France,* April 1869.

Joseph, Andrew C. "The Settlement of the Jews in Canada." *Publications of the American Jewish Historical Society* 13 (1905): 117–20.

"Literary Notices." *New Dominion Monthly,* June, December 1876.

Price, Julius J. "Proceedings Relating to the Expulsion of Ezekiel Hart from the House of Assembly of Lower Canada." *Publications of the American Jewish Historical Society* 23 (1915): 43–53.

———. "Unpublished Canadian State Papers Relating to Benjamin Hart." *Publications of the American Jewish Historical Society* 23 (1915): 137–40.

Roy, Pierre-Georges. "L'émancipation politique des Juifs au Canada." *Le Bulletin des Recherches Historiques* 11 (March 1905): 89–91.

Scott, J. McP[hail]. "The Jew in North America." In *World Wide Evangelization.* New York, 1902.

"The Shame of Canada," broadside, Montreal, March 1900.

Smith, Goldwin. "The Jewish Question." *The Nineteenth Century,* October 1881.

Sulte, Benjamin. "La Maison Hart." *Le Monde Illustré,* 11 March 1893, 18 March 1893.

Tassé, Joseph. "Droits Politiques des Juifs en Canada." *Revue Canadienne* 7 (June 1870): 407–25.

Some Later Works Relating Directly to Canadian Jews

BOOKS AND PAMPHLETS

Abella, Irving and Harold Troper. *None Is Too Many: Canada and the Jews of Europe, 1933–1948.* Toronto, 1982.

Abrams, Alan. *Why Windsor?* Windsor, 1981.

Anctil, Pierre, and Gary Caldwell, eds. *Juifs et réalités juives au Québec.* Quebec, 1984.

Audet, Louis-Philippe. *Histoire du Conseil de l'Instruction Publique de la Province de Québec, 1856–1964.* Montreal, 1964.

Baron de Hirsch Institute. N.p., n.d.

Le Baron Maurice de Hirsch et la Jewish Colonizaton Association. Paris, [1931].

Belkin, Simon. *Through Narrow Gates.* Montreal, 1966.

Bercuson, David. *Canada and the Birth of Israel.* Toronto, 1985.

Betcherman, Lita-Rose. *The Swastika and the Maple Leaf.* Toronto, 1975.

Caiserman, H[ananiah] M[eir]. *Two Canadian Personalities.* Montreal, 1948.

Canadian Jewish Congress: Fifty Years of Service. Montreal, 1970.

Cashman, Tony. *Abraham Cristoll.* [Edmonton, 1963].

Chiel, Arthur A. *The Jewish Experience in Early Manitoba.* Winnipeg, 1955.

———. *The Jews in Manitoba.* Toronto, 1961.

Clark, Gerald. *Montreal: The New Cité.* Toronto, 1982.

Cohen, Zvi, ed. *Canadian Jewry: Prominent Jews of Canada.* Toronto, 1933.

Crestohl, Leon. *The Jewish School Problem in Quebec.* [Montreal? 1926?].

Cukier, Golda. *Canadian Jewish Periodicals.* Montreal, 1969.

Davies, Raymond Arthur. *Printed Jewish Canadiana, 1685–1900.* Montreal, 1955.

De Sola Pool, David and Tamar. *An Old Faith in the New World.* New York, 1955.

Douville, Raymond. *Aaron Hart.* Trois Rivières, 1938.

The Emanu-El Story. [Montreal], 1960.

England, Robert. *The Central European Immigrant in Canada.* Toronto, 1929.

Feinstein, Marnin. *American Zionism, 1884–1904.* New York, 1965.

Fifty Years of Community Service Highlights. Montreal, 1967.

Figler, Bernard. *Lillian and Archie Freiman.* Montreal, 1961.

———. *Louis Fitch, Q. C.* Ottawa, 1968.

———. *Rabbi Dr. Herman Abramowitz, Lazarus Cohen, Lyon Cohen.* Ottawa, 1968.

———. *Sam Jacobs, Member of Parliament.* 2d ed. Ottawa, 1970.

Figler, Bernard, and David Rome. *The H. M. Caiserman Book.* Montreal, 1962.

Frank, Solomon. *Two Centuries in the Life of a Synagogue.* N.p., n.d.

Gibbon, John Murray. *Canadian Mosaic.* Toronto, 1938.

Goodman, Paul. *Bevis Marks in History.* London, 1934.

Gottesman, Eli, comp. *Canadian Jewish Reference Book and Directory.* Montreal, 1963.

Grossman, Vladimir. *The Soil's Calling.* Montreal, 1938.

Gutkin, Harry. *Journey Into Our Heritage.* Toronto, 1980.

Hamilton, Ross, ed. *Prominent Men of Canada, 1931–32.* Montreal, 1932.

Hart, Arthur Daniel, ed. *The Jew in Canada.* Toronto and Montreal, 1926.

Hertz, Joseph H. *The First Pastoral Tour to the Jewish Communities of the British Overseas Dominions.* London, 1924.

A History of Beth Jacob Congregation. [Hamilton], 1969.

History of the Corporation of Spanish and Portuguese Jews of Montreal, Canada. Montreal, 1918.

Horowitz, Aron. *Striking Roots.* Oakville, Ontario, 1979.

Hughes, Everett Cherrington. *French Canada in Transition.* Chicago, 1943.

Hyamson, Albert M. *Jews' College, London, 1855–1955.* London, 1955.

———. *The Sephardim of England.* London, 1951.

Hyman, Paula. *From Dreyfus to Vichy.* New York, 1979.

Israelite Press: The Hundredth Anniversary Souvenir of Jewish Emancipation in Canada and the Fiftieth Anniversary of the Jew in the West, 1832–1932. Winnipeg, 1932.

Jewish Daily Eagle Centennial Jubilee Edition. Montreal, 1932.

Joseph, Samuel. *History of the Baron de Hirsch Fund.* N.p., 1935.

Kage, Joseph. *The Dynamics of Economic Adjustment of Canadian Jewry: A Historical Review.* Montreal, 1970.

———. *With Faith and Thanksgiving.* Montreal, 1962.

Kallen, Evelyn. *Spanning the Generations.* Don Mills, Ontario, 1977.

Katz, Irving. *The "Beth-El" Story: Jews in Michigan Before 1850.* Detroit, 1955.

Kay, Zachariah. *Canada and Palestine.* Jerusalem, 1978.

Korn, Bertram Wallace. *The American Reaction to the Mortara Case, 1858–1859.* Cincinnati, 1957.

Lambert, Richard S. *For the Time Is at Hand.* London, [1947].

Lande, Lawrence M., comp. and ed. *Montefiore Club.* [Montreal], 1955.

Leonoff, Cyril Edel. *The Architecture of Jewish Settlements in the Prairies.* N.p., 1975.

———. *Pioneers, Pedlars, and Prayer Shawls.* Victoria, 1978.

Levitt, Joseph. *Henri Bourassa and the Golden Calf.* Ottawa, 1969.

Levitt, Sheldon, Lynn Milstone, and Sidney Tenenbaum. *Treasures of a People.* Toronto, 1985.

MacLennan, Hugh. *Two Solitudes.* Toronto, 1945.

Marcus, Jacob Rader. *Early American Jewry.* 2 vols. Philadelphia, 1951, 1953.

Marrus, Michael. *The Politics of Assimilation.* Oxford, 1971.

Maynard, Fredelle Bruser. *Raisins and Almonds.* Toronto, 1965.

Meyer, Isidore S., ed. *The American Jew in the Civil War*. Philadelphia, 1961.

Newman, Peter C. *Bronfman Dynasty*. Toronto, 1978.

Paris, Erna. *Jews: An Account of Their Experience in Canada*. Toronto, 1980.

Rasminsky, Louis, ed. *Hadassah Jubilee*. [Toronto, 1928].

Reisen, Zalman. *Leksikon fun der Yiddisher Literatur, Presse un Philologia* [Yiddish]. 4 vols. Vilna, 1929.

Report of the Royal Commission on Bilingualism and Biculturalism. Book 4. The Cultural Contribution of the Other Ethnic Groups. Ottawa, 1969.

Report of the Special Commission on Education of the Province of Quebec. Quebec, 1925.

Rexford, Elson I. *Our Educational Problem: The Jewish Population and the Protestant Schools*. Montreal, [1924?].

Rhinewine, Abraham. *Canada: Ihr Geschichte un Entwicklung* [Yiddish]. Toronto, 1923.

Richler, Mordecai. *The Street*. London, 1971.

Rome, David. *Clouds in the Thirties,* 4 vols. Montreal, 1977.

———. comp. and ed. *Early Documents on the Canadian Jewish Congress, 1914–1921*. Montreal, 1974.

———. *The Early Jewish Presence in Canada: A Booklover's Ramble Through Jewish Canadiana*. Montreal, 1971.

———. *The First Two Years*. Montreal, 1942.

———. comp. *Jews in Canadian Literature: A Bibliography to 1964*. 2 vols. Montreal, 1964.

———. *On the Jewish School Question in Montreal, 1903–1931*. Montreal, 1975.

———. *Recent Canadian Jewish Authors and La Langue Française*. Montreal, 1970.

———. comp. *A Selected Bibliography of Jewish Canadiana*. Montreal, 1959.

Rome, David, Judith Nefsky, and Paule Obermeir. *Les Juifs du Québec: bibliographie rétrospective annotée*. Quebec, 1981.

Rose, Albert, ed. *A People and Its Faith*. Toronto, 1959.

Rosenberg, Louis. *Canada's Jewish Community: A Brief Survey of Its History, Growth, and Characteristics*. Canadian Jewish Communities Series: Canadian Jewish Population Studies 7. Montreal, n.d.

———. *Canada's Jews*. Montreal, 1939.

———. *Changes in the Geographical Distribution of the Jewish Population of Metropolitan Montreal in the Decennial Periods, 1901–1961*. Research Papers: Series A. Montreal, 1966.

———. *A Gazetteer of Jewish Communities in Canada Showing the Jewish Population in Cities, Towns, and Villages in Canada in the Census Years, 1851–1951*. Canadian Jewish Communities Series: Canadian Jewish Population Studies. Montreal, n.d.

———. *Growth and Change in the Distribution of the Jewish Population of Montreal*. Canadian Jewish Communities Series: Jewish Population Studies: vol. 1, no. 4. Montreal, 1955.

———. *Jewish Children in the Protestant Schools of Greater Montreal in the Period from 1878 to 1958*. Research Papers: Series E, no. 1. Montreal, 1959.

———. *The Jewish Population of Canada: A Statistical Summary from 1851–1941*. Canadian Jewish Communities Series: Canadian Jewish Population Studies. Montreal, n.d.

———. *Language and Mother Tongue of Jews in Canada*. Population Characteristics Series: Canadian Jewish Population Studies. Montreal, 1957.

———. *Population Characteristics of the Jewish Community of Montreal*. Canadian Jewish Population Studies. Montreal, 1956.

Rosenberg, Stuart E. *The Jewish Community in Canada*. 2 vols. Toronto, 1971.

Rosenbloom, Joseph R. *A Biographical Dictionary of Early American Jews*. [Lexington, Kentucky], n.d.

Roth, Cecil. *The Nephew of the Almighty*. London, 1933.

Rowley, Owsley Robert. *The Anglican Episcopate of Canada and Newfoundland.* Milwaukee, 1928.

Roy, Raoul. *Lettre aux Juifs de Montréal.* Montreal, 1979.

Rumilly, Robert. *Histoire de la Province de Québec.* Vol. 13. Montreal, 1943.

Sack, Benjamin G. *History of the Jews in Canada.* Translated by Ralph Novek. Montreal, 1965.

S.-Louis-du-Sacré-Coeur, B. *Un Lis Fleurit Entre les Epines.* Montreal, 1955.

Schull, Joseph. *Laurier.* Toronto, 1966.

Sclick, Abel, ed. *History of B'nai B'rith in Eastern Canada.* Toronto, 1964.

Shaffir, William. *Life in a Religious Community.* Toronto, 1974.

Silcox, Claris, and Galen M. Fisher. *Catholics, Jews, and Protestants.* New York and London, 1934.

Simons, John, ed. *Who's Who in American Jewry.* Vol. 3. New York, 1938–39.

Sissons, C[harles] B[ruce]. *Church and State in Canadian Education.* Toronto, 1959.

Speisman, Stephen. *The Jews of Toronto: A History to 1937.* Toronto, 1979.

Statistical Tables on Languages Spoken by Jews and Other Ethnic Groups According to Census Statistics, 1931–1951. N.p., n.d.

Stern, Malcolm H., comp. *Americans of Jewish Descent.* Cincinnati, 1960.

Swiss, Irwin A., and H. Norman Shoop. *Rabbi Aaron M. Ashinsky.* Pittsburgh, 1935.

Tcherikower, Elias. *The Early Jewish Labor Movement in the United States.* Translated and revised by Aaron Antonovsky. New York, 1961.

Teboul, Victor, *Mythe et images du Juif au Québec.* Montreal, 1977.

Upsilon Chapter of Zeta Beta Tau, 1913–1923: A History. Montreal, 1923.

Vaugeois, Denis. *Les Juifs et la Nouvelle France.* Trois Rivières, 1968.

Vineberg, Ethel. *The History of the National Council of Jewish Women of Canada.* Montreal, 1967.

The Vision and Understanding of a Man. [Montreal, 1954].

Wallace, W. Stewart, comp. *The Dictionary of Canadian Biography.* Toronto, 1926.

Waller, Harold M. *The Canadian Jewish Community: A National Perspective.* Jerusalem and Philadelphia, 1977.

Warschauer, Heinz. *The Story of Holy Blossom Temple.* Toronto, 1956.

Waterman, Esther, ed. *Golden Jubilee: Canadian Hadassah-WIZO, 1917–1967.* Montreal, 1967.

Weinfeld, Morton, William Shaffir, and Irwin Cotler. *The Canadian Jewish Mosaic.* Toronto, 1981.

Women of Canada. Montreal, 1930.

Woodley, E. C. *The House of Joseph in the Life of Quebec.* Quebec, 1946.

The YM-YWHA Beacon Dedication Issue. [Montreal], 1929, 1950.

ARTICLES

Abramowitz, Herman. "Samuel William Jacobs." *American Jewish Year Book,* 1939.

Arnold, A[braham] J. "Inside Canada: The Role of the Jews in the Opening of the West." *Pioneer Woman* (February, March 1969).

Becker, Lavy M., and Louis Rosenberg. "Jewish Education in Montreal." *Jewish Education* (winter-spring 1950–51).

Bennett, A. B. "The Jew in Canada: A Reply." *The Canadian Forum* (May, 1934).

Blaustein, Esther I., Rachel A. Esar, and Evelyn Miller, "Spanish and Portuguese Synagogue (Shearith Israel), Montreal, 1768–1968." The Jewish Historical Society of England *Transactions* 23 (1971): 111–142.

Bloomfield-Schachter, Evelyn and Jean Claude Lasry. "Jewish Intermarriage in Montreal." *Jewish Social Studies* 37 (summer-fall 1975).

Bouchard. T.-Damien. "Climbing the Hill." *Le Haut Parleur,* July 26, 1952.

Boyaner, Eli. "The Settlement and Development of the Jewish Community of Saint John, N.B." *Jubilee Edition of the Jewish Daily Eagle,* 1957.

Brogan, Denis. "Twentieth Century Huguenots: Jews and the English Establishment." London *Jewish Chronicle,* 9 September 1966.

Brown, Michael. "The American Connection of Canadian Jews." *AJS* (Association for Jewish Studies) *Review* 3 (1978): 21–77.

———. "The Americanization of Canadian Zionism," in *Contemporary Jewry: Studies in Honor of Moshe Davis.* ed. Geoffrey Wigoder. Jerusalem, 1984. pp. 129–58.

———. "The Beginnings of Reform Judaism in Canada." *Jewish Social Studies* 34 (October 1972): 322–42.

———. "Divergent Paths: Early Zionism in Canada and the United States." *Jewish Social Studies* 44 (Spring 1982): 159–83.

———. "The Empire's Best Known Jew and Little Known Jewry," in *Community and the Individual, Essays in Honor of Lavy M. Becker,* eds. Ronald S. Aigen and Gershon D. Hundert. Philadelphia, 1986. Pp. 156–70.

Caiserman, H[ananiah] M[eir]. "Builders of Canadian Jewry." *Canadian Jewish Year-Book,* 1939.

———. "Edmund Scheuer: Grand Old Man of Toronto Jewry." *Canadian Jewish Year-Book,* 1940.

Clough, Edwin. "Raphael de Sola Has Suits for All Seasons." *Weekend Magazine,* 12 December 1967.

Cohn, Werner. "English and French Canadian Public Opinion on Jews and Israel: Some Poll Data." *Canadian Ethnic Studies* 11 (1979): 31–48.

Davids, Leo. "Canadian Jewry: Some Recent Census Findings." *American Jewish Year Book,* 1985.

Davis, Moshe. "Centres of Jewry in the Western Hemisphere: A Comparative Approach." *The Jewish Journal of Sociology* 5 (June 1963): 4–26.

Dictionary of Canadian Biography. 11th ed. 1982. S.v. "de Sola." By Carmen Miller.

Dictionary of Canadian Biography. 11th ed. 1982. S.v. "Joseph, Abraham." By Annette R. Wolfe.

Edelstein, Hyman. "Canada's First Jewish Poet." Toronto *Jewish Standard,* October 1951.

Fergusson, C. Bruce. "Jewish Communities in Nova Scotia." *Journal of Education* 11 (October 1961): 45–48.

Figler, Bernard. "History of the Zionist Ideal in Canada." *Canadian Jewish Chronicle,* 3, 10, 17 November 1961.

———. "Hyman Edelstein (1859–1957)." *Canadian Jewish Chronicle,* 21 February 1958.

Friedman, Lee M. "Canada's Jews." *Journal of Jewish Bibliography* 3 (October 1942): 132–35.

Friedman, Reena Sigman. ' "Send Me My Husband Who Is In New York City": Husband Desertion in the American-Jewish Immigrant Community 1900–1926.' *Jewish Social Studies* 44 (winter 1982): 1–18.

Gaon, S[olomon]. "Some Aspects of the Relations between Shaar Hashamayim of London and the Shearith Israel of New York." In *Migration and Settlement: Proceedings of the Anglo-American Jewish Historical Conference.* London, 1971.

Gartner, Lloyd P. "North Atlantic Jewry." In *Migration and Settlement: Proceedings of the Anglo-American Jewish Historical Conference.* London, 1971.

Gibbon, John Murray. "The Hebrew and Canada." *Canadian Jewish Year-Book,* 1941.

Ginsburg, M. "The King George Sick Benefit Association in the Last 15 Years." In *Souvenir: King George Sick Benefit Association of Montreal.* Montreal, 1946.

Glazer, Gabriel. "French Canadian Nationalism and the Jews." *In the Dispersion* 4 (winter 1964–65): 33–38.

Goeb, Jan. "The Maritimes." *Viewpoints,* winter-spring 1973.

Goulston, Michael. "The Status of the Anglo-Jewish Rabbinate, 1840–1914." *The Jewish Journal of Sociology* 10 (June 1968): 55–82.

Greening, W. E. "Guilty as Charged," *The ADL Bulletin,* April 1964.

Groulx, Lionel. "Le vingt ans de l'A.C.J.C." *l'Action française,* June 1924.

Hayes, Saul. "Antisemitism in Canada." *The Facts.* May 1949.

––––––. "Canadian and United States Jewry: Some Differences." *Congress Bi-Weekly,* 21 November 1966.

Helfield, Tilya Gallay. "Quebec." *Viewpoints,* winter-spring, 1973.

Herstein, Harvey H. "The Growth of the Winnipeg Jewish Community and the Evolution of Its Educational Institutions." *Transactions of the Historical and Scientific Society of Manitoba* 3 (1965–66): 27–66.

"The House of Joseph in the History of Quebec." *Congress Bulletin,* May 1959.

Kantrowitz, Jack. "Jews in the New Quebec: Where Do We Go From Here?" *Viewpoints* (Spring 1979).

Kattan, Naim. "Les Juifs du Canada." In *Juifs et Canadiens,* edited by Naim Kattan. Montreal, 1967.

––––––. "Mosaique Canadienne." *Les Nouveaux Cahiers* 9 (spring 1967): 60–65.

Katz, Irving. "Ezekiel Solomon: The First Jew in Michigan." *Michigan History* 8 (September 1948): 20–24.

Katz, Yossi. "The Plans and Efforts of the Jews at Winnipeg to Purchase Land and to Establish an Agricultural Settlement in Palestine before World War One." *Canadian Jewish Historical Society Journal* 5 (spring 1981): 1–16.

Kronitz, Leon, "Zionism: Creator of a State, Guardian of a People," *Canadian Zionist,* November 1972.

Langlois, Conrad. "Montréal Anglicise les Juifs Nord-Africains, Réfugiés au Québec par Milliers Pour y Parler Français." In *Studies and Documents on Immigration and Integration in Canada,* edited by Joseph Kage. Montreal, 1965.

McCullough, Stewart. "The Future of the Jew in Canada." *Canadian Forum,* April 1934.

Malchelosse, Gérald. "Les Juifs dans l'histoire Canadienne." *Les Cahiers des Dix* 4 (1939): 167–95.

––––––. "Premières organisations Juives au Canada." *La Revue Nationale* 5 (October 1923): 301–99.

––––––. "Premières Synagogues à Montréal." *Le Bulletin des Recherches Historiques* 50 (May 1944): 155–56.

Marcotte, Gilles. "Le Romancier Canadien-Français et son Juifs." in *Juifs et Canadiens,* edited by Naim Kattan. Montreal, 1967.

Massicotte, E. Z. "Le Rameau Catholique des Joseph." *Le Bulletin des Recherches Historiques* 40 (December 1934): 751–55.

Miller, Evelyn. "The Learned Hazan of Montreal: Reverend Abraham de Sola, L.L.D., 1825–1882." *American Sephardi* 7–8 (1979): 23–43.

––––––. "The Montreal Jewish Public Library." *Congress Bulletin,* November 1973.

Morris, Richard. "The Jews, Minorities, and Dissent in the American Revolution." In *Migration and Settlement: Proceedings of the Anglo-American Jewish Historical Conference.* London, 1971.

Neusner, Jacob. "The Role of English Jews in the Development of American Jewish Life, 1775–1850." *YIVO Annual* 12 (1958–59): 131–56.

Osofsky, Gilbert. "The Hebrew Emigrant Aid Society of the United States (1881–1883)." *Publications of the American Jewish Historical Society* 49 (March 1960): 173–87.

Perel, Shlomo. "Quebec's Nationalist Movement and the Future of Its Jews." *Israel Horizons,* April 1977.

Phillips, N. Taylor. "Clarence I. De Sola." *Publications of the American Jewish Historical Society* 28 (1922): 269–72.

Reich, Nathan. "Montreal: The Quebec School Question." *The Menorah Journal,* June 1929.

Rome, David. "Literature of Jewish Canadiana." *Jewish Book Annual* 18 (1960–61): 44–53.

Rosenberg, Louis. "Chronology of Canadian Jewish History." *Canadian Jewish Chronicle,* 30 October 1959.

———. "The Demography of the Jewish Community in Canada." *Jewish Journal of Sociology* 1 (December 1959): 217–33.

———. "The Earliest Settlers in Canada: Facts vs. Myths." In *Canadian Jewish Reference Book and Directory,* compiled by Eli Gottesman. Montreal, 1963.

———. "Some Aspects of the Historical Development of the Canadian Jewish Community." *Publications of the American Jewish Historical Society* 50 (December 1960): 121–42.

———. "Two Centuries of Jewish Life in Canada, 1760–1960." *American Jewish Year Book,* 1961.

Rosenberg, Stuart E. "Canada's Jews: the Sacred and the Secular," *Conservative Judaism* 24 (spring 1970): 34–44.

———. "French Separatism: Its Implications for Canadian Jewry." *American Jewish Year Book* (1972): 407–427.

Ryan, Claude. "A French Canadian Looks at the Jews." *Viewpoints* (October 1969).

Sack, Benjamin G. "A Suit at Law Involving the First Jewish Minister in Canada." *Publications of the American Jewish Historical Society* 31 (1928): 181–86.

———. "When Did David S. Franks Last Leave Canada?" *Publications of the American Jewish Historical Society* 31 (1928): 234.

Sarna, Jonathan. "The Canadian Connection of an American Jew: The Case of Mordecai M. Noah." Canadian Jewish Historical Society *Journal* 3 (fall 1979): 115–129.

———. "Jewish Immigration to North America: The Canadian Experience (1870–1900)." *The Jewish Journal of Sociology* 18 (June 1976).

Schiff, Mortimer. "Separatism in Quebec," *Midstream* 11 (March 1965): 69–78.

Schoenfeld, Stuart. "The Jewish Religion in North America: Canadian and American Comparisons." *Canadian Journal of Sociology* 3 (February 1978): 209–231.

Silver, Arthur. "Some Aspects of Anti-Semitism in Quebec." *Jewish Dialog,* summer 1975.

Szajkowski, Zosa. "The Alliance Israélite Universelle in the United States, 1860–1949." *Publications of the American Jewish Historical Society* 39 (June 1950): 389–443.

———. "The European Attitude to East European Jewish Immigration (1881–93)." *Publications of the American Jewish Historical Society* 41 (December 1951): 126–63.

———. "Some Facts Regarding Alsatian Jews in America." *YIVO Bleter* 20 (September, December 1942): 312–18.

"Tax-Supported Jewish Schools in Montreal in the 1890's." *Congress Bulletin,* February 1953.

Tennenhouse, Patty. "My Grandfather and His Girl." In *Israelite Press Centennial Issue,* 1967.

Trépanier, Léon. "Un Montréalais du siècle dernier: l'immigrant juif Louis Marchand." *Les Cahiers des Dix* 30 (1965): 131–48.

Tulchinsky, Gerald. "Recent Developments in Canadian Jewish Historiography," *Canadian Ethnic Studies* 14 (1982): 114–25.

———. "Clarence De Sola and Early Zionism in Canada." Paper delivered at Conference on Jews in North America. Toronto, April 1983.

Waller, Harold M. "Canada." In *Zionism in Transition,* edited by Moshe Davis. New York, 1980, pp. 111–120.

Wallot, Jean-Pierre. "Les Canadiens français et les Juifs (1808–1809): l'Affaire Hart." In *Juifs et Canadiens,* edited by Naim Kattan. Montreal, 1967, pp. 111–22.

Warsen, Allen A. "Cadillac and the Lost Ten Tribes of Israel." *Michigan Jewish History* 2 (March 1961): 13–17.

Weinberg, Henry H. "The Image of the Jew in Late Nineteenth-Century French Literature." *Jewish Social Studies* 45 (Summer-Fall 1983): 241–50.

Weinfeld, Morton. "The Jews of Quebec: Perceived Antisemitism, Segregation, and Emigration." *The Jewish Journal of Sociology* 22 (June 1980): 5–20.

———. "La Question Juive au Quebec." *Midstream* 23 (October 1977): 20–29.

Winston, Milton. "The Jews of Quebec: Two Views." *Jewish Dialog,* spring 1980.

Wisse, Ruth R. and Irwin Cotler. "Quebec Jews Caught in the Middle." *Commentary* (September 1977): 55–59.

Wolff, Martin. "The Jews of Canada." *American Jewish Year Book,* 5686 (1925–26).

Yarosky, Michael. "The Jewish Community of Quebec: Bridging the Past and the Present." *Journal of Jewish Communal Service* September 1979).

Index